The Significance of Consciousness

The Significance of Consciousness

CHARLES P. SIEWERT

PRINCETON UNIVERSITY PRESS

PRINCETON, NEW JERSEY

Library of Congress Cataloging-in-Publication Data

Siewert, Charles P., 1959–
The significance of consciousness / Charles P. Siewert.
p. cm.
Includes bibliographical references and index.
ISBN 0-691-02724-2 (hardcover : alk. paper)
1. Consciousness. I. Title.
B808.9.S54   1998
126—dc21   97-32848   CIP

This book has been composed in Sabon

Princeton University Press books are printed on acid-free paper and meet the guidelines for
permanence and durability of the Committee on Production Guidelines for Book
Longevity of the Council on Library Resources

http://pup.princeton.edu

Printed in the United States of America

1 2 3 4 5 6 7 8 9 10

CONTENTS

ACKNOWLEDGMENTS

THIS BOOK has emerged from much revision and reworking of my doctoral dissertation, written at the University of California at Berkeley. Thus the first debt I would like to acknowledge is to the members of my dissertation committee: I thank John Searle, for his steadfast encouragement over many years of struggle with this (once unfashionable) topic, and for his usefully (and characteristically) direct criticisms; Hubert Dreyfus, for helping me to keep my confidence and to heed my phenomenological scruples; and Stephen Palmer, for helpful remarks regarding my discussion of blindsight. From my days at Berkeley I would also like to thank Bernard Williams and Richard Wollheim, for the impetus a joint seminar of theirs gave to the early development of some of my ideas; in this way, too, I am indebted to Donald Davidson and Bruce Vermazen for their seminar on self-knowledge, held when I first started to put this project together. Also during this period, conversations with two fellow students at Berkeley, Kirk Ludwig and Kayley Vernalis, were especially valuable to me. My interest in philosophical questions about consciousness was inspired as well by a seminar conducted by George Myro that I was allowed to attend before becoming a student at Berkeley. I count myself very fortunate to have been not only George Myro's student, but also, as an undergraduate, the student of two of his students, George Bealer and Neil Thomason. All three have provided me with important guiding examples of philosophical attitude and practice.

I would like to thank colleagues and students at Reed College for their feedback in talks and classes, particularly Mark Bedau, Seth Crook, Claire Curtis, Ezra Gollogly, Mark Hinchliff, Zeke Koch, Robert Paul, Bill Peck, David Reeve, and Dan Reisberg.

I am grateful also for comments and questions from colleagues at the University of Miami, in particular Ed Erwin, Alan Goldman, Howard Pospesel, Harvey Siegel, David Wilson, and Eddy Zemach. Also at Miami, discussions with participants in a graduate seminar on consciousness, while undoubtedly adding to the time it has taken to finish revisions, have, I hope, helped me improve my views considerably. Among those to whom I am especially grateful in this regard are Maria Frapoli, A. J. Kreider, and Corina Vaida.

Though I am thankful to both reviewers of my manuscript for Princeton University Press, David Chalmers and another who remains anonymous, I want specially to acknowledge the incalculable benefit I have received from Chalmers's support, good words, and detailed critical comments.

To my wife, Lisa Park, I am grateful for helpful conversations about both philosophical and stylistic concerns, as well as for her forebearance with the seemingly unending demands this project has made on my time. My son James I thank for his heartfelt encouragement.

Finally, my thanks both to those of whom I am most critical in the following pages, for the opportunities for learning my disagreement with them has given me, and to all those teachers and authors I have encountered who have shown me how such opportunities can be realized.

The Significance of Consciousness

INTRODUCTION

The Project

To understand consciousness is to understand something deeply important about us. This may sound truistic to some, but even so, it is not a truism apparently much honored in the past century's leading views of mind, meaning, and behavior. In fact, to judge by such accounts, one might easily think what is most significant about consciousness is just its surprising insignificance. Or one might think what is supposed significant is not consciousness itself, so much as its seeming to create for theories of mind some oddly persistent nuisance.

Perhaps such attitudes have abated of late: at least, books and articles featuring the frequent and unembarrassed use of the term 'consciousness' have proliferated enormously in recent years. But I think these efforts have not fully reversed (and some have reinforced) certain habits of downgrading the importance of consciousness. The habits I have in mind find their mildest expression perhaps in the familiar view that, though consciousness plays some genuine part in human psychology, still, the larger portion of this—and what most deserves our attention—lies in what is *not* conscious: the "unconscious mind." In another (less mild) expression of such tendencies, one might, while granting the reality of consciousness, maintain it to be quite inessential to mind, psychology, or cognition—and at most, of some peripheral or derivative status or interest. Finally, one may devalue consciousness by failing or refusing to recognize its reality in one's theorizing about the mind; at its extreme, this emerges as the notion (whether disguised or forthright) that consciousness is some kind of illusion.

In speaking of a standing tendency to marginalize consciousness, or to diminish its significance, I speak only of a diffuse, loosely identifiable intellectual trend, not a shared precise doctrine, or a theoretically unified movement. Psychoanalysis, behaviorism, cognitive psychology, and a variety of philosophical approaches stressing the importance of society or language have all displayed in diverse ways the tendency to which I refer. That views from such various sources, as dissimilar as they are, have often persuasively blended some antagonism or indifference to consciousness with hopes to supersede apparent common sense, has helped, I think, to inculcate a vague prejudice we have not yet quite overcome: that any advanced, critical, or scientific way of thinking about ourselves will inevitably tell us that consciousness is, in some way or other, really not as great as we may have supposed.

But I think that, if we are not content to be carried along by some general theoretical drift, and we seriously want to reconsider for ourselves the place of consciousness, we are hindered most not by such powerfully vague and various presumptions against it. What stymies us most is a failure to locate adequately our topic of discussion. Efforts to discuss or explain consciousness, to find its place in relation to other phenomena and assess its importance, are often marred by blurred distinctions and false preconceptions that keep us from even sufficiently identifying for ourselves what should be the focus of study.

In what follows, I offer a way of understanding consciousness that will eventually lead us to grant this feature a central place in our conception of ourselves and our minds. Rather than considering consciousness, if at all, as an afterthought, fitting it into some theory conceived in its neglect, requiring it to conform to this or else be scorned, we should, on my view, first carefully cultivate some understanding of what consciousness is, and insist on organizing accounts of mind around a respect for this. Consciousness, in the sense I want to explore, is—though vulnerable to theoretical neglect—extremely important. But this will not be adequately appreciated, I believe, unless I make it clear what I am talking about when I talk about consciousness, and explain how some ways of thinking inhibit its recognition, and how these can be overcome.

A FIRST-PERSON APPROACH

Some philosophers (Nagel 1974, 1986; Searle 1992) stress that the "first-person" or "subjective" point of view is somehow crucial: if we shun this in favor of an exclusively "third-person" or "objective" perspective, we will miss just what is special and interesting about consciousness. I will leave aside the contrast between "subjective" and "objective" perspectives, since I find it too unclear and potentially misleading to provide a good starting point. But I do wish to make a specifically first-person approach in a way crucial to my project of clarifying a certain sense of 'consciousness.'

Let me explain this. Many people who write about consciousness start by saying that, though our use of the word stands in need of clarification, we should not expect to begin our discussion with a definition in general terms of the expression 'conscious' or its cognates. I agree with this, and I will accordingly explain what I mean by 'conscious' by appeal to examples— both of what is conspicuously and univocally conscious in the sense I want to employ, and of what is not, or would not be, conscious in this sense. Thus I want to make it clear what feature I intend to pick out by the term 'consciousness' by drawing attention to cases in which its occurrence is, I believe, most unmistakable, and by contrasting these with cases, both actual and merely hypothetical, in which consciousness is made conspicuous by its absence.

Part of what makes the way I propose to use this method of explication a specifically "first-person" approach is this: I will describe types of conscious experience, as well as cases in which certain kinds of conscious experience are or would be lacking. In considering actual instances, as well as the hypothetical situations I will describe, I ask you to turn your attention to the first-person case. That is, I would like you to consider instances *in your own life* of the types of conscious experience I will describe, and where I describe merely hypothetical situations in which someone has or lacks certain kinds of conscious experience, I would like you to conceive of being a person who has or lacks the relevant sort of experience. These will be cases in which one could truthfully assert or deny one had a certain sort of experience by use of the first-person singular pronoun, cases where one could assert or deny, for example: "That noise sounded louder to me than the previous one"; "I was visualizing the front door of my house"; "It looks to me as if there is an X there"; "I feel a pain in my right hand."

Why do I make a point of asking you to focus on the first-person case? Because I think that if instead you consider only the third-person case—that is, if you think only of instances, whether actual or not, in which someone other than yourself might be said to have or lack a given sort of experience—you are liable to attend not to the difference between consciousness and its lack, but to the differences in behavior that would warrant your either affirming or denying that another person had conscious experience of a certain kind. Thus you may interpret my use of 'conscious' by reference to dispositions or capacities to do what could manifest one's possession or lack of conscious experience to an observer. And this, I will argue, would be a misunderstanding.

This rationale for my approach presupposes that first-person claims or beliefs about experience are not warranted in just the same way as third-person ones are. For otherwise, the danger to which I say a third-person approach is vulnerable would haunt my approach as well. Confining ourselves to cases where one would make or withhold third-person attributions of experience would involve no risk we could reasonably hope to avert by turning to the first-person case. Furthermore, my approach assumes not only that first-person claims about experience are not warranted in the way third-person ones are, but also that we do have warrant of some sort for making the first-person claims. For I wish, by appeal to examples in the first-person case, to explain a sense of 'conscious' in which we do indeed have experience that is conscious. To clarify only a sense in which someone *could* have conscious experience is not enough for my purposes, since I also want to assess the importance of our having the sort of conscious experience we do. If we had no warrant to claim—in a certain sense, no right to say—that we do actually have conscious experience, then we would have no warrant for saying it is or is not important in some way that we have it.

So, if my appeal to the first-person case is to show us a sense in which we do have conscious experience, and prepare us to consider its importance, and if this approach is to have the sort of rationale I have suggested, then I need to assume that the way we know the truth of first-person beliefs or claims about our minds differs from the way we know that third-person claims about minds are correct. More precisely, I hold that one has a type of warrant for some of one's beliefs or claims, assertible using a first-person singular pronoun to attribute some experience (or attitude) to *oneself*, that differs from the type of warrant had (ordinarily, at least) for any beliefs or claims, whose assertion would constitute the attribution of some experience or attitude only to someone other than the speaker. This view I shall variously refer to as the "distinctiveness thesis" or the "claim of first-person warrant"—the claim that we have a distinctively first-person knowledge of our own minds, or a distinctively first-person warrant for beliefs about our own minds.

GUARDING AGAINST PEREMPTORY REJECTION

What I have said may well spark certain suspicions that could make the reader unwilling to cooperate in my enterprise, and unwilling to accept the results at which I think we can arrive. My talk of consciousness, and a proposed reliance on a distinctively first-person knowledge, will likely elicit from my audience patterns of response formed by the legacy of Descartes, whether or not I want this. Modern Western philosophy has been pervasively affected by a long history of reactions to the (now notorious) claims by Descartes ([1641] 1985, 171) that "there is nothing in the mind . . . of which it is not aware," and that this awareness (some would say *consciousness*) gives us a special sort of self-knowledge that forms the indubitable basis for constructing and justifying an all-encompassing account of the world. This history has left contemporary intellectual culture suffused with ways of thinking about the mind apparently hostile to reputedly "Cartesian" notions. Thus I suspect that some will want to dismiss my first-person approach and my claim that through it, we can arrive at an account that puts consciousness at the center of our self-conception, because they think these notions are inevitably bound up with some fusty Cartesian view that has been long since discredited, or that has at least gone hopelessly out of fashion. So I imagine that some may decline my invitation, because they think I must be suggesting that we base our investigations upon private nonsensory observations, with "introspection's immaterial eye," of the "ghostly" happenings on the mind's "inner stage," or that we rely upon the "privileged access" that makes the mind "transparent" to itself, and sets knowledge of one's own mind above and apart from all claims to know other minds, and the "external world." "But *surely*," one will say, "since Ryle, Wittgenstein, and Quine, and in the wake of modern psychology—from Freud and Skinner to Chomsky and Marr—we're having no more of that sort of foolishness."

Since my proposal is liable to excite some set of associations of this sort, often nestled around the term 'Cartesian,' I probably need to spend some time explaining and defending what I assume in the investigation of consciousness I propose—the "distinctiveness" thesis. Part of this involves making explicit (what I believe are) some genuinely Cartesian assumptions about mind and self-knowledge to which I am *not* committed, so as to forestall certain misguided objections that may arise. I am not, for example, presupposing that consciousness enables one to know one's own mind by some kind of peculiarly "direct" quasi-visual "inner sensing"—"introspection." In fact, I will be most concerned to criticize this conception of consciousness later on.

But I want to make it clear that if I am not aptly described as a follower of Descartes, I also cannot embrace certain influential anti-Cartesian modes of thought. For example, I certainly cannot go to the extremes of anti-introspectionism that have led some to deny that there is any distinctively first-person knowledge of mind—whether because, like Gilbert Ryle (1949), they would deny there is any difference in kind between knowledge of one's own and that of others' minds, or whether because, like certain behaviorists and eliminative materialists (Quine 1960; Stich 1983; P. M. Churchland 1981), they would say there is no knowledge of mind, period—since the claims we might suppose we know here are all constitutive of some primitive doomed theory of behavior. To some, it seems, if the "inner eye" offends, we must pluck it out and cast it away. But clearly, since I claim we do have a distinctively first-person knowledge of our attitudes and experience, to correct what is wrong with thinking of self-knowledge as the deliverance of an "inner eye," we need, in my view, some therapy more subtle than amputation. However, it may not be obvious just what other claims about self-knowledge, consistent with my approach, are available, and with what right we make them, if we do not help ourselves to a Cartesian view of consciousness and self-knowledge.

Explaining what I mean by claiming that we have a distinctively first-person knowledge and warrant regarding our attitudes and experience, and saying why I think we are entitled to rely upon it in thinking about consciousness, will take a little while—the first two chapters of this work. Some readers may be impatient to get on with what I have billed as the main feature—consciousness—especially when I admit that what I have to say about self-knowledge will be far from a thorough, positive account of it. In my view, we will not be in any shape to give that kind of account of self-knowledge until we are clearer about consciousness. But I believe some methodological prolegomenon is indispensable. For assumptions about knowledge and justification have a large potential to distort or thwart our thinking about consciousness. And clarifying my assumptions about knowledge will involve explaining my use of certain key terms, as is needed if the reader is to understand and fairly assess much of what I go on to say. In any event, the issues about mind and knowledge that will turn up in the course of the first two chapters are philosophically interesting in their own right.

A Look Ahead

Even if one is ready to accept without complaint my refusal to launch into the main topic right away, one might still reasonably want some idea of what lies ahead once I do start, in Chapter 3, to turn my attention directly to consciousness. Here is a rough orientation.

The job of Chapter 3 is to provide a core understanding of the feature I intend to identify by the term 'consciousness'—enough to give us a foothold, and to avoid certain mistakes I argue cause consciousness to be unjustly neglected, even in writings ostensibly dedicated to giving some account or theory of it. In Chapter 4 I point out ways in which consciousness can be and has been neglected in certain theories, and in Chapter 5 I examine some reasons one might have for thinking this neglect is not so unjust after all. Here I hope to discourage consciousness neglect by criticizing certain views I think promote it.

In Chapter 6, I concentrate on what I take to be a basic source of distortions in our understanding of consciousness—which I will have partially exposed already in earlier chapters—a tendency to confuse consciousness with some form of self-directed intentionality or self-representation, such as is found, for example, in thoughts about one's own experience. Here I say why I do not accept the perennially tempting view that consciousness is in some way the mind's perception of itself. In order to sort out this issue, as well as prepare the way for later discussions, I say how I understand the notion of intentionality, or intentional features—the directedness or about-ness of thought, experience, symbols, pictures—in a way adequate to my purposes.

Then I go on to say something about how I think consciousness *is* related to intentionality, first in the case of vision (Chapter 7), and then in the case of thought (Chapter 8). This is at the same time a discussion of the *phenomenal character* of these kinds of experience (roughly, the way it seems to us to have them, or the way in which conscious experiences may differ from one another, in virtue of being conscious). For I see the question of how consciousness relates to intentionality as the question of how the phenomenal character of our experience (or, our phenomenal features) relates to our intentional features. I argue that our phenomenal features *are* intentional features.

We need, I believe, a firm grasp of the points developed in Chapters 1 through 8, and a resolute wariness of the kinds of error I criticize there, before we can fruitfully consider the question at which we finally arrive in Chapter 9—that of the importance of consciousness. There I argue that, once we have properly identified for ourselves the phenomenal character of our experience, we can recognize that in a certain sense, we strongly value having it (and others' having it) for its own sake, and partly for this reason, for many of us, life without consciousness would be little or no better than death. This is to accord consciousness no small importance. So the neglect of consciousness is no small slight.

That my discussion leads up to this issue of the *importance* of consciousness helps explain why I have chosen *The Significance of Consciousness* as the title for this work. But as should now be clear, I am interested in the 'significance' of consciousness in two other ways as well: for I want (first) to explore and clarify one significance (or sense) we may give the term 'consciousness,' and then to discuss how (as we might say) conscious experience *signifies* (that is, its intentionality)—to argue that experience does not have its significance as *signs* do, derivatively: in some way, consciousness has significance already built into it.

The use of the definite article in my title should not be taken to suggest I intend my treatment to be somehow final or exhaustive. Even after my relatively long discussion, there will, I recognize, be many important questions about consciousness I will not have posed or considered—including those whose answers seem to be what we yearn for, when we ask that consciousness be explained—where that means something like showing why we have conscious experience, or why we have the forms of it we do. But I think we need not rush to provide a theory we should want to call "the explanation of consciousness," or to make pronouncements on the prospects for such ambitions. To say, in detail, what accounts for our having the forms of experience we have, or any conscious states at all, would clearly be a worthy thing. But efforts to reach this goal will only take us farther from it and foster confusion, if we are not first sufficiently clear concerning what we want to talk about. And we will not understand what makes the explanation we seek so desirable, unless we begin to articulate how and why consciousness matters to us. Thus I believe claims to explain consciousness, or to show why it cannot be explained, need to be informed by careful reflection on the matters I will discuss, and that this can provide an understanding of consciousness as fully important as any explanation of it we would hope to have.

CHAPTER 1

First-Person Knowledge

1.1 ATTITUDES AND EXPERIENCE

I have proposed taking a first-person approach to consciousness—one that enjoins us to rely on a distinctively first-person knowledge of our minds. Before I defend the claim that we have such knowledge on which to rely, I want to make it a little plainer still just what my proposal does and does not involve. However, this clarification is not entirely separate from the task of defense, since, in averting certain misunderstandings by making explicit what I am *not* assuming, I hope also to help save my views from being mangled in the molds of some ready-made critique. In the course of saying how I wish to draw distinctions involved in my claim that first-person knowledge differs in kind from knowledge of others, I want to enable the reader to interpret and assess what I will later say, by explaining how I use certain terms crucial to my entire discussion, which may have already caused some puzzlement, notably 'attitudes,' 'experience,' and 'warrant.'

When I speak of a distinctive self-knowledge or first-person knowledge, what am I supposing this is knowledge *of?* "Self-knowledge" may suggest something fine and momentous, knowledge of one's Self, of who one is— what makes one wise in the face of life-changing decisions, and gives one confidence without conceit. But an account of such self-knowledge ideally would be rooted, I think, in an understanding of knowledge more common, and not always quite so estimable. When I talk about self-knowledge, or knowing your own mind, I am simply talking about your knowledge that you have certain *attitudes* and *experiences*. But knowing this need involve nothing more profound than knowing that you just recalled where you parked the car, or that you were thinking about what to say in a letter, or that you feel an itch in your left foot.

I use the term 'attitudes' to include the usual company of "intentional states" that we attribute to ourselves in ordinary talk. When, for instance, we speak of ourselves *believing, intending, wanting, desiring, remembering,* or *perceiving* something, we speak of the attitudes we have. One knows that one has certain attitudes, and what one knows may often be expressed by sentences of the form, "I F . . . ," where "F" is replaced by an appropriate form of one of the verbs listed above (e.g., "believe," "intend," etc.) and the ellipsis is filled by expressions of variously appropriate grammatical forms, depending sometimes on the type of verb employed (for example: "I believe *that the post office is closed now*"; "I want *to go for a walk*"; "I see *a sign in the window*"; "I see *that her hair is wet*").

When one knows what sort of an attitude one has, it is not always the case that what one knows oneself to have at that time is reasonably identifiable as an *occurrence* of a certain sort. For instance, it may be true at a certain time that one believes that the moon is smaller than the earth, though nothing is happening at that time properly identifiable as the occurrence of this belief, or the event of one's having this belief. We see this most clearly when we note that one may rightly be said to have this belief even at such time as one is deeply and dreamlessly asleep, or even comatose—in which circumstances it surely seems reasonable to say there is *no* actual event at that time suited as a candidate for the role, "occurrence of the belief that the moon is smaller than the earth" (if any event is ever so suited).

But not all attitudes one knows oneself to have are like this—some attitudes are also occurrences, events, or happenings. These I shall count as "experiences." So when I say that one knows that one has attitudes *and* experiences of various sorts, I do not mean these two classifications to exclude one another. Many occurrences of what I broadly call *thought* or *thinking* count as both experiences and attitudes, where I take this to include (at least on some applications of these terms) *supposing* something is so; *wondering, considering,* or *doubting* whether it is; *judging, concluding, conjecturing* that it is; *deliberating* about what to do; *deciding* to do it; as well as *daydreaming, remembering,* and *imagining* (e.g., *visualizing*). Other attitudes that can be classified as experiences (but do not fall naturally under the heading "thought") are: *feeling* a *desire* or an *urge* to do something; *feeling angry, depressed, ashamed, elated, nervous,* or *disgusted* at or about something; and *feeling affection, jealousy,* or *pity* for someone. And sense-perception in its various modalities provides examples of what can be both attitude and experience: its *looking, sounding, smelling, tasting* some way to someone, or its *feeling* some way to someone (where feelings are taken to include feeling by touch, feeling warmth and cold, and feeling the position and movement of one's body).[1]

I have said that the experiences I have listed are also attitudes. But it may be that there are experiences that are *not* attitudes of any sort. On some views, this would be the case with regard to what are called 'sensations,' for example, pains, itches, tickles, and after-images. It would be correct to say of such experiences that they are not attitudes, if they do not have intentionality, or if the possession of such experiences is not the possession of intentional features. For having an attitude of some sort is an intentional feature.

But what is intentionality? Saying that attitudes are necessarily intentional features does little to explain what attitudes are, or why someone might want to say certain kinds of experience are not attitudes. There is no clear or obvious common usage on which to rely, where the term 'intentionality' is concerned. I could say, by way of introducing this term, that intentional features are those that make thought, speech, and pictures "about" or "of" things, or that intentionality is the "directedness" of these to things, a kind of directedness of which sense-perception also partakes. But appealing to these prepositions, and this metaphor of "direction," though somewhat suggestive, does not by itself get us very far. We might try to develop this further by trying to explain "directedness" as a special relation to certain kinds of objects. But I am not going to take this course.

My approach to the notion of intentionality has at its core the observation that assessments of truth and falsity, accuracy and inaccuracy, are made regarding people and things in virtue of certain features they have. So, for instance, if I believe there is a pen in my top desk drawer—if I have that feature—and there is a pen in my top desk drawer, then what I believe is true. And if there is no pen there, then what I believe is false. So, I want to say, I am assessable for truth in virtue of this feature: believing that there is a pen in my top desk drawer. Similarly, if it looks to me as though there is a glob of toothpaste on the faucet—if I have that feature—and there is such a deposit of toothpaste there, the way it looks to me is accurate. But under other conditions—say, if there is nothing protruding on the faucet's surface, but only a reflection from the shower curtain—the way it looks to me on this occasion is inaccurate. Thus I am assessable for accuracy in virtue of its looking to me a certain way. On my understanding of 'intentionality,' it is *sufficient* that someone or something have features in virtue of which he, she, or it is assessable for truth or accuracy in the way illustrated, for that person or thing to have intentional features, to have intentionality. Later (in Chapter 6) I say more about what I mean by this.

But the examples I have offered will have to do for now as explanation of what I mean by 'attitudes and experiences' when I say we have a distinctively first-person knowledge of what attitudes and experiences we have. And what I mean by 'mind' (and so, by 'knowing one's own mind') is also to be understood by reference to this. One has a mind if one has attitudes or experience of some sort; one knows one's own mind if one knows that one has attitudes or experience of a certain sort. Any more elaborate, precise, or metaphysically imposing notion of what constitutes having a mind is unnecessary for current purposes.

1.2 Knowledge, Belief, and Warrant

But what is it to say that knowledge that someone has attitudes and experience is "distinctive" where that "someone" is oneself? I have said this much already: my contention is that the type of warrant one has for first-person belief about attitudes and experience *differs* from the type one has (ordinarily at least) for third-person beliefs. And this is how I understand the claim that the way in which one knows one's own mind differs from the way in which one knows others' minds. But this stands in need of clarification.

Just what do I mean by 'warrant'? One occasionally hears it said outside of philosophy that someone does or does not have warrant for saying something, or that what they claim is or is not warranted. The term is encountered in philosophical discussions as well. But in neither place is it always used against quite the same background of assumptions as inform my usage, or at least, it will not be obvious that this is so. Thus I had better explain how I want it to be taken. I speak of one's having warrant for a belief one has, or for a claim or assertion one makes. Having warrant for a belief is closely related to, but distinguishable from, both its *being* true, and one's *knowing that it is* true. As I understand these matters, if one believes that p, and one knows that p, then one has warrant for believing that p. However, one may have warrant for believing what is not true, or lack warrant for believing what is. But, if one wants to say what is true, and one has warrant for one's belief that p, then one has a reason to assert that p (in the sense in which one might be generally said to "have a reason" for doing something). In that sense, warrant, though distinct from truth, at least must have a certain "affinity" with it, for warrant gives one who aims at speaking the truth a reason to speak.

Some examples will perhaps make these statements and distinctions clearer. First, consider an illustration of having true belief without having warrant for it. Suppose Bob believes that his next-door neighbors are quarreling, and this is true, and further, that Bob believes this because he hears shouting coming from next door. But now suppose also that the angry voice he hears is coming not from one of his neighbors, but from their television. In such a case, we could say that Bob's belief was, as it happened, true, but *he lacked warrant for holding it.*

Or should we say that in this sort of case, Bob has at least has some, a little, warrant for believing what he does? Even so, I think we can still find a distinction between having a true belief and having warrant for holding it intelligible. For to say Bob has some or a little warrant for holding this belief, is not to say it is only a little bit true—it is no more or less true than it would be if he were an eyewitness to his neighbors' furious bickering (in which case, he would presumably have much more warrant for his belief). And we can make sense of the claim that if Bob formed his belief about the neighbors based on certain mistaken notions—for example, superstitions, or claims to "psychic powers"—then even if what he believed just happened to be true, Bob had no warrant at all for believing it.

Now, consider also cases where one has warrant for a belief, though it is false. Suppose Bob knows that one of his neighbors habitually (and successfully) seeks to annoy the other by turning up the television volume. One day he sees the two walk, sour-faced, into the apartment, and soon notices what sounds like the television suddenly roaring with noise. This all leads Bob to conclude that his neighbors are quarreling. Then he would have warrant (surely, at least *some* warrant) for his belief. But this would still be so even if his neighbors were *not* quarreling, and the abrupt rise in the television's volume were just coincidence.

These examples might suggest that having warrant for one's belief not only (as I said) gives one a reason for asserting it, provided one wants to say what is true, but also involves having an ability to *state* what these reasons are, so as to produce an *argument* or *evidence* for what one believes. For we will suppose Bob could do this. But this will seem strange when put beside the thought that one *knows* that one has attitudes and experiences of various kinds, and that when one also believes that one has them, one has *warrant* for one's belief. This will seem odd because typically one is not asked for, and cannot give, supporting reasons of this sort for assertions about one's own mind. For example, if you were to say you thought your next-door neighbors weren't getting along, an ordinary question for me to ask would be, "How do you know?" And an ordinary reply for you to give might be, "I heard a lot of shouting coming from their house last night." But it would be strange and confusing if this prompted me to say: "I wasn't asking how you knew that the neighbors were at odds; I was asking how you knew that you *thought* they were." It would be strange, too, if I asked how you knew that you heard shouting, and, getting the response, "Well, it *sounded* like shouting to me," I replied, "Okay, but what I'm driving at is: how did you know that it sounded like shouting to you?"

In these circumstances, the "How do you know?" question would be considered out of place. I would seem to be asking that you state reasons giving an argument or furnishing evidence for your claim that you thought such and such, or that something sounded a certain way to you. For whatever reason, this is regarded as an inappropriate request. And, though someone making first-person assertions about thought or experience would generally be unable to fulfill it, this inability is not thought somehow to render these assertions doubtful, as it would in other contexts in which the "How do you know?" question, posed in the wake of some assertion, brought forth no statement of argument or evidence.

This state of affairs could lead one to think either that one does not ever know, for example, what one thinks or how something to sounds to one (and has no warrant for assertions on such matters), or perhaps that the "How do you know?" question, in this context, simply makes no sense. I would disagree with both claims. I do not think my inability to support my first-person claims about attitudes and experience with argument or evidence implies that I do not know that they are true. And I think the question of *how* I know they are true does make sense, provided that one interprets it as the question, "What type of warrant do I have for these assertions?" Now, I agree this is not an *ordinary* question, but that is not enough to show that it is *unintelligible*. So I do not think we can simply assume that having warrant for a belief, and knowing it to be true, always requires that one is able to offer reasons supporting it, as argument or evidence. It may be that first-person knowledge, and the warrant one has for first-person belief, is in this sense nondiscursive: having it does not require that one be able to state reasons supporting the belief in question with argument or evidence, nor even that one be able to state what type of warrant one has for it at all.

Furthermore, it may be that having the kind of warrant one sometimes has for first-person beliefs and assertions about attitudes and experience does not consist in having reasons that even *could* be cited as argument or evidence supporting these claims, in the way we often require when we pose the "How do you know?" question. For it may be that the conditions under which one has this type of warrant for first-person assertions include the truth of those very claims.

Indeed, this might explain why we do not normally ask, "How do you know that you think such and such?" or "How do you know that it sounded that way to you?" For "How do you know?" questions ordinarily would have a point only where one's knowledge of the truth of one's assertions required that one have reasons that could be cited in support of the assertion, *without* reasserting it. And if part of what gives you warrant for saying that, for example, something sounds a certain way to you—part of what gives you a reason to say this—is just that something *does* sound that way to you, then, to say what your warrant is for making your assertion would involve reiterating it, and that would not be regarded as providing an argument for it, or saying what evidence supports the claim. Such reassertion in response to the "How do you know?" query, made in the face of first-person claims, could hardly serve any purpose in an ordinary context, since it would not give the questioner any new reason to believe what was first asserted. And the prospect of acquiring such a reason is ordinarily part of what motivates such a question.

The crucial point right now is simply this: Although having warrant for a belief one holds does involve having a reason to assert it, I do not assume that this necessarily involves having the ability to *say* what one's warrant is for the belief, nor, more particularly, do I assume that having warrant for a belief requires that one be able to produce an argument, or state evidence supporting that belief—as we presume Bob would be able to do, in the case of his beliefs about the neighbors. Knowledge and warrant *may* be, in some cases, nondiscursive. This is not a possibility we can reject out of hand. In fact, I think we will find good reason to believe (as we may already be inclined to believe) that knowledge of one's own attitudes and experience is, in this way, often nondiscursive. And further, I do not think we should assume that having knowledge or warrant always requires that one have reasons that could be cited as argument or evidence for one's claim, without reasserting it.

I need to draw attention briefly to a few more points about warrant before my explanation of how I want to use that notion is complete. First, we should recognize that there is a sense in which one can lack warrant *for* one's belief, even though that belief is warranted. In one of my earlier examples, Bob's belief that his neighbors are fighting is warranted—it is just that *he* does not have (much) warrant for believing it. This is because Bob lacks evidence for the belief, or takes as evidence for it something that turns out not to bear the right sort of relation to it. But, since the circumstances offer good reasons to be found for believing what Bob believes, even if Bob hasn't found them, we could say that his belief is a warranted one.

Second, one person may have warrant of a type different from that which another possesses, even though they both possess warrant for the same belief. You may believe that the mail has not arrived yet because you see that the mailbox is empty, and you have the only key to open it, while I may believe the mail has not arrived yet because I have been sitting on the front steps all morning and haven't seen the mail carrier. We may suppose both of us have warrant for our shared belief that the mail has not yet arrived, but the warrant we have is in each case of a different sort, in some respects. And this leads to a further point. To say that the types of warrant we have differ is not necessarily to make any comment on the superiority or inferiority of my warrant over yours. Warrant does indeed come in "degrees"—one can have more warrant for one belief than for another. But there are also differences in *kind*, distinct from differences in *degree*, of warrant. It may be that you and I have different sorts of warrant for our shared belief about the mail, though neither of us has more warrant than the other for holding this belief. Likewise, you and I may both believe that something looks green to me. And my first-person belief is either similar or identical to your third-person belief.[2] But while the warrant I have for my belief may differ in kind from that you possess for your belief, this does not by itself imply that I have any more or less warrant for my belief than you have for yours.

1.3 WHY I AM NOT A CARTESIAN

A large potential source of misinterpretation remains that I think should be discussed here at the outset. This has to do with the suspicion that my first-person approach does not deserve a try, since its illegitimacy is guaranteed by its devotion to some "Cartesian" view we can (supposedly) be quite sure we have long since surpassed. I now want to describe four strands, variously combined and woven together by various thinkers, that make up what I will call the "Cartesian View" of psychological knowledge. I will not make much effort to justify the historical accuracy of labeling the account they provide "Cartesian"; it is enough for my purposes if the four doctrines I describe here are widely associated with Descartes and his influence, and are recognized to have (or at least to have had) an important intellectual appeal. Having identified this "Cartesian View," I will indicate my own attitude toward it.

The first component of this view I call the "perceptual model" of consciousness and self-knowledge. It involves either the view that consciousness *is* in some sense the "perception" of mental items of some sort, or else the claim that some general *analogy* between consciousness and sense-perception provides us with an account of what is special about the former. Any view that defines consciousness as the perception of one's own "ideas," or of what "passes in one's mind," or that takes consciousness to be a kind of "inner sense," or that somehow holds that consciousness relates to one's own states of mind as seeing does to things seen (or hearing to things heard, etc.), subscribes to this aspect of the perceptual model.[3] This perceptual model of consciousness is then situated in an account of self-knowledge. The idea here is that first-person knowledge differs from third-person knowledge, because the former comes from perceiving (or doing something analogous to perceiving) one's own mind, whereas the latter, knowledge of others, is not had in this way, since one does not in this way perceive another's mind. This way of thinking about consciousness and self-knowledge is suggested by the metaphor buried in the term 'introspection,' and use of this expression often signals that the perceptual model is at work.

Sometimes the difference between knowing one's own mind and knowing others' minds is described by saying that while one "directly" or "immediately" perceives one's own mind (one's own thoughts, experiences), or one is "immediately" or "directly" conscious *of* one's own states of mind, one only "indirectly" or through inference knows what attitudes and experiences others have. This contrast leads us to the second strand of what I am calling the "Cartesian View." On this view, the warrant for our third-person psychological beliefs, to the extent we possess this, lies specifically in the inferential relation these bear to a scrupulously "dementalized" conception of the body one perceives (on a strict Cartesian view, the body one only *indirectly* perceives), when one perceives another human being. That body is conceived of as an extended mass of flesh following various trajectories through space, described in a way that involves no talk of attitudes and experience, and no terms whose application we understand by relating it to such talk. So, when encountering another, one observes the shape of a certain body, the frequent twists, wrinkling, stretching, and contortions of its trunk, digits, limbs, and skin, and a sequence of fantastically complex noises constantly bubbling out of its mouth—and when it comes to saying what another *perceives, wants, feels,* or *thinks,* one can know what one says is so, only if it is possible to justify one's claims entirely on the strength of their providing the best explanation of the behavior of bodies so conceived. But—on this picture—one's *self*-knowledge is not, and need not be, justified in this way.[4]

Now, the third strand of the Cartesian view has to do with a type of invulnerability supposedly characteristic of first-person belief. One adheres to this third part of the Cartesian view if one holds that, with at least some first-person beliefs, if one has them, what one believes makes one's belief logically insusceptible to one or another sort of epistemic flaw: some beliefs are such that their content bestows on them a certain epistemic invulnerability. On such a view, it follows from one's first-person belief's having a certain sort of content, that a certain sort of condition could not possibly obtain that, were it to obtain, would entail that one did not know one's belief was true. The very content of one's belief necessarily protects it against certain knowledge-threatening eventualities.

For example, one might hold that for some values of p, it is a necessary truth that, if one believes that p, and this is a first-person belief, then p is the case. So, for instance, one might hold that it is necessary that if I *believe* that I am in pain, then I *am* in pain. To accept this sort of view would be to maintain a strong kind of content-determined invulnerability for first-person belief, a kind of *infallibility* thesis. Another possible form of invulnerability: one might propose that where some values of p are concerned, it is necessary that, if one believes that p, and this is a first-person belief, then one cannot with reason doubt that p (or perhaps: one can have no warrant for doubting that p). This would attribute to first-person belief a certain kind of content-determined *indubitability*. And here is a third invulnerability proposal: for some p, it is necessarily the case that, if one believes that p, and this is a first-person belief, then no one has warrant for contradicting one's belief that p. This sort of claim could, I think, reasonably be called a kind of content-bestowed *incorrigibility* thesis: where certain first-person beliefs are concerned, that one believes what one believes entails that no one can with warrant challenge and correct this belief.[5]

The fourth and final strand of the Cartesian account of self-knowledge involves the notion that self-knowledge enjoys a certain kind of independence from knowledge of others. What kind of "independence" do I have in mind here? Consider some ways in which one might claim that self-knowledge *does* depend on knowledge of others. One might, for example, hold that one could not apply mental or psychological predicates to oneself, if one could not (accurately) apply them to others. This seems to be the upshot an argument of P. F. Strawson's (1958). And one might extract from those remarks of Wittgenstein's (1953) taken to argue against the possibility of a "private language" some thesis that psychological or mental terms, or terms for attitudes and experience, can make sense to us at all only if we are able to use them successfully in the third-person, that is, only if we can make third-person assertions employing such terms, and in doing this, say what is so. Or one might argue for the inseparability of speaking truthfully and intelligibly about one's own mind, and of speaking thus about others' minds, by in some *other* way working from the idea that language is, and must be, something "public" or "social."

Such views might be taken to show that self-knowledge is dependent on knowledge of others, by showing that one could not know any of what one believes about one's own attitudes and experience, unless one could know that some of what one believes about others' attitudes and experience is so. I assume it is the Cartesian's business to deny some form, or forms, of such dependence. The Cartesian needs first-person knowledge to be in some strong way third-person independent, for it is essential to his view of knowledge that first-person beliefs enjoy warrant of a sort that permits them to serve as a distinctively privileged basis by reference to which one's adherence to other beliefs is to be justified. Though first-person beliefs are, on this view, invulnerable to one or another sort of epistemic weakness, this can afflict other beliefs, including those about others' minds, en masse. So, it is said, for example, that one could doubt whether any of one's third-person beliefs were true, while leaving untouched by these doubts (at least some important) beliefs about one's own attitudes and experience. But I take it that on at least some versions of the view that first-person knowledge and warrant are third-person dependent, beliefs about oneself could not remain invulnerable to this or other sorts of epistemic weakness, while the entire body of one's beliefs about others was left to suffer from them.

This, then, is the picture of psychological knowledge I am calling "Cartesian." It is formed from the following four claims.

1. *The perceptual model*: Consciousness is a special sort of perception of one's own states of mind, or can be accounted for on analogy with sense-perception, and it is somehow through such perception of one's own mind that one has knowledge of it.

2. *Third-person belief as a theory of dementalized movement*: One knows other minds, only if one's third-person beliefs can be justified solely on the grounds that they provide the best explanation of the dementalized movements of others.

3. *The invulnerability of first-person belief*: It is necessarily true that first-person beliefs with certain sorts of content do not suffer from one or another sort of epistemically relevant weakness, such as fallibility, dubitability, or corrigibility.

4. *The independence of first-person knowledge*: It is not necessary that one know something of another's mind, if one is to know something of one's own.

My own attitude toward this picture can be summed up as follows. I premise my discussion on none of the above claims. I argue against (1) and (2), while neither asserting nor denying either (3) or (4). I identify this set of views ([1]–[4]) as the "Cartesian" picture, and emphasize my lack of support for it, in order to orient us toward an understanding of my own proposed reliance on first-person knowledge and its defense, by explicitly dissociating it from assumptions to which readers may be prone to attach it, but which I regard as quite inessential to a first-person approach. This is partly so that, if readers are inclined to criticize reliance on the "first-person point of view," when (allegedly) this is known to be some "Cartesian" blunder, or some discredited "subjectivism," or "introspectionism," they may be encouraged to be exact about the nature of their objections, and to be careful not to attribute to me some view I do not hold.

But now, even if I disavow this "Cartesian View," neither do I wish to join those who would use the term 'Cartesian' as a rhetorical cudgel, marking whomever one drubs with it as some sort of philosophical pariah. This is partly due to the proliferation of styles of anti-Cartesianism fundamentally at odds with what I *do* want to say. For, first, I do think that there is a nondiscursive, distinctively first-person knowledge and warrant with regard to attitudes and experience. Second, I treat this as crucial to understanding consciousness. And finally, I believe that having conscious experience is essential to the warrant one possesses for believing one has it. To some, this all will no doubt make me unbearably "Cartesian," even once it is clear that I have no attachment to the "Cartesian View" sketched above. So now I want to declare my disengagement from certain varieties of *anti*-Cartesianism and, by doing this, to prepare the way for explaining how I want to defend my proposed first-person approach to consciousness.

It is clear already I cannot accept the kind of anti-Cartesianism Ryle affirmed, which holds that there is no difference in kind between first- and third-person epistemic situations. And it is obvious I oppose those who would say that we have no first-person knowledge of mind because there just is no knowledge of mind, period. But I cannot be noncommittal on the issue of whether there is or is not some distinctively first-person knowledge. For I have conjectured that a relentlessly third-person perspective is potentially the source of mistakes about consciousness, and I have accordingly proposed that we guide our investigations by first-person knowledge. Now I want to add: not only must I reject views that would stay aloof from first-person knowledge of mind, but I also must decline certain possible strategies for showing that we do have a distinctive kind of warrant and knowledge in the first-person case. Since I believe consciousness plays an essential role in our knowledge of it, I cannot base my endeavors on accounts of this knowledge that leave consciousness out of the picture.

This leaves me unable to avail myself of a certain family of philosophical views about self-knowledge, such as are found in Rorty (1970); in remarks about self-knowledge in Armstrong's (1965), Lewis's (1972), and Putnam's (1960) expositions of functionalism; or in Davidson's account of the "asymmetry" between first- and third-person beliefs about mind (1973, 1984b, 1987). These views about the distinctiveness of our knowledge of first-person beliefs or claims are all anti-Cartesian, in that they involve a peculiar kind of inversion of the Cartesian scheme. In the Cartesian story, I am to take my knowledge of my own mind as primary, and justify judgments about others' minds by inferring them from what I can know of my own. But in the sorts of account just mentioned, it is, on the contrary, from what *others*—my interpreters or observers—can know about what I mean and think and feel, that my knowledge of myself is derived. The idea, roughly, is: if I know that I have certain attitudes or experiences, that is only because this follows from the fact that I present others with warrant for holding that I am able to represent my own mind accurately, where they are not. Thus, instead of deriving knowledge of other minds from knowledge of one's own, here, in a sense, one proposes to derive knowledge of one's own from knowledge of other minds—that is, from what other people can know of what is *for them* another mind—namely, one's own! One might say, here one takes up a third-person, observer's perspective on oneself, and tries to reconstitute one's self-knowledge from that perspective.

However non-Cartesian my view may be in some respects, I cannot defend my first-person approach to investigating consciousness by such maneuvers, because I believe that consciousness itself is essential to a distinctively first-person warrant for judgments about conscious experience, whereas in the views of the philosophers I mentioned, consciousness plays no role. In fact, consciousness, as I understand it, finds no place at all in these philosophers' schemes. And this will not be too surprising, if my conjecture is correct—that an attempt to base one's account of mind ultimately only on the type of warrant available for third-person claims about it is liable to inhibit a recognition of consciousness. In view of all this, it would not make much sense for me to try to justify my reliance on first-person knowledge by reference to this strategy of inverting the Cartesian picture. And, in any case, it would be unwise for me to build upon the views I have just mentioned, since in my judgment they contain serious difficulties, even apart from their omission of consciousness.

1.4 THE SHAPE OF THE ARGUMENT

We each know about our own attitudes and experience in a way we do not know about those of others. This is a claim we are, many of us, disposed to find plausible—even stunningly obvious. But does this commit us to the "Cartesian View" of self-knowledge? I do not want to argue for the legitimacy of my approach by defending or appealing to the conviction that we each have the ability to "directly perceive the contents of our minds," and that this bestows a kind of invulnerability to doubt, error, or challenge upon first-person judgments, and provides us with a knowledge of our own minds independent of any knowledge of the world outside of them. But then, can I argue for our right to adhere to this claim that we have a distinctively first-person knowledge without trying to derive our possession of it from a third-person perspective? It seems I cannot begin by offering an account of the conditions under which I do think we know our own minds. For I hold that we need a proper understanding of consciousness before we are in a position to state this, but a development of that understanding still lies ahead, and, I claim, requires us to rely on the very sort of first-person knowledge to be accounted for. So I cannot justify my proposed reliance on first-person knowledge by first saying what I take it to consist in, and *then* proceed to deal with the obscurities surrounding consciousness.

Perhaps it will seem I must simply take as basic or primitive the claim that we have and can make use of a distinctively first-person knowledge. But I think more can be done. Let's be clear about what is at issue. The question is not just one of whether you know that certain claims—those in which you attribute attitudes or experiences to yourself—are correct, but one of whether you know this in a way in which others do not. This question is to be understood as that of whether or not you have a certain *type of warrant* for them: a type of warrant had (ordinarily) only in the first-person, not in the third-person case. So we are concerned not just with a question about what we know, but about how we know, or (as we might put it) about the sources of knowledge: the conditions under which we have warrant for believing or asserting what we claim to know. Claims about such matters—general claims that we do or do not (would or would not) have warrant for certain kinds of assertions or beliefs (or knowledge of their truth) under certain kinds of conditions, let us call "epistemological claims." Thus the thesis of first-person warrant is an epistemological claim, since it says that the conditions under which one has warrant for first-person beliefs about mind differ in some way from the conditions under which one has warrant for third-person beliefs about mind. The issue now is: if claims about when one has warrant for a given kind of belief are put into question, how are we to try to arrive at a reasoned view of the matter?

We are disposed to make certain judgments about what we know, or what we have warrant for claiming or believing, even where our making such judgments does not depend on some inference from epistemological claims. That is to say, our being disposed to make these judgments regarding what we know or have warrant for believing at a certain time, is not contingent on our being able to infer them explicitly (i.e., verbally) from epistemological claims. We learn to make such judgments, and acquire dispositions to make them, in the absence of acquiring any ability to infer them from epistemological claims to which we are prepared to assent. For example, it is just possible that you are not only inclined to say that you know what you are (or were) thinking of, what you believe, or want, or how things look, sound, etc., to you—you might also be able to infer these assertions about what you know from certain epistemological claims, such as are found in some philosopher's theory of self-knowledge. But that, I take it, is *not* a precondition of your having been disposed to judgments that you know about such matters in the first place, but a fairly unusual ability, a late-born product of philosophical debate and reflection.

Now, what I propose first is that we examine such "pre-epistemological" judgments of knowledge or warrant, and see what they commit us to holding. That is, I want us to consider what we are inclined to assert we know (or have warrant for saying), even without any ability to infer such assertions (and perhaps thereby justify them) from epistemological claims to which we adhere. And I want us to take note of whether such judgments as we are inclined to make commit us to any view about the matter at issue—the thesis that we have a distinctively first-person warrant for assertions about our minds. I argue, in this chapter, that they do commit us to this very "distinctiveness thesis." The question I then want to pose (in the next chapter) is whether we have some good, non-question-begging reasons for abandoning this commitment and the judgments that lead us to it. That is, I want us to consider whether, without simply assuming the falsity of the distinctiveness thesis, we can find sufficient reason to reject the judgments we would otherwise be inclined to make about what we know (or have warrant for claiming) regarding our own attitudes and experiences. My assumption is that if we can find no good reason to abandon our pre-epistemological judgments about warrant and knowledge, we are entitled to keep them (or are warranted or justified in doing so), along with the epistemological claims to which they commit us. And so I will argue that since we have no adequate reason to deny what we pre-epistemologically would judge about our knowledge of our minds, we are entitled to proceed on the assumption that we do have a distinctively first-person knowledge of mind, and to rely on such knowledge in our inquiries about ourselves, in lieu of the discovery of some compelling reason not to do so.

This is how I intend to defend the legitimacy of the first-person approach to consciousness. This way of trying to argue for epistemological claims that may be in dispute is not, I will certainly admit, guaranteed to secure agreement. There may be a lack of accord about what would count as a good reason to reject our pre-epistemological judgments about what we know and when, and we may be unable to find a way to resolve such disputes. But even if that is so, at least we will be clearer about where the source of disagreement lies, and that is progress of a sort, which may open the way for further discussion.

However, I should point out that my procedure assumes from the start what may be open to doubt: that our pre-epistemological judgments are presumed to carry some authority, and deserve our continued acceptance, until we can find some reason to reject them. This way of proceeding would not please someone who thinks we should, when philosophizing about knowledge, suspend and set aside all our pre-epistemological judgments, and then somehow, independent of them, work out what the *correct* epistemological principles are, so that only once we have grasped these are we entitled to claim, by inference from them, that we know or have warrant for saying that such and such is the case in some particular instance. But I shall only say that I do not know how we are to determine what the correct epistemological principles are, if we are not allowed to grant some presumptive, if defeasible, authority to our pre-epistemological judgments about what we know. And if someone says that we must somehow independently determine what the right epistemology is, or else embrace a universal skepticism, I can only wonder why we should adopt that particular epistemological standard.

Now, you might have trouble identifying the sorts of pre-epistemological judgment regarding what you know about yourself to which I will refer, for the following reason. You might say:

> I don't have any disposition to make these judgments, though perhaps I once would have. Since I have become enlightened about what psychological knowledge requires, I have extirpated all the primitive superstitions to which you might

appeal—that I know I have certain "attitudes and experiences," identified in ordinary language. For now I can tell that the everyday standards by which I would have claimed to know such things about myself were totally inadequate.

If something like this is *your* view, I ask only that for now you consider what kinds of pre-epistemological judgments you once would have made, prior to your conversion to the allegedly advanced view of knowledge that demanded you change your ways. Once it is clear what such pre-epistemological convictions would commit one to holding, we can face afresh the question of whether there is indeed some superior perspective that permits us to put ourselves above or beyond the norms guiding ordinary talk, and so to break any commitment to the notion of a distinctively first-person knowledge of mind to which these may once have tied us.

But we are not ready for these questions yet. First we need to examine just what pre-epistemological claims we are (or would be) inclined to make, to see whether these do implicate us somehow in the view that the kind of warrant we have for first-person claims differs from the kind ordinarily had for third-person claims.

1.5 KNOWING WHAT ONE PERCEIVES

The following, I take it, holds true for many of us. One often either asserts, or is prepared to assert, that something looks, sounds, tastes, smells, or feels some way to one, or that one sees, hears, tastes, smells, or feels something. And one would say that these assertions of first-person beliefs are not just guesses, hypotheses, or proposals, but that one knows that they are correct. So, one often has various first-person beliefs about one's mind—in particular, beliefs about one's perception, or sense-experience—and one believes one knows these to be correct. One did not acquire such convictions, and the ability to form them, by acquiring the ability to state epistemological claims, and from these infer claims to know such things about oneself. Thus one has certain pre-epistemological convictions about one's knowledge of one's own perceptual experience.

I will come back in a little while to consider what to say to a way of trying to motivate a denial that we have such convictions. For the moment, I will assume that you are often disposed to assert that things look, sound, smell, taste, or feel a certain way to you, and that you know they do. Now, if you would say that you believe you have experiences of these sorts, and that you know you do, it follows (granting the connection between knowledge and warrant spelled out in 1.2) that you would also say you have warrant for certain first-person beliefs about your mind. But the question now is whether you are committed to holding that the type of warrant you have for these differs from the type of warrant ordinarily had for the corresponding third-person beliefs—the type someone else would ordinarily have for believing that something looks, sounds, tastes, smells, or feels a certain way to you.

Let's first note what we ordinarily assume would be required for one to have warrant for third-person beliefs about someone's perceptual experience. I think we can agree that ordinarily we know how others perceive things, if we do, through such observation of their bodies' position and movement, and of their effects on their environment, as can be made without examination of their nervous systems. By saying we agree to this, I intend to leave open the question of what exactly is observed, and how this relates to the relevant third-person beliefs to make for knowledge. So again, I do not, for instance, assume this knowledge rests entirely on some inference to the truth of these third-person beliefs from observed dementalized bodily movements. Furthermore, by saying that we *ordinarily* know about others' experience through observation of the sort described, I just want to call attention to the fact that if some sort of "extra-sensory" third-person knowledge is possible—either by using some imagined neuropsychological gadgetry hooking up one brain to another,[6] or by alleged parapsychological means—these are not the ways we actually take ourselves to know about others' experience in most or all cases. And it is the warrant with which we usually, ordinarily take ourselves to know about others' minds that I want to contrast with the sort we often take ourselves to have in the first-person case. Finally, although the word 'observation' may seem a little cold and detached to describe the kind of perception we normally have of other people by which we know of their experience, I do not think this should provide an obstacle. By 'observation' I simply mean any sensory modality by which one sometimes perceives things other than one's own body or its condition: for example, sight, hearing, smell, taste, and touch. (By contrast, that manner of perception by which each of us feels or senses the position only of his or her own body does not count as observation.)

Now, of course, you can and do observe your own body and what it does. You see your own hands, and hear your own voice, for example—that I don't want to deny. But what I want to draw attention to is this: the sorts of observation by which you ordinarily know what perceptual experience others have, are not ones by which you know what perceptual experience you yourself have. If I am to know how something looks to another person, and thus to have warrant for a certain third-person belief, I need to observe the movement of his body, or something produced by these movements, or reports from someone else who has made such observations. Although it is not clear that self-observation—perceiving one's own body via the sorts of sensory modalities by which one perceives another's body—is not *somehow* involved in knowing about one's own perception, what is clear is this. The sorts of observation required for someone else to know what, in particular instances, one knows about one's own perceptual experience are just not such as one actually makes oneself.

For instance, though I know on a particular occasion that one piece of cake looks bigger to me than another, the observations of me that another person would ordinarily need to make if he or she were to know that the one piece of cake looks bigger to me than the other are not any that I, as a matter of fact, make of myself. For another would need to observe something of the following sort: my bodily orientation; my eyes, and their movement and position; my hand and arm movements (e.g., those involved in pointing to one piece when asked, "Which is bigger?"); or my speech (e.g., my saying, "This one looks bigger to me"). Perhaps in certain cases, in order to know how something looks to another, all one would really need to observe is an appropriate speech act (though certainly it does not seem that one could know how things looked to other people if all anyone ever observed of another was his speech). But these complications needn't detain me, if it's clear enough that often I know how something looks to me, without observing even my speech. And it does happen sometimes that I do not see (or otherwise observe) my eyes, or hear (or otherwise observe) my speech, when I know that this piece of cake looks bigger to me than that one.

I use this example of a piece of cake, but, of course, any case of something looking as though it had a certain size, or position, or shape, or color, would do. And although I use this example of something's *looking* some way to me, there is nothing preventing us from using instances of knowing that one *sees* something, or sees that something is the case. You may think the belief that something looks some way to you is more certain, less dubitable, or in some way or other less epistemically vulnerable, than the belief that you see something, or that something is so. Still, you probably would be inclined to think you know that you see, even when you do not observe of yourself what another ordinarily would have to observe, if he or she were to know, on those occasions, that you see what you see. So the point I am making applies equally well where talk of seeing is concerned. And the same sort of point can be made regarding each of the sensory modalities, and what we experience or perceive through these.

Now, if your pre-epistemological convictions are of this sort—and I trust I am not alone in having these beliefs—you will be committed to holding that the type of warrant you have for first-person beliefs regarding perceptual experience is different from the type of warrant had for the corresponding third-person beliefs. For you think that there are instances in which you know that certain first-person beliefs about perceptual experience are correct, even though you do not make the observations that would ordinarily be required for another to know that corresponding third-person beliefs are correct. And what the third-person beliefs thus require from these sorts of observation is what they would need for anyone having them to possess warrant for them. So this is the situation: you know that certain *first-person* beliefs are so, and thus you have warrant for them, but you lack what one ordinarily would need to have warrant for the corresponding *third-person* beliefs—certain kinds of observation. Therefore, the type of warrant you have for these first-person beliefs is not the same as the type of warrant one ordinarily needs for the corresponding third-person beliefs.

Thus our pre-epistemological judgments commit us to the view that we possess a type of warrant for at least some of our first-person beliefs (those having to do with perception) distinct from the type we ordinarily possess for the corresponding third-person beliefs. Briefly put: even if circumstances are such that another does know at a given time what you know about your own perception, you do not know, as the other does, by observation, simply because you often simply do not make the required observations of yourself.

1.6 A WITTGENSTEINIAN CHALLENGE

Some may reject what I said in the last section because they resist from the start the notion that it even makes sense to speak of your *knowing* how things look or feel to you. They might say that the norms governing our use of ordinary terms for what I call "attitudes and experience"—far from condoning the kinds of first-person claims to knowledge that I contend express our pre-epistemological convictions—actually require us to regard such "claims" as complete nonsense. Such, at any rate, might be the response of someone influenced by famous remarks of Wittgenstein. If this objection stands, then clearly my argument has gotten off to a bad start. So perhaps I had better pause to reflect on what would give rise to these Wittgensteinian worries, even if this involves something of a digression; I shouldn't dismiss what has struck many thoughtful people as compelling and incisive (or at least intriguing), when this appears to halt my first few steps.

A prime instigator of this objection to what I have said so far might be Wittgenstein's remark that one cannot say, "I know I'm in pain" (for this would be *nonsense*), or one can say this only as a *joke*, or, only if it is taken to *mean just the same* as "I'm in pain" (1953, sec. 246). Some may believe that not only is this correct about 'know' and 'pain,' but it also goes for other talk ostensibly about "perceptual experience"—for example, "This shirt looks blue to me"; "It smells like smoke in here"; "This cake tastes to me as if it has rum in it."[7]

Now, clearly I think it does make sense to say that I know that something looks, smells, or tastes some way to me, and (although I haven't discussed this specifically) I would also say that it makes sense to say that I know that I'm in pain. And I do not think these make sense only if one refuses to treat them as literal assertions, or only if one takes them to mean nothing more than what one would mean in asserting, by itself, what comes after "I know that . . ." in each of these cases. Should Wittgenstein's remarks somehow persuade me otherwise?

Someone impressed by Wittgenstein's claim, "It can't be said of me at all (except perhaps as a joke) that I know I am in pain," might think it shows that "I know I'm in pain" cannot intelligibly be taken as a literal statement, since we cannot see what motivation someone would have in uttering this sentence, unless he were joking. And if someone is joking, he doesn't mean what he says—it's not to be taken literally. But the fact that someone might utter this sentence as a joke (even if this were the typical use of this sentence) does not show that it cannot be used to make literally intelligible statements. On the contrary, it seems to me the most plausible explanation of why "I know I'm in pain" might be said as a joke *requires* that generally it could be used to make an intelligible, literally true statement when the speaker is in pain. I agree it would indeed usually seem odd to say that one knows that one is in pain, but why is this? It is not, I suggest, because "I know I'm in pain" is *senseless*, but rather because it is normally assumed that one *does* know when one is in pain. Where it is clear that someone is in pain on account of the circumstances and what she does in them (and these may include her saying, "I'm in pain"), it is taken for granted that she knows she is in pain; this is not something anyone would think of denying or doubting. So to assert that one knows that one is in pain would be to say something that, though true and intelligible, is otherwise spectacularly uninformative. Since in speaking one typically tries to be somewhat informative to one's audience, someone who simply notes what all would consider glaringly obvious, which leads to nothing else that is not so, flagrantly violates our understanding of what it is appropriate to do in conversation. The absurdity of such a violation is just the sort of thing that sometimes strikes us as funny. (Though admittedly, in this case, the joke is not exactly side-splitting.)

But what can we make of Wittgenstein's other suggestion, that if "I know I'm in pain" means anything, it means the same as "I'm in pain"? One follower of Wittgenstein elaborates on this by claiming that "I know I'm in pain" is simply an emphatic way of saying "I'm in pain."[8] But why should we think this? Surely the initial presumption is that the word 'know' functions merely as a kind of exclamation point no more when used in "I . . . that I'm in pain" than when used in "I . . . that she's in pain." Why would it seem plausible to override this presumption? The best I can do to motivate this is to consider some scenario like the following. Suppose Irene says, "I'm in pain." Bob then objects, "But surely that couldn't have really hurt" (perhaps because it seems to him the stimulus was too mild to induce pain). Then Irene replies, rather testily, "But I *am* in pain!" We might also, it seems, just as well imagine Irene to have responded here, "But I *know* I'm in pain." In either case, Irene's reply is somehow supposed to overcome Bob's reasons for doubting her original assertion. And we might think this is supposed to work in either case in the same way—through the force of emphasis.

But it seems to me that Irene's responses in the two variants of this scenario would typically work in somewhat different ways, and to somewhat different ends. In the first variant ("I am in pain!"), we should imagine that Irene is trying to overcome Bob's suspicion that she is dissembling or exaggerating. Irene's reiteration of her words, with emphasis, is supposed to convince Bob of her *seriousness* and *sincerity*, and it works, if it does, because many of us most of the time find ourselves reluctant or unable to assert emphatically and unfalteringly what we believe to be definitely untrue to those we think will take us seriously. However, I find it implausible to suppose the second variant response ("I know I'm in pain") would be offered against a suspicion of insincerity or exaggeration. Why then *would* anyone make such a response in such a situation? We can make sense of this, if we suppose that Irene is trying to overcome Bob's doubts by reminding him, in effect, that however inadequate *his* grounds might so far seem, in the given circumstances, for asserting that Irene is now in pain, *she* has a distinctive sort of right to beliefs about such matters, entitling her on this occasion to assert that she definitely is in pain, enabling her to *know* (even if *he* does not) that she is in pain.

So it appears that Wittgenstein has offered us three choices: "I know I'm in pain" is nonsense; or it is a joke; or it means the same as "I'm in pain." And the problem is, when I try to think of why anyone would find the latter two options plausible, I find myself denying the first option, and concluding that "I know I'm in pain" can, after all, express a significant, even true, proposition. Thus Wittgenstein's remarks do not make me want to deny that first-person claims to know what sort of experience one has are sometimes true and intelligible; if anything, they bolster precisely the opposite conviction.

But perhaps one will in another way bring Wittgenstein to bear witness against the intelligibility of what I claim to be our convictions about experience and self-knowledge. Some may point to the suggestion that it makes no sense to suppose that one could be mistaken about, or doubt, or be ignorant of, one's own pain. And if such suppositions are senseless, then (so the suggestion runs) talk of one's knowing that one is in pain is also senseless. For there is a place here for knowledge, only if there is a place for error, doubt, or ignorance. And maybe such considerations also apply in the case of other putative first-person claims to know what one experiences, to which I have made appeal.[9]

But what kind of error are we talking about here? What would constitute an error regarding one's own pain? One would presumably be mistaken about one's own pain if one asserted sincerely that one was in pain, even though one was not in pain. Now, it is at least plausible to suppose that one could not be in this way mistaken about being in pain (at least, not in the "standard" case).[10] For we might reasonably think typically that if someone says, "I'm in pain," when she is not in pain, and there is no reason to think she is not speaking sincerely, then she could not mean by this utterance that she is in pain. Something similar may also hold for certain other first-person sentences, such as, "It looks green to me." And one might argue that if this kind of mistake is not possible, then it is not possible for one to doubt or to be ignorant of the fact that one is in pain, or that something looks green to one.

However, even if this kind of error, or doubt, or ignorance is not possible, that does not imply that it makes no sense to say, "I know I'm in pain," or "I know it looks green to me." How could anyone think it did? There may be a couple of reasons. First, one might fail to distinguish between the claim that it is impossible for someone mistakenly to assert that he is in pain, and the claim that it is senseless to say that he mistakenly asserts that he is in pain. Moving from the first claim to the second, one might go on to infer that it is senseless to say that someone doubts or is ignorant of the fact that he is pain, and then to the conclusion that it is senseless for someone to say that he knows that he is in pain. But we should not be led down this trail, for we ought to distinguish between claims about what is not possible on the one hand, and impossible claims—that is, senseless ones—on the other.

One might also be tempted to infer the senselessness of certain first-person knowledge claims from the notion that one cannot make certain kinds of mistakes about one's own experience, if one fails to distinguish between the kind of mistake just discussed—a mistaken sincere assertion that one is in pain—and another kind of mistake, an incorrect use of the English sentence, "I'm in pain." Now, clearly, this second kind of mistake does need to be possible if it is to make sense to say, "I know that I'm in pain." For this makes sense only if a speaker can use "I'm in pain" to assert that he is in pain. And for this, it must be possible for a speaker to use the sentence "I'm in pain" in a way that shows that he does not understand it to mean that he is in pain, that is, in a way that would allow us to say that, *relative to this interpretation*, his use of this sentence is mistaken or incorrect. If this kind of mistake were not possible, if it were not possible to use this sentence in a way that was not in accord with a certain understanding of it, then there would be nothing that counted as either a correct or incorrect use of this phrase, and then we would indeed have to say that it was nonsense, or didn't mean anything. And if "I'm in pain" were nonsense, "I know I'm in pain" would also be nonsense. But never fear: this kind of mistake *is* possible. So we do not have to worry about what follows from its impossibility.

Thus my thoughts about the relevance of mistakes regarding one's own pain come down to this. The claim (a) that I cannot utter, "I'm in pain," to make a sincere but false assertion that I am in pain, is consistent with the claim (b) that I may utter this sentence in a way incompatible with a certain interpretation of it, for example, one that takes it to be an assertion by the speaker that he is in pain. And only the kind of mistaken use that (b) involves needs to be possible for the statement, "I'm in pain," to make sense. If this makes sense, then I see no objection to saying, "I know I'm in pain" (and "I know this looks green to me," etc.) make sense.

Someone may here wish to draw our attention to still another suggestion of Wittgenstein supposed to bear great consequences for our conception of experience and self-knowledge, namely, that we liken "I'm in pain" to the cries, groans, or grimaces whereby we express our pain, that we think of an utterance of "I'm in pain" as "pain behavior."[11] What are we to say to this?

Well, maybe there is some analogy here—maybe the utterance of this sentence does "replace" the cries, groans, etc., as part of one's learning to use it, and maybe both the utterance and the groans are in some special sense "criteria" by which another judges that the utterer/groaner is in pain—at least, both give another warrant to believe one is in pain. However, none of this shows that "I'm in pain" is not—as groans are not—used to make a true statement.[12] And again, if this is so, why shouldn't it make sense to use this sentence to state something one knows?

But I do not simply want to respond to these Wittgensteinian suggestions about the senselessness of saying one *knows* what sort of experience one has. For I do not want to leave the impression that what is crucial to my thesis turns entirely on our willingness to use the word 'know' to make certain first-person assertions—"I know I'm in pain," "I know this looks blue to me," etc. What I am most concerned with here is our commitment to the claim that we have a type of warrant for first-person beliefs about our attitudes and experience that we do not ordinarily have for the third-person beliefs; an appeal to an inclination to say one knows that one has certain kinds of experience is just a way of demonstrating this commitment. But we can still bring this out, even if we set aside the word 'know' for a moment, and speak just of *warrant*.

I assume it makes sense to say that another may have warrant for claiming or believing that I am in pain. Am I to say that while this other may have warrant for asserting that I am in pain, *I have no warrant whatsoever* for believing that I am in pain? This seems strange. But then, if I do say that I also have warrant for the belief at issue, then commitment to the distinctness thesis will ensue, by a now-familiar route, for I may lack the sort of warrant the other needs to have from observation for the claim that I am in pain. (I perhaps do not observe myself wincing, groaning, etc.)

But what is wrong with saying that only my observer has warrant for believing that I am in pain, while I have no warrant whatsoever for this claim? If this position does not already seem absurd enough, one might bring this out by noting some of its consequences. Consider: one way in which you may have warrant for believing that I'm in pain is by hearing me assert that I am. Now, I can hear myself make this assertion just as well as you can, so there seems to be no obstacle in principle to my having some sort of warrant for my belief about what sort of experience I have. I can at least have the same sort of warrant from observation for my first-person belief as you can have for the corresponding third-person belief about me. Now, of course, this does not show that I have a distinctively first-person warrant for the belief in question. Perhaps I can have warrant for first-person beliefs about my experience only when this warrant is of the same type as would be had for the corresponding third-person beliefs. But this is untenable. For I can *intentionally misrepresent* my experience to my hearer, in circumstances in which he or she would have warrant for accepting the falsehood I tell. I might intentionally falsely assert to you that I'm in pain when I am not, though conditions are such that you have warrant for believing what I say. But then, if I can have no warrant for my first-person assertion here but what is ordinarily available to others, then I can never have any warrant for thinking I am lying in such circumstances. I will then inevitably have more warrant for believing my own lie than for believing what I do believe, which is true. But surely *this* seems absurd. And so I can have warrant for thinking what I say to another regarding my own experience is false, even where he or she is none the wiser. So we should reject the assumption that would have us say otherwise, that one can have no warrant for first-person assertions about one's experience but what others have. Thus we are brought back again to the thesis of first-person warrant.

I conclude that certain Wittgensteinian challenges to the claim that one has a distinctively first-person knowledge and warrant regarding what sort of perceptual experience one has fail to undermine this claim, and indeed, even reinforce it. You may feel a little funny about saying that you know that you're in pain, or that something looks green to you, because typically you find no occasion to make such assertions. But further consideration of the sorts of (atypical) circumstances in which you might want to make them (as a joke, or to overcome your hearer's doubts) only serves to strengthen the conviction that, however unusual it might be to *say*, "I know I'm in pain" (or "I know this looks green to me," etc.), it is not at all unusual for such claims to be *true*. And if it is hard, or even impossible, to conceive of how one could, in a standard case, be mistaken about such matters, the difficulty in making this kind of mistake casts no reasonable doubt on the intelligibility of the relevant first-person assertions, or the claim to know they are true. Finally, once we shift from talk of knowing to talk of warrant, and once we allow that one obtains warrant for third-person beliefs about experience from first-person assertions, we are led to recognize that first-person beliefs about experience have warrant of a distinctive type, or else to embrace the absurdity that you cannot have warrant for thinking you have deceived others about your experience. And if you allow that you can have a distinctively first-person warrant for claims about your experience—the crucial point at issue—it would seem that only a quibble could make you still refuse to say you often know you have perceptual experiences of various sorts. And so it seems to me there should be no reasonable resistance to my earlier way of showing our commitment to the distinctiveness thesis—from examples in which we know how things look (sound, etc.) to us, but not by self-observation.

The possibility to which I appealed a moment ago, where one knowingly and intentionally misleads others about one's own (pain) experience, points to another way of bringing out our commitment to the distinctiveness thesis, which will help broaden the range of attitudes and experience about which we recognize we have a distinctively first-person knowledge. For part of what makes us think the kind of deception to which I alluded possible is that we think one can sometimes be in a position to know what is the case regarding one's own experience, when no one else is. In the next section, I consider some of the implications of this.

1.7 SOLITARY SELF-KNOWLEDGE

I want us now to consider instances in which one believes, as it seems one often does, that one knows what one is thinking, or has been thinking, though, as it happens, *no one else does*. We might call these cases of "solitary self-knowledge." That sometimes self-knowledge is solitary does not, by itself, tell us that it involves a different sort of warrant than that involved in knowledge of others. After all, one may at various times know all sorts of things of which the rest of the world happens to be ignorant, though it is fairly easy to see how another could have come to know, by observation, had he or she just happened to be in the right place at the right time. I alone know now that there is an ant crawling across my desk; though no one else happens to be in on this, they could have easily established it for themselves, and with the same source of warrant: namely, by looking. The mere fact that I know and no one else does is clearly not enough to establish that I did not know by the same sort of observational route another could have used.

But in many cases of such solitary self-knowledge, given one's actual behavioral history up until and including the time one is thinking something or other, it is very hard to see how anyone else could have been in a position to know, by any ordinary observation, what one is thinking. Though you may enter and see, and know, as I do, that a tiny insect is making its way across my desk, you will not know, unless and until I tell you, that as I was watching this ant I was wondering why I dislike ants so much; you will not know that I was then reminded of an "ant farm" I had as a child, that I was at that moment recollecting the cheap green plastic farm props inside, the barn and the silo, and the pathetic ants inside, some dead, some barely struggling, wiggling in the white sand. That you couldn't care less about this is not to the point; the point is, until I tell you, you will not know, and could not, it seems, reasonably be expected to, through any ordinary observation of my body, its movements, reactions, or creations throughout its entire history up until and including that moment. I, on the other hand, do not have to wait to be told; I know already.

Now, if things sometimes happen as in my story about my ant thoughts, then it happens that no observations such as another might ordinarily make of my body, its movements, etc., could have at a certain time given them warrant for their belief or claim that I was then thinking (wondering about, recollecting) certain things, given the history of my body's movements and its interaction with the world around it—and yet I nonetheless did have warrant for my belief, since I knew what I was thinking. And so it follows that the type of warrant I had for my first-person belief was not just the same as the type of warrant someone might ordinarily have for the corresponding third-person belief, since, while I had warrant for my first-person belief, the type of warrant ordinarily to be had, through observation, for the relevant third-person belief was, under the circumstances, simply not available. So what followed from my initial convictions concerning my knowledge of perception follows also here, in these nonperceptual cases.

Here again, as in the perceptual cases earlier discussed, I ask the reader to consider whether he or she has similar convictions in similar circumstances, that is, whether it happens that you take yourself to know that you were thinking of or about something, or thinking such and such, even though, at the time, such of your behavioral history as is observable by ordinary means does not offer adequate opportunity for an observer to have warrant for the relevant third-person beliefs. If so, it will follow that you are committed to holding that you possess a kind of first-person warrant that differs from third-person warrant of the ordinary sort.

I want to offer just a few more stories illustrating this kind of solitary self-knowledge, inviting you to consider whether these bear a relevant resemblance to occurrences known firsthand. I hope this will help draw out the convictions about self-knowledge on which I want to focus, and the commitments they entail. I hope also it will make clear to a cooperative reader the great abundance and variety of what we would take ourselves to know of this sort. For I fear that one may too easily lose sight of this, when accustomed to consider claims about the distinctiveness of self-knowledge only with regard to the rather limited range of examples so often found in discussions of the alleged "incorrigibility" of first-person statements about "sensation," especially pain.

So, suppose one Sunday morning you emerge from sleep, still too tired to move, or even open your eyes; retaining some dim awareness of a dream, you wonder what it was about. You recall only a few fragments, though a firm sense of the larger narrative eludes you: you were swimming underwater in a large, dimly lit pool, others swimming around you, when suddenly you realized: *this is a pool for blind people*—and you became apprehensive about colliding with them. . . . You think of getting up, but you still feel tired; you think of what you will do after getting up: breakfast. You wonder what you might make to eat: you begin to imagine French toast frying in a pan on the stove, its look, its smell, the spongy warm eggy taste, mixed with thick liquid sweetness.

Maybe not everyone has spent an early morning remembering swimming dreams or thinking of French toast, but I think the reader will be able to recognize that broadly the same kind of thing has happened to him or her. That is, on some occasions, you believe you are, lying there in bed, able to know that these kinds of things are going on: that you are thinking of breakfast and of something you might have for breakfast, that you are trying to remember a dream, that you recollect some aspects of it, and so on. And yet, as far as other people may know, standing there watching you—still, eyes closed, quietly breathing—you might be asleep. And it doesn't matter how attentively they watch you, or how skilled they are at observation, or even if they had been observing you every moment since birth: they still do not know, nor could they be expected to know from ordinary observation of you, that you are, say, thinking about French toast.

Perhaps the solitude of this self-knowledge is particularly striking in such circumstances, where one lies motionless, eyes closed, withdrawn from the world to some quiet sanctuary. But one can easily enough have such solitary self-knowledge while obviously awake, and amidst the turmoil of humanity—riding the subway, for example. Do Bob's fellow passengers know that he is at this moment worrying about his taxes, dreading the expense and the effort, feeling frustrated at the way life seems to get eaten up by all these tiresome unwanted tasks, as he sits there staring at an advertisement? Bob knows. And he knows he feels regret about what he said last night to Irene, as he wonders whether the tension that was there this morning will still be there when he sees her again this evening, wonders also how he could set things right. Again, Bob knows all this is happening right as it is happening, though no one else does. And how could they, even if they had subjected Bob's entire life until that point to the most intense scrutiny?

Now, there are, I trust, in each of our lives occasions on which we, like Bob, take ourselves to know that we are worrying about something, or feel frustration at or regret about something, or recollect something that has occurred, or wonder about what will happen and what we will do. And on many such occasions, one has offered up for ordinary observation nothing that would give others, at that time, the wherewithal to know what one then takes oneself to know about oneself.

Perhaps instances where we would take ourselves to have solitary self-knowledge of this sort are more striking where the attitudes and experience in question are not directed at one's immediate surroundings, and where it is a matter of someone reflecting, musing, daydreaming, or engaging in "silent soliloquy." But, although confining our attention to such cases would already make the phenomenon ubiquitous, we should recognize that one may often take oneself to know oneself in instances where others' observations are powerless to help them know what one knows, even though the attitudes one believes one has are concerned with one's immediate surroundings. Irene is rifling through a desk drawer looking for a certain photograph it suddenly occurred to her she wanted to see. She knows what she is looking for, but it could easily happen that none of the rest of us could tell this from what has been available to us to observe. Or again, Irene is walking down the street, and for a moment, a man approaching her looks to her like Bob, but then the next instant she sees that he is a stranger. She knows that this little episode of mistaken identity has occurred, but, as it happens, no one else does, nor has Irene done anything up to this point that would enable them to know, by ordinary means. Again, the conviction that such things actually happen in our own lives should be familiar to us. We each sometimes take ourselves to know what we are doing, or how something or someone looks to us, in such circumstances as do not happen to allow another to know, at this time, that these things are so.

Now, in all these stories I've been telling, one takes oneself to know one's own mind, to know, that is, what attitude or experience one has, at a time when no other person knows nor could have known this, by any ordinary means, given one's behavioral history. I am confident that the verisimilitude of such stories to the reader's life will be evident, even if the experience found there is often not nearly as drab, but wonderfully profound, and full of wit and poetical nuance. And if I pass over, for the time being, many fascinating and important, if common, aspects of experience, this is only because of their relative elusiveness; I find it best to start with examples more easily recognizable.

One may say, of course, that wherever situations do arise such as those in my stories, though others do not know what the solitary self-knower at that moment knows, they could perhaps *guess* correctly what was on the person's mind. But this is not to the point; confirming the accuracy of the guess will require that something more than mere guessing is possible, and it is just some such "something more" that one takes oneself to have in one's own case, though all others lack it. And it is irrelevant that each of my stories could be elaborated or altered in ways that allowed others to know through ordinary observation what the self-knower knows; this may be true, but the point is that we can also suppose that things do not happen so as to allow any other to know this when the self-knower knows it, and in supposing this, we are not supposing things to be otherwise than they often are in fact.

1.8 But Do We Know Our Minds?

We have discovered two general ways to bring out pre-epistemological convictions committing us to the view that we have a first-person warrant different in kind from third-person warrant of the ordinary sort—the thesis of first-person warrant. The first way proceeds from examples illustrating that one takes oneself to have warrant for first-person beliefs, *even when one does not observe* what is ordinarily required for possession of warrant for the corresponding third-person beliefs. The second way proceeds from examples illustrating that one takes oneself to have warrant for first-person beliefs, even when what is ordinarily required for possession of warrant for the relevant third-person beliefs is *just not there to be observed*. Either way, it follows that the warrant one takes oneself to have in first-person cases is not the sort third-person beliefs ordinarily have.

Notice now that I have presented the thesis that first-person knowledge differs from knowledge of others in a way that shows we are committed to it by our initial convictions, but that avoids the "Cartesian View" earlier identified. I have made appeal neither to the notion that one "directly perceives" one's own states of mind, nor to the notion that some first-person beliefs are somehow infallible, indubitable, or incorrigible. Nor have I contrasted first-person knowledge with knowledge of others by saying that the latter, but not the former, somehow involves or requires one to infer claims about attitudes and experience as a theory to explain observed, dementalized bodily movements. And I have not claimed that our knowledge of our own attitudes and experience is somehow generally independent of third-person knowledge of mind. The convictions to which I have appealed to show we believe that we have a distinctively first-person warrant are not ones acquired through exposure to the Cartesian tradition of philosophical theorizing, but rather are such as we learn to form just in learning to employ some garden-variety terms in our language. And, while my exposition has not relied on Cartesian sympathies, I also have not approached the topic of self-knowledge through an inverted Cartesianism, trying to derive our possession of first-person warrant from the third-person point of view.

I would like to remark also that, however modest my results so far, it would be quite misleading to say I have done no more than point to some "commonsense intuition" that self-knowledge differs from knowledge of others. For I have not simply appealed to some inclination we may have to assent to the general proposition that the way in which we know our own minds differs from the way in which we know others' minds. Rather, leaving aside at first whatever such general assertions we might be inclined to make about how we know our own minds, I have shown that examination of our convictions about what we know of our own minds in specific instances leads us to recognize a commitment to the thesis of first-person warrant. Also, partly for this same reason, it would be wrong to say I appeal to some "feeling" we have that first-person knowledge generally differs from third-person knowledge. But we ought to avoid this way of putting matters for another reason as well; I have not tried to infer the thesis of first-person warrant from some belief we may have that a certain kind of "feeling" accompanies certain of our experiences, a "feeling of knowing"—whatever that may be. Again, I have inferred our belief in the thesis of first-person warrant from our convictions about what we know, and from the character of the circumstances in which we would claim to know.

Nevertheless, if these are our pre-epistemological convictions, maybe they should not be our *post*-epistemological ones. If we are inclined to say we know such things about ourselves in such circumstances, maybe we *ought not* say this, once we have considered matters more carefully. And so, perhaps we ought not to be committed to the claim of first-person warrant, but to its denial. Recall that I earlier imagined a reader who was confident that no claim about a distinctively first-person knowledge of mind I could draw from our pre-epistemological convictions would be worthy of allegiance, a reader who held that there are higher standards to which to devote oneself, which reveal the hopeless naivete of our unprofessional, homespun claims to self-knowledge. Such a reader, I supposed, would disclaim the kind of self-knowledge I assume many of us would be ready to assert we have.

Now, the question is whether we really ought to think an epistemology that would ask us to forsake the kinds of claims to self-knowledge to which I've referred offers salvation from error, or whether such abandonment is itself just philosophical folly. I would grant that we have no right to assume that our pre-epistemological convictions about self-knowledge are beyond question, or that they give the final word. We cannot rule out the possibility that we may find reason to change our view of what we know about ourselves and when we know it, even where the sorts of first-person claims I have been discussing are at issue. So we must examine what reasons we think there are for doubting our convictions. Nonetheless, if we find these reasons wanting, we should stand by such convictions, unintimidated by appeals to some vaguely identified, allegedly more sophisticated perspective—no matter by what labels of intellectual advertising (e.g., 'empirical,' 'objective,' 'scientific') one touts it.

Third-Person Doubts about First-Person Warrant

2.1 THIRD-PERSON DOUBTS

Should we hold to our belief in first-person warrant? Or do we have reason to say our claim to even the mundane self-knowledge I've illustrated evinces only some quaint, pretheoretical naivete? If one is to refute the thesis that we have a distinctively first-person knowledge of mind, one will need to attack the pre-epistemological convictions in which we discerned a commitment to it. But it may be difficult to see where one could look for reasons to doubt such beliefs.

What we are willing to count as a serious reason to doubt here depends on what we are willing to assume is required for knowing what attitudes and experience one has. Now, I do not assume that knowledge of the truth of some genre of beliefs or claims requires they be somehow secured against even the *possibility* of falsehood. I do not think we need to demonstrate somehow that it is strictly impossible for one's first-person claims to be largely false, in order to be entitled to claim to know they are true. Also, as I said in Chapter 1, I am not willing to assume that knowledge is always discursive—so it will not count as a convincing reason to doubt our claims to self-knowledge, that where we think we know, for example, how things look to us, or what we are thinking, or that we are in pain, we are unable to state an argument or cite evidence that shows what our warrant for making these claims consists in. And, I said, I do not think we can assume that an account of what one's warrant for making such claims consists in would comprise an argument or statement of evidence supporting these claims, of the kind we usually want when we ask, "How do you know?" For part of what is crucial to having a distinctively first-person warrant for such claims may just be their truth, and to reassert the truth of first-person claims would not be to state an argument or cite evidence in their favor.

However, this is not to say there is nowhere to seek some way of casting doubt on the distinctiveness thesis. For I am willing to grant that first-person assertions about mind are defeasible, in at least some circumstances, and further, that knowing our first-person beliefs are correct in the sorts of cases to which I made reference in the last chapter requires at least that we are able to form accurate beliefs of this sort with some regularity. This seems to give some opening to doubt. For we might ask whether we can find reason for saying that the sorts of first-person assertions earlier illustrated, which we would claim to know are correct, are not, in fact, regularly correct, but are chronically prone to error. If we can find reason to say this, then we can find reason to overturn our pre-epistemological convictions, and with them our commitment to the claim of first-person warrant.

Now if, in order to attack the notion of a distinctively first-person knowledge, we seek some warrant for convicting ourselves of chronic error in our first-person claims about attitudes and experience, it will make no sense to look for this by appeal to claims for which we have a distinctively first-person warrant—that would clearly be a self-defeating strategy. So our warrant for finding ourselves endemically in error in the relevant first-person beliefs will have to be of the sort available to third-person claims about our attitudes and experience. Thus what we have to consider is whether there is reason to hold that the kind of evidence we offer to observation somehow supports the claim that we have no distinctively first-person knowledge of our minds.

You may dismiss the suggestion as preposterous. How could we seriously deny that each of us knows how things look and feel to us, and what we are thinking, as no one else does? How could we deny that when we speak of such things in the first person, we speak with a special sort of right? But some, excited by the thought that experimental research can establish what once seemed absurd as sober fact, may suppose that through it we can ascend to some vantage point from which we can and should look down to pass cold judgment on all our initial convictions about self-knowledge. Hasn't modern psychology debunked "introspection," and shown "privileged access" to be a myth? Although I have refused to characterize first-person knowledge of attitude and experience with such phrases, some may suspect that criticism of views expressed in these terms has, in any case, thoroughly discredited my claims as well.

To attempt through theories justified by observation to discredit and rob us of the claim to a first-person knowledge of mind would be to try to undermine first-person warrant by third-person means. In this chapter I argue that there is no good reason for thinking that observationally based experimentation or theorizing has given us, or will likely give us, grounds to deny that we know what attitudes and experience we have in circumstances that show we possess first-person warrant. Our confidence in the possession of such knowledge of our minds is, I contend, not sapped by such third-person challenges as we can contrive for it, but strengthened and renewed by the endurance of our initial convictions in the face of these doubts. And this result gives us all the more right to rely on the sort of warrant involved in first-person knowledge in further inquiry.

2.2 Experimental Assaults on "Privileged Access"

We may disarm the suspicion that some third-person evidence generally overturns our convictions about self-knowledge, once we note just how humble are the claims that lead us to the thesis of first-person warrant. And once we recognize that many much-criticized beliefs often associated with doctrines of self-knowledge—for example, the various strands of the "Cartesian View"—do not, after all, underpin the thesis of first-person warrant, we may find ourselves at a loss to locate evidence we think likely to refute it. Consideration of the kinds of claims under attack in prominent experimentally based criticisms of "introspective" or "privileged" access bears this out: the claims there under threat are simply not essential to the distinctiveness thesis on which we have focused.

Consider, for example, the famous, much-cited article in which Nisbett and Wilson (1977) collect a variety of studies supposed to "cast doubt on the ability of people to report on their cognitive processes," studies that they say "suggest" we lack a peculiarly "privileged" or "introspective" source of first-person knowledge regarding "mental process."[1] As it turns out, the sort of distinctiveness-claim about self-knowledge they think they can debunk assumes that first-person assertions about mind issue from an "introspective" knowledge, only if they enjoy an accuracy *superior* to corresponding third-person assertions. For Nisbett and Wilson argue against first-person "privileged access" to, or "introspection" of, "mental processes," on the grounds that studies show that if observers are given enough information about a person, they will predict that person's behavior no less accurately (or inaccurately) than that person will himself.[2]

Now, many (though not all) of the examples of inaccurate or nonexistent first-person reports of mental process to which Nisbett and Wilson draw attention involve cases where subjects were asked to *explain why* something had happened, or *predict* what would. For instance, insomniac subjects were asked why they had increased or decreased difficulty falling asleep on certain occasions; subjects were asked how they arrived at solutions to problems; or they were asked to say how the presence of other people did or would influence their "helping behavior"; or they were asked about the influence the position of merchandise presented to them had on their choice of which to buy, or about how differences in a literary passage did or would affect the degree of readers' emotional response. Apparently, from a lack of superior first-person accuracy in subjects' explanations and predictions in such cases, we are to infer that they lack an "introspective" kind of knowledge of what they will do or why they do what they do, and this is taken as an indication of our general lack of introspective knowledge of "mental process."

But clearly this kind of criticism Nisbett and Wilson make of what they call "introspection" gives us no reason to question our adherence to the thesis of first-person warrant. For first of all, this thesis simply does not, of itself, presuppose that first-person reports enjoy some superior accuracy. And second, our acceptance of many of the examples of self-knowledge manifesting our commitment to this thesis does not require us to believe that first-person reports enjoy any greater accuracy than third-person reports do. You and I may both know at the same time, *and both just as accurately believe*, that I see the car parked in front of the house, or that I smell smoke, or feel pain, but still the circumstances show that I do not have the same type of warrant for my belief as you have for yours.

We may note that this difference in the type of warrant we possess for such claims does also make for a difference between your and my knowledge of what Nisbett and Wilson would term my "mental processes"—if a difference in our knowledge of *explanations* or *predictions* of my behavior is sufficient for that. For these sorts of claims may be offered in explanation of what I have done, or as a prediction of what I will do, and so the difference in the type of warrant we have for them will result in a difference in the type of warrant we have for these explanatory or predictive accounts—though again, there may be no difference in the accuracy of our accounts.[3] So if I have a distinctive first-person knowledge that I feel pain, or smell smoke, I may on account of this also know why I am buying aspirin, or searching the building for some sign of fire. The warrant for my beliefs about why I'm doing what I'm doing will then be different in kind from that anyone else has for beliefs about why I am doing these things. But this shows that there just is no need to assume some disparity in the *accuracy* of first- and third-person belief to arrive at a difference in *type of warrant* possessed for reports of "mental processes."

Admittedly, acceptance of some of the examples to which I have appealed—the cases of solitary self-knowledge—does indeed require us to believe it often happens that at a given time one knows about oneself what no one else can then know by ordinary observation, given what is so far available to observe. And so, I suppose, in these cases, first-person beliefs—and, presumably, the predictions and explanations that employ them—are likely to be at least temporarily more accurate than certain third-person beliefs. I say "at least temporarily" because I do not claim there is anything in principle *irremediable* about this difference in the accuracy of first- and third-person reports. It may happen that subsequent to the time at which one's self-knowledge is solitary, others come to know by observation what one already knew. So, for example, I may be able accurately to "predict" that I'm going to make a phone call when you would not predict this, because I know that I just remembered that I needed to make a phone call, though I keep it to myself. But you will also be able to predict what I'm going to do as accurately as I, if I go on to announce, "I've got to make a phone call now."

However, if Nisbett and Wilson intend to deny that first-person beliefs are often in this way at least temporarily more accurate than certain third-person beliefs, they certainly do not make this clear; in any case, I cannot find in any of the evidence they present anything that would support such a denial. Insomniacs sometimes give bad explanations of their sleeplessness; shoppers sometimes give mistaken explanations, or have none to give, for why they chose one variety of an item they wanted over another. Is this really supposed to give us reason to think we do not, for instance, ever know that we are about to make a phone call when no one else does? It would be pretty reckless to think so. For the cases of solitary self-knowledge that would show we sometimes know what we are about to do, or why we are doing or did something, are cases in which we would claim to possess (or to have possessed) a knowledge of what attitudes or experience we have (or had), at the time we have (or had) them, which no one else is (or was) in a position to get by observation of us. But the erroneous first-person claims that Nisbett and Wilson tell us people make are *not* of this sort. The claims the research is supposed to show are false are *not* assertions by subjects that they had attitudes or experience, which they would have said they knew they had at the time of having them, when no one else was then in a position to know this by observation. So it does not seem that the cases in which Nisbett and Wilson would impugn a claim to "introspective access" include cases of apparent solitary self-knowledge that would reveal a distinctive first-person knowledge of one's state of mind, and thus of "mental process" as well.

Also, even if Nisbett and Wilson *did* draw our attention to cases in which people thought they knew something about their current attitudes and experience, when the evidence showed they were mistaken, this would still be far from giving us a reason to deny that there is solitary self-knowledge that involves first-person warrant. For that result, we would need much more. We would need also to argue (1) that in correcting the error we did not rely on any solitary self-knowledge; (2) that *what* was erroneously believed about one's attitudes or experience is relevantly similar to what one believes about them in other cases where one takes oneself to have solitary self-knowledge; and (3) that errors of this type occur with such frequency as to show that similar first-person belief in putative cases of solitary self-knowledge is not reliably correct.

So studies like those that Nisbett and Wilson cite do not really even come close to threatening our right to claim first-person knowledge of attitudes and experience. Now, if someone wants to make the claim that first-person reports of mental processes are *invariably* more accurate than third-person reports, and wants to define 'introspection' as the faculty by which such reports are generated, then I suppose Nisbett and Wilson can say their evidence shows that there is no such thing as what this person would call "introspection." But they offer us no reason to deny the claims to a distinctive self-knowledge in which we are now interested.[4]

The same conclusion also holds for Gopnik's more recent (1993) experimentally bolstered attack on the distinctiveness of self-knowledge. The assumptions at which she directs criticism are again inessential to the thesis of first-person warrant and the examples that bring out our commitment to it, and she presents no evidence that should give us reason to retract our preepistemological convictions about self-knowledge.

Gopnik collects evidence from studies in developmental psychology to show that three-year-old children, while they can use some of the terms in our everyday vocabulary for talking about attitudes, consistently make errors in their statements about their own recently past beliefs when those

beliefs differ from their current ones. For example, children presented with
what they themselves say they think is a box full of candy will, upon discovering it a moment later to be full of nothing but pencils, consistently deny
that they *ever* thought it had candy in it. And Gopnik has found this first-
person error parallels difficulties children have in reporting the beliefs of
others. She takes this to suggest that neither young children nor we adults
enjoy a first-person knowledge of intentionality that is "privileged" over, or
"profoundly different" from, third-person knowledge of intentionality.

Gopnik purports to arrive at this result by contending that, if there *were*
a distinctively first-person knowledge of attitude, it would enable the three-
year-olds to report accurately what their recently past, but since revised,
beliefs were. This is apparently because she supposes that (1) if there were
first-person knowledge of intentionality, it would involve a "direct" or "immediate," "noninferential" link between one's attitudes and what could be
described as an "experience" of them;[5] and (2) if self-knowledge involved
such a direct experiential link to one's own attitudes, this sort of link would
hold in the case of the young children's recently past, no longer held beliefs.[6]

But there is no reason to suppose our convictions that we have self-knowledge in instances such as those I illustrated in the last chapter depend on any
assumptions against which Gopnik presents evidence. For first, our convictions are not based upon, and do not require us to adopt, the (allegedly
"commonsense") direct-perception model of self-knowledge Gopnik wants
to criticize—our claims to self-knowledge just do not assume (1).[7] And anyway, she never makes it clear why the direct-perception story about self-
knowledge falls afoul of her evidence, that is, why we should accept (2).
Finally, there is just nothing in the thesis of first-person warrant, or the examples committing us to it, that is incompatible with admitting that three-
year-olds are typically unable to report their recently revised beliefs.

So—not only does belief in the distinctiveness of first-person knowledge
not depend on the direct-experience or direct-perception view of self-knowledge, but also, whether one understands first-person knowledge in this way
or not, one has no commitment to the claim that three-year-old children
ought to have "an experience of their past belief." Assuming all one means
by saying that they lack such an experience is that they fail to recollect their
recently abandoned beliefs (what else could it mean?), then it seems incon-
testable that they do lack this—but just why should the believer in first-
person knowledge, even the believer in the "direct-perception" account of it,
need to say otherwise?

Maybe one will shift ground a bit at this point, and say that since the
three-year-olds' errors in attributing just-past beliefs to themselves are similar to their errors in attributing these to others, it is probable that there is
some common explanation of these errors. Then that in turn is evidence (or
perhaps just "suggests") that the way they make *correct* reports about, and
know, their own beliefs does not significantly differ from the way they correctly report on and know others' beliefs. But first, notice: it does not explain

why the children make the errors to say that when they do know what they believe, they know this in the same way they know what others believe. And it is quite unclear why saying this should put us in any better position to explain the errors. Second, suppose we grant that the children fail to recall their own beliefs for the same reason they fail to recall others' beliefs. That is entirely consistent with saying that when children learn to form beliefs about their own beliefs, the warrant they have differs from that they have for beliefs they learn to form about others' beliefs.

Is the idea perhaps that if we try to give some common explanation of the children's errors, the most plausible account will require us to deny that we have first-person knowledge of our attitudes? The case for this would need to be made. In the meantime, I suppose one might try casting around for a plausible strategy of finding a common explanation and see what happens. Here is a suggestion. First, it is a truism that people forget or fail to keep track of information when they cannot make use of it. Now we might ask: why do we bother remembering what we once believed, after we've changed our minds? And why do we bother remembering what others once believed, when we ourselves don't believe it and don't think they now do either? One reason: it can be useful to keep explicit track of what errors you and others have made even after you have corrected them, so that you can talk yourself out of repeating these mistakes, or persuade others not to make them. But now consider this ability to articulate a kind of inference about the way things are in your actual environment, without using it yourself to form a belief, and to evaluate it by reference to its failure to lead to right results on some occasion. This may be a trick that the average three-year-old has not learned well yet. So, a suggestion might be, perhaps: given their capacities for explicitly reasoning their way to claims about their circumstances, three-year-olds usually do not have much use for recalling what they once said about the way things are, after they have changed their minds, or for recalling what other people once said, when the children themselves (at least now) believe otherwise, and (as far as they can tell) so do these other people. In short, maybe the children do not recall this kind of thing because they are unable to do anything with this information that is useful to them. This kind of explanation would admit that children's first- and third-person errors in attributing beliefs have a common explanation, but it involves no denial of first-person knowledge. (Incidentally, if some explanation of roughly this sort is right, what is revealed by young children's errors in reporting past beliefs is not [as Gopnik argues] the peculiar way in which they are theorizing about the mind, but, on the contrary, how little they are yet able to engage in the kinds of reasoning characteristic of theorizing.) I am not arguing that this, or something like it, is the correct explanation, but it illustrates the point that there may be a common explanation to the children's first- and third-person errors in belief attribution, completely compatible with admitting first-person knowledge of intentionality. And, whether or not this suggestion about how to understand what is going on here is on the right track, the point remains that the existence of the kinds of error that young children make in reporting recently past, revised beliefs is quite compatible with the claim that we have a distinctive first-person knowledge of our attitudes, and with the ordinary convictions that reveal a commitment to it. And no good reason has been given for thinking the correct explanation of these errors (whatever that is) will require us to deny either this claim or these convictions.

At first glance, it may seem that either Gopnik's article or that of Nisbett and Wilson marshals experimental evidence to support some astonishing denial of our possession of a distinctively first-person knowledge of mind. But it turns out that Nisbett and Wilson's arguments are directed against the claim that first-person mentalistic explanations and predictions of response are somehow generally superior in accuracy to third-person ones, whereas the distinctiveness thesis that I maintain simply does not entail this. And the convictions about when we know our own minds to which I appeal either do not imply any superiority in the accuracy of first-person beliefs, or, where they do, are not overturned by the kind of evidence Nisbett and Wilson present. As for Gopnik's arguments, they seem to be aimed only against some "direct-perception" account of self-knowledge that would somehow preclude one's failing to recall that one recently had a belief one no longer holds. It is more than a little unclear who would maintain a direct-perception account with such consequences; in any event, such a view is not implied by the distinctiveness claim of which I speak, or by the convictions that lead us to it.

2.3 Why Third-Person Investigation Will Not Banish First-Person Warrant

One might think I should find no great consolation in the fact that the research just discussed does nothing to falsify the thesis of first-person warrant; for if such studies cannot lay claim to this result, perhaps some others can, and if no actual studies can, maybe future ones will. Can we say anything about the prospects for such a discovery?

It seems such a discovery would require us to employ such resources as provide warrant to third-person beliefs about mind, to show that we never actually know what attitudes and experience we have, on occasions where our having such knowledge would imply our possession of first-person warrant. Now again, I do not know how we could find reason to conclude we had made such a discovery, unless we found reason to think that the accuracy of our first-person beliefs on such occasions is so poor as to show them regularly liable to error. But if this is the form the challenge takes, we have little reason to fear it. For if we grant the (fairly modest) assumption that we do have attitudes and experience of the kind attributable in the everyday idiom used to make first-person claims, we should regard as futile any attempt to destroy the general credibility of these through third-person evidence, for this reason. Our very standards for forming and assessing third-person beliefs about these kinds of attitudes and experience frequently puts them *in accord with* first-person beliefs.

We can start to see this when we consider first just how often, and how pervasively, third-person belief conforms with the assumption that another's stating that she has or had this or that sort of attitude or experience is a strong reason to believe that she does or did. That someone *says* that she perceives (sees, hears, etc.) something, or that something looks (sounds, smells, etc.) some way to her, or that she feels pain or feels tired or glad, or that she wants something or intends to do something, or that she thinks, believes, suspects, fears, regrets, or hopes something: these are frequently considered good reasons for believing that she does perceive or see something, that something does look or sound some way to her, and so on.

This is not to say that in any given instance, first-person assertion about attitude or experience stands alone, independent of anything else one might perceive or believe, as sufficient reason to judge that another has the attitude or experience that he says he does, nor is it to say that such first-person statements are immune to challenge. But the fact is, the way we actually form and evaluate third-person claims, acceptance of first-person claims often counts for something, and frequently for quite a lot, in determining what we think it is correct to say about someone else's mind. So, far from offering to undermine the claims of first-person warrant, our practice of assessing the warrant for third-person belief actually proceeds in accordance with the assumption that first-person reports are often accurate. If we follow this practice, we can see that there is no reason to suppose our claims to first-person knowledge will quite generally face a serious challenge from third-person doubts.

However, one may suggest that, though our actual practice of forming and assessing third-person claims is in this way friendly to first-person assertions, it ought not to be: perhaps we will discover the illegitimacy of this practice, if we draw on sources of third-person warrant other than first-person reports. But I think we find here that, to the extent that we do rely on additional sources of warrant for forming third-person beliefs about mind, distinct from the authority granted first-person statements, our third-person verdicts again often either do not contradict, or actually coincide with, the first-person claims. This is just to say that people who assert that they have a given attitude or experience often otherwise act in ways that confirm they do. The man who says he wants to go to the grocery store to get some milk is soon found at the check-out counter clutching a carton and handing over his cash; someone who says she feels a pain in her right ankle, grimaces when it is moved; the person who says he feels dizzy and frightened in high places keeps his head turned rigidly to the left as we drive along a mountain road with a sheer hundred-foot drop to the right; the person who says she just remembered she wanted to check her mail proceeds forthwith to go

downstairs to her mailbox and look inside. These sorts of occurrence are not
the least bit unusual.

And this point does not fail to apply where we would regard ourselves as
having self-knowledge, in instances that demonstrate commitment to the
thesis of first-person warrant. One can easily enough imagine the examples
I have just given as also illustrating this. The man who wants to go to get
some milk, and the woman who remembers she wants to check her mail,
may have already known this about themselves, before they either asserted
what they knew, or otherwise acted in a way that gave others warrant for
believing it true. So what they had first-person warrant for believing about
themselves, others later came to have third-person warrant for believing
about them. And the woman who feels a pain, and the man who feels frightened by heights, know this about themselves, though they do not observe
what others observe that simultaneously gives them warrant for the relevant
third-person beliefs. The crucial point is that, in imagining these little scenarios, we are only imagining circumstances that we would say often occur in
our own lives. We sometimes take ourselves to know that we want, remember, feel, or fear something in circumstances that indicate our warrant for
our first-person beliefs is not of the sort others ordinarily have for such beliefs about us, and we act in ways that give others observing us warrant for
believing about us what we think we know about ourselves. Such states of
affairs are utterly commonplace. They show that third-person warrant often
accords with, and so does not undermine, the first-person beliefs we would
claim to know are true with a distinctively first-person warrant.

This accord between first-person belief and the verdicts supported by
third-person warrant is so ordinary we may not notice it. And we should not
be suprised if psychological research does not try to draw it to our attention.
For such research, naturally enough, often seeks evidence for attitudes of a
sort we did not think we had, or whose possession we would have denied.
The psychologist would like to tell us something new, to add to our knowledge, to surprise us, or maybe even to shock us. But this interest in the unusual or the unsuspected can make us grossly overestimate the extent to
which third-person evidence casts first-person assertions into doubt. So we
may neglect how common it is for the deliverances of third-person observation to agree with first-person belief.

For example, as earlier noted, Nisbett and Wilson make much of evidence
that people are sometimes unable to offer or would even reject the correct
psychological explanation for something they do, and that they sometimes
fail to make, on the basis of attributing attitudes to themselves, correct predictions of what they will do, even where observers' predictions succeed.
However, the studies Nisbett and Wilson cite do not, even according to these
authors, provide evidence of the falsity of people's claims that they have
certain attitudes and experiences.[8] And if few studies have been published
presenting evidence that people often do act in ways that confirm their first-
person reports of attitude and experience, I suspect this is not because such

evidence would be so scarce, but because of its bland ubiquity. Maybe no one has done a study, or even submitted a grant proposal, to find out whether, for example, restaurant customers' claims about what they want to eat and drink are confirmed by subsequent observation of their behavior, when they are presented with, or denied, the purported objects of their desires. But if no one has done this, surely that is not because the hypothesis seems too farfetched, but rather because no one really doubts what the results would be. We must beware of vague or careless generalizations about the inaccuracy of first-person reports, or the unreliability of "introspection," based on experimental studies. If someone puts forward the evidence of such studies as an objection to first-person belief in a given instance, we should ask what reason there is for thinking that what led to first-person error or obliviousness in other cases is also at work in the case at hand. To cast reasonable doubt on a given belief that one has some attitude or experience, it is surely not enough merely to point out that sometimes beliefs about one's own attitudes and experience have been shown incorrect by others. For while what guides our formation and assessment of third-person beliefs can put them into local conflicts with first-person beliefs, it often leads them elsewhere to accord with these.

2.4 SELF-KNOWLEDGE AND THE ELIMINATIVIST PROSPECT

But this may drive someone reluctant to admit first-person knowledge of mind to seek a more extreme form of opposition. The argument of the last section starts from the premise that people do have attitudes and experience of the sorts attributable in the everyday idiom I have used in my examples. But mightn't we reject this? Eliminative materialist philosophers would seem to claim we have reason to say it is false. For they propose that attributions of such attitudes and experience rest on a "radically false theory" about human behavior—a "folk psychology," as it has been condescendingly called—that will be "displaced," "eliminated," in favor of a new account, in a new vocabulary—the correct theory of human beings. Typically, this replacement theory is envisaged as a much-advanced account of the organization and patterns of activity in the human nervous system.[9]

So, if first-person knowledge of attitudes and experience seems unassailable by third-person means as long as we continue to say there are attitudes and experience to be known, this final option suggests itself: argue that the evidence compels us to declare all this everyday mind talk entirely false. On this picture, the kinds of claims I have used to illustrate and argue for the thesis of first-person warrant are all simply applications of a theory, shown to be radically false on "empirical" grounds—that is, as an explanation of our "behavior." The sort of warrant available for third-person claims about us, through *confirming* some up-and-coming theory, *disconfirms* attributions of attitudes and experience in the everyday idiom, including first-person claims, en masse. Though this view may not quite entail that we have no warrant at all for first-person claims, it would at least mean that whatever first-person warrant we might have for affirming them is weaker than the third-person warrant had for denying them. And this is bad enough from my perspective, since the point of my focus on first-person warrant is to prepare us to rely on this for an investigation of consciousness, and it would hardly be desirable to rely on a kind of warrant we identify only through our possession of it for claims that we have greater warrant for deeming false. So even if eliminativism does not entail that we have no first-person warrant for claims about attitudes and experience, it leaves us at best with a claim to first-person warrant so weakened as to be useless.[10]

The kind of view that would figure in the argument against first-person knowledge I have sketched is eliminative materialism in its most radical and straightforward incarnation. But those most clearly associated with this doctrinal label—Paul and Patricia Churchland—sometimes indicate they mean by it a less harsh proposal, a prediction that the ways of classifying things we invoke in speaking the everyday idiom of attitude and experience will likely undergo considerable revision of some kind over time as our understanding of the brain progresses.[11] To see whether an eliminativist perspective in the philosophy of mind has untoward consequences for my proposed reliance on first-person knowledge, I need to focus on the bolder and less vague variant. For only this seems to provide the materials needed to block acceptance of the thesis that we have a distinctive first-person warrant for our claims to have certain attitudes and experience, and give us reason to reject my proposed reliance on it. It hardly gives us reason to reject the claim that we sometimes have first-person knowledge that we remembered something, or that we were thinking about something, or that something looked to us a certain way, and so on, merely to predict that some of our ways of classifying mental phenomena will alter in some way as a result of future research. So then, in order to assess this strong eliminativist attack on first-person knowledge, we need to be very clear from the start about what it would hinge on—namely, the thesis that our anticipated acceptance of developing new theories and vocabularies for talking about the brain gives us reason to conclude that talk about attitudes and experience embodies a radically erroneous theory of some sort: *everyday mind talk and brain science are supposed to be incompatible.* But to this we must ask: "Why?"

A key part of the answer would seem to lie in the idea that the explanations we offer in terms of attitudes and experience are to be seen not only as constituting a theory (whatever that comes to exactly), but as constituting a theory that is *inferior* to that which neuroscience does or will provide. And then, we are told, if this inferior theory cannot be somehow subsumed under or incorporated into the superior one, by reducing the former to the latter via "bridge laws" (or perhaps in some other way), the inferior theory must be discarded, displaced, eliminated. Finally, it is argued, or suggested, that the laws constituting our commonsense psychology cannot be reduced to neuroscientific laws or in any relevant way subsumed under the superior theory. Therefore, the inferior theory, along with all of what it "posits"—attitudes like believing, wanting, doubting, recognizing, regretting, and all the rest—is to be eliminated.

But the fact that theory A is a better theory than theory B, according to some general canons of theory quality, does not by itself tell us that acceptance of A gives us reason to reject B unless B can be subsumed under A. Surely it matters *in what respect*, and *in relation to what*, the superior theory is superior. So we need to know: in what way and with regard to what is commonsense psychology inferior to neuroscience, and why does *that* sort of inferiority require us to dump the first, if we cannot subsume it under the second? Here perhaps is a clue. Paul Churchland (1981) tells us that the everday forms of explanation we employ by attributing attitudes to ourselves fail to explain a number of things—for example, mental illness, differences in intelligence, sensorimotor coordination, how the retinal image gives rise to visual perception in three dimensions, and how we remember things. Also, he says we have not, over the centuries, appreciably improved at explaining things by reference to our attitudes ("folk psychology" is "stagnant"). And third, there are many phenomena our ancestors would have explained in this way that we no longer do—so: we (some of us) no longer say that weather, disease, or earthquakes are explained by the attitudes of deities. (Thus "folk psychology" is "retreating.")

So we might infer that lay mentalistic explanation is inferior to neuroscience in these three respects. For, first, neuroscience *will* explain mental illness, differences in intelligence, etc. Second, we are becoming, and will continue to become, better at explaining things in this way. And third, the scope of what we will explain in this way is expanding. So then the argument appears to be: because everyday-attitude psychology is inferior to brain science in these ways, then unless it can be regimented into a theory reducible to neuroscientific theory, our acceptance of the latter gives us reason to count all attitude attributions as false.[12]

But clearly the argument is still seriously incomplete. Just why should everyday mind talk's inferiority to neuroscience *in these respects* force this subsumption-or-rejection dilemma on us? It is unclear, to say the least, that our warrant for making attributions of attitudes in the situations in which we typically make them depends *in the slightest* on success in using such modes of description to explain the sorts of phenomena of sensorimotor coordination, memory, depth perception, mental illness, and intelligence to which Churchland alludes—most of which few, if any, have ever even *tried* to explain in such terms. And to suggest that our right to attribute attitudes to ourselves is seriously jeopardized by the rejection of either animistic or theistic explanations of weather, disease, etc., seems, on the face of it, rather gratuitous. Finally, it is far from evident just why our warrant for speaking of our attitudes is threatened by the fact (if it is one) that we are not much better at explaining things about people in these terms than our ancestors were. Does every form of description we employ for explanatory purposes need to evolve continuously in the direction of greater explanatory power, if we are to be entitled to retain it? Suppose, at least for the sake of argument, that a couple of millennia ago or so we got about as good overall as we are ever going to get at explanation in terms of attitude attribution. Why isn't that good enough to allow us to keep talking about attitudes?[13] And finally, if it is a mystery why any of these limitations on what we can successfully explain in everyday mentalistic language should be taken to affect our warrant for attribution of attitudes generally, it is even more a mystery why they affect our warrant for using this language *so* adversely as to justify a rejection of all claims made in such terms, unless the forms of explanation they offer can be subsumed under theories not suffering from the same limitations.

So there is quite a gap in the eliminativist argument thus far. There is some prospect of filling it, I believe, only if we make explicit further assumptions that seem to lie behind eliminativist thinking. The problem facing the eliminativist is that the ways we have listed in which "folk psychology" is held to be inferior to present or future neuroscience so far give us no reason why we should think we have to "save" the former by subsuming it under the latter, or else conclude that attributions of attitudes are all false. I can see why this might seem so only if we make two assumptions. First, we assume that everyday mind talk comprises a theory that, if it explains anything, explains nothing other than the things neuroscience does or will explain. Second, we assume that we have more warrant for saying sentences about ourselves using such terms for attitudes and experience are true than for saying they are false, *only if* they belong to a theory that either explains these things better than any theory that lacks such terms, or is subsumable (through, e.g., reduction) under another theory that explains them better. This is to say, we must see our attitude talk as a theory whose *explananda* are entirely included among those of neuroscience, and we must see our warrant for attitude talk as wholly dependent on its success in handling just these *explananda*. Only on some such assumption, it seems, can everyday attitude talk and neuroscientific talk be viewed as "rivals," so that accepting the truth of the latter forces us to admit the falsity of the former.

But now, just what is the shared explanatory goal, relative to which the truth of all our talk of our attitudes and experience is to be evaluated? It will be said here that both "folk psychology" and neuroscience are theories of "human behavior." Now, it may not be immediately obvious exactly what conception of "behavior" we are to employ here, but this much at least is clear: the eliminativist argument needs to hold that our warrant for making statements in the everyday idiom of attitudes and experience depends entirely on their success as explanations of what is conceived of in wholly *other* terms—terms that completely *exclude* the everyday idiom. That is to say, when we describe the behavior to be explained, we are not allowed to make claims using the terms to be eliminated, nor may we speak of people in any terms the use of which we would explain by making claims about them in such terms. If the conclusion is to be that mind talk is all false, then we can no more employ it in our conception of the *explananda* than in our conception of the *explanans*. (Someone could, of course, propose that what attitude and experience talk fails to explain [because neuro-talk explains it better] is, in part, this: what attitudes and experience we have. But that person would be an *epiphenomenalist*, not an *eliminativist*—that is, this would not be a philosopher who denied that we have any attitudes and experience, but one who denied only that our possession of some of these ever accounts for why we have others.)

So the picture that emerges is this. If explanations in terms of attitudes and experience cannot be subsumed under (e.g., reduced to) neuroscientific ones, then we have more warrant for describing ourselves in lay psychological terms than for not doing so, *only if that provides a better explanation than neuroscience would of what is described in a way that thoroughly dispenses with all such terms.*

This epistemological view should be somewhat familiar to us from the earlier discussion of the Cartesian conception of psychological knowledge. Recall that, on this view, our warrant for attributing states of mind to others requires that we be able to justify this entirely on the basis that it provides the best explanantion of their bodily movements, conceived of in a thoroughly "dementalized" way. We arrive at the eliminativist picture by adopting the Cartesian view about knowledge of other minds, then discarding the contrast between this and a direct, perceptual knowledge each mind has uniquely of itself. In the eliminativist story, *all* warrant for talk of attitudes and experience is conceived of on the model the Cartesian constructs specifically for the third-person case.

This points to another interesting parallel between the eliminativist philosophy and Cartesianism. Descartes granted a certain privileged epistemic status to our judgments about what is "in our minds" relative to judgments about what is "outside of them," in the realm of matter. And the eliminativist recognizes a similar asymmetrical epistemic relation between the "mental" and the "physical"—only the assignments of privileged and subordinate status are reversed. Our right to claims made in a mind-including idiom is made to depend entirely on their providing the best theory of what is conceived of in a mind-excluding one, while our right to apply this latter conception does not in turn depend on our warrant for claims about attitudes and experience. And this inversion of Cartesian epistemology leads to an ontological inversion as well. Just as frustrations with the Cartesian attempt to base a justification of claims about material bodies wholly on knowledge of the "ideas in one's mind" made it look attractive to philosophers to deny the reality of matter, so apparent difficulties in justifying claims about attitudes and experience as a theory of bodily movement en-

tice some to deny the reality of mind. Of course, the fact that the epistemology eliminativism presupposes can be traced back to Descartes does not
give us reason to reject it. But neither does it give us reason to accept it.
Should we?

Well, we might say, isn't it clear that our warrant for attributions of attitudes and experiences depends on how well these explain things? And isn't
it clear that what these explain, if anything, is our observable behavior?
Affirmative answers to both these questions may seem to indicate that we
accept the epistemological picture eliminativism requires. Now, it is true
that we assess our warrant for at least some attributions of attitudes and
experience by considering how well these explain things about the persons
of whom they are made. However, for the most part we make this assessment relative to how well these explain other attitudes people have, and
what they do, described in terms whose application we understand by reference to attitudes and experience. For first, what we want to explain by appeal to lay psychological terms, we often describe *in* these same sorts of
terms—we want to know why people *thought, felt, wanted, preferred, expected,* or *feared* something; why they were *attending to (looking at, listening to)* this or that; why this *reminded* them of that; why this was *interesting,
attractive,* or *exciting* to them, or why that was *boring,* or *repulsive,* or *dis-
gusting* to them. And when we describe some "behavior" we want to explain, we often do not describe it in terms divorced from attitudes and experience at all, but rather in ways we understand by reference to these. This is
true, for example, where the behavior we want explained is some sort of
speech act—for example, someone's *saying* (i.e., stating) that something is
so, or *asking* for something, or *promising* to do something, *apologizing,
threatening, warning, greeting,* and so on. For we would explain what it is
to do these things by reference to attitudes. And this is also the case, where
we identify movement by reference to what attitudes or experience they typically reveal: a *pained,* or *calm,* or *cheerful* expression; a look of *surprise,* or
recognition, or *disgust,* or *embarrassment*; an *angry,* or *welcoming,* or *nervous* gesture, and so on.[14] Also, many of our ordinary ways of describing
what people are doing, which we explain by means of their attitudes and
experience, we take to apply to them in virtue of what attitudes or experience they have. So when we say people are *looking* (searching) for something, *reading* something, *pointing* at something, *waving* hello or goodbye,
beckoning, dancing, singing, playing, and *fighting,* we imply that they have
attitudes or experience of a sort appropriate to these activities. (If we come
to think they lack certain of these attitudes or experience, we think these
descriptions do not apply after all.) And where we describe people doing
things that may be understood with reference to some result (*cooking a
meal, repairing a bicycle, driving to work, combing hair*), our willingness to
describe them in these ways still typically depends on the assumption that
they want certain ends. For we will not think we were wrong to describe
them in these ways, if the result is not achieved, provided that they had the

appropriate attitudes: for then, even if the bike is not fixed, or one never makes it to work, we still will think it right to ask why the person was repairing the bike or driving to work (or at least, why they were *trying* to do so).

Thus, generally where we do assess the warrant of our attributions of attitudes and experience to people by how well it explains, we describe or think of *what is to be explained* in terms whose application we understand by reference to attitudes and experience. So it is not at all clear that the fact that we evaluate such attributions by considering how well these explain something commits us to saying that we have warrant for such attributions, only if we can describe human behavior in a completely dementalized fashion, and then justify these attributions en masse, by arguing that they provide a better explanation of behavior thus described than any alternative.

But here one might point out: wouldn't we withdraw our attributions of attitudes and experience to people if we found some nonpsychological alternative that better explains some piece of their behavior? For instance: if we thought Irene did not raise her arm, but her arm simply rose because metal attached to it was attracted to a powerful magnet, or if we thought Bob did not smile, but only had a spasm of facial muscles, we probably would not explain these movements by appeal to their attitudes. However, the fact that we would abandon attitude explanation under such circumstances is not enough to show that we would do so because we assume the epistemology under consideration: that all everyday mind talk must ultimately be evaluated relative to its offering the best explanation of the motions and sounds of our bodies. Our withdrawal of attitude explanation in the cases just imagined may be based on different assumptions altogether. We might think that, if Irene's and Bob's movements are due to external causes of the sorts described, it would not feel to Irene as it does to raise her arm, and it would not feel to Bob as it does to smile. And then we would think: in that case, she was not raising her arm, and he was not smiling, and Irene's and Bob's movements, if they are not arm raisings or smiles, probably are not to be accounted for by appeal to their attitudes and experience. (Although they *might* be: we might have evidence that Irene intentionally had the metal put in her hand, and flicked a switch that turned the magnet on, or that Bob arranged for his muscles to be contracted in that way through implanted electrodes.) So the fact that in some circumstances we would abandon a "folk psychological" explanation in favor of an alternative, while redescribing what is to explained in dementalized fashion, does not by itself commit us to the view that the truth of ordinary mind talk as a whole is to be assessed relative to some such conception of our behavior.

But still we might suspect such a commitment can be detected in this: where we hold that what we do is explained by reference to attitudes, we will also accept that what we do can be described in a dementalized manner; and further, we will agree that the attitude explanation still holds true of what is so described. But then, what if we say we can show that, in every case, attitudes do *not* explain the behavior so described, because something else (described nonmentalistically) does? We might say this would show that attitudes do not really explain what we do, no matter how it is characterized. And then we might argue that if that is so, then we have no warrant for attributing attitudes at all. And if we argue in this way from a failure of everyday mind-talk explanations of dementalized behavior, to the conclusion that such talk is unwarranted, we show we accept the eliminativist epistemology.

But first, it is not clear that there cannot be more than one correct explanation of some episode of behavior. So I might explain why Irene raised her arm, by saying she wanted to ask a question, and also explain her arm's rising, without attributing to her any attitudes or experience. What we might count here as the same behavior described in different ways can receive different correct explanations. Perhaps "mere movements" can also be explained in the idiom of attitude and experience, in part because they can (with warrant) be described in ways understood with reference to that idiom. (There need not be any vicious circularity here. I can explain Irene's arm rising by saying she wants to ask a question, because her arm rising can with warrant be described as her raising her arm. But it is not the case that my warrant for this description requires the truth of my belief that she wants to ask a question.) If something along these lines is right, our warrant for attributions of attitude and experience to others is not to be assessed entirely on the basis that it best explains what is conceived of in a thoroughly dementalized fashion, even if such attributions do explain what is conceived of in this way.

Second, suppose one grants we are just mistaken to think that attitudes and experience explain our movements or sounds, for one grants there can be only one correct explanation of these. One might still hold that one can have warrant for beliefs about others' attitudes, because these explain their behavior, understood in ways tied to attitude and experience, better than *other* attitude attributions would. That is, one might think that psychological features are, in a certain sense, "epiphenomenal" with respect to behavior, and still think that one can form correct beliefs about what attitudes and experience others have, by describing their behavior in terms understood relative to attitudes and experience, and asking which attitude attribution best explains what is so described.

This would leave unanswered the question of just how one arrives at such characterizations of other people's behavior in the first place. But that is a question that has no obvious answer in any case. For as far as we can tell, we typically *start* our assessment of attitude explanation of other people from description of the *explananda* already rich with assumptions about attitudes and experience. We know we are able to describe others in this way somehow partly because we perceive their utterances and movement, but we have little to say regarding how exactly the perception relates to the description. Someone may say that these descriptions and tendencies to offer them are the fruit of some brain process that generates them from sensory information we encode, representing others' movements and sounds in some thoroughly dementalized fashion. It is not clear to me that the way we perceive other human beings when we are able to "read" their attitudes is accurately characterized in this manner. But suppose it is. Does it follow that we ought to evaluate the truth of our explicit attributions of attitude and experience as a whole by asking how well these explain behavior described in mind-excluding terms? I do not see that it does. It does not follow, even if we suppose further that the attributions we make or are prone to make tend to be those that would explain the dementalized behavior of those we encounter better than other such attributions. In sum: that our attributions of attitude to others are caused by the perception of their nonmental features does not show that we should evaluate the truth of these attributions by asking whether they excel all other forms of explanation in accounting for the occurrence of such features. And it does not show this, even if we say the perceptions that trigger these attributions represent others as mere moving shapes or noise makers.

It may still be thought that the fact we can pose to ourselves the *problem of other minds* shows that we do conceive of our warrant for beliefs about others' attitudes and experience in this way. For we may think: "I can consider the possibility that others have no attitudes and experience, and then ask myself what justifies my thinking that they do. It would be question-begging to answer: I know they do because attributing some attitudes and experiences explains other ones they have—for the question is, whether they have any such at all. Thus I must justify my belief that they have minds as the best hypothesis to describe the motions and noises they make."

But that is merely one way of looking at the "problem of other minds"; it is not the only way. Another way would be to argue (as some have, under Wittgenstein's influence) that if our ways of forming beliefs about others' attitudes and experiences do not give us knowledge, then we do not understand what we mean when each of us talks or thinks about his or her own attitudes and experience. Since we do understand what we mean, our way of forming third-person beliefs about attitudes and experience does give us knowledge. On another approach, we might reason along these lines: "My way of forming third-person beliefs about attitudes and experience would turn out pretty good results were someone else to apply it to me. If I have no reason to think that others to whom I apply it differ from me in some way that would make it work badly when applied to them, and if I do have some reason to think that they don't relevantly differ from me, then I've got more right to hold that others have attitudes and experience than to deny it." And if neither of these ways of dealing with the problem of other minds actually succeeds, that is no objection for the eliminativist to raise. For she cannot claim that her favored way of viewing the warrant for third-person attributions of attitudes and experience succeeds where these fail: she wants to claim that none succeed.

I will have a bit more to say about these "other minds" issues later. For now, the point is, this philosophical problem is not one that demands to be addressed on the assumption that claims about others' attitudes and experience are to be assessed in the way the eliminativist requires—as a theory explaining the motions and noises of a certain class of bodies. So it would be wrong to assume that our ability to pose this problem reveals a commitment to the Cartesian epistemology of third-person claims about attitudes and experience.

So: when we look at what we actually talk about when we give explanations using claims about people's attitudes and experience, we find no commitment to the claim that their truth is to be evaluated by regarding them as a system of "posits" to explain bodily movements described in dementalized fashion. Where we treat an interest in how well our attributions of attitudes and experience explain as relevant to our assessment of the truth of the attributions, we are *not* committed to claiming the attribution makes an otherwise unavailable addition to a theory for explaining human behavior described in mind-excluding terms. Rather, we measure the success of our explanation against a conception of what is to be explained that is itself rife with attributions of attitudes and experience. And it is most unclear what should persuade us to adopt the rather different conception of how attitude explanation warrants attitude talk, which the eliminativist argument would urge upon us.

The next point is this. Sometimes—most notably in first-person cases like those described in the last chapter—we think we know what attitude or experience we have, without assuming any need to justify this by reference to what it explains. I simply do not try to evaluate the truth of my claim that it looks to me as if this piece of cake is bigger than that one, or that I was thinking about what to make for breakfast, by reference to something else this is supposed to explain—certainly not my bodily movements and noises. So, even if we ignore the difficulty in showing why we should endorse this account of what is required to have warrant for such *third-person* claims, we are still wanting an argument for the view that the warrant for *first-person* claims about attitudes and experience is to be assessed by taking them to comprise a theory for explaining what is described in wholly other terms.

One might try to deal with this problem by maintaining that having warrant for first-person claims requires that appropriate third-person statements about mind be warranted, and this is so only if these are justifiable entirely by arguing that they provide the best theory for explaining behavior conceived of in mind-excluding terms. But notice that here we are dealing not with just *any* claim that first-person warrant is dependent on the warrant for third-person beliefs, but with one that builds in a very particular conception of what this third-person warrant requires. And it is not clear why I should accept the thesis that I have warrant for my claims about what I am thinking, how things look to me, etc., only if someone else can (1) conceive of the movements and sounds of my body in a way that completely strips them of any relation to attitudes and experience, and (2) justify attribution of these to me as providing the best theory to explain these movements and sounds. One could not arrive at this thesis simply by appeal to the conviction that there must be some "public" (third-person) way of making attributions of attitude and experience, if there is to be a "private" (first-person) way of doing this. Even supposing that I can know my own mind only if I can make it public to others, it is by no means clear that it has to become public to others through their being able to justify a mentalistic theory as the best explanation of the mass of my dementalized movements.

I conclude that not only do we not, in the way we actually form and assess claims about people's attitudes and experience, make explicit use of the principles by which the eliminativist would govern our acceptance of such claims, we are also not somehow implicitly committed to these standards. But then, I see no reason why we should adopt this conception of our warrant for talking about ourselves, and rule our speech by it. Before we sacrifice to some epistemological idol our readiness to claim that we sometimes recall incidents from our past, or feel thirsty, angry, tired, or afraid, or that some things look bigger to us, or farther away, than others, or that we have sexual fantasies, or worry about paying our bills, or expect great discoveries in neuroscience, or decide, doubt, dream, and so on, we need, I think, a very good reason to accept the authority of rules that would lay waste to so much. I do not believe this has been offered.

The epistemology I have seen lying behind eliminativism is not generally made explicit. But it seems to me needed, if one is to run an eliminativist argument sweeping enough to throw out the sorts of attitudes and experience by reference to which I have argued the thesis of first-person warrant. The eliminativist should not be allowed to get by unchallenged with a claim that, if we do not argue that neuroscience, or some projected scientific psychology, will "save" or "vindicate" "folk psychology" in some proposed manner—either by intertheoretic reduction, or by identifying states of belief with discrete states of the brain, or by finding sentences in "brain writing" with the same meaning as those by which we express our attitudes in English, Urdu, or Mandarin—then we will have reason to say we have no attitudes at all. We should request a justification for the demand that we seek some such "salvation" for our talk of attitudes and experience. If this request is not adequately met, argument that our attitudes and experience *cannot* be reduced to or identified with our brain states (if it is provided) will show us not that we entirely lack attitudes and experience, but just that certain forms of physicalism are wrong. But how are we to justify the claim that everyday mind talk must be saved through relating it in this or that way to what is found in the brain, or else be damned to elimination? It seems we must appeal to the idea that brain talk is destined to triumph in some *competition* with attitude and experience talk, unless talk of the second sort proves itself worthy of rescue by its superior. But to see our everyday mind talk in this way standing before brain science as either doomed rival or anxious supplicant is to try to assess our warrant for it as a whole, relative to some supposed shared explanatory aim, defined in a manner purged of all association with attitude and experience. Thus the defense of eliminativism seems inevitably to drive us to the sort of epistemology I have criticized.

If we have insufficient reason to adopt this epistemology, we ought not accept the eliminativism it is needed to support. And if we do not accept that philosophical doctrine, then we should be unpersuaded by any argument against first-person knowledge in which it would figure. Thus I discover in eliminativist philosophy of mind no good reason to relinquish the pre-epistemological convictions that found us in possession of a distinctively first-person knowledge of our attitudes and experience. Now, I do not, of course, deny that we should try to investigate what sorts of relations do in fact hold between what we can describe in the everyday idiom and what we come to know in accounts of the brain's anatomy, chemistry, and microstructure. I just want to say that we do not have to ward off the specter of the kind of mass extinction of attitude talk that some seemingly relish to contemplate, by first erecting and arguing for some theory purporting to describe a general and systematic relation between "folk psychology" and brain science.

Does this mean I maintain that *nothing* could reasonably make us change our "folk psychological" ways in any significant respect, that the claims and explanations we give in the everyday idiom are somehow completely immune from revision or falsification? No, and the thesis of first-person warrant does not require that we assume this. It would be a mistake to try to "rule out" any rational change in the way we classify our own attitudes and experience, based on experimental and clinical research. Nor do I see any good reason to say that *neuroscientific* research could not contribute to such change. But any proposed innovations and the cases for them will have to be assessed as they arise. I suppose we might imagine our current way of talking about ourselves gradually giving way to another we will regard as so different, and we will become convinced that what we once said about ourselves was so full of confusions, misleading suggestions, and false implications, that we will no longer count much of it as true. Though, as an erstwhile champion of eliminativism has pointed out (Stich 1996), it is unclear on what grounds we are to imagine ourselves concluding that we were earlier wrong to say we had the features or states we reported in the old way, rather than that we merely used to have some seriously mistaken notions about those (real) states and features. What sorts of discoveries should convince us not just that some commonly accepted claims about beliefs were mistaken, but that we were mistaken to claim that we had beliefs at all? It seems to me that it would be difficult to make a strong argument that it is likely our ordinary self-conception, as expressed in our everyday lexicon for attitude and experience, will undergo a revision *so extreme* that we would be justified in saying that practically none of our ordinary attributions of attitude were ever true.

However, we might note that even rather big revisions would not necessarily show that the thesis of first-person warrant was wrong. After all, we may make a transition away from our old way of understanding ourselves not only as a result of new observational evidence, but also partly on the strength of first-person warrant. Perhaps, as we work out implications of some of what we are now inclined to say, expose hidden assumptions, take into account a fuller range of examples and experimental evidence relevant to new questions we pose, and forge and ponder unsuspected alternative ways of describing ourselves, we will gradually come to believe that the first-person warrant we think we have for what we now say about ourselves actually better supports a profoundly different way of speaking of ourselves than that with which we had previously been content. If we revise our conception of ourselves in this way, the new way of speaking of ourselves—once we work ourselves into it—will also be such as we can apply to ourselves, and such as we know applies in first-person cases, though not by observation. So we will be able to rewrite the argument of Chapter 1 in our new vocabulary, after we have come to use it. Thus, one can allow that even the sorts of claims we make in the everyday idiom may be, all of them, in principle subject to revision. But to contemplate the prospect of such a far-reaching revision, one need not agree they would be falsified in toto if they did not furnish, or reduce to, the superlative theory of bodily movement, and one need not give up the thesis of first-person warrant.

2.5 Lingering Methodological Anxieties

I conclude that we need fear no third-person evisceration of first-person knowledge.[15] For I find no convincing reason to think that the kind of warrant we can have for third-person claims does or will support an account of us that effectively undermines our commitment to first-person warrant. Not only does research aimed at establishing the unreliability of first-person reports disappoint in this regard, but we have reason to think it will continue to do so, as long as we grant that the terms we use to assert our first-person beliefs are also suitable for stating what third-person knowledge of mind we have. And the eliminativist argument—that our claims to first-person knowledge are about to be swept away by a theory of behavior rooted in neuroscientific investigations—depends on an epistemology we do not have good reason to accept.

Can we now conclude we've criticized our convictions about self-knowledge sufficiently to permit us to proceed on the assumption that we do indeed have the sort of first-person knowledge of attitudes and experience to which they point? I am almost ready to move on, but before I do, I would like to address just a few concerns I think may still persist, which might still inhibit some. I have in mind roughly the sorts of objections that have been made in the past against the methods of so-called introspectionist psychologists. It will be said that, though I disavow the perceptual model of self-knowledge suggested by this label, in advocating reliance on a uniquely first-person sort of knowledge of mind, I commit the same sort of methodological errors for which the introspectionists were so insistently booed off the stage. One can see how such a criticism might take hold if one recalls the old behaviorist complaint against the introspectionists, something like: "Since 'introspection' can be performed only on oneself, we are dealing here with a sort of observation that cannot be confirmed by others, as they cannot introspect one's states of mind. And surely confirmability of claims by multiple investigators is a prerequisite to a sound methodology; it is what distinguishes science from activities that rely crucially on the supposed special authority of particular individuals or texts, characteristic of religion." Translated into my terminology, the objection might run: if we rely on first-person claims for which the claimant supposedly possesses a kind of warrant no one else does, we rely on claims that are not subject to confirmation by others, and thus we make our investigation dependent on the words of an authority, whose claims others are not accorded the wherewithal to check.[16]

But we are now in a position to see we needn't be deterred by this kind of worry. First, it should be clear, I am not asking you to accept *my* authority, or that of some hallowed text or institution, regarding the character of *your* experience; I am asking you to accept your own authority, tempered by careful reflection and criticism, for speaking of your experience. Second, I do not deny that first-person beliefs can be confirmed from the third-person point of view, nor do I assert that the evidence available to another ought never cause one to revise one's first-person beliefs about attitudes or experience. The fact that I have for a given first-person belief a kind of warrant that you do not ever have for a corresponding third-person belief just does not imply that you do not or cannot have warrant for it. One's mere possession of first-person warrant for some statements about attitudes and experience does not in principle block others from confirming or disconfirming first-person statements by means available to them from their point of view. However, I do not think we have to assume that you can know nothing about your experience unless it is confirmed by someone else. Such confirmation would in any case frequently be rather trivial, since your assertion about your experience will, in many ordinary circumstances, and given what else one has reason to believe about you, often be taken to constitute confirmation that your experience is as you say it is.

This might provoke one to ask: "But under just what circumstances does third-person evidence *disconfirm* first-person claims, if you do not deny that it can?" I do not view it as an obligation to try to set out at the beginning a general account of just when and where third-person evidence does or may overrule first-person claims; in fact, I do not think it is desirable to try this, since I believe that we cannot get a good grip on this issue until we have a more positive understanding of first-person warrant, and this awaits clarification of the notion of consciousness. It is enough for now that I signal my readiness to consider whether such a view as I will offer, and will claim is supported by first-person warrant, is somehow overturned by observational evidence.

More generally, I do not think that reliance on a kind of warrant has to be preceded by some general theory about just what possession of that warrant consists in, and when it is lacking. For example, we can, I think, have perceptual knowledge, and depend on it in our research and our everyday lives, without first solving the puzzles that can arise once one attempts to say anything substantive about just how sense-perception provides our beliefs with warrant, and under what conditions. And we can also rely on first-person knowledge of experience in discussions of it, without first providing and arguing for a positive epistemological theory about it. I might say roughly, for what it's worth, that one knows one's own mind in a distinctively first-person way by having the attitudes and experience one believes one has, just as I might loosely say, one knows truths about one's surroundings by seeing that they're so. But such remarks would clearly leave us with many philosophical questions about the circumstances in which such conditions could provide knowledge, and what general principles we can use to evaluate specific claims to knowledge of these sorts. Satisfactory answers to such questions are not easy to come by, attempts to give them are caught in controversy as deep as any, and some will doubtless say the effort to provide this sort of epistemology is futile. But whether or not that is right, if you would demand that we first argue for some more positive account of the conditions under which we have first-person warrant before we are entitled to rely on it, I would ask whether you also demand that we first provide something similar regarding the conditions of perceptual knowledge, before we might rely on it. And I have, it seems to me, actually provided more to defend a proposed reliance on first-person knowledge than is usually demanded as preface to reliance on sense-perception, since I have defended the claim to such knowledge against such general skeptical attacks as I could see contrived against it.

But now comes the objection: if I do not deny that we can know about someone from the third-person perspective what I claim we know about ourselves with first-person warrant, why bother with the latter at all? Isn't this methodologically otiose? Not necessarily. As I have already suggested, while it may be that one can know about another's mind by observation, if, when we think of examples by which to explain what we might mean by 'consciousness,' we focus just on cases in which someone would assert or deny that another has experience of a certain sort, we may be liable to confuse what warrants third-person attribution of conscious experience with conscious experience itself. And so, if a first-person approach to consciousness can help us avoid this error, it will be useful.

But my comments so far do not confront a likely lingering source of anxiety, which might be heralded by invoking a vaguely articulated ideal of "objectivity." The kind of worry I have in mind comes down to a concern that my proposal will provoke intractable disagreements; it is a worry that if we proceed in the way I suggest, we will not be able to achieve *consensus*. And we should ask of a way of inquiry that it assist inquirers in achieving consensus.[17] This again has been the source of many polemics against the introspectionist psychologists of the past: their reliance on a first-person approach (it is alleged) led psychology to become bogged down in hopelessly irresolvable disputes.

This is not the place for a detailed reappraisal of the source of the controversies whose character brought disrepute upon the introspectionists. But it is not clear to me that the inability of the disputants in these controversies to resolve them should be blamed on their use of a distinctively first-person warrant for psychological claims; it may have had more to do with other, deeply entrenched differences in the theoretical assumptions with which they were operating. As for the general concern about achieving consensus, I would urge, first, that we not prejudice ourselves about what consensus we may achieve as we go along the path I am indicating; let us first proceed, and see what we find. We may discover that we can avoid mistakes that in the past have led to discouraging impasses, and, even if we encounter certain areas where further talk seems unable to resolve ardent disagreement, we may find other areas regarding which worthwhile consensus can be found. Second, though we may hope to achieve a certain amount of consensus, we ought not to assume that the extent of knowledge is only as great as the consensus we know how to create among sane, intelligent people. Where the psychological is concerned, profound disagreements may be especially likely; but I do not think this should make one give up the effort to arrive at a warranted view of these matters. Finally, if we decide to ban certain ways of inquiry on the grounds that they invite dissension we do not know how to resolve, and if we exclude people who refuse to play by these rules from our community of inquirers, we may be achieving consensus among those who remain only on the basis of shared error—or we may wind up so restricting our conception of what is available for discussion that we leave out much, or even most, of what is interesting.

Phenomenal Consciousness

3.1 THE TASK OF CLARIFICATION

We can do little to judge the efforts of those who purport to explain consciousness, and little to assess its relation to other features or its importance, if the notion of consciousness at issue is obscure to us. 'Conscious' and its cognates are notoriously slippery terms, and the sense I want us to consider in which our experience is conscious can be elusive: eminent theorists have used 'consciousness' in ways that indicate either a denial that we even have experience conscious in this sense, or else a remarkable lack of commitment on this point. So if I tried to do no more than to clarify a certain sense in which we can rightly say our experience is conscious, I do not think I would set myself too paltry a task.

That some proposed treatments of consciousness (or the mind generally) somehow neglect, leave out, or implicitly deny the occurrence of consciousness is not a new complaint. Nor am I the first to suggest that a tendency to neglect consciousness grows from an intellectual hostility to the "first-person point of view." But one aspect of the confusion surrounding this topic lies in the difficulty of saying just what constitutes either a denial or a neglect of consciousness, implicit or otherwise, and what one is committed to, in accepting the reality of consciousness. In explaining what I mean by 'conscious,' I want not only to secure recognition that we do indeed have conscious experience in this sense, but also to propose a way of distinguishing such recognition from its absence or rejection, and to make it clearer how such a difference in attitude can turn on whether one accepts or rejects the legitimacy of a first-person approach. If nothing else, this will, I hope, help clarify our thinking about what there is for us to notice, account for, or explain, where consciousness is concerned. This is worthwhile, partly because our possession of experience conscious in the sense I want us to acknowledge makes the questions posed about consciousness—in philosophy, in psychology, and in neuroscience—especially challenging. If we fail to grasp this sense, we will not appreciate the challenge. But, even apart from this, our conscious experience is something fascinating and valuable in its own right—or so it seems to me. To ignore it would be a shame.

Some will want to identify the sense I have in mind by speaking of the *phenomenal character* or *subjectivity* of experience, or of *qualia*, or by saying that there is *something it's like* to be what has conscious experience for what has it, or *something it's like* for one to have it. I am content to label the sense of the term I intend to invoke 'phenomenal consciousness,' and it would be right to think that I am interested in a sense that relates in the way just suggested to this "what it's like" idiom that Thomas Nagel and others have made prominent. However, I am not satisfied to depend on these phrases, or on any of the other expressions I've noted, to explain what I mean; I am concerned that they are themselves too beset by obscurities, ambiguities, or misleading associations to bear this burden alone.

I should also say that I will not employ certain well-known, if controversial, thought-experiments that have been used to isolate the notion of consciousness. I am alluding here, for example, to the suggestion that one could undergo a kind of "inversion" of color experience, while certain other of one's features remained constant (the "inverted spectrum"),[1] and also to the suggestion that some creature very like us in form and behavior might nonetheless have no conscious experience whatsoever (the possibility of "zombies").[2] I do not want to deny the value of such thought-experiments in aiding our understanding. However, I think they are, in a way, too ambitious for my purposes. That is, they put a greater strain on our conceptual powers than is needed for us to demonstrate our grasp of consciousness. So although I myself will make considerable use of thought-experiments in what follows, I want to try keeping such flights of imagination as close to the ground as I can.

I have said I want to adopt a first-person approach to the task of clarifying a certain notion of consciousness; the last two chapters have been devoted to defending this proposal. Now that the time has come to carry it out, it will perhaps be useful to review briefly just what this proposal amounts to, and how we have been led to it.

I have said—as have many others who have ventured into this territory—that it would not be fruitful to start by offering a definition of 'consciousness' in general terms. Instead I will try to convey an understanding of what I mean by 'conscious' with an appeal to certain (I hope) judiciously chosen examples. So, in this chapter, I first identify a class of actual cases that share the feature of being conscious, in the relevant sense. Then I contrast the occurrence of certain varieties of conscious experience with cases, real and hypothetical, in which it is lacking. This contrast consists largely in describing an extended thought-experiment, suggested by the phenomenon known as "blindsight." By this procedure, I hope to throw into relief what I mean by 'consciousness,' and in the process warn us off certain ways of thinking that may obscure this sense.

Now, what is specifically first-person about this is manifest partly in that, when I ask you to consider actual instances of conscious experience, as well as the hypothetical cases I will describe, I want you to think of the first-person case. That is, I would like you to consider actual occasions of the types of conscious experience I will describe, drawn from your own life, and, when I describe certain situations that I do not ask you to maintain are actual, I would like you to conceive of being a person in such situations, a person who has or lacks certain kinds of conscious experience.

Implicit in my advocacy of this approach are two assumptions: first, that we do have warrant for first-person judgments about our conscious experience; and second, that the type of warrant we have for these differs from the type had (ordinarily) for the corresponding third-person judgments. For I want to focus on a sense of 'conscious' in which we actually do have a right to say our experience is conscious. And I explained my appeal to the first-person case by pointing to a danger I suspect attends our focusing on the circumstances in which we make third-person judgments about conscious experience—a tendency to confound what typically gives us warrant for such judgments with consciousness itself. So—I have spent the last two chapters arguing for the legitimacy of the assumptions behind the first-person approach I recommend.

And now, in what follows, I ask that you make use of this distinctively first-person knowledge of your own experience. I ask that you attend to what you know about your own experience with the sort of warrant identified in the examples I argued reveal our commitment to the distinctiveness thesis—the sort of warrant you have for judging how things look to you, and what you are thinking about. Notice that I am *not* asking you merely to consider *what you are inclined to say* about your experience, as part of the third-person evidence for a theory about your mind. I am not asking you to elicit first-person "verbal reports" about experience, and then venture theories to explain how these are generated; I am not proposing what Dennett (1991) calls "heterophenomenology." Rather, I am asking you to consider your own experience, and what you can judge about it, with the kind of warrant with which you can make everyday first-person assertions.

I do not argue that you cannot possibly understand consciousness unless you do as I request. But if you find that, when refusing to consider these matters as I propose, you have trouble agreeing that you have conscious experience in the sense I characterize, or difficulty in understanding it, I ask that you do sincerely try to adopt the approach I recommend before concluding that you do not know what I am talking about.

3.2 SILENT SPEECH

So, what do I mean by 'consciousness'? Let's begin by noting, in our own lives, as events strikingly illustrative of phenomenal consciousness, instances of this remarkable general fact: *Often we talk to ourselves without making any noise.* The phenomenon is, I think, utterly familiar, though it seems hard to draw attention to it without sounding paradoxical: this kind of "speech" is unvocalized. You can "speak" in this way perfectly well while suffering from laryngitis, and others cannot hear it. You can talk to yourself in this way on a crowded bus, saying the most insulting things imaginable about those only inches away, without suffering the slightest reaction. You also might say, paradoxically, you "hear" yourself speaking to yourself, but not with your ears—this is a "nonaural" kind of hearing of a nonvocal kind of speech (plugging your ears does not muffle or stop it).

But also: you might "hear silent speech" even when it is not a case of either voluntary or intentional utterance; these you would probably not describe as cases of "talking to yourself." And you may "hear" phrases in this way though you do not mean anything by them. They include *recollections* of utterances, your own as well as others, and also what the schizophrenic reports when he says, "I hear voices." So I want to say, by way of illustration, when you "speak" to yourself, or merely "hear" utterances in this way, something is happening, something occurs, and this is an occurrence or episode of consciousness.

It is hard to know how to report such occurrences without using scare quotes. Our language for imagery is clumsy and potentially misleading (we may, for instance, draw too simple or too crude an analogy between seeing a picture and forming a "mental image"). But it seems we should classify such silent speaking as "aural imagery"; we could say that, as we visualize things we might see (a face, a shape), so we can "auralize" things we might hear, like verbal utterances. Such phenomena have been called "internal monologue" or "silent soliloquy"; I prefer the term "silent speech," for these other phrases suggest we are concerned only with intentional speech acts, or even, only with notably eloquent ones. Now, I want not only to appeal to occurrences of silent speech as paradigm cases, but also to emphasize that although they provide valuable illustrations of conscious states, they are just one kind of conscious state among others. Not all occurrences of consciousness are instances of auralized utterance. Other kinds of imagery, as well as sense-experience, can be conscious in the very same sense as silent speech.

We might put this another way. If we describe unvocalized utterance as silently saying what one is thinking, or experiencing (e.g., visualizing, seeing, smelling), and call this silent verbalization of thought and experience, we can say that not all episodes of consciousness are occurrences of silent verbalization. And not only are many conscious states not themselves instances of verbalization, many are not accompanied by silent verbalization *of* them, either. For that matter, occurrences of consciousness are often not, in this sense, verbalized at all, either silently or out loud. What we perceive or imagine we often do so consciously, without *saying* what we perceive or imagine.

To understand that there is a sense in which one knows that one's silent speech is conscious, in which also other imagery, and at least much sense-experience, is conscious, and to distinguish this shared feature from that of being verbalized, whether silently or aloud, is to take the crucial first steps in understanding what I mean by 'conscious.'

These points may seem too obvious to bear mentioning. But I want to emphasize them because some renowned authors (and, presumably, many of their readers) seem to overlook them. And unless one firmly acknowledges them at the outset, one may neglect altogether the sense of 'conscious' I am after. When I say that some have overlooked these points, I do not mean they explicitly state that consciousness somehow *is* verbalization, but rather that they make remarks indicating they have not clearly distinguished a state's being a conscious one from its being an instance of verbalization, and from its being verbalized.

The psychologist Julian Jaynes, for instance, theorizes that Homeric Greeks totally lacked consciousness, because, he thinks, they routinely hallucinated voices they interpreted as those of gods speaking to them, but never auralized utterances they considered as their own (Jaynes 1976). This suggests that Jaynes would say there is no sense in which the Greeks of this era had conscious experience. But his (pretty dubious) claim about verbal auralizations of Bronze Age Greeks could count as a reason for denying that they had conscious states, only if he means by 'consciousness' something very different than I do, for as I understand the term, not only can the aural hallucination one takes for the voice of a god count as a perfectly good occurrence of consciousness, so will other states involving no *verbal* imagery at all. So, even granting Jaynes's odd speculations about the attitude the real-life counterparts of Achilles and Agamemnon had toward their verbal auralizations, it would not even begin to follow that their lives were devoid of occurrences of phenomenal consciousness.

Other writers do not reveal as clearly as Jaynes an insensitivity to the distinctions I want to make, but still they give no indication that they would recognize them. The neurobiologist William Calvin says, after casting about for various ways of taking the term, that he is "with Jaynes" in his understanding of 'consciousness,' and that he wishes to restrict this term to having to do with what he calls "the narrator of experience" (Calvin 1990, 76–79). He leaves the connection between consciousness and "narration" vague, so it is not clear that he outright identifies consciousness with some kind of verbalization; he also does not make it clear that he would distinguish the two, and his claim of kinship with Jaynes suggests that he is not clear about this himself.

The failure to distinguish verbalization and consciousness adequately can manifest itself in a still more indirect way. The appeal of certain claims some make about consciousness seems to me sustained by a failure to heed the distinctions of which I've been speaking. I have in mind here the suggestion bandied about that consciousness has some special connection to the notion of a "serial processor." Dennett, for example, says that, even though the processes of the brain are "massively parallel" in nature, the "seriality" of consciousness lends itself to characterization in terms of the "programming architecture" of a "von Neumann machine."[3] But I find it extremely obscure why we should be tempted to say that occurrences of consciousness generally relate to one another in this manner, and so contrast them with nonconscious "parallel" processes. This picture seems to depend on our thinking of the temporal succession of episodes of consciousness in a given person's life as the successive production of small batches of symbols, such as might lend itself to description as the implementation of a set of instructions, von Neumann-style, one at a time. But why *should* we think of them in this way?

Dennett seems to encourage such thinking by his remarks likening "the stream of consciousness" to a "stream of narrative," and so this serial-processor talk appears to find some surface plausibility in thinking of conscious experience as a "stream" of words (Dennett 1991, 113). But why should we think of it thus, when episodes of verbalization exemplify only one sort of conscious experience, and nonverbal and unverbalized imagery and sense-experience are conscious in the same sense as is silent speech? Possibly one thinks of conscious experience as a stream of narrative because, first, one thinks of it as a temporal "stream" of occurrences, and second, one thinks of *all* "mental" or "cognitive" processes (both those involving what is conscious and those involving what is not) as operations on languagelike symbols of some sort. But still, in that case, and if we have reason to think, as Dennett says, that the brain's processes, and so mental symbol manipulations, are *generally* "massively parallel," why should we want to make an exception to this wherever conscious experience is concerned? It seems that, in the absence of reason to think otherwise, we should suppose that the way a given stretch of visual experience (for example) relates to other experience, nonconscious states, and behavior, is no more "von Neumannesque" than the way brain events relate to one another generally.[4]

In sum, it seems to me that, in pursuit of the notion that there is some special connection between consciousness and verbalization, certain authors have lost track of the occurrence of nonverbal imagery and unverbalized sense-experience, and so have lost touch with the notion of phenomenal consciousness.

3.3 CONSCIOUSNESS: NOT JUST TALK

But perhaps some doubts are beginning to crop up about the firmness of the distinctions I have drawn, and so about my notion of consciousness—for evidently many have found the authors I have named compelling. And whether they seem persuasive or not, it may help to ease our way into thinking about consciousness—a topic that can, in any case, quickly become an amazing engine of confusion—to start with some relatively simple points. How could we make my distinctions clear to ourselves, should they prove at all elusive?

One way to do so would be to consider actual occurrences one might classify as cases of "aural imagery," in addition to those of silent speech. One can, for example, make various silent *nonverbal* noises to oneself: one can hum a tune, or mimic machine or animal noises "to oneself," "in one's head," silently, and these events are every bit as conscious as silent speech, and in the same sense. Not only are these occurrences of consciousness not themselves episodes of silent speech, they also are typically not accompanied

by any such episodes of verbalizing them (or for that matter, by any utterance at all). Hum "to yourself" "Yankee Doodle," the opening to Beetho-
ven's Fifth, or "Louie, Louie," and you will not find that you *say* what you
are humming, as this occurs (whatever that could mean), but this occurrence
is still conscious. And further, imagery in sense-modalities other than aural
also provides us with examples of conscious states that neither consist in nor
are accompanied by some kind of verbalization. If you can visualize or "picture" some familiar object or shape—say, an umbrella, a wheel, a triangle—
you can know that, though of course you sometimes may concurrently say
to yourself "umbrella" as you imagine an umbrella, and so on, there are
occasions on which you do *not* say to yourself (or, for that matter, to
anyone) what you are visualizing or picturing. For you may say *nothing* to
yourself or you may just say *anything*—whether it applies to what you are
visualizing or not (so you may picture a triangle, while saying "square,"
"umbrella," "mitochondria," etc.). And the occurrence of such visualization
is still conscious, in the same sense as is silent speech.

And not just sensory imagery, but sense-*perception* furnishes perfectly
good examples of (what we might call) "mute" consciousness. Take note of
occasions when something looks dark blue to you, or round, or flat, or
bumpy, or too far to reach. Or think of times when you know that something sounds some way to you: for example, like a dog barking, a wave
crashing, or a baby crying. Or consider occasions on which you know that
something smells to you, for example, like rotting vegetables, meat cooking
on a grill, gasoline, or pine trees, or where you know that something tastes
sweet to you, or bitter, or like a peach, or like chocolate ice cream; or that it
feels smooth to you, or jagged, slippery, or sharp-edged. There are occurrences we may in such ways report that are conscious in the same sense as
silent speech. And in such cases, provided one is not subject to some kind of
hallucination, one might also say that one *consciously perceives* something;
one consciously sees, hears, smells, tastes, or feels something. One can also
say, in this sense, that one consciously perceives one's own body. One consciously perceives being touched, caressed, poked, or pushed; one's own position and movement; muscular tension and relaxation. We can include here
also cases of sense-experience that are not so clearly perceptual, and often
are grouped under the term 'sensations,' such as feelings of "bodily" pain
(that is, the sort involved in headaches, jabs with sharp objects, and muscle
cramps), feelings of nausea and heartburn, and itches, tickles, and tingles (as
occur when you try to move a foot that has fallen asleep).

Such occurrences all may be known to be conscious in the very same sense
as episodes of silent speech are, though they are not experiences of utterances, silent or aloud, nor does one always verbalize them, silently or aloud,
when they occur. And if this is not already obvious, one has only to think of
cases where one's auralized or, for that matter, one's vocalized verbal utterance concerns something *other* than anything of which one has conscious
sense-experience at the time. What one is saying on a given occasion—

silently or aloud—often has nothing whatsoever to do with what one is perceiving at the time, though one may be consciously perceiving quite a lot. You may be talking with someone about your grandparents, the fall of the Berlin Wall, or the dent in your new car, and though none of these things are there to be seen, you still see, for example, your interlocutor, and something of your surroundings, and this seeing is conscious all the while you are gabbing away, not saying a thing about what you are seeing. And you may be talking to yourself about a childhood pet, plans to buy a house, or what is meant by 'postmodernism,' while gazing out the window of an airplane at the farms below, and this seeing is still conscious, even if verbally unremarked. Furthermore, one may have conscious perception where verbal utterance, silent or otherwise, has come to a complete halt. Though some of us may find that when we shut our mouths the "internal" chatter rarely ceases, I think even the most compulsively verbal will know occasions when all silent voices are stilled, though conscious perception continues—say, when attention is absorbed in some manual task, or in listening to music.

The reflections invited so far may seem too elementary. But contempt for simple observations can get theories off to a bad start. We can see that, though they do not make this clear, theorists of consciousness who want to speak to us of some putative "narrative" sense of consciousness apparently want just to pass phenomenal consciousness by, without acknowledgment. Or else they unwittingly conceal it from themselves. For any effort to identify phenomenal consciousness with some sort of "narrative" seems, in light of the points I have noted, quite mistaken. In considering the examples that help us to make this plain, we manifest our understanding of consciousness—a feature strikingly illustrated by occurrences of silent speech, but that belongs also to nonverbal imagery, and sense-experience.

However, I do not want to suggest that *only* what is thus described is phenomenally conscious. So I will want to say, for example, that it is not just the auralized utterance I make that is conscious, but also the thought I have by making that utterance. It is not just my auralizing, "There's a beer in the fridge," that is phenomenally conscious, but also my thinking that there's a beer in the fridge. And my thinking is typically in this way conscious, where I speak not silently, but audibly. That point may not be sufficiently clear; I discuss it at length later. Until then, I should note that I will occasionally speak of conscious thought in ways that indicate this is my position; if you have doubts on this score, I ask you to be patient.

I should also note that I have not discussed at all whether the kinds of feelings we are likely to classify as *emotions*—such as anger, pity, pride, lust, sadness, amusement, and fear—should be included as examples of conscious experience. I think they should, and in fact, these and other examples of experience I gave at 1.2 I would consider instances of conscious experience. For I regard the expression 'conscious experience' as pleonastic: in my lexicon, there can be no sort of experience that is *not* phenomenally conscious. It may be useful to speak, redundantly, of *conscious* experience, though. For not only will there undoubtedly be those whose use of 'experience' does not carry this implication, it also may not be obvious even to those who would ultimately accept it, while the relevant interpretation of 'conscious' has yet to be explained. But—to return to the point about emotions—I do not offer a list of emotional feelings as paradigms of conscious experience, for I think it would be misleading to set such a list alongside thought and perception as more examples of conscious states, as this suggests that such feelings should be seen as distinct from thought and perceptual experience, in something like the way these last two are distinct from one another—a suggestion I believe is untrue. But sorting this out is a job I must set aside.

Having alerted you that I do not assume conscious experience is restricted to episodes of imagery and sense-experience, I will excuse my initial choice of illustrations by saying that it can be useful to start by gathering together and concentrating on humble, easily identified examples of such experience, for this will make us less liable to overlook consciousness. However, what I have said so far may not yet be sufficient to induce you to attend to it.

3.4 MAKING CONSCIOUSNESS CONSPICUOUS BY ITS ABSENCE

One can explain what one means by a term—as I have been doing—not only by drawing attention to instances to which it applies, but also by contrasting these with cases, real or hypothetical, in which such instances are lacking. And so, I now want to pursue my task of clarification further, by contrasting the presence of conscious experience with its absence.

At first glance, this might seem easy enough. For surely we can point to many occurrences we would want to say are not themselves occurrences of consciousness, in the sense in which we know silent speech, imagery generally, and much perception and sensation to be. One will want to say that most of what happens, both inside and outside our bodies, are not episodes of consciousness—for instance, the circulation of our blood through our arteries and veins, the absorption of food through our intestinal walls, the secretion of insulin, the shaking of a tree's leaves in the wind, the rush of water from this tap, the combustion of gasoline in this car's engine, the revolution of the earth around the sun, to name a few. If there is supposed to be a problem about our saying we *know* that these events are not conscious, and if there are people (either panpsychists or phenomenalists) who would maintain just the opposite, we need not be sidetracked by this. For if these are occurrences of consciousness, we do not know this with first-person warrant, as we do in the other cases. So if we cannot straightforwardly contrast instances of consciousness with events that unquestionably lack this feature, we can at least contrast cases where we know with first-person warrant that it is exemplified, with cases in which we do not in this way know that is, if it is. And this serves the purpose of clarification just as well.

However, this kind of contrast does not go as far in warding off potential misunderstandings as I would like. For suppose one responds to the foregoing by saying one understands well enough what this feature, consciousness, is—namely, just the feature of being a *mental* event. This would not be an adequate way of stating what I am driving at, because there are various sorts of "mental"—or, at any rate, "representational"—goings-on to which we, or our brains, are alleged by various theories to play host, that I would *not* want to say are known by us to be conscious.

But then, if this is a problem, why do I not simply list some of these supposedly mental states, processes, or whatever they are, and explain what I mean by contrasting my earlier examples with these? It would not be necessary for me to commit myself to the truth of whatever claims I might, for this purpose, draw from—for example, some psychoanalytic account, or a theory of vision or language. I could just say that, *if* the events such theories purport to describe occur "in our minds" or in our brains, they are not such as we know to be conscious in the relevant sense.

But I would rather not assume our grasp of notions special to theories that may not be well understood, and I would prefer not to mix up my account with whatever complications swarm around them. I also doubt it would help to appeal here to examples of states of mind that are not phenomenally conscious, of the sort we might attribute to one another in the course of nonprofessional psychological explanation. Though it may be that some of the *beliefs* and *intentions* we so attribute are not conscious in the sense I want to illustrate, I do not want to rely on such cases for the needed contrast, because I do not think it is clear enough what we mean by saying of beliefs or intentions that they *are* conscious, and whether this involves just the same sense as I have been discussing, or only a related one.

So, I would like to explain what I mean by 'consciousness' by contrasting instances of this feature with cases in which they would be lacking, without simply taking for granted our understanding of explanations (professional or otherwise) that appeal to nonconscious "mental," or "cognitive," or "intentional," or "representational" states or processes. Here, then, is what I propose. I would like you to try to employ the notion of consciousness so far illustrated to conduct a thought-experiment, falling into roughly four stages, in which you consider certain situations I will describe. This will, I hope, allow us to contrast the presence of conscious experience with its lack in a way that will help to refine our understanding of consciousness.

3.5 PROMPTED BLINDSIGHT

The initial stage of my thought-experiment requires that you imagine being a person of the following sort. You are seated, facing a screen, at the center of which you consciously see a small light. That is to say, it looks to you as if there is a small light there, this is a conscious experience, and you are not subject to some kind of illusion or hallucination. While continually maintaining your focus on this light, you also consciously see, intermittently, either an X or an O briefly flashed somewhere to the left of the point of visual focus. You see these figures only briefly, but still this seeing is conscious, in the same sense that your seeing the light on which you have focused is conscious, and in the same sense that your saying to yourself silently, "I saw an X," or your visualizing an X with your eyes closed, may be conscious occurrences.

Now suppose you find yourself suffering from the following calamity. You find that in circumstances in which you formerly would have consciously seen certain things located to your left, now you no longer see things so placed, or at least, you do not see such things *consciously*. This change in the extent of your conscious vision becomes especially obvious to you when you are set once more before the screen described above and find that, as long as you fix your focus as before on the dot of light at the center, you no longer consciously see the X's and O's flashed, or anything at all there, where you formerly would have, to the left of the light on which you focus, and as you still do consciously see X's and O's flashed in the right portion of the screen.

What I am asking you to imagine here might be put this way: your field of conscious vision has "shrunk" or "contracted" on the left side. That is to say, the range of items before you of which you have conscious vision has considerably diminished. In such circumstances, you would probably be inclined to say that you were suffering from some kind of partial blindness. You now no more consciously see things located on your left, where once you would have, than you ever have consciously seen (without mirrors or cameras) of things located behind your head. You now no more consciously see the X's and O's that you once would have, than you do those things on your right lost to conscious vision when, with gaze fixed, you shut your right eye.

Now suppose something further. Though you still lack conscious vision of stimuli in certain locations in circumstances in which you formerly would have had it, nevertheless, in controlled experiments, when required to "guess" what sorts of stimuli—from among a short list of options—were presented in this area of deficit, you evince an ability to discriminate verbally at least some of them with a remarkable degree of accuracy. For example, when asked to guess whether an X or an O was flashed to the left in the sort of setup described above, you are able to guess correctly, at a level well above chance. The tests show that somehow the light reflected from these stimuli onto your retinas and the resulting neural activity enable you to make successful discriminations of this kind, but *without your consciously seeing the stimuli*. These discriminations, we may suppose, are not produced by some direct or remote-control manipulation of your brain or your muscles by something other than visual stimuli—no high-tech puppetry, or miracle, or act of God jerks them out of you; these responses to what you do not consciously see are as much a product of what goes on in you as are the responses you make to what you do consciously see.

You would probably be surprised when told of the results of these tests, but that is not to say such an scenario is not possible. In fact, as many are aware, there is evidence that what you have just imagined happening has actually occurred to some people, such as the subject of Lawrence Weiskrantz's famous case study, D.B. (Weiskrantz 1986). This is the phenomenon on which Weiskrantz and others have bestowed the paradoxical name "blindsight."

3.6 Spontaneous Blindsight

I now want to sharpen our understanding of 'conscious' a little more, by altering this scenario slightly. Again, suppose you find yourself subject to a loss of conscious vision with certain optical discriminatory powers intact, as described above—blindsight. But you find also that, while the former extent of your conscious vision is not restored, you are on occasion struck by the thought, as by a powerful hunch or presentiment, that there was something of a certain sort just present in the area of your deficit—say, an X or an O—*even though you have not been prompted or required to guess about these matters.* You may, if you like, imagine this thought expressed through a verbal auralization of the sort earlier discussed, a silent utterance of "X there!" or "O to the left!" But, though we may well say this thought is itself an occurrence of consciousness, it is no more an instance of *consciously seeing* the items in question—an X, an O, or whatever—than would be the sudden "feeling" that you might get that someone directly behind your head is staring at you, or than would be an allegedly psychic hunch that there is an X hidden from view behind a screen. But now, as it turns out, experiments show that you reliably have such spontaneous unprompted thoughts about what is before you just when your retinas actually do receive light from these very sorts of stimuli, even though you do not consciously see them. And again, we assume these thoughts come just as much from within you as do those you have about what you do consciously see.

These accurate thoughts about what sorts of figures are on your left are, we may suppose, "spontaneous," not only in that you have them without being prompted by multiple-choice questions concerning what was there, but also in that they are, as we might say, "seemingly noninferential." That is to say, your having them is not contingent on your having any inclination or ability to *justify* the claim in question—that there is an X on your left—by making some others from which this one may be inferred, or by which you state what evidence you have for it. The thought simply occurs to you that there is an X on your left: it just "pops into your head," as we say. And though this thought of yours may be what we might call a "hunch," that will not necessarily prevent your having a fair degree of confidence in, and commitment to, its truth. So we might speak here of a spontaneous *judgment* that there is an X. And finally, though one might make such a judgment as a result of an effort to say (or of "willing" oneself to say) something about what is on one's left, we need not suppose this is essential; we may conceive of such thoughts occurring, on occasion, quite unbidden.

Now, we can suppose further that one makes such spontaneous discriminatory judgments about visual stimuli that one does not consciously see, in relation to a variety of simple shapes or patterns, not just X's or O's. How widely can we coherently suppose this ability to range—over just what types of stimulus? Presumably, at least this far: whatever types of visual stimulus that the evidence indicates *actual* blindsight subjects can discriminate *with* prompting, we may suppose a *hypothetical* blindsighter able to discriminate these spontaneously, *without* prompting. So, for example, as Weiskrantz's actual blindsight subject has apparently demonstrated a prompted ability to discriminate whether his visual stimulus consists of lines or is a homogeneously shaded area, as well as whether lines are oriented this way or that, so the hypothetical blindsighter, whom you imagine being, would have a capacity spontaneously to discriminate such differences verbally, without consciously seeing the stimuli. And surely we can go a little further than this. There are at least some relatively simple and restricted types of difference in visual stimuli for which evidence of actual blindsight is relatively more controversial, or even nonexistent, which we can readily suppose may be discriminated without conscious vision, either with or without prompting. Suppose, for example, your left-visual-field stimuli cause you to make unprompted accurate judgments about what colors are present there, though you do not consciously see anything there. It just occurs to you that there is something green, or blue, or yellow on your left, in your area of deficit, when and because there actually is something of that sort there. Suppose you are even able to say, with accuracy, that there is something green above something yellow, or that the green area is larger or smaller than the yellow, or that the color now present is lighter or darker than the previous one. Suppose you are able to make spontaneous judgments of this sort about which among three colors in your left field were most similar—without consciously seeing them there.

To conceive of this, we need not try to think of the blindsighter as somehow instantly and spontaneously uttering terms (aloud or silently) that would classify *all the different types of stimuli* that actual prompted blindsight can apparently discover in a given kind of stimulus situation. That is, we need not suppose the hypothetical spontaneous blindsighter would produce a (silent or noisy) complete running commentary on all the kinds of figures that she could discriminate, as they occured in her "blind" left visual field, reporting their relative size, position, and color. Rather, we need suppose only that, without conscious sight, retinal stimulation affords the subject the *ability* to make this range of verbal discriminations, with no exposure to options for verbal response during or just after the time of stimula-

tion, and in the absence of any disposition to justify the response, by reference to other claims providing argument or evidence for what was said in
response. So—we may suppose that, from among the responses such a subject can make to stimuli not consciously seen, only *some* will, on a given
occasion, actually be manifested spontaneously in thought or verbalization,
without this happening because of a question the subject has put to herself,
or because of one put to her, or in response to some effort she is making. But
we may imagine also that she is *able*, spontaneously and verbally, to discriminate with blindsight *other* stimuli, when relevant efforts are made or
questions (that are not "forced choice") are posed. Thus, for example, the
thought that there was an X on her left might pop into her head, but then
also, if she is asked or wonders, for whatever reason, whether there was any
other figure there, she finds herself able to say there was an O as well, below
the X, of the same color.

Thus we may consider a form of blindsight that differs from the prompted
(and apparently actual) kind in that it involves an ability to discriminate
spontaneously, in verbal fashion, a range of visual stimuli. These types of
stimuli, however, we are not supposing differ much from those that actual
blindsight subjects have been alleged to discriminate—they are relatively
simple visual stimuli: simple shapes, patterns, areas of color, lightness and
darkness, and relative position.

But one might now worry: in expanding the forms of blindsight we consider in this way, beyond what the actual clinical cases seem to present, do
I ask us to assume that our neurophysiological makeup would allow us to
become such blindsighters? No, I am not asking us to indulge in presumptions about what alterations the human brain can admit. It does not undermine the reflections I invite if, given the organization of the human visual
system, neither lesions nor surgery can produce any blindsighters such as I
have described. It does not matter for my purposes if *we* cannot become such
spontaneous blindsighters, as long as we have human brains, organized in
the way those naturally are. And as far as I am concerned, we may even
assume that having such brains is something essential to us. But whether or
not your becoming such a blindsighter is, in this way, an impossibility, it is
not, in any case, a transformation I ask you to contemplate. Rather, I ask
you to suppose that *some* kind of being (perhaps with an internal organization rather different from ours) enjoys the kinds of discriminatory power
without conscious vision of which I have been speaking. Even if sometimes
I ask you, for the sake of convenience, to suppose that you can make such
and such responses without conscious sight (instead of asking: conceive of
being someone who would), you need not conceive of a scenario in which
you yourself are such a subject; you need merely conceive of being such a
subject—much as you might conceive of being someone fifteen feet tall,
without trying to conceive of a situation in which *you yourself* are fifteen feet
tall. You and I can try to conceive of being spontaneous blindsighters, without trying to entertain the possibility that you, the person reading this book,
and I, its author, become blindsighted.

3.7 AMBLYOPIC BLINDSIGHT

Relieved of any worry that I have asked us already to fantasize more wantonly than a respect for the physiological facts should allow, one may now wish to press a concern of a contrary sort: perhaps we should feel no reluctance to hasten on to conceive of deficits in consciousness involving much greater departures from the actual. For, as long as our hypotheticals are unconstrained by the physiology of human vision, mightn't we go on from here to consider even more fanciful and elaborate forms of spontaneous blindsight, where the visual discriminatory capacities of someone with no conscious vision at all would match those of a normal, consciously sighted adult human being? Mightn't we conceive of a form of blindsight that enabled one to perform whatever feats of bodily coordination and dexterity normal conscious vision does? It may seem we can in thought conjure up some sort of "premium-quality" blindsighters who use their "vision" to drive taxis, play baseball, and even do brain surgery, needlepoint, and carpentry. Such "super-duper" blindsighters (as Ned Block [1995] has called them) would have powers of visual discrimination as high-grade as those of any normal consciously sighted person.

This seems somewhat harder to imagine than those more conservative scenarios earlier suggested. But if we were successfully to push our thought-experiment in this direction, to this extent, then it would be clear that the contrast we are considering here, between the presence of conscious visual experience and its lack, *is not simply a contrast between higher and lower grades of visual discriminatory power*. This latter admission is indeed one I think we should make. But I do not intend to elicit it by asking you to contemplate a form of blindsight that would be nearly as amazing as that just mentioned.

It is crucial to keep in mind here that even conscious visual experience, of the sort that would be missing in the spontaneous blindsight just described, may enable one who has it to do little else but make discriminatory judgments and movements of a *very* feeble sort. Consider: those of us who wear glasses or contact lenses notice on their removal a change in our conscious vision of roughly the sort familiar even to those more optically fortunate when the movie projector goes out of focus. This sort of change occasions a precipitous and general drop in the kinds of visual stimuli we can discriminate, verbally and otherwise. And this impoverishment of conscious visual experience can be quite extreme—as it is with those who fall firmly within the classification "legally blind." People can have no better than the very crude visual discriminatory capacities characteristic of severe amblyopia, without losing conscious vision of stimuli entirely.

This brings us to the third stage of our thought-experiment. Notice now that we might contrast a case in which one has lost conscious vision of stimuli in one's left visual field, not only with a case in which one has *normal* conscious sight of things in one's full visual field, but also with a case in which, while one's right field vision is unimpaired, one has only *severely amblyopic conscious vision* of stimuli in but *part* of one's left visual field. Consider again for a moment the case of Weiskrantz's subject, D.B. Although soon after an operation on his visual cortex he reported that he saw nothing in roughly the left half of his visual field, later he claimed to have regained sight in an isolated portion of his left field, although he was able to discriminate stimuli here with only very low acuity. Thus Weiskrantz called this area of apparently restored conscious vision an "amblyopic crescent." Somewhat surprisingly, D.B.'s prompted blindsight discriminations of stimuli in his left visual field *outside* this "crescent" in some ways displayed greater acuity than his discriminatory judgments about what lay *within* the amblyopic crescent, where he had conscious vision (Weiskrantz 1986, 22–23, 30–31).

We might alter the features of this case somewhat as before, when we first turned our regard from what I took to be actual blindsight to spontaneous blindsight. Suppose, much as before, that, while in your right field conscious vision remains, you do not consciously see what lies in your left visual field, *except*, now, *in some isolated portion* of it, you do have very blurry, *conscious* visual experience of areas of color, lightness, and darkness, their extent and relative position. We may suppose your acuity here is much too low to be able to distinguish even the large letters at the top of the eye chart, viewed at close range—you cannot tell if it is an X or an O you are looking at. And suppose you have in the rest of your left visual field—outside the region of conscious amblyopic vision—some powers of spontaneous *blindsight* discrimination. Now consider the (rather limited) kinds of unprompted verbal discriminations of color, shape, position, etc., you could make of stimuli in your "amblyopic crescent." We may, it seems, also conceive of being a blindsighter who lacks this crescent of blurry left-field conscious vision, one who consciously sees *no* left-field stimuli at all, but who is *no worse off*, with respect to his capacity for spontaneous discrimination of left-field stimuli. That is, you may suppose your capacity for spontaneous verbal discriminatory judgment about left-field visual stimuli is generally the same, whether you are someone who consciously sees none of them at all, or whether there is an isolated area on your left of which you have amblyopic conscious vision. And if we can suppose this, surely we can suppose behavioral responses to stimuli in an area of which conscious visual experience is entirely missing to be no less acute or rapid or extensive than are those responses certain forms of legally blind conscious vision enable one to make. In other words, we can conceive of a kind of left-field blindsight that provides one with powers of spontaneous discrimination, as manifested in verbal and other behavior, equivalent to those afforded by extremely poor, blurry conscious vision. This we might call "amblyopic blindsight."

We make this all the easier to conceive of, the more degraded and simple (the more severely amblyopic) we suppose the conscious vision with which we contrast its hypothetical blindsight counterpart. Thus we may conceive of being someone who consciously sees only a blurry patch of various shades of gray in part of his left visual field—and who has the ability to judge spontaneously, of the visual stimulus there, no more than that it is a patch of gray, now brighter, now darker, and to indicate these judgments in an indefinite range of observable behavior—whether linguistic utterance, hand movements, ear wiggling, etc. And we can fairly readily contrast this with the case of a blindsighted analogue of such achromatic amblyopic experience, who would duplicate the relatively unimpressive feats of spontaneous discrimination, but without consciously seeing the stimuli. Such a blindsighter would clearly be much more limited in visual ability than Block's virtuoso blindsighter, who, we are to suppose, may blindsightedly play tennis, repair watches, and so on. What I want to emphasize here is that although we may, for whatever reason, find the contemplation of the latter form of blindsight conceptually daunting, we need not try to stretch our imaginations this far in order to appreciate a point that would follow from it, which is crucial to grasping the phenomenal sense of 'consciousness.' That is, again, the point that the contrast between phenomenally conscious vision and its lack is not merely a contrast between greater and lesser abilities to respond discriminatively to visual stimuli. A premium-quality or super-duper blindsight would make this clear, but spontaneous, amblyopic blindsight is enough to do the job.[5]

3.8 Is "Blindsight" Real Sight?

In preparation for the last stage of our thought-experiment, I think it will help to try to clarify the sense in which blindsighters could properly be said to *see* the stimuli that they discriminate. The term 'blindsight' looks like an oxymoron—if you are blind, then surely you cannot have sight? Some reflection on how we can interpret this expression, without absurdity, to refer to a form of sight or vision seems appropriate, in any event.

If one says that, yes, "blindsight"—or at least the hypothetical "spontaneous" variant I have mentioned—is literally a form of sight, then this will, I suppose, be because one wants to treat the kinds of judgment or other discrimination it would occasion as in some sense visual (in fact, I myself have already been speaking of it this way), and one is happy to talk of sight and seeing wherever there is discrimination or judgment that is visual in this sense. But in what sense would these be visual? We might say: well, the discriminations are of, and the judgments are about, *visual stimuli*. And to say that stimuli are visual, I take it, is to say that they bring about a response through affecting a subject's light-sensitive organs.

But now we will probably want somehow to allow that there can be a properly visual judgment, and a properly visual discriminatory response, even in cases where they are not triggered by the types of stimuli they are about, or are discriminatory of. This would be so in cases where a visual judgment is false: for example, one visually judges that there is an X on one's left, though there is nothing X-shaped there at all. We can, however, make room for this, if we say it is enough to make the judgment or response visual, that it is *the effect of what is typically brought about by a type of light stimulus*, about which the judgment in question would be true (if true), or to which the response would be a discriminatory response, were such stimuli present. Now, I am not interested in trying to refine further this conception of 'visualness'; I just want to concede for the sake of discussion that one might have some notion of the visual, applicable to blindsight capacities, that makes being suitably causally related to light-sensitive organs sufficient for rendering some judgment or other a discriminative state or some response a visual one. And I want to allow that, possessed of some such notion of what counts as visual, one may sensibly speak of blindsighters as literally *seeing* the items of which they lack conscious sight.

All I insist on at present is that we reserve talk of "consciously seeing an X" only for those cases where one has the kind of experience of left-field X's that we suppose missing in a blindsight case. Notice that this leaves open the possibility that a person could make a spontaneous conscious judgment, or could have a conscious thought, that was, in a certain sense, visual, even without consciously seeing the stimuli of which it was true. Thus we need to distinguish between saying that *one consciously sees an X*, and saying that *one makes a conscious visual judgment or has a conscious visual thought about an X*. A blindsighter's conscious visual hunch is to be distinguished from a conscious visual experience. Further, we are not supposing that the conscious experience missing in the blindsighter's case is simply whatever, distinct from visual judgment, serves causally to link such judgment to visual stimulation. For we will suppose that the blindsighter's proximal visual stimuli and visual judgments are also *somehow* causally mediated—but not by conscious visual experience. One might want to go on to say that such a causal intermediary itself should be termed a 'visual representation' of some sort, or should be thought to "encode information" about visual stimuli. I am not interested here in either affirming or rejecting this way of talking—I only ask that you recognize, if you want to speak this way, that such a visual representation would not be a conscious visual experience. And so, if you were a blindsighter, you might intelligibly say you are making a conscious visual judgment that there is an X on your left, and that you have a nonconscious representation of an X in your visual system, even while you say you still do not consciously see anything to your left, so that there is a type of conscious visual experience of an X you still lack.

One natural way to describe this condition would be to say that, though you now consciously *think* or *judge* that there is an X on your left (at least, you consciously auralize an utterance, "There is an X on my left," that expresses that thought or judgment), it does not *look* to you as if there is an X on your left—or anything there at all, where formerly it did. On this way of understanding 'look,' to say that it looks to you as if there is an X on your left would be to report the occurrence of a kind of conscious visual experience such as may be conceived to be absent, even assuming you had the capacity to make conscious judgments about and triggered by visual stimuli. I endorse this use of 'looks' to describe what the blindsighter lacks in lacking conscious sight, or conscious visual experience. But again, it is not essential to my purposes to say that the blindsighter does not, in any sense, see what he does not consciously see—what does not *look* any way to him. And finally, my terminological choice here leaves us free to adopt theories that would populate blindsighters' brains (or our own) with nonconscious visual representations, or nonconscious encodings of visual information.

3.9 Reflective Blindsight

With this point of clarification behind us, we are ready to pass to the fourth stage of our thought-experiment. Now I would like you to suppose again that you (or more properly, the blindsighter whom you conceive of being) lack conscious vision of stimuli to your left, but enjoy unprompted blindsight capacities of the sort I have described, though now with the following difference. Suppose that it often spontaneously occurs to you not only that there is, say, an X on your left, when in fact there is, but also that this judgment you make is a *visual* one, in the sense in which I said just a moment ago we might regard such a blindsight judgment as visual. That is, you think your blindsight judgment is visual, in that it is appropriately causally related to effects on your light-sensitive organs—your eyes. Consider, then, a blindsighter to whom it spontaneously occurs that his or her judgment is a visual one, and who would regard it as sufficient for this, that it be the effect of something internal, typically caused by light stimuli, of a sort of which the judgment would be true, if true. For this is what this person means by 'visual,' when saying without prompting, "I have a visual hunch that there's an X on the left," or a bit more formally, "I visually judge that there's an X on the left." So, you would not only have a spontaneous thought that there's an X (or an O, or something green) on your left, you would also have, we might say, a thought about your thought—namely, that it is a visual one.

You need not suppose that your inclination to think of your blindsight judgment as visual is something for which you are prepared to offer some argument or evidence. You need not suppose that you would argue that your judgment "must have been visual" on the basis of something else—say, the fact that your eyes are open, and you have demonstrated a blindsight capacity to discriminate visual stimuli of the relevant type in the past. For you may suppose that sometimes, when you have your eyes open, you have spontaneous thoughts you are *not* inclined to classify as visual, about things of *that* type. You might regard these others as manifestations of some "extrasensory" power of discrimination you have, or, less eccentrically, you might simply lack any spontaneous conviction about their source.

I see no reason why, if we can conceive of someone making spontaneous blindsight judgments, we cannot also conceive of someone making spontaneous judgments about their provenance. One might, it seems, make spontaneous judgments about all sorts of things, and one might be quite confident that they are correct—as people sometimes recklessly are. (Consider self-proclaimed psychics.) Now, someone in the kind of blindsight condition I have just described I want to call a "reflective blindsighter." For here the visual stimulus triggers a thought, not just about that stimulus, but also about *oneself and one's representation of the stimulus*—though all the while, one lacks phenomenally conscious visual experience of it. Here, what "pops into one's head" is not just the ("first-order") thought that there's an X on one's left, but the reflective ("second-order") thought that this is a *visual* thought.

We need not, it seems to me, suppose these are two distinct events. Suppose you are visually exposed to an X, and the thought occurs to you, "I visually judge there's an X on my left." Perhaps the best way to describe this would be to say that this occurrence is both a thought about the X, and a thought about that thought. In any case, we may conceive of a subject who spontaneously has both the first-order thought and the reflective thought about it, but who does not consciously see an X, since the X in question is flashed in the portion of her visual field from which phenomenally conscious visual experience has receded. In describing this, I have been focusing on an example of blindsight regarding X's. But I assume we may extend our conception of the reflective blindsighter to incorporate the previously discussed elaborations. So we may conceive of a reflective blindsighter who has the visual discriminatory capacity afforded by severely amblyopic vision, and who, being "reflective," is able to make unprompted judgments about the visual judgments wherein that power to discriminate visual stimuli is manifest. Thus we may conceive of being an *amblyopic reflective blindsighter*: one who is inclined to think not only that there is a splotch of gray on her left (where she consciously sees nothing), but that her thought that this is so is visual in source.

This ends the thought-experiment I wanted us to conduct. It has proceeded through roughly four stages—from what I supposed was the case of *actual* or *prompted* blindsight, to a hypothetical form I labeled *spontaneous*, to an *amblyopic* variety, and finally, to the kind I called *reflective*. By conceiving of being someone subject to such deficits in conscious experience, I hope we can be clearer than we might otherwise have been about what feature I intend to pick out with the term 'consciousness.' By using the sense of 'conscious,' earlier illustrated with reference to actual experience, to contrast the occurrence of certain kinds of episodes of consciousness with their absence, one manifests one's understanding of 'phenomenal consciousness.'

3.10 How Experiences Differ: Phenomenal Character

By means of both positive examples of conscious experience and negative examples of its absence, I have tried to secure a recognition of what episodes of consciousness have in common. But to understand consciousness, one needs to understand not just what conscious experiences share, but also a certain way in which they differ. I have in mind here the kind of difference sometimes recognized by saying that experiences differ in their "phenomenal," or "subjective," or "qualitative" character.

Earlier I announced my dissatisfaction with anchoring an explanation of what one means by 'conscious' in talk of "phenomenal feels," "subjectivity," and "qualia," since these terms can bring with them unnecessary or unwelcome implications, suggestions, or restrictions. However, I have elected to use the phrase 'phenomenal character'—and I do think its use can be more readily detached from assumptions I do not want to endorse than can the use of these others. But I still would not want to rely exclusively on this phrase to point out to the reader differences of this sort. 'Phenomenal character' may seem as alien as any clump of jargon; I need to offer some explanation of how I want it to be understood.

One way to start to see what I mean by 'phenomenal character' is to consider an erroneous way of thinking about what would be missing when certain kinds of conscious vision are missing in blindsight. I said that in a case of spontaneous blindsight, someone might want to theorize that, even though the subject lacks a conscious visual experience of an X, she has, distinct both from the discriminatory verbalized judgment that there is an X, and from the retinal stimulation by the X, a representation of an X in her brain, in her visual system—albeit a nonconscious one. I said that I was not concerned to deny the possibility of such visual representations. But now, if one did believe that there would be such a nonconscious representation of an X in the blindsighter's visual system, one might be tempted to think also that she *would* possess the kind of visual experience of an X that we supposed her to lack, if only that visual representation of an X had added to it this one extra feature: the general feature of phenomenal consciousness, which her blindsight visual thoughts and her right-field visual experiences share.

We can see that this would be a mistaken way of thinking about what she lacks. For what the blindsighter's *nonconscious* visual representation of an X would lack—which, were it not lacking, would make it the conscious visual experience we imagined absent—is a feature that many of her *conscious* experiences would lack as well. If the missing feature is not simply one that belongs to episodes of phenomenal consciousness generally, then the nonconscious visual representation could not somehow be transformed into a conscious visual experience of an X by adding to it this general feature. What is missing here is not just something that all episodes of consciousness share, but a way in which consciously seeing an X would differ from other experience, yet that would not characterize any nonconscious visual representation. That is to say, what we supposed was lacking when we conceived of ourselves in the blindsighter's situation—the conscious visual experience of an X—has a certain *phenomenal character* that neither various other kinds of conscious experience nor any of our nonconscious mental representations (whatever we take these to be) would have.

We might identify the sort of phenomenal character we supposed missing by saying that it does not *seem* to the blindsighter the way it *seems* to us normally sighted people, for it to look to us as if there is an X on our left. So I might distinguish between my visually judging that there is an X, and its seeming to me the way it does for it to look to me as if there is an X. Only where the latter occurs may I speak of a conscious visual experience of an X, or of consciously seeing an X. And thus I might report that I have experience with the phenomenal character mine has when I consciously see an X by saying, "It seems to me the way it does for it to look as if there's an X on my left." (Where I use a personal pronoun in connection with only one of these verbs 'seem' and 'look,' the person to whom it seems and the person to whom it looks are assumed to be identical.)

So: *the way it seems to me* for it to look as if there is an X on my left is the *phenomenal character* of the experience I would report by saying, "It seems to me as it does for it to look as if . . . etc." And, I will say, its seeming this way to me is a *phenomenal feature*, a feature I attribute to myself in such a report.

Why do I resort to this curiously double locution—"The way it seems to me for it to look as if . . ."? Why do I not simply say that I attribute a certain phenomenal feature to myself by saying, "It looks to me as if there's an X on my left"? It is not as though I think the event of its *seeming* to me this way is any other than that of its *looking* some way to me. And I have already said that I want to interpet 'looks' in such a way that for me to assert, "It looks to me . . .," is to report that I have a conscious visual experience. However, I resort to this locution because of certain subtle questions about just what constitutes a difference in phenomenal character, or distinct phenomenal features. We need to be careful not to build into our way of talking about phenomenal character potentially controversial assumptions about what kinds of phenomenal differences there are. It is not immediately clear that if it looks to me as if p, but it does not look to you as if p, this entails that we have distinct phenomenal features—even if we understand 'looks' here so that it could look to me as if p, only if I have conscious visual experience, and not if I have only blindsight.

Suppose, for instance, it looks to me as if your right front tire is a little low, but it does not look to you as if it is, even when you look at the tire from just where I am standing—and it does look some way to you. We may assume that it could not, in this sense, look to me as if the tire is low, or to you as if it is sufficiently full, if we had only blindsight. However, it is not clear that, in our situation, we should say that the *phenomenal character* of your visual experience differs from that of mine. Perhaps we should say that the way it seems to me for it to look as if the tire is low does not differ from the way it seems to you for it to look as if the tire is full. Maybe we should say that all that differs here are the *visual judgments* we are each inclined to make, in some sense, on the basis of our phenomenally indistinguishable visual experiences, and maybe this difference in visual judgments is not to be thought of as involving any difference in the phenomenal character of our experience.

So we should not pretend that there is no difficulty in being clear about just what constitutes a difference in the phenomenal character of experience. However, that is not to say that *all* such differences are equally difficult to recognize. We can achieve a basic understanding of what phenomenal character is if we first consider differences in phenomenal features that are particularly striking and obvious, those we will be able to recognize, if we are able to recognize any. Where the phenomenal character of sight is concerned, it seems to me that color vision furnishes examples of this sort.

Think of an occasion on which you consciously see something, and it looks to you as if it is yellow. (You may as well think of seeing something flagrantly yellow—like a sunflower.) Now again, I want to say that it seems a certain way to you on such occasions, in a sense in which it would not if you lacked a certain kind of conscious experience. It would not seem to you the way it does for it to look to you as if there is something yellow, if you had only a blindsight capacity for discriminatory color judgment, such as we might imagine. Suppose you had only achromatic conscious vision of your surroundings, so that all you consciously saw were white and black and varying shades of gray, and the whole world looked to you no more colored than a black-and-white movie. Still, we may suppose that you make accurate unprompted judgments about what color things are in your environment. But in a sense, it would never be the case that it seems to you the way it does (or would) for it to look as if something is yellow (or blue, etc.).

You might also, as before, conceive of having a kind of blind color sight regarding visual stimuli of which you have no conscious vision at all. If you were such a person, you could not truthfully say, when something yellow is presented only in the blind part of your visual field, that it seems to you the way it does for it to look as if there is something yellow there, even if this stimulus triggers the spontaneous judgment, "There's something yellow over on the left," or some such.

Now, not only does it sometimes, in this sense, seem to you as it does for it to look as if something is yellow, but also, the way it seems to you then *differs* from the way it does for something to look as if something is blue (or red, or some other color). Finally—and here is the crucial point—not only does the way it seems to you typically differ when you consciously see differently colored things, so that one has different kinds of conscious experience, but also any state one is in, or event in one's brain, that differed from others just as these experiences differ among themselves, would be a conscious experience.

For example, any state or event that differed from others, in just the way its looking to you as if something is yellow differs from its looking to you as if something is blue (or red, etc.), would be an episode of phenomenal consciousness. These experiences differ as nothing could differ without being an episode of consciousness. The differences in question are these: the way it seems to you for it to look as if something is yellow differs from the way it seems to you for it to look as if something is blue, and both of these differ from the way it seems to you for it to look as if something is red, and so on.

Now, of course, if you had blindsight for color, nonconscious events that triggered your discriminatory judgments of color might differ from one another in some ways that conscious experiences also differ from one another. For instance, its looking to you as if something is yellow typically depends on visual stimulation from yellow things and enables you to judge accurately that they are yellow, and so would certain nonconscious events in a hypothetical case of color blindsight. Also, if we suppose that certain events or states of the blindsighter's visual system were to be regarded as "visual representations," we might say that they would differ in the "information" they contain, or in the "representational" or "intentional" features they would have: for one is accurate only if there is something yellow on your left, and the other is accurate only if there is something blue on your left. And the conscious visual experience the normally sighted person has might be said to differ in the same way. Thus both conscious color experience and nonconscious blindsight-producing occurrences could share certain features, and differ from other experience and occurrences in the same respects.

However, the events we may suppose could produce reliable judgments of color without conscious color vision still would not differ from one another in just the way in which you know that, for instance, its looking to you as if something is yellow differs from its looking to you as if something is blue. If we suppose these two differing color experiences absent in the blindsight case, what remains in their stead would lack not only what these two experiences shared—the general feature of consciousness—but also something in respect of which they differed. The visual experiences do not differ from one another just in respect of what kinds of stimuli typically cause them, and what visual judgments they typically cause. And its looking to you as if there is something yellow on the left does not differ from its looking to you as if there is something blue on the left, in only the way a representation of something yellow differs from a representation of something blue. After all, one's visual judgments would differ in *this* way—but they do not differ from one another just as the visual experiences do. This further respect in which our color vision varies, which would be missing in the case of a person with blindsight for color, is a difference in phenomenal character.

The fact that these differences in phenomenal character are distinguishable from the differences in representational features that can characterize what is not phenomenally conscious may lead us hastily to assume that phenomenal features are somehow "nonrepresentational" or "nonintentional."

I would like to raise a warning flag here. It may be that there are intentional or representational features that what is conscious experience shares with what is not. But that does not entail that phenomenal features are never themselves certain kinds of intentional features. We might want to say that, typically at any rate, the phenomenal character of our experience is, in some sense, inherently intentional. But that is an issue to be addressed later.

Now, I said that, in the face of unclarity about just what constitutes a difference in the phenomenal character of experience, color experience furnishes a good initial example of such variation. But we should not for a moment suppose that differences in the phenomenal character of vision are confined to color experience. We can make analogous points in connection with visual perception of *shape*. Consider again our old friends, the X's and O's.

We can understand the claim that it looks to you as if there is an X on your left, so that this is true only if you have a conscious visual experience of a certain kind—the kind we supposed missing in the blindsight thought-experiment. So suppose you do have an experience of this sort: it seems to you the way it does for it to look as if there is an X on your left. You are able to know with first-person warrant that the way it thus seems to you differs from the way it seems to you to have other experiences—the way it seems to you for it to look as if there is an O on your left, for example. And again, the crucial point is that whatever differs in just the first-person knowable ways such experiences differ among themselves—in respect of the way it seems to you to have them—is a conscious experience.

Of course, if you had blindsight regarding shape, the events that provoked your discriminatory judgments of shape might differ from one another in some ways that conscious experiences of shape also differ from one another. Its seeming to you as it does for it to look as if there is an X is typically contingent on visual stimulation from X-shaped things and enables you to judge accurately that they are X-shaped, as would be nonconscious occurrences we might suppose at work in the hypothetical blindsight case. However, the events that we may suppose could so trigger reliable judgments of shape without conscious vision would not differ from one another in *just* the way in which you know that, for instance, its looking to you as if there is an X on your left differs from its looking to you as if there is an O on your left. And again, we might want to suppose the blindsighter would have, besides his visual judgments about figures in his blind field, nonconscious visual representations of figures there, but the missing visual experiences of the X's and O's differ from one another not just as a representation of an X differs from a representation of an O. This is clear, because even the visual judgments differ from one another in this respect. But neither they nor any nonconscious states or events display the difference we may pick out by saying: the way it seems to you for it to look as if there is an X on your left, differs from the way it seems to you for it to look as if there is an O on your left. If we suppose two such differing visual experiences absent, as in blindsight, their substitutes would lack not just what these two experiences *shared*—the general feature of consciousness—but also something in respect of which they *differed*—namely, the way it seems to have them. Just as the analogous points made regarding color vision did not apply merely to the examples of perceived colors chosen, but to an indefinite variety of visible color, so, too, the considerations just raised concern not merely the visual perception of X's and O's, but that of an indefinite variety of consciously visible shapes.

If it is not initially obvious just what the range of variation in the phenomenal character of vision is, we can, I believe, at least agree that our phenomenal features can differ in the ways just illustrated—the ways it seems to us for it to look as if things are variously colored and shaped. And the contrast with hypothetical cases of color and shape blindsight helps us to distinguish the kind of difference I am calling "phenomenal" from other differences, such as might obtain among nonconscious states or events. This gives us an initial understanding of what kind of variation is at issue.

We might also illustrate and familiarize ourselves with this notion of phenomenal character, by making points similar to those I have made about vision in relation to other sensory modalities. So we might talk about differences in how it seems to us for things to sound, feel, smell, and taste certain ways. For example, the way it seems to me for something to feel slippery differs from the way it seems to me for something to feel rough. And the way it seems to me for something to taste like coffee differs from the way it seems to me for something to taste like beer. To extend this manner of talking about differences in phenomenal features to *imagery* experience, I would say, for example, that the way it seems to me to visualize a square differs from the way it seems to me to visualize a circle. And the way it seems to me to auralize an utterance of "It's raining" differs from the way it seems to me to auralize an utterance of "It's pouring."

To develop a vivid sense of what a difference in phenomenal character is, it might also help to consider certain irksome differences of this sort that are particularly hard to ignore. There may or may not be occurrences or states we should want to call feelings of pain or nausea that are not episodes of consciousness. But obviously such feelings are at least sometimes phenomenally conscious, and when in my case they are, I could rightly say that it seems to me as it does to feel pain, or to feel nausea—where it seems to me in these ways only if I have certain phenomenally conscious experiences. The way it seems to me to feel pain differs from the way it seems to me to feel nausea. Further, any state or event that differed from others in just the first-person knowable manner these do would be a phenomenally conscious experience. Though we might want to recognize a category of "nonconscious pain" and say that what falls under this heading shares certain features with conscious feelings of pain, in respect of which it differs from, for example, conscious feelings of nausea, any state or occurrence that differed just as a conscious feeling of pain differs from a conscious feeling of nausea would be a conscious experience. Nonconscious pain and nausea—whatever we might suppose those to be—would not differ from one another in just the way that conscious feelings of pain and nausea do.

Now, you might wonder here why I do not make this point more simply by saying that the way it feels to be in pain differs from the way it feels to be nauseous. I have no objection to this way of putting it, but I frame this point instead in terms of how it seems to one to feel pain or nausea, only because I wish to draw attention to a wider range of phenomenal features than talking about "ways of feeling" permits. The difference between the way it seems to me for it to look as if there is an X on my left, and the way it seems to me for it to look as if there is an O on my left, is a difference of *the same kind* as that between the way it feels to me to be in pain, and the way it feels to me to be nauseous. But I cannot speak of "the way it feels" for it to look to me as if there is an X on my left. Or else, if I do, it will appear that I am talking about a certain kind of *emotion* I feel when I see X's on my left (whatever that could be). And this, incidentally, points up the inadequacy of talking about differences of the sort I want to discuss as differences in "phenomenal feels." So I employ this talk of "the way it *seems*" to have an experience in order to have a unified way of talking about variations in phenomenal character, applicable across the range of conscious experience.

However, this locution does lend itself to what in my view is a misinterpretation. There may be some temptation to understand my saying that it seems a certain way to someone to have such and such an experience to mean that it seems to someone *that* he has such and such an experience. And if you take this to mean that someone *thinks* or *believes* that he has such and such an experience, then you may suppose that the phenomenal character of your experience is somehow a matter of having certain kinds of thoughts or beliefs about it. Or else, you might think that when I say it seems to me a certain way to have an experience, I mean that the experience seems to me or appears to me a certain way, so that somewhat as things I see appear colored or shaped a certain way, so their appearing *also* appears to me—though there is a difference between "inner" and "outer" perceptions, appearances, or presentations. But I would regard such ways of understanding what I mean by speaking of how it seems to have experience as mistaken. The reasons why, I can make clear only later. However, I can at least emphasize here that I do not intend that my way of discussing phenomenal character be taken in these ways.

But now, what if someone just does not want to accept that there *are* any differences in phenomenal character, as I have described these? I said that my talk of phenomenal character was meant to capture the sort of thing I believe people are after when they speak of the qualitative character of experience, and there have certainly been people who have said they wanted to deny qualitative character or qualia. But though I suppose that some would deny that experience ever has phenomenal character, as I have explained this notion, and would profess not to understand this talk of "the way it seems to feel pain" in the way I intend, typically the defenders of such views would resist even the claim that there are episodes of consciousness, in the sense made out in the previous two chapters. It would be strange, I think, for someone to grant the substance of what I have had to say there, and yet reject my claim here that conscious states differ in phenomenal character. And in the next two chapters, I will look at some ways one might try to doubt altogether that we have phenomenally conscious experience.

But mightn't someone admit that experiences are phenomenally conscious, yet deny that they differ from one another in ways accessible to first-person knowledge, in which *only* what is conscious may differ? We might imagine someone holding that, though conscious states differ, there is no first-person knowable way in which they differ from which it follows that they are conscious states. In that case, for it to seem to me the way it does for something to look red is just for there to be an occurrence that has the general feature of consciousness, plus some other characteristic, the possession of which does not imply that it is a conscious state. So on this view, there is some description D, satisfiable by nonconscious states, such that necessarily it seems to a person S just as it does for something to look red to S, if and only if there is some event in S's life that is both conscious, and satisfies D.

Clearly, I do not believe there is any such description D. And if someone should sincerely wish to claim otherwise, I can only point to examples of the kinds of difference among conscious experiences that resist capture in any such characterization. I have done this partly by noting that, where it seems we can locate differences among conscious states that nonconscious states might *also* exhibit, the conscious states would still differ in ways in which the nonconscious states would not. So even if there could be what we might want to call "nonconscious color vision," or "nonconsious perception of shape," or even "nonconscious pain and nausea," in virtue of what occurrences so called shared with conscious sight and feelings, still, if we are to maintain that they are not conscious, they would not differ from other states just as we know that the corresponding conscious experiences do. One could not say that occurrences of "nonconscious pain"—whatever exactly we suppose these to be—differ from other events in just the respect we pick out by saying that the way it seems to us to feel pain differs from the way it seems to us to have other kinds of experience. Any state of being in pain that did differ from other events in just this respect, could not be other than a conscious feeling of pain.

This introduction of the notion of phenomenal character completes my preliminary clarification of consciousness. Again, some may have found much of what I have had to say too obvious to dwell upon. But the topic of consciousness is, in my view, especially lavish with opportunities for confusions and false starts that can entirely vitiate efforts to discuss it. So we should not be ashamed to approach the subject cautiously, with resort to fairly simple examples, and to be explicit about what may strike us as elementary points.

But the difficulties that greet us here, and threaten to sabotage our attempts even to reach a substantial and shared conception of what it is we want to pick out when we talk about consciousness, are too numerous, complex, and obscure for us to hope to deal with all at once. And I worry that in my effort to avoid certain confusions by beginning with what I regard as relatively simple points, I myself will have unwillingly invited other errors. For concentration on certain examples of conscious experience I think are readily appreciated at the start may unfortunately—as I mentioned earlier—lead one to a much too narrow and too thin conception of what is involved in episodes of consciousness, and what kinds of phenomenal features there are. I can only try, as I go along, to point out and remedy some of what I would regard as mistakes of this kind, and I can only hope that the foothold we have in the topic now will allow us to recognize these as errors.

Of course, what I have said so far gives me nothing so secure that it cannot provoke dissent, and I suspect it is liable to do so, as I begin to use it to argue that others have neglected phenomenal consciousness—for they will probably not want to admit to this. So part of my task as I continue will be to consider and respond to some of the misgivings I imagine some will have about accepting the notion of consciousness it has been my business to elucidate. But first I will need to clarify what I would take as a sign of its rejection.

3.11 How to Deny Consciousness

The thought-experiment I have had us conduct to contrast consciousness with its lack, and thereby sharpen our understanding of the difference, has required a certain amount of care and concentration, and demanded a willingness to consider at least some nonactual situations—for, as far as I know, there is no reason to think any spontaneous or reflective blindsighters have ever walked the earth. Still, these reflections do not, it seems to me, call for any leaps into the conceptual stratosphere.

But my asking you, as I have, to "suppose" you are, or to "conceive" or "imagine" being, a blindsighter—prompted, spontaneous, amblyopic, or reflective—and your successful compliance with that request, may seem to leave unresolved a large question of potentially great import to our theories of consciousness. That is: Are these *conceivable* situations also *possible* situations? It will be said that one may conceive of something's being the case, without its being possible, and we must distinguish possibility—"metaphysical" possibility at any rate—from mere conceivability; the former does not follow from the latter. (Such remarks have become habitual among philosophers since Kripke's [1972] and Putnam's [1975a] writings on meaning and necessity.) Relatedly, one may press questions about the kind of necessity involved in the notion of phenomenal character. To say that nothing *could* differ just as conscious experiences do without being occurrences of consciousness indicates that some notion of necessity is at work. But what kind? Logical? Metaphysical? Natural or nomic?

Let me first respond to the question about the possibility of the situations described in my thought-experiments. Just what we think about this can indeed affect what we think consciousness is, and whether we acknowledge that we have experience that is conscious in the sense I have aimed to clarify. One effect is this: if you believe that what I have asked you to conceive of is, in a highly restrictive sense, impossible, then, on my reckoning, you are committed to denying that we even have phenomenally conscious experience.

But what would it mean to say, in a requisitely restrictive sense, that one of the forms of blindsight I have asked you to consider is impossible? I have already indicated that it would not be enough for this, to say that spontaneous blindsight, for example, is not "*humanly* possible." That is, it would not be enough to say only that it follows from the truths of human neuropsychology that no one whose brain is constituted and organized in the way actual human brains generally are would ever be a spontaneous blindsighter—and in that sense, there *could not* be such people. Again, perhaps *that* is true, but saying so does not, in my book, constitute a denial that we have conscious visual experience. Now I would extend this point further. Saying that *human neuropsychology* is incompatible with the forms of blindsight discussed not only would be insufficient to commit one to a denial of consciousness, it also would not be enough for this, if one held that these forms of blindsight are impossible for any sighted organism inhabiting the actual world. That is: you might hold that each set of psychophysiological principles governing the visual capacity of some species of consciously sighted organism in the actual world, is such as would be violated by the supposition of a spontaneous blindsighter from that species. Still, you would not deny the possibility of blindsight in such a manner as to preclude the recognition of phenomenal consciousness.

But suppose you went further, and held first, that there is some set of psychological principles, true of entities in the actual world, that governs not only every actually occurring natural species of sighted animal, but also any sighted being that comes to be—whether through artificial or natural means—out of the physical constituents of the actual world. That is, suppose you held there are some psychophysical principles from which it follows that any organism or artifact constituted out of the physical particles available in the actual world, that had the sorts of visual functions I have attributed to my "reflective amblyopic blindsighter," would also have the sort of conscious visual experience of left-field stimuli I have asked us to suppose such a one would lack. Then, if we take the claim that a certain type of sighted entity is impossible to be the claim that its existence is inconsistent with principles such as I have just described, we might say that, in a certain sense, my blindsighters are impossible. We might put this by saying that such blindsighters are strongly *infeasible*—incapable of being brought about either by us or by nature, given what there actually is to work with in the world, and the psychophysical principles that govern it. This is a strong claim, and it is not clear what would justify it. But supposing you thought it was true—would it follow *then* that you denied the existence of phenomenal consciousness?

No. You would deny phenomenal consciousness by denying the possibility of one of my forms of blindsight only if you added to this sort of assertion of strong infeasibility another, even stricter claim of impossibility. Suppose you claimed not just that the existence of one of my blindsighters would violate some principle governing what kinds of visual functions without conscious sight would be had by beings made out of what is available in this world, but went on to say that there is no possible world in which such a blindsighter could occur. This would be to claim not just that there are in fact laws predicting that anything made out of what is in this world, having one or another of the visual capacities of my "blindsighters," will not really be a blindsighter after all; it would also be to deny that what these laws say is so, might have been otherwise. On this view, not only is it the case that if something or someone comes to be in this world, exercising visual functions such as I have attributed to my so-called blindsighters, then it will *consciously see* what I say such subjects would not, but also: *things literally could not have been any other way.* This would be to claim that at least one of the forms of blindsight I describe is not just strongly infeasible, but, as we might say, *strictly impossible.* And it would be to claim that it is *strictly necessary* that anyone exercising the visual function of my "blindsighters" would consciously see what I asked us to suppose these would not. To commit oneself to these claims would be to refuse to interpret 'conscious' in the manner I am urging; and it would suffice to deny the reality of *phenomenal* consciousness.

Why do I draw the line here—why do I make this assertion of impossibility a test for consciousness denial? Partly this is a terminological stipulation, a decision about how I want the term 'consciousness' to be interpreted in this discussion—but the decision is not, I think, an unmotivated one. For I would like to have a way of identifying the feature I want to express by the term 'phenomenal consciousness,' which allows us to understand why theories of mind can seem to some to neglect consciousness, where their defenders recognize no just cause for such complaint, and which helps us to see how such divergence of views may stem from a difference between adopting and repudiating a first-person approach to the study of consciousness. Notice that if you would be committed to saying that occurrence of one or another of the forms of blindsight described above is strictly impossible, and not just strongly infeasible, then it seems that you would inevitably find *inherently misleading* the sort of first-person reflection by which I have tried to lead us to identify phenomenal consciousness. To think of consciousness in that manner, is to think of a feature that is known with first-person warrant to belong to silent speech, imagery generally, and a variety of sensory modalities, *and* to think of someone lacking certain instances of *that feature* (someone lacking certain kinds of visual experience), while exercising the discriminatory skills I have attributed to my blindsighters. If thinking about consciousness in this way leads you to think anything regarding the question of whether or not consciousness is a feature, shared by these paradigms, of which someone exercising those discriminatory powers might possibly lack certain instances such as I have described, it will lead you to think that consciousness is indeed such a feature. But, if you hold that, on the contrary, it is strictly impossible for there to be such blindsighters, then you say that consciousness is *not* such a feature, and that the thought-experiment I've asked you to perform leads to a mistaken conception of what you're thinking about, when you're thinking about consciousness—a conception so radically mistaken, in fact, there is no feature we can think of by employing it. For then you would say there is *no* feature satisfying the description by which one is led, through first-person reflection of the sort I have encouraged, to express one's conception of consciousness: there just is no feature one knows with first-person warrant to be shared by the paradigms, relevant instances of which blindsighters, as I have described them, might lack. And since the allegedly mistaken conception at issue is one to which first-person thought about experience fairly readily lends itself, though it is powerless to correct the error, the suggestion would be that such first-person reflection tends to misdirect us about what feature we can rightly attribute to our experience by calling it 'conscious,' and misleads us to such an extent that it yields a conception that fits no feature whatsoever.

On the other hand, suppose my thought-experiment embodying a first-person approach to consciousness is *not* fairly accused of conducing in this way to illusion. Then we will find it is instead the theory of mind that would make such an accusation that really perverts the understanding—and does so to such an extent it invites the criticism that it asks us to turn our backs on consciousness altogether. For one may reasonably think: if it were true that, as some theory tells us, this concept of consciousness to which first-person reflection leads is entirely chimerical—for no feature fits that concept—then there really would be no phenomenal consciousness at all, since whatever consciousness is, it is not a feature about which first-person thought so thoroughly misleads us. But if a theory is mistaken in impugning first-person thought about experience so radically, then it is wrong to tell us there is no phenomenal consciousness, and by this denial merely shows its neglect of reality.

Thus I suggest we try to to locate what divides those who think some theories of mind leave out consciousness from those who admit no such lacuna, by considering attitudes toward the claim that various hypothetical forms of blindsight are impossible. Perhaps in the end there is some better way of achieving this end that I could be persuaded to accept. I hope at least that this way might help various parties in the disputes over consciousness to be more precise about their commitments. But such reflections will have the desired salutary effect only if there are indeed ways of thinking about the mind that can reasonably be taken to commit one to the claim that one or another form of blindsight is strictly impossible. And how might such commitments be manifest?

Such commitments would, I believe, be implicit in the claim that the impossibility of such blindsighters follows either from what we can mean by 'conscious' (i.e., by what concept of consciousness we can form) or from what consciousness *is* (i.e., from what the property or feature of being a conscious experience consists in). For I take it that if one says that it is impossible for a certain description to be true of anyone, because of what is meant by it, or on account of the concepts it expresses, one invokes a kind of impossibility—a "conceptual" or "broadly logical" impossibility—distinct from that I have called "strong infeasibility." I assume that even if (for example) spontaneous blindsight is incompatible with such laws as govern the sorts of sighted beings our world will afford, it may not be impossible in the sense that would follow from consideration of what we mean or understand by 'conscious vision.' For to show it is *logically* impossible for there to be such blindsighters—rather as round squares are said to be impossible— would be to show more than that certain principles that govern our world are incompatible with these forms of blindsight; it would be to show that principles governing what visual capacities require conscious sight could not have been otherwise, given what is meant by 'consciousness.' Similarly, I take it that if one says it is impossible that a certain feature or property be present or absent under certain conditions, on account of what that property or feature is, one invokes a kind of impossibility—sometimes called a "metaphysical" impossibility—that goes beyond what is entailed by incompatibility with the sorts of principles I have mentioned. I assume that even if (for example) spontaneous blindsight is incompatible with such laws as govern the sorts of sighted beings our world will afford, it may not be impossible in the sense that would follow from what it is to consciously see something, or from what the property or feature of visual consciousness is, or consists in. For to show it is *metaphysically* impossible for there to be such blindsighters—rather as water that is not H_2O is said to be metaphysically impossible—would be to show more than that certain principles that obtain in the actual world are incompatible with these forms of blindsight; it would be to show that these principles governing what visual capacities require conscious sight could not have been otherwise, given that they concern the feature or property of being a conscious visual experience.

So, I would count someone a denier of phenomenal consciousness who said that all he *means* by saying—and all he can *understand* by my saying— that someone *consciously sees* an X, is that she exercises a capacity to discriminate, spontaneously and visually, a stimulus of a certain type, and so he finds "spontaneous blindsight" to be quite impossible. Likewise, I would regard someone a repudiator of consciousness who would deny the possibility of spontaneous blindsight on the grounds that *being a conscious visual experience*, just is (or is "nothing but," or "nothing over and above") *being a state that enables what is in it to make spontaneous visual discriminatory judgments*. More generally, to back a claim that *any* of the forms of blind-sight we have considered are impossible by means of such conceptual or metaphysical assertions, would be to assert claims of strict impossibility—and it is just such claims of impossibility that I want to say are incompatible with an acceptance of consciousness.

Although I have used the labels 'conceptual' and 'metaphysical' for speaking of strict impossibility, I should make it clear that I do not mean to take on board some particular way of distinguishing between conceptual and metaphysical "modalities," or even to endorse the view that they are, at bottom, distinct.[6] My claim is just that a commitment to the belief that the types of blindsighter I have discussed are more than strongly infeasible, that they are either logically or metaphysically impossible, is tantamount to a denial that we have phenomenally conscious experience. But this leaves the question: if I say such denial of possibility would preclude recognition of the phenomenal consciousness I want acknowledged, do I then ask us to affirm that certain kinds of blindsighter are either logically or metaphysically possible, on the basis of our capacity to imagine or conceive of being them?

I should say first that, although I have sometimes asked you to imagine this or that in carrying out our thought-experiment, I do not mean to have made its successful performance a feat of imagination only. We can distinguish, as we should, between the ability to *imagine* (e.g., visualize) something on the one hand, and the ability to *conceive* of it on the other. But I expect *both* such faculties to be brought into play in cooperation with my requests in this chapter—and my claim is that we can achieve success at least in conceiving of these forms of blindsight. That is, I do not think that these are merely imaginable, but not conceivable (as we might say, e.g., of the spatial arrangements in Escher's famous "impossible" drawings).[7] But beyond this, I should say that I do not make recognition of consciousness contingent on adopting some positive thesis regarding some "strict" type of possibility, and its relation to the blindsight scenarios I have invited you to consider. I would not make recognition of certain forms of possibility, and attempted resolution of the many perplexities to which the notion of possibility generally gives rise, a prerequisite for recognizing consciousness. But if acknowledgment of consciousness does not require us to affirm certain conceptual or metaphysical possibilities, adopting a view that would have us deny them can, I believe, promote consciousness neglect.

If I do not wish to bind recognition of consciousness to views about just what kinds of necessity there are, don't I still need to have us somehow understand a kind of necessity bound up with the notion of phenomenal character and phenomenal features? If states that differ in phenomenal character differ as nothing but conscious experiences *could* differ, are we not saying that it holds with some kind of necessity that whatever differs in this way is an occurrence of consciousness? And if it follows from the attribution to someone of a phenomenal feature, that he or she has a phenomenally conscious experience, then how does it follow: from laws of nature, of logic, of metaphysics?

The kind of necessity with which it is true that experiences differing in phenomenal character are conscious, I would say, is this: the strongest necessity available. Suppose we recognize different "strengths" of necessity, in the following sense. There are two distinct kinds of necessity, such that everything necessary in the first of these ways is necessary in the second, but not conversely. Then the first kind of necessity is stronger than the second. For example, we might say that every proposition that is true as a matter of logical necessity is also naturally (or nomically) necessary (or at least, the contrary of what is logically necessary is never naturally [physically or nomically] possible). However, it is not true that everything naturally necessary is logically necessary (or, it is not true that everything naturally impossible is logically impossible: there is a sense in which the laws of nature might have been otherwise). And this would be to say that logical necessity is stronger than natural necessity. Now, I may not be altogether sure how many grades of necessity there are, or just how to distinguish them—at least, recognition of differences in phenomenal character ought not to depend on some doctrine about these matters. But however many different grades of necessity one recognizes in this sense, and however one sorts them, the necessity with which differences in phenomenal character are differences among conscious experiences will be a necessity of the strongest sort (or, if we recognize two or more equally strong modes of necessity, stronger than all others, it will be in this class of strongest necessities). And from its seeming to you as it does for it to look some way—from your possession of some visual phenomenal feature—it follows that you have a conscious visual experience, with a necessity of the strongest kind there is. Finally, if you would abstain from all talk of necessity and possibility, you may content yourself with acknowledging the truth of this: whatever state differs from another in phenomenal character, is a conscious experience.

Such comments regarding necessity and possibility I will consider sufficient to help us interpret my efforts to explain what phenomenal consciousness is, in a way that will allow us to distinguish its friends (those who acknowledge its occurrence) from its foes (those who would deny this).

3.12 SUMMARY

In the next chapter I will say why I think there are some whose use of the term 'conscious' or whose theorizing about the mental seems to imply a denial of the possibilities I have described, or near relatives of them, so as to evince or promote a neglect of phenomenal consciousness. And in the chapter following that, I will reply to some of what I imagine might reasonably be said in defense of such a posture. But even if you would not dream of denying the reality of phenomenal consciousness, you may now be troubled by the following thought. Though you have kindly cooperated with my request to consider real and hypothetical examples of conscious experience, you still have no crisp, concise response to give to the question, 'What is consciousness?'—which by itself would suffice to identify for anyone puzzled about this what feature I want to speak of when I use this term.

Maybe there is some such account of consciousness to be had; I, at any rate, do not have it. (Surely if I did, I ought to have offered it at the start.) I will not say that there is no direct, snappy answer to give to this question that is as good as my decidedly indirect, unsnappy one. But if I cannot argue that the way I suggest we clarify our understanding of consciousness is the only possible way to do it, it is at least an available way to do it; it is better than nothing, and, as I will try to show, it can help prevent mistakes we are liable to make.

Nevertheless, isn't it possible for me to offer *some* summary of the understanding of consciousness I have been attempting to secure in this way? I could say this. Phenomenal consciousness is that feature we know with first-person warrant to be shared by episodes of silent speech, other imagery, and sense-experience—a feature whose occurrence one would deny, if one held any of the various forms of blindsight earlier described to be strictly impossible. What one would lack in such cases of blindsight, where certain kinds of conscious experience are missing, are certain phenomenal features; experiences with a certain phenomenal character would be absent. For you to have a phenomenal feature is for it to seem a certain way to you to have an experience—for example, its seeming to you as it does to feel pain, or its seeming to you as it does for it to look as if there is something blue in a certain place, etc. Differences in the way it seems to you to have the experiences you do, differences in their phenomenal character, are such as can be distinguished with first-person warrant, and could obtain only among conscious experiences.

Such is my summary. When considering it, I would ask that you keep these two points in mind. First, do not assume this provides a full picture of the kinds of conscious experience there are, or the full range of phenomenal features—I have concentrated on examples I think will provide us with a relatively uncontroversial starting point, and I have not tried to take a comprehensive view of the forms of phenomenal consciousness. Second, a summary statement of the sort just offered is no substitute for the process of reflection summarized. The understanding of consciousness I am trying to cultivate lies in that process, and without it cannot be conveyed by such summary.

Varieties of Consciousness Neglect

4.1 A Test for Neglect

You may or may not have enjoyed lingering over examples of your conscious experience. And you may or may not have found it interesting to conceive of being someone who suffered from hypothetical deficits in visual consciousness. But you should not doubt the value of such reflections because you think consciousness is already unmistakable and obvious. I hope to make this clear by drawing attention to some ways in which the distinction between consciousness and its lack is liable to serious theoretical neglect, even amidst extended efforts to explore the territory where it is found.

You neglect something, I take it, if you do not notice or acknowledge it, when your situation would lead a reasonable person to expect that you do so. Of course, neglect is sometimes remedied fairly easily: it would have been averted had one's attention merely been rightly directed, and it does not persist, after one is alerted to it. Perhaps this holds true of the theorizing about consciousness I criticized in 3.2–3 above, which links consciousness to a "narrator" or a "stream of narrative" in a way unsuited to phenomenal consciousness. Maybe proponents of such narrative accounts would readily enough admit what I have said they ignore—that we are sometimes properly said to have conscious experience when that experience is neither verbalized nor an instance of verbalization—and afterwards revise or clarify their views so as to take this into account. But if they either refused to affirm or denied this point, we would be dealing with a form of neglect more stubborn and deeply rooted. For it both would persist after the mistake had been pointed out and would be unacknowledged—the relevant parties would deny they had neglected anything. Furthermore, such neglect would involve a denial of facts so seemingly ordinary that, if *we* acknowledge them, while others appear to deny them, this would indicate to us that others actually do not mean by 'conscious' what we do. And, if they also use no other term whose correct application we would reasonably take to require the occurrence of conscious experience, this would show their failure, not just to recognize the occurrence of certain instances of a given type, but to recognize this type of occurrence at all: phenomenally conscious experience. So, in a sense, this neglect would be not only persistent and unacknowledged, but pervasive as well. It would involve not just an unremedied and unavowed failure to recognize that a certain feature is instanced on this or that occasion, where one might reasonably have expected success, but also a failure to acknowledge, when called upon to do so, that it has any instances at all.

Since it seems reasonable to expect one who aspires to a general account of consciousness or mind to acknowledge that we have phenomenally conscious experience, I think it fair to say a theory that betrays a lack of this recognition suffers from a form of neglect. I argue in this chapter that some would-be discussions of consciousness, and accounts of the mind generally, do indeed display, or else can be taken to encourage, a pervasive neglect of phenomenal consciousness.

An explicit denial that we have phenomenally conscious experience would clearly be a direct indication of such neglect. And some philosophers *have* explicitly denied the reality of what they term 'consciousness' or 'qualia.' But they seem to assume that experience is conscious or has "qualitative character" only if it has certain special features, and base their denials on the claim that it has no such features—though these, in my view, form no essential part of its being conscious. Partly for this reason, I think we cannot assume that consciousness neglect will be reliably revealed by direct evidence. But indirect evidence of it may be found. One source of such evidence is suggested by the discussion of consciousness and narration above. If someone makes remarks about consciousness and narration like those considered, but will not admit that what that suggests about their relationship is untrue of conscious experience in at least one sense, we may take this as a sign that the "consciousness" of which the theorist speaks is not phenomenal consciousness, and that this has been left out in the cold. More generally, we can say we've found evidence of consciousness neglect, if we discover that the way of speaking about ourselves proper to a certain philosophical or psychological account of our minds, even if it employs the term 'consciousness,' nonetheless in some way or other lacks the resources needed to distinguish phenomenal consciousness from other features.

But what else—apart from an inability to distinguish consciousness from some kind of "inner" narrative—would manifest such a lack of theoretical resources? Recall that, on my interpretation of 'phenomenal consciousness,' one would deny the reality of phenomenal consciousness altogether, if one said that the forms of blindsight I have described are strictly impossible—if one said they were conceptually or metaphysically impossible. So, suppose the claims proper to a certain theory or account of mind or consciousness, reasonably interpreted, offer us no acceptable way of leaving open the possibility of these forms of blindsight. Then the theory would not allow us the intellectual means for distinguishing phenomenal consciousness from other features, and acknowledging its occurrence. I will argue that, by this measure, certain accounts of mind and consciousness manifest a neglect of the phenomenal character of our experience. For they either commit us to saying these hypothetical forms of blindsight are strictly impossible, or they would have us say that closely related situations are strictly impossible, while offering us no principled basis on which to leave open the one possibility while denying the other. And I can find no way to extricate them from this predicament, without abandoning assumptions their adherents would not wish to reject. So, if we recognize no consciousness but what such theories allow us to recognize, or if we acknowledge no distinctions in the mental or psychological domain but what they would have us acknowledge, then we do not recognize or acknowledge phenomenal consciousness.

4.2 SEEMING, JUDGING, AND DISCRIMINATORY TALENTS

I start by looking again at some remarks Dennett makes, for I think these furnish a particularly notable recent example of how one may fail to recognize consciousness, even while ostensibly theorizing about it, elaborately and with much ingenuity. And his remarks are broad enough that they will suggest a framework for investigating a variety of ways, evident in other authors, in which accounts of mind may make us numb to consciousness.

First consider what Dennett says about "seeming" and "judging." He discusses a perceptual illusion in which, when we look at a certain specially designed drawing (reproduced on the back cover of his book), in some sense there seems to us to be a pinkish glowing ring, although in fact there is no pink on the paper where it seems to us there is. He pointedly warns us of what he thinks is a trap we risk falling into here, that of supposing there is, as he says, a "phenomenon of really seeming—over and above the phenomenon of judging in one way or another that something is the case" (1991, 364). On Dennett's story, what happens to you when you look at this drawing, and it seems to you as if there is a pinkish glowing ring, is just the occurrence of a certain "presentiment"—it just suddenly occurs to you "that there is something pink out there, the way it might suddenly occur to you that there's somebody standing behind you" (ibid.).

Notice how this appears to rule out the possibility of the sort of condition—spontaneous blindsight—consideration of which was essential to our identification of consciousness. For there, recall, we conceived of a case in which one lacked conscious visual experience of an X on one's left (it did not look to one as if there was an X there), though one was struck by the thought (as by a hunch or presentiment) that there was an X there. Now, its looking some way or another to you (e.g., as if there is an X, or a pinkish glowing ring) would be plausibly regarded as a "phenomenon of really [visually] seeming." So Dennett's remarks then appear to suggest that its looking to someone as if there is an X on her left is *nothing over and above* her being struck by the thought that there is one there (presumably on account of appropriately visual stimulation). And *that* could reasonably be regarded as committing him to saying that it is strictly impossible for one to have such a visually triggered thought (or judgment) without a conscious visual experience of an X. That is, one could not make the visual judgment without having the visual experience, since the latter is nothing but the former. Regardless of what we might have thought we were supposing, spontaneous blindsight is strictly impossible. Thus this proposal that we absorb "visual seeming" entirely into some manner of visual judging appears to require that we commit ourselves to a claim of impossibility incompatible with recognizing the reality of phenomenal consciousness.

Perhaps, however, this appearance is misleading. For Dennett has also said, with regard to a spontaneous blindsight response to simple figures like X's and O's, that he "agree[s] that it is readily imaginable" (1993, 151). Does this concession mean he would *not* deny the possibility of spontaneous blindsight? What he says is that, though he can imagine making a spontaneous blindsight judgment to the effect that there was an X on his left, he cannot imagine what would induce him to decide that he had (even if he wanted to say he had)—an ability to make discriminatory judgments about visual stimuli, just as "rich" in informational content as those we can typically make with normal conscious vision, but without consciously seeing them. The point seems to be that, while he won't deny that spontaneous blindsight judgments with rather poor or sparse contents (e.g., that there's an X on the left, that there's some green on the left) are possible, he would deny that it is possible (it is not, he seems to think, even imaginable, i.e., conceivable) that one justifiably think one was making much fancier blindsight judgments.

But does this give Dennett a way of identifying visual appearance with visual judgment, without ruling out the possibility of spontaneous blindsight, and thus neglecting phenomenal consciousness? Perhaps his idea is this. Since one could never justifiably think that one was a "virtuoso" blindsighter—one of the premium variety—all we must think is missing, when we suppose conscious vision is missing in spontaneous blindsight of *simple* figures and color patches, is just an ability or talent for judging that something more *complex* is the case. So what would be missing in blindsight is not some kind of visual seeming, distinct from visual judging, but just an ability to make visual judgments particularly rich in informational content. The following remarks suggest this is indeed Dennett's proposal.

> They [actual blindsight subjects] exhibit sensitivity to a very limited or crude repertoire of contents; they can guess well about simple stimuli, and very recently . . . evidence of color discrimination has been secured . . . but there is still no evidence that [they] have powers beyond what can be manifest in binary forced choice guessing of particular widely dispersed properties.
>
> My contention is that what people have in mind when they talk of 'visual consciousness,' 'actually seeing,' and the like, is nothing over and above some collection or other of these missing talents (discriminatory, regulatory, evaluative, etc.). (Dennett 1993)

So, Dennett's thought seems to be that all we have in mind, when we suppose someone would make spontaneous discriminatory judgments about his visual stimuli, even though he does not consciously see them, is just that he would be able to make certain crude judgments of this sort, even though some additional sort of discriminatory, regulatory, evaluative, or other talent—involving less "limited" and "crude," more complex "content"—is lacking. And this missing talent would presumably be of the sort involved in the ability to make content-rich judgments about visual stimuli—so that it would be a matter of lacking an ability to judge that something is the case, not an absence of "real seeming."

But now recall the point I emphasized back at 3.7—someone may have conscious vision in part of her visual field (somewhat as D.B. had in his "amblyopic crescent") that gives her only very meager visual discriminatory talents. Thus it would seem that her spontaneous visual judgments about stimuli in that area would be correspondingly meager or sparse in "informational content." So the suggestion that all we have in mind when we say there is a lack of conscious visual experience is a talent to discriminate, via information-rich visual judgments, seems quite misguided. For what we have in mind when we speak of conscious visual experience (or, if you like, visual consciousness) includes the sort of extremely blurry visual experience that yields only information-*poor* visual judgment.

Dennett might say here that, however poor conscious sight might be, it could never conceivably be as poor as some form of spontaneous blindsight. So, consider someone who has in her left visual field only a poor blurry patch of conscious vision, and contrast her with another hypothetical subject, who has no conscious vision of left-field stimuli, but only spontaneous blindsight abilities with respect to them. The suggestion is that the first subject must be able to make visual judgments at least *somewhat* informationally richer than the second: for again, all we have in mind when we contrast the two is a relative difference in this sort of talent. But this would have us declare strictly impossible (because inconceivable) the sort of situation we considered in stage three of our thought-experiment—"amblyopic blindsight." There we contrasted a pair of subjects, one of whom had on her left conscious vision of only extremely low acuity, and one of whom had on her left only spontaneous blindsight—no conscious vision there at all. And we said the two were peers in respect of the types of left-field stimuli they were able to discriminate spontaneously, whether verbally (either aloud or in thought) or through other behavior: that is to say, they were equally bad at it. Call the first such subject "Connie" and the second "Belinda" and, to make the point most strikingly, suppose Connie's conscious left-field vision is very poor indeed—the sort that enables her to judge that there is a patch of light on her left of indefinite shape, in varying shades, of varying relative brightness and extent, but that leaves her helpless to discern even simple shapes like X's and O's, or to distinguish the orientation or spacing of lines, or to discriminate red from blue. So the idea is that Belinda, with her left-field blindsight, would match—judgment for judgment—the rather paltry and colorless, but spontaneous, discriminations of her counterpart, when exposed to the same conditions of stimulation, even though she (Belinda) has no conscious visual experience of left-field stimuli: for example, it does not look to her as if there is a grayish blob of light on her left, which is becoming brighter.

Now, if Dennett is proposing that all we have in mind (and so, presumably, all we mean or think) when we speak of an absence of conscious vision and the like, is a lack of a talent for making relatively information-rich visual judgments, then the situation I have just described would on his view be literally inconceivable, and in this way, strictly impossible. It would be as if I had just asked you to suppose that Connie and Belinda were precisely the same height, though Connie was twice as tall. If my earlier description of Connie and Belinda does not strike you as absurd in this way, then you should not agree with Dennett about what you have in mind when speaking of visual consciousness and the like, *unless* you can come up with a good reason to think there is some secret incoherence in the description of these hypothetical subjects. To maintain that there is a hidden incoherence in the notion of Belinda's kind of amblyopic blindsight would be to maintain that the very notion of phenomenal consciousness, as I have introduced it, is incoherent. And, if you think I require us to be able to conceive the inconceivable, as a condition of recognizing our possession of a conscious experience, then you will have to deny recognition of phenomenal features at all. But if we can find no adequate reason to embrace this thought, and this denial—which Dennett apparently encourages—with respect to phenomenal features, then we can only conclude that his remarks evince and promote their disregard.

Similar considerations would apply where a denial of Belinda and Connie's possibility is motivated, not by claims about "what we have in mind"—what our concepts are, what we mean or understand by what we say—but rather by claims about what the feature or property of consciousness is, or by claims about what being a conscious visual experience is or consists in. So one might say that being a conscious visual experience just is, in part, being a state that has relatively rich visual information, so that the difference between any subject who consciously sees a given stimulus, and one who has only blindsight with respect to it, consists partly in the former's having a richer array of information with respect to the relevant part of her visual field than the latter has. On this view, then, the existence of Belinda and Connie, as I have described them, would be, as the saying goes, "metaphysically" (and thus strictly) impossible. For Belinda was supposed to make spontaneous visual judgments as informationally rich (or rather, as sparse) as Connie's, even though Belinda had blindsight where Connie had conscious vision. But if having conscious vision just consists partly in having more visual information than could be had with blindsight, then it is metaphysically ruled out—it is somehow ruled out by the "essential nature of things"—that a Belinda might match a Connie's discriminatory feats. (Just such a view, I believe, is suggested by Tye's [1995] theory of consciousness.[1])

Now again, if we declare this form of blindsight, this deficit in visual consciousness, to be strictly impossible, then we cannot recognize our possession of phenomenal consciousness. One may try to offer reasons for endorsing the denial of possibility at issue (something we will consider in the next chapter), but until one has compelling reasons for this in hand, we have to see theories incorporating such denial as offering us no alternative to consciousness neglect.

What I have been arguing so far is that proposals that we collapse any distinction between having conscious visual experience and making visual judgments, or that we make out the difference between conscious sight and its lack in terms of the relative richness of visual information available to the subject, yield theories that do not allow a recognition of phenomenal consciousness. But now, in order to be clearer about what recognition of consciousness involves, I think it would be helpful to go back to something I quoted from Dennett—his contention that "what people have in mind when they talk of 'visual consciousness,' 'actually seeing,' and the like, is nothing over and above some collection or other of these missing talents (discriminatory, regulatory, evaluative, etc.)." Does such an assumption inevitably lead to, or embody, consciousness neglect? The first thing to note: unless we have some more definite idea of the kinds of talents at issue here, this claim will escape the accusation of theoretical blindness only in virtue of its vacuity. For the contention would become trivial if no restriction at all were placed on the type of "discriminatory, regulatory, or evaluative" talent concerned. For then we might say, for example, that the (discriminatory, etc.) talent we must suppose absent, in a person with blindsight, is just this: the ability to *consciously* see them. But this we would all accept, and would not serve to distinguish Dennett's view from those to which he is evidently opposed.

Maybe we can see what substantive restriction on the relevant talents Dennett has in mind here if we consider that he does want to rule out the possibility of (what I have called) premium blindsight, and apparently considers it crucial to his view of consciousness that we do so. So perhaps the sorts of missing talents Dennett thinks are all we have in mind when we contemplate the absence of visual consciousness, are such as a premium blindsighter would have, if there could be one. The idea is: that kind of blindsight is inconceivable, because all we have in mind when we say someone does not consciously see is that he lacks one or another of the sorts of talents that such a putative blindsighter would possess. This suggests that the talents with whose exercise we are to identify conscious visual experience would be what we might call *manifest* talents—the capacities we can have warrant for thinking we have, without having to observe anything hidden literally inside us (for example, in our skulls). For the visual ability the premium blindsighter would have that made him premium quality—the ability to make judgments about, and behaviorally respond to, visual stimuli—would be something manifest, not hidden inside him. To have such a feature would be to have a feature of a sort either he or we could have warrant for thinking that he had, without having to look inside his, or anyone's, head, or rely on the reports of someone else who had.[2]

Now we have seen that to identify the possession of conscious visual experience with the exercise of a talent for making relatively information-rich visual judgments, as Dennett appears to propose, would leave us no alternative to the consciousness neglect that first seemed implicit in his remarks about judging and "real seeming." And we have seen that the neglect persists if we formulate the claim not as a conceptual one, but as a metaphysical one, about what the difference between visual consciousness and its lack essentially consists in. But Dennett's rather vague reference to discriminatory and other talents invites the question of whether there might be some other, nontrivial way of making out the contention in which this list figures, that does *not* invite consciousness neglect, but still holds to the thought that the talent in question would be of a manifest, not hidden, sort.[3]

I find that when I try to imagine what *substantive* claim might be advanced by saying that a conscious visual experience of an X, or of something green, is nothing but the exercise of a manifest discriminatory, or regulative, or evaluative talent of some sort, I encounter only one or another form of consciousness neglect. I think it will be worth explaining why I say this, by exploring various ways of trying to identify consciousness with one or the other of the sorts of talents at which Dennett gestures, for this will help us to ferret out a number of possible ways of neglecting phenomenal consciousness, to which other writers also make us liable. This will improve our understanding of consciousness, I believe, by helping to inoculate us against doctrines that can make us intellectually oblivious to it.

4.3 LEARNING VISUAL JUDGMENT

In describing my hypothetical blindsighters, I was silent about how we might suppose they came to acquire their peculiar abilities.[4] I set us to conceiving of being someone who judged, unprompted, that there was a figure or patch of light on her left without consciously seeing anything there, but told no story about how she arrived at the position of confidently making such visual discriminations, without the conscious visual experience that normally seems to occasion them. We might wonder whether there is, necessarily, some (manifest, not hidden) difference between the way a blindsighter like Belinda would have learned to form her visual judgments, and the way someone such as Connie would have come by hers. If there is, we might ask whether this would allow us to vindicate Dennett's suggestion, by maintaining that the difference between having and lacking certain conscious visual experiences is nothing over and above the difference between having and lacking visual discrimination that gives one certain talents for learning to judge visually.

For this to work, we would need to find some difference in the way our hypothetical subjects could learn to discriminate left-field stimuli, which we could nontrivially identify with the difference between the one's having and the other's lacking a certain phenomenal feature, and this difference in learning would have to be such as could be evident either to them or to an observer, without some kind of (literally) internal examination. So certain differences we might think would inevitably separate Connie and Belinda would not be relevant to cite here. For instance, we might say that the physical constitution or configuration of whatever allowed them to do what they each do equally well (or poorly) with respect to left-field stimuli would have to differ. Or we might point out that the learning abilities of the two would inevitably differ in this respect: Connie could learn to discriminate left-field stimuli by consciously seeing them, whereas Belinda could not. But this would not help to show, in any interesting sense, that conscious vision is nothing but discrimination that gives one a certain manifest talent. For in the first instance, we would appeal to a difference in hidden, not manifest, talents, and in the second, we would buy truth for the proposal only by trivializing it.

With this in mind, let's explore the proposal at hand by considering how we might plausibly think Belinda had come by her special talents. On one scenario, we might suppose, she suffered some sort of damage to her visual system, and after a period of simply denying she saw anything on her left when asked to identify stimuli there, and offering no claims about them, she became convinced by researchers that she had exercised, and possessed, an ability to respond with reliable accuracy when posed certain questions, which offered a choice of answers. ("Did a light just flash there or not? Was it brighter than the last or not?") Then we might imagine she was trained to give accurate responses, but *without* being posed questions suggesting responses. So, when asked simply what, if anything, was on her left, she said, "A light just flashed on my left, brighter than the one a moment ago (though it didn't *look* any way at all to me)." Then she found that such thoughts, on occasion, began to occur to her without her being directly asked anything, and the information about her left field was simply available to her, if it became relevant to some task she was engaged in (say, an experimenter asked her to press a button whenever there was a flash—once if less bright than the previous flash, twice if brighter). And we might suppose that by this time, if not before, she had adjusted her behavior to left-field stimuli spontaneously and in certain characteristic ways—for example, when there was a sudden change in the intensity of light in her left field, she moved her eyes so as to bring the stimuli into view in her (conscious) right field.

We may focus on the part of the story in which she moves from a "forced choice" kind of blindsight to an unprompted variety, and suppose that this transition is made partly via some piece of inductive reasoning on her part. Perhaps she says to herself, "According to these people observing me, I make reliably accurate claims about what kinds of things happen on my left where

I (consciously) see nothing, when given certain options for response. So I can in the future trust my inclinations to say this or that is there, should I have them." Then, she is put through training sessions, in which she is asked to say "whatever she thinks" is on her left, where she has no conscious vision, and finds that thoughts do just come to her about what is there, and then again is reassured by her teachers that her responses are correct. Gaining confidence, she finally finds herself spontaneously responding generally in thought and behavior to visual stimuli she does not consciously see as well as another pathological subject, who has an amblyopic patch of conscious left-field vision—Connie—responds to those she thus sees only blurrily.

Now, one might suggest that there is a necessary component to Belinda's learning process that need not have been present in any discriminating Connie learned to do with respect to what falls in her area of blurry conscious vision. Belinda, one might say, had to *infer* from her observers' responses to her trials that she was getting things right, and from this *further* infer that she would get things right in the future. Blindsight learning, we might propose, would inevitably need the support of some kind of inductive reasoning that learning with conscious sight does not require. It may be that the particular judgments the blindsighter eventually learns to make are spontaneous, not only in that they are unprompted by suggestive questions, but also in that the subject can (at that time) offer no reason why she should have been inclined to affirm their truth—why she should have been inclined to say there is an X rather than an O on a particular occasion. But her learning to have these verbal inclinations that were spontaneous in this sense, is (so this story goes) dependent on her having offered (or been able to offer) to herself or others, at some time in her past, reasons why, generally, she should be confident in the truth of what she found herself inclined to say about such matters: others have confirmed the reliable accuracy of such judgments. So although now (perhaps) she cannot explain and justify her judging that there is an X there rather than an O, at one time at least, she was able to justify her degree of confidence in the visual responses she found herself making, by appeal to some reasoning from evidence about their general accuracy, to the truth of these particular claims—and the fact that she once was like this partly explains how she came to be the spontaneous blindsighter she is today. This leads us to the thought that the essential difference between conscious seeing and blindseeing ultimately consists just in this: the former enables you to learn, *without this sort of background history of inductive reasoning*, to make spontaneous visual discriminations that nonconscious sight could afford you only through this process of inductive learning. This would be the manifest talent whose absence in blindsighters—of whatever variety—is their lack of conscious visual experience.

But this line of thought fails once we reflect that, with little effort, an alternative, and apparently equally possible, story can be told about Belinda and Connie's learning history, which erases this difference between them, while leaving them dissimilar with regard to their phenomenal features. Suppose that each has had her visual deficit from birth, and that each learns to respond, verbally and otherwise, to visual stimuli, including those in their left fields, in the way children generally do, by being exposed to them in the presence of another person who says what they are, and encourages the child to do likewise. It will have been noticed that both children had quite impoverished discriminatory abilities toward things on their left that others did not; perhaps it will have been thought for a time that they had no abilities here at all. And since children's command of nuances of psychological vocabulary proceeds somewhat fitfully, it may not be immediately apparent through their words that one has visual experience the other lacks. But after the two acquire a firmer hold on talk of how things look to them, it becomes apparent that while Connie will say, when asked if it looked to her like there was a light on her left, as there had been on her right, "Yes, but it was all fuzzy," Belinda will say, "No, it didn't look like a light, but there was one there I think." And it seems we may suppose that the learning process that brought each child to this point was equally "inductive" or "noninductive." In any case, we may suppose neither child verbalized to herself or to others some reasoning from the observed responses of her elders to conclusions about her abilities reliably to use certain terms accurately—nor was either child disposed to offer some such inductive argument at any stage in her learning. Little Belinda came by her confidence partly in the way Connie did—through feedback and reinforcement from her teachers. I see no reason to think such a situation impossible, if the original contrast between Belinda and Connie did not describe an impossibility.

But we may well think that this scenario does not completely erase essential differences in the relevant learning history associated with Belinda's left-field blindsight and with Connie's correlative conscious "blursight." For it seems somewhat plausible to say that Belinda's learning to judge about visual stimuli in her left, blind field would be somehow dependent or parasitic on her learning to judge about the same kinds of stimuli in her right field, of which she has conscious vision, in a way in which Connie's would not be. That is, there is some pull toward the idea that Belinda would not have been able to learn to judge that there was light on her left, of varying relative brightness, had she not learned to judge this about stimuli on her right of which she had conscious vision. The idea is: she never would have been able to grasp the concept of light, or of varying brightness (and hence make judgments about light and brightness), if she had nothing but her left-field blindsight with which to work. Connie, on the other hand, could have acquired this talent for judgment, through learning to discriminate verbally left-field stimuli of which she had conscious, albeit extremely poor, vision, without any reliance on her conscious right-field vision. She could have managed, if she had no conscious right-field vision at all.

Whatever seems appealing about this suggestion is, I suppose, whatever seems appealing about the Humean claim that a man blind from birth can form no notion of color. This traditional empiricist idea makes its appearance here in the suggestion that (a) Belinda would be able to learn to make spontaneous visual *left-field* judgments, only if she has learned to make spontaneous visual *right-field* judgments, for the reason that (b) she would be able to learn to make certain spontaneous visual judgments at all, only if she has conscious visual experience (and on her left she has none of this). Now, we might think this *consciousness empiricism* is too strong. For we might think one could learn to make blindsight judgments, no matter what is judged, without conscious vision, at least if one first learned to judge such things—acquired the use of relevant concepts—in some other way. But (b) rules this out. However, we might still opt for a similar, weaker claim that is entailed by, but does not entail, (b), namely: (c) She would be able to learn to judge that something or other is the case, *in part by learning to judge visually and spontaneously that it is*, only if she had conscious visual experience.

The weaker claim (c) does not deny that a person entirely lacking conscious vision might learn to make spontaneous verbal responses to visual stimuli, and thereby express judgments about them; it says just that what she learned to judge of things spontaneously and visually, she first would have had to have learned to judge in some other way. She first would have had to have acquired the relevant concepts in some way other than by learning to make spontaneous visual judgments. For, according to (c), only if she consciously sees what she is responding to, will her learning to make spontaneous verbal responses to visual stimuli contribute to her ability to understand—and thus to express judgments by—the words she utters.

The idea might be illustrated by considering a hypothetical blindsighter similar to Belinda, but who has no conscious visual experience at all. Totally blindsighted from birth, she learns to make, on the basis of visual stimulation, spontaneous verbal responses like those Belinda makes to left-field stimuli (using terms like 'light' and 'brighter'). If Belinda is not deemed impossible, there seems no good reason to think a blindsighter of this sort—call her "Linda"—could not exist. We may suppose Linda also learns to use the words figuring in her visual responses when speaking with others, in other ways we would regard as appropriate to their English meaning—for example, in making inferences ("If you turn off the light, it will be too dark in here for you to read") and stating general truths ("The Earth gets its light from the Sun"). But since she has no conscious visual experience, if you accept (c), you must say that she would not have learned—and would be unable to learn—to make judgments about light and brightness partly by learning to make her verbal responses to visual stimulation. Her learning to make these would have contributed *nothing* to her coming to understand the words she utters—though perhaps her learning to make inferences containing the word would have contributed to her understanding, and she would eventually count as someone who understands what 'light' means. What (c) says is that although one can learn what 'light' means partly by learning to make spontaneous visual discriminations of light using this term, this will be so, only if one *consciously* sees the light one discriminates; blindsight discrimination (like Linda's) could enable one to learn to utter the word 'light' in response to light stimulation, but it could not in this way help teach one to make judgments about light by uttering this word. We might put this briefly by saying: conscious visual experience is essential to "acquiring concepts visually."

Now only (b), the stronger claim, would support (a), the suggestion that there would have to be an asymmetrical dependence of blindsight judgment on that of conscious vision. But what is more significant for present purposes is that either the stronger or the weaker claim might suggest to us a way of identifying conscious vision with a kind of manifest discriminatory talent— a talent for *learning* to discriminate in a certain way. The suggestion would be something like: (d) All we have in mind or mean when we say the blind-sighter Belinda would lack conscious visual experience in her left field—or, all there is to her lacking the feature she would then lack—is her missing the talent/ability for *learning to judge what she was unable to judge before, partly by learning to judge this visually and spontaneously about things to her left*. All she would lack is an ability to acquire concepts visually on her left side.

In response to this, I do not intend to deny that a blindsighter, in lacking conscious vision, would necessarily lack some noninductive concept-learning ability: maybe so. However, I will argue that, even if it is true, it will not make a proposal such as (d) acceptable, and so will not provide us with an acceptable way to endorse the idea that an absence of conscious vision is nothing more than the absence of a manifest discriminatory talent, without denying phenomenal consciousness.

First, if (d) is true, then all we have in mind or mean when we say the blindsighter Linda would lack conscious visual experience, or, all there is to her lacking the feature she would then lack, is that she does not have the ability to acquire concepts visually. Now consider someone (call her "Glenda") who, unlike Linda, has, in her left visual field, the sort of poor conscious visual experience Connie was supposed to have there (and, let's suppose, no other conscious vision), but who is otherwise as much like Linda as this difference between them would allow. Their utterances of the term 'light' in response to visual stimulation and in conversation, we may suppose, would be more or less the same—except perhaps in this: Linda would never be inclined to say she consciously sees light, but only that she visually judges that there is light. According to (d), then, all we have in mind when we say Linda would lack the conscious visual experience Glenda has, or all we would attribute to Glenda and withhold from Linda in saying this, is Linda's lack and Glenda's possession of an ability to acquire concepts visually. So: Glenda's utterance of the word "light" in response to visual stimuli would help her to learn what 'light' means; but Linda's doing this would teach her nothing of the sort.

Now I take it that, if Linda and Glenda would differ in regard to this sort of ability, there must be some other way in which they would differ as well, relevant to the difference in their ability to understand. That is, if Linda lacks the ability to acquire concepts visually (or to learn what words mean partly through visual stimulation), and Glenda has this, then they must differ (or be disposed to differ) in some other respect (feature, attribute). And either it would follow from their differing in this way that Glenda was learning what the words meant by visual stimulation, while Linda was not, or else a difference of that sort is one that could warrant a judgment that one was coming to understand a term (acquire a concept) and the other was not. We might put this by saying that if Linda and Glenda differ in the concept-acquiring capacities as proposed, they would have to differ (or be disposed to differ) in some way that would display this difference in their abilities. I assume it would be absurd to say that Glenda is able to learn what 'light' means by visual stimulation, but Linda is not, though there is no way in which they differ, or are liable to differ, that would display this difference in their abilities—no other difference between them by which anyone (including themselves) might ever discern the presence or absence of understanding, nor any from which this would follow. Furthermore, I think it is not too bold to assume that the feature or features in respect of which they must here differ must be *manifest*, not *hidden*. Linda may have a hole in her brain where Glenda does not, but it is reasonable to think this hidden difference between them would display Linda's lack of understanding, only if it would display this through its relation to some manifest feature Glenda has that displays her possession of the concept-learning ability Linda is supposed to lack.

Now, granted that Linda and Glenda's differences in understanding capacities must be, in the sense explained, *manifestly displayable*—how *could* they be, given what we have said about them, if we assume the truth of (d)? We cannot respond: the difference in their abilities to acquire concepts is displayable in just this way—Glenda has conscious visual experience; Linda does not. For, *ex hypothesi*, that would not describe a feature in which they differ other than the ability to acquire concepts visually, and so would not describe a feature that *displayed* this difference in ability; it would simply state that they did differ in this ability. So, we must ask—given that the one has Connie-poor conscious vision and the other blindsight, is there any *other* way in which they could differ, in respect of manifest features, that would display the alleged difference in their powers of understanding?

Perhaps it is true that Linda could not be like Glenda in this manifest respect: they could not both be inclined to think they consciously see things. But, however plausible this might otherwise seem, it is not tenable, *if* we assume (d) is true. For remember, according to (d), all Glenda would have in mind if she thought she consciously saw, or all she would attribute to herself in thinking it, over and above the kind of visual discrimination Linda has, is the ability to acquire concepts visually. But surely Linda would be able to think she had that ability too. To say otherwise, we would need to hold that it is impossible for anyone to deny consciousness empiricism. If it is not impossible for Linda and Glenda to share the visual discriminatory abilities we have ascribed to them, it is not impossible for someone (including Linda herself) to believe that Linda's blindsight-generated verbal responses would contribute to her understanding her utterances, and that she would not lack the ability to acquire concepts visually. Then—assuming (d)—there is no reason to think Linda and Glenda, if they were as similar as they could be, given that they differ experientially, would not both believe that they consciously saw things. Now, I think that if one cannot maintain that Linda and Glenda would have to differ even in this manifest respect—in respect of their ability to think they consciously see—there is really no way they would have to differ *manifestly* at all, which one can reasonably maintain would display their respective ability and inability to acquire concepts visually.

Where does this leave us? If (d) were true, Linda and Glenda would have to differ in their abilities to acquire concepts visually—for on this proposal that is all there is to the one's having, and the other's lacking, conscious vision. But then we said they must also differ or be disposed to differ in some other way, some way that would manifestly display the acquisition of understanding in the one, and its absence in the other. And if, as (d) would have it, all we attribute to Glenda and deny Linda, in saying the former has but the latter lacks conscious vision, is the ability to acquire concepts visually, then their differing experientially will *not* display their difference in understanding. But then, given what else we have said of them, and assuming what (d) would have us assume, there would then be *no* manifest way in which they would differ that would display the relevant difference in understanding. And from that we can infer that there would be no such difference in their understanding at all, contrary to the hypothesis (d). Thus (d) requires us to presuppose some form of consciousness empiricism (expressed by [b] and [c]) that then (on reasonable assumptions) ultimately undermines it—so (d) ultimately undermines itself. And so it offers us no acceptable way of accounting for the difference in visual consciousness separating Glenda and Linda (or Connie and Belinda) as a difference in manifest discriminatory talents.

One could, of course, reject the argument by saying that it is strictly impossible for two persons to share the talents for discriminating visual stimuli that we originally supposed Belinda and Connie would, while differing in their experience. But that would be to deny the reality of phenomenal consciousness. So, in exploring how visual learning may be related to conscious vision, we *may* have found a manifest discriminatory talent—one for acquiring concepts—that is missing whenever conscious vision is missing. But we still have found no acceptable way to say an absence of the latter is nothing but an absence of the former, while leaving open the blindsight possibilities. We have not found an acceptable way to interpret Dennett's contention so that it yields anything other than consciousness neglect.

4.4 INNER DISCRIMINATION, SENSORY QUALITIES, AND HIGHER-ORDER THOUGHT

But perhaps we have been looking in the wrong place for the "discriminatory talent" whose absence is the absence of visual consciousness, by focusing on talents with regard to the discrimination of *visual* stimuli. For maybe the relevant talent is one involving the discrimination of something else. This may seem hopeless right off: pretty clearly it is no good saying that the person with total left-field blindsight must be less talented in discriminating nonvisual *sensory* stimuli (sounds, smells, etc.) than the person with a patch of conscious amblyopic vision on the left. But recall what I labeled the "perceptual model" of consciousness, and identified as a strand of the Cartesian heritage—the idea that consciousness is somehow the perception of what is in one's own mind. Whatever draws one to that way of thinking might suggest that the discriminatory talent any blindsighter would be missing is not one with respect to "outer" or sensory stimuli of any sort, but involves rather a kind of "inner" discrimination—not, to be sure, a sensory perception of one's own body, but a kind of discrimination of one's own sensory discriminations. On this suggestion, what the chromatic blindsighter would lack, in lacking conscious visual experience of green, is simply a talent for discriminating her own visual discrimination of green.

We can readily see this is unacceptable as it stands, if we recall stage four of our thought-experiment—the case of the reflective blindsighter. Such a person we supposed not only spontaneously thinks that there is something green on her left, without consciously seeing anything green there, she also spontaneously thinks that this thought she has is visual, in the sense that it is of a sort that tells her about what is affecting her eyes. She thinks: "I visually judge there's something green on my left." So she not only visually discriminates (judges) that there is something green, but also discriminates (judges) that she makes this visual judgment. All the same, we supposed, she does not consciously see green; she has no visual experience of green; it does not seem to her the way it would for it to look as if there is something green on her left. But if we say that the absence of conscious visual experience is nothing over and above the missing manifest talent for discriminating one's own visual discrimination, then we rule out the possibility that someone might exercise that talent, though the object of her visual discrimination did not look any way to her at all—the possibility of reflective blindsight. And declaring this impossible is incompatible with recognizing the reality of phenomenally conscious experience. So far, then, taking an absence of consciousness to be nothing but a lack of inner discrimination offers no alternative to neglect.

But I think it is worth lingering a while longer here, for the notion that consciousness is a kind of inner discrimination can take a number of forms, and the consciousness neglect they embody may not always be readily apparent. I would like us to consider, in this connection, the account of consciousness developed by David Rosenthal (1986). He proposes that we think of consciousness as the possession of a certain sort of "higher-order thought." That is, on his account, what "makes a conscious state conscious" is that it is a mental state that causes one, seemingly without inference, to think that one is in that state. One might take this as a proposed account of a *concept* of consciousness we have (what we mean by, or what we have in mind when speaking of some state of mind as, 'conscious'), an account perhaps involving some revision, in response to hidden inconsistencies and unclarities in our thinking. Or else one might take this as a proposal that tells us what being a conscious state is, one about the *property* attributed to some state or event, in calling it 'conscious.' And one might say these are distinct proposals. But on either construal of the idea that what makes a conscious state conscious is its being the object of a higher-order thought, we can ask whether this would provide an account of *phenomenal* consciousness.

Again, it clearly will fail to do this, if it tells us that what constitutes having a phenomenally conscious visual experience of green is your thinking—seemingly without inference—that you visually judge that there is some green, when in fact you do. For if it held that this is all there is to visual consciousness, the Rosenthal-style theory would declare reflective blindsight strictly impossible, and so would not recognize the occurrence of phenomenal consciousness. But the question arises whether some other, reasonable way of construing a Rosenthalian view of consciousness would have it account for, and not neglect, phenomenal consciousness. As we have just seen, an affirmative answer here minimally requires that we find some way of understanding the kind of visual mental state the theory would allege one to be in and to think one is in, just when having a conscious visual experience, so that being a visual judgment is not sufficient for being a visual state of this kind. So we need to look around for an appropriate sort of mental visual state we might be able to plug into the account.

But before we proceed in this way, we may be blocked by an objection that to do so would be to misinterpret Rosenthal's efforts. His claim is, roughly, that what makes a conscious mental state conscious is that one has a certain sort of thought to the effect that one is in it. But maybe this does *not* commit him to holding that it is strictly impossible (as either a conceptual or a metaphysical matter) for someone to have a certain kind of experience that is phenomenally conscious, without having this sort of thought about it. For, someone might suggest, all that he wanted to say was that some (logically and metaphysically contingent) lawlike regularity holds, such that people have phenomenally conscious experiences of a certain type just when they spontaneously think they are in states of that type. Alternatively, Rosenthal might say that he does indeed recognize the reality of phenomenal consciousness and its distinctness from mentalness-about-which-one-has-a-higher-order-thought; he just uses the term 'consciousness' differently. Maybe it is just that he employs his term 'sensory quality' for what I call phenomenal character. Perhaps it would be misguided, then, to worry ourselves over whether phenomenal consciousness and "higher-order-thought consciousness" are one and the same, since maybe no one (Rosenthal included) ever dreamed of asking us to think they were other than distinct, and equally real.

However, if by saying (as he does) that states with "sensory quality" are sometimes not conscious, Rosenthal means that they are sometimes not objects of higher-order thought, and "sensory quality" is just his expression for phenomenal character, he will not be proposing that phenomenally conscious experience does occur in the suggested lawlike relationship with the relevant sort of higher-order thought after all. And in any case, even if he *did* propose this, that would not appear to explain what makes experience (phenomenally) conscious. Suppose it happens that we do think that we have a Rosenthalian "visual quality of green" just whenever we have the conscious visual experience of green. Still, if we also distinguish between having that sort of thought when true, and having visual experience with a certain phenomenal character—if we distinguish higher-order-thought consciousness from phenomenal consciousness—then it is extremely unclear why we should regard the former as in any way *explaining* the latter. (Why not suppose, rather, that your having the experience accounts for your having the thought about it?)

Further, though Rosenthal's talk of "sensory qualities" may seem redolent of "sensory qualia" and "qualitative," hence phenomenal, character, he has not, I think, made it clear that his use of the term involves a recognition of (what I call) phenomenal consciousness. And, when we look into this, I think we will find that really it does not. That people may use terms like 'sensory quality' in theories that nonetheless leave the phenomenal character of sense-experience out of account is important enough that we should take a moment to make this clear.

Consider what Rosenthal offers to persuade us that common sense would countenance the claim that we have states with sensory qualities, which are nevertheless (in his sense) not conscious. Common sense, he says, allows us to say that we are sometimes in pain throughout most of the course of a day (from a headache), though we are intermittently so distracted from our pain that we are no longer conscious of it (Rosenthal 1991). He also thinks this makes it plausible to say we are sometimes *in* pain, when we have no *feeling* of pain. Let's concentrate just on the notion that we are sometimes in pain or have a pain, even when, temporarily, because of distraction, we have no feeling of pain. I do not think "common sense" is clear here. Does common sense tell us that sometimes feelings of pain come and go and come again, and while they are gone one is in pain but has no feeling of pain, or does it say that when feelings of pain come and go, one is only intermittently in pain? This seems to be just the kind of picky question common sense would be content to leave alone.

In any case, it is reasonably clear that the way it seems to feel pain can change, depending on how much attention one is paying to the way it feels. And perhaps when the extent to which you are attending to your pain is greatly diminished, you would want to say that in some sense you are no longer "conscious of" how it feels at all. But still: should we say that sometimes we are so distracted from a pain that it does not feel any way at all to us, though we still "have" it? It is hard to say when, if ever, one should describe one's situation in quite this way, because it is hard to say just when a relatively unattended, "background" feeling of pain ceases. But if we *do* want to describe certain occasions in this way, then I think it will be because we recognize that a condition partly like feeling pain in its causes and effects can persist even when one ceases to feel pain, or even when what normally would make one feel pain is prevented from doing so. Thus by saying one is "in pain," in this sense, one implies no more than that one is in such a condition. One would use 'pain' in such a way that someone who, under the influence of an anesthetic, does not *feel* any pain could still rightly be said to be in pain. Now, if we do say this, then we will be saying that someone is in pain, even though he does not have an experience that feels to him the way pain does—he lacks an experience with that phenomenal character, he lacks a phenomenally conscious feeling of pain. Thus if Rosenthal wants us to take such a use of 'pain' to introduce his notion of a sensory quality, then it is clear that to have a state with that quality is *not* to have an experience with the phenomenal character of pain, that is to say, a conscious feeling of pain, in my sense. Rosenthalian "sensory quality" does not entail phenomenal consciousness.

This is evident also from what Rosenthal says about visual sensory qualities. He says there is a family of properties, visual somehow, that can belong to states of ours that are *not* (in his sense) conscious, that resemble and differ among one another in a way "homomorphic" to the resemblances and differences among the color and shape properties of physical objects we see. So, for example, when I see red, I am in a state with some quality that is more like another such quality involved in seeing orange than it is like one involved in seeing blue, *and* this pattern of relative similarities systematically maps on to a pattern of likeness among the corresponding "physical" properties—red, orange, blue, etc. The idea seems to be that to have a state with a visual quality of a certain sort, is to be in a state, visual in some sense, that stands in a network of relations of greater and lesser amounts of similarity to other visual qualities, of the same sort as that in which a corresponding property of visual stimuli stands to other properties of visual stimuli.

Complexities arise once one tries to elaborate on just what properties of light reflectance one wishes to identify with "physical" red, blue, orange, etc., and one explains whether one wants to distinguish different dimensions in respect of which the relative similarity of a given visual quality to others is to be characterized, and if so, how. But without worrying about these, I think it will be clear that Rosenthal's "visual quality" is not just another way of talking about the phenomenal character of visual experience. For consider: someone who had the sort of chromatic blindsight we considered at 3.6 above could presumably be said to have internal states bearing relations of likeness and difference isomorphic to those among the physical color properties she discriminates. So if we do not rule out that kind of blindsight, we should not deem it impossible that one could have states with the visual qualities of colors, in Rosenthal's sense, while lacking visual experience with the relevant phenomenal character—so nothing looks red or blue or green to one. But if 'visual quality' is just another term for the phenomenal character of vision, then it follows that we should not deem it impossible that one could have states with these visual qualities of colors while lacking states with those visual qualities. However, surely we *should* rule out that possibility. So "visual quality" is not the phenomenal character of vision.

To make the point another way, we might say that Connie's states of colorless amblyopic *conscious* vision, and Belinda's corresponding *blindsight* states, could each rightly be said to bear amongst themselves relations of similarity isomorphic to the same network of relations of similarity holding among properties of the stimuli, regarding which Connie and Belinda had equally good discriminatory talents in their left visual fields. This is to say, if we do not deem Belinda impossible, we have no reason to deem it impossible that her blindsight might have Rosenthalian "visual qualities"— since it could presumably bear the appropriate isomorphism to grayish light. But blindsight is a lack of conscious sight. So if to say that a state had "visual quality" were just another way of saying that it was a phenomenally conscious visual experience, then it follows that we have no reason to deem it impossible that what is not a phenomenally conscious visual experience (Belinda's blindsight) might be a phenomenally conscious visual experience (might have "visual quality"). And surely we do have reason to deem *that* impossible. So, if we do not rule out the possibility of a blindsighter like Belinda (as we must not, on pain of neglecting phenomenal consciousness), it is clear that 'visual quality' is not another term for visual consciousness in my sense. More generally, sensory quality à la Rosenthal is not phenomenal consciousness.

So it would be a mistake to think Rosenthal acknowledges phenomenal consciousness under the term 'sensory quality.' Thus it is not misguided to try to see whether phenomenal consciousness can be accounted for in a Rosenthal-like higher-order-thought story about what makes conscious states conscious. For if (as we have seen) sensory quality is not phenomenal character, and now we find that higher-order thought also does not account for phenomenal consciousness, then Rosenthal will have left it out of account altogether.

Now we are ready to rejoin the issue raised earlier. Is there some kind of visual state, such that we can account for, and not neglect, conscious visual experience, by identifying its possession with one's being in a visual state of that type and thinking (seemingly noninferentially) that one is? We saw that this would require that we make out some way of being a visual state, distinct from that of being a visual judgment, and the question is: what way might that be? I assume that we will not find acceptable a way of specifying the relevant sort of visualness to plug into the higher-order-thought story, if doing this would undermine any claims the resultant thesis might have to constitute a genuine account or explanation of phenomenal consciousness. And, I take it, this claim *would* be undermined, if we said that the way in which a state must be visual, so that being in such a state, and thinking you are, makes you have a phenomenally conscious visual experience, is just this: it must have the phenomenal character of visual experience. For you would presumably not furnish an account or explanation of what makes experience phenomenally conscious by saying that it satisfies a number of conditions, an essential one being that it be *phenomenally conscious*. And the just-mentioned manner of saying what kind of visualness is appropriate to filling out the Rosenthal-style account amounts to saying exactly that. So, to be successful, this kind of account needs a nontrivial way of specifying what is enough to make visual experience conscious, which appeals to its being a certain kind of visual state, targeted by a certain kind of thought. And for this we need a way in which a state can be a visual one, distinct from being a visual judgment, which is also, as we might say, *consciousness neutral*, or *nonphenomenal*—a way of being a visual state to which being a conscious experience is not essential.

Here is where our earlier consideration of Rosenthal's "sensory qualities" comes in handy. For there it seemed we were dealing with an ostensible visualness of the required type, one that could be instanced even in a blindsight case—"visual quality." So this leads to the suggestion that what makes you have a conscious visual experience of (for example) green is that you are in a state with the nonphenomenal visual quality of green, and seemingly without inference think that you are in a state of that type. Roughly, the idea is that you add to a state of mind that has some nonphenomenal sensory quality the thought that you are in a state with that quality, and it becomes phenomenally conscious sense-experience; take away the thought about it, and the state loses its phenomenal character.

One immediate difficulty: just how would this deal with the reflective blindsight problem? Though Rosenthal's remarks about sensory qualities may give us some idea of what could be meant by talk of a visual quality possessed in the absence of conscious visual experience, one that we could not deny a blindsighter, what they do not tell us is why a reflective blindsighter should not be regarded as thinking that she has just such a visual quality, in thinking that she visually judges that there is (say) some red on her left. There appears to be no reason to think the property of being a visual judgment that there is some red does not bear a relation of relative similarity to visual judgments about orange, blue, and so on, appropriate to putting it in that special isomorphism to the similarity relations "physical red" bears to "physical orange," and so on, that would make it the "visual quality of red." For it seems right to say, for example, that judging there to be red is more like judging there to be orange than it is like judging there to be blue, and so on.

One might reply here that this is not a problem, because the blindsighter would not, properly speaking, think that she had the visual quality. For the notion of a visual quality, understood in terms of some complex isomorphism of similarity to properties of the physical stimulus, would not be part of her *notion* or *concept* of a visual judgment. So it is not part of what she spontaneously thinks, not part of the content of the thought she expresses when she says, "I visually judge. . . ." She does not think that her judgment possesses a visual quality in this special sense, even if being a visual judgment entails having a visual quality, for she is not aware of this entailment. And, one might say, since she lacks the thought she would have if she were so aware, she lacks conscious visual experience. But more problems now present themselves. If one does not deny the possibility of reflective blindsight, I can see no reason to deny its possibility in a case where the subject *is* aware of the entailment in question—where it *is* part of her notion of visual judgment that it is a visual quality in something like Rosenthal's sense. Furthermore, though it is indeed likely that we first conceived of a reflective blindsighter who lacked the relevant notion of visual quality (a rather abstruse notion, after all), something similar might be said of actual normal people who consciously see: they typically lack this esoteric notion of visual quality as well, and so could hardly be said to apply it to themselves continually, in spontaneous thoughts about their visual states. But then, it is quite common for people to have conscious visual experience, even though they lack the higher-order thoughts that, according to the proposal, they ought to have, since these are needed to make our conscious states conscious.

I can see a couple of likely tactics a fan of higher-order-thought consciousness might try in response here, but they are ultimately blocked by new forms of the difficulties. In response to the reflective blindsight problem, one might, for instance, try to tinker with the notion of a visual quality, so as to make of it something visual judgments would not exemplify. So, for example, one might cook up some conception of a special kind of visual representation that does not belong to visual judgment, but to visual experience. Perhaps something like Tye's (1995) idea that belief (and hence, presumably, judgment) is represented in the brain in a "sentencelike" fashion, whereas experience is a "maplike" or "matrixlike" representation, could be pressed into service here (though in a way Tye would not endorse). If matrical visual representation could be had by blindsighters (why not?), and the reflective blindsighter judged only that she made visual judgments (which are not matrical), then one might claim to have found a construal of "visual quality" that we could plug into a higher-order-thought account of consciousness, without neglecting phenomenal consciousness by denying the possibility of reflective blindsight.

But this strategy still has the problem that we typically simply do not have the higher-order thoughts the account would attribute to us. This may be brought into focus by considering the following situation. Suppose you are seated in a tightly sealed lightless room, staring straight ahead, but unable to see anything around you. Then a green light, which you consciously see, is flashed briefly to your left. Now, suppose you are a left-field blindsighter in the same situation. When the green light is flashed, you consciously see nothing, but it spontaneously occurs to you that there is something green briefly on your left, and that this thought is a visual one. We may suppose that in both cases you make (and think you make) a spontaneous visual judgment that there is something green on your left. But, on the proposal we are examining, there must be something else you have, both when you *consciously see* the green, and when you only *blindsee* it—a visual quality somehow associated with this visual response, which normally you spontaneously think you have. But just what is that? The only kind of "visual state" I normally and seemingly without inference think that I have, which I can distinguish from visual judging, is just the kind I suppose a blindsighter would *not* have— namely, a conscious visual experience: its seeming to me the way it does for it to look as if there is something green to the left. Another way of putting this: I cannot find a way to interpret any phrase, whether it be, "I have a visual experience of green," or "It looks to me as if something is green," or "I have a visual sensation of green," etc., such that this would express a thought that actually spontaneously occurs to me when I consciously see green, that is also distinct from the thought that I visually judge that something is green, *and* that could be true of me, even if I did not consciously see anything at all. When I think that it looks to me as if something is green, what I think I have, distinct from visual judgment, is exactly what I think the blindsighter would not have.

The problem here is not just that there are plenty of people who consciously see, but lack any notion of a "matrical" (as opposed to "sentential") form of visual representation in the brain, and so cannot be said to think continually that they possess matrical visual representations. One might hope to tackle *that* problem by claiming that while we do not have such a concept of our visual experience, we can pick out the feature of which it is a concept—and one does so when one spontaneously thinks: "I have *this* visual quality," where "this" refers to the feature of being a certain kind of matrical visual brain representation (though we may not think of it as such). But whatever the merits of such a maneuver, it still leaves unaddressed the basic problem. The visual quality we are supposed to attribute continually to ourselves in thought, which makes us have conscious visual experience throughout the day, is supposed to be one that could belong to someone who lacked the relevant conscious vision—a blindsighter. But now, even if I do not object to the notion that I can pick out by some sort of demonstrative thought ("My experience has *this* visual quality") the feature of being a certain sort of brain representation I cannot identify as such, I may still object to the notion that at almost every waking moment, I somehow attribute to myself a kind of visual state that visual judgments are not, but that could be had without having conscious visual experience. Maybe I can be ignorant in certain ways about the features I spontaneously attribute to myself or my experience in thought, but I am not *totally* ignorant about what features I think I have. And here is something I know about what features I think I possess, in thinking that it looks a certain way to me, or that I feel pain— these are features one would not have, if one had no sight but blindsight, or if one was under anesthesia: thus these are not nonphenomenal "sensory qualities." Again, you might insist that I am simply wrong about what features I think I have. But if, once it becomes clear to me that visual qualities are supposed to be features of visual experience of a sort compatible with blindsight, I sincerely deny that there are any such features it ever spontaneously occurred to me I had, the burden of proof rests squarely on one who maintains I am mistaken in this denial.

This is not to deny that I might come to think that I possess a visual state of the relevant sort, which a blindsighter would share with me. I may have this thought, having been exposed to this special notion of visual quality, and having inferred that whenever I have experience of a certain phenomenal character, I also am in a state of the corresponding nonphenomenal visual quality. But the thought to which such inference would lead me is not one I have been in the habit of having whenever I think about my experience. And it is, in any case, indeed a thought to which *inference* appears to lead me, not, in the relevant sense, a *spontaneous* higher-order thought, of the sort supposed to make conscious states conscious. Similar considerations apply also in the case of feeling pain.[5]

The point is this. In order to try to avoid denying the possibility of reflective blindsight, while recognizing none but a "higher-order-thought" sort of consciousness, one winds up saying that we have conscious sense-experience, only so long as we are in a sensory state of a type that is not judgment-like, and to which phenomenal consciousness is not essential; and we spontaneously think we are in states that are of such a type. But this does not give us an acceptable way to save the theory from a denial of phenomenal consciousness. For I, at least, do not spontaneously think I am in sensory states of that sort, whereas I do have conscious sensory experience galore.

I do not deny that there could indeed be someone who not only possessed sensory qualities that were of a nonphenomenal sort, but also (unlike me) spontaneously thought she had them. But apart from the fact that this takes nothing from the point that sensorily conscious beings (such as myself) actually often do not fit this description, there remains the question of whether someone who *did* fit that description would have to have conscious sense-experience of the relevant sort. I said earlier that we cannot say they would, if we lack a notion of nonphenomenal sensory quality that excludes sensory judgment; for otherwise we would have to deny the possibility of reflective blindsight. But now I want to add that it does not really help the case for a higher-order-thought account of consciousness, if we manage to construct for ourselves some reasonably clear notion of, for example, nonphenomenal visual sensing (as opposed to visual judging). For we do not deem it impossible for a blindsighter to think spontaneously: I *visually judge* that there's an X. But then there is no good reason why we should declare it strictly impossible that a blindsighter might spontaneously think: I *visually sense* an X.

Remember, the Rosenthalian account requires that I am sometimes in a state that bears a nonphenomenal visual property corresponding to green and that I seemingly without inference think I am in a state with this property. And it requires that a blindsighter could be in a state with this property. But if such a thought could just occur to me, why could it not occur to a chromatic blindsighter? Why could this thought not occur to one who discriminated colors in visual judgment but never consciously saw them, either because he consciously saw nothing there at all, or because things looked only black and white to him?[6] To the extent that I can form some rough idea of what the required sort of "visual sensing" might be, if not conscious visual experience, I discern nothing in the difference between the thought that one visually judges and the thought that one "visually senses" that permits only the first thought to occur spontaneously when true, in the absence of conscious visual experience, while precluding the possibility that the second will do so.

In reply one might say that, while no difference in the thought that one visually senses rules out the possibility that when one lacks conscious sight one may spontaneously (and correctly) think one visually senses, still there is something in the nature of visual sensing itself, which distinguishes it from visual judgment, that does this. But again, it is a complete mystery why anyone should think that the nonphenomenal ways of distinguishing sensing from judging at which some theories point would make this kind of difference. What, for example, is it about the nature of the difference between "matrical" and "sentential" representations (supposing that is what separates sensing from judging) that would not preclude the reflective blindsighter's thinking she visually *judges*, but that would make it strictly impossible for her to think she visually *senses* (as we allegedly think, whenever we consciously see)? The problem is, we lack any principled basis for declaring one of these situations impossible, but not the other. So, if we recognize no consciousness but Rosenthal's "higher-order-thought consciousness," we have left ourselves no reasonable alternative but to deem *both* impossible—and thus to neglect phenomenal consciousness.

One might try to resist this conclusion by saying that it is difficult to imagine that someone could make spontaneously in judgment the kinds of subtle discriminations among nonconscious sensory states that we can make among our conscious sense-experiences. We can detect in thought, and report, rather subtle differences in how it feels to us, or in how something looks to us, by saying or thinking: "This feels/looks different (similar) to this." And we may have a hard time imagining that a blindsighter could differentiate her nonphenomenal visual qualities quite so finely. This may lead one to doubt the conceivability of a blindsighter's reflective judgment discriminating visual states as well as that of someone with conscious vision. And this might seem to give one good reason to deny the possibility of a type of reflective blindsight for visual sensing, which one leaves open in the case of visual judging. So my present objection to a higher-order-thought theory of consciousness would not block the move of taking conscious vision to be nothing but visual sensing that is relatively finely discriminated by the subject's reflective judgment.

This, however, won't successfully answer the objection. The alleged difficulty here does not concern whether there could be reflective blindsight for nonconscious visual sensing. The suggestion is just that reflective judgment could never differentiate nonconscious visual states as finely as it does conscious experiences. But now, recall that we need not suppose conscious sense-experience is very finely differentiated: the rather paltry visual experience of grayish blobs that we supposed Connie had in her left visual field would be relatively poor in qualitative differentiation. Thus any nonphenomenal visual qualities she would have, the discrimination of which someone might tell us made for conscious experience of what is in her left visual field, would presumably be neither very finely differentiated in themselves, nor very finely distinguished by her in thought. So, in order to conceive of a reflective blindsighter of Belinda's ilk discriminating her "visual qualities" as finely as Connie would, we do not need to conceive of her discriminating them *all that finely*. So it seems to me that conceiving of reflective blindsight for visual sensing presents no difficulty that does not already afflict us when the blindsighter's reflection is assumed to be trained on her visual judgment.

But I suspect we still may be troubled by misgivings here, similar to those that gave rise to the discussion at 4.3, having to do with how we are supposed to imagine that someone learned to be a reflective blindsighter. The worry is this: While there may be no grounds for denying that someone might form a notion of a nonphenomenal difference between sensing and judging—a difference that could obtain in the absence of conscious experience—and ultimately somehow come to apply such a distinction spontaneously in first-person thought, it may seem to us inconceivable that someone could have *originally* come to grasp a distinction between sensing and judging, by learning to apply that distinction to himself spontaneously, without having any phenomenally conscious experience to which to apply it. We may think a blindsighter like Belinda just could not have acquired the concept of visual sensing partly through spontaneous first-person discrimination of her (nonconscious) visual sensing. But (allegedly) the consciously sighted can do this. If there is this inevitable difference in learning ability between the blindsighted and the consciously sighted, mightn't there still be some hope for some higher-order-thought account of visual consciousness? Mightn't one say that this is all there is to the difference between having conscious visual experience and lacking it: the first is such as can help you acquire the concept of visual sensing through spontaneous first-person discrimination, the second is not?

The suggestion might be made clearer still by considering it in this light. If we do not rule out the possibility of reflective blindsight for visual sensing, there is no good reason to think that someone blindsighted from birth, and *entirely* lacking conscious vision—Linda again—could not have at least learned to make spontaneous *verbal* discriminations of her visual sensing, of the sort that would (if uttered by another) express judgments. (She could be trained to utter the words, "I visually sense a light to my left," when what we would mean by this phrase is true of her.) But the suggestion is that such a person, because she lacked conscious sight, would lack a crucial ingredient, without which her learning to make these verbal responses to her own mental states would contribute nothing to her understanding the meaning of the words she utters. She (unlike the consciously sighted) would not learn the distinction between visual sensing and judging by learning to employ this distinction in spontaneous thought about herself. I will not try to say whether this is true or false. I only want to argue that although, if this is true, there is indeed an essential difference between the manifest talents of someone with conscious sight and those of someone without it, such a difference will not give us an acceptable proposal that absolves the higher-order-thought account from the charge that it neglects phenomenal consciousness.

Such a proposal would look something like this: All we have in mind when we speak of an absence of conscious visual experience, or all there is to lacking a conscious visual experience, is the absence of a talent for learning the distinction between visual sensing and other sensory and mental states, by learning to discriminate them in spontaneous higher-order thought. And so all we have in mind when we say someone has conscious visual experience (or all we attribute to her in saying this) is a state of visual sensing, of the sort that enables one to acquire the concept of visual sensing partly through spontaneous first-person discrimination.

This would depart quite a bit from Rosenthal's idea that what makes conscious states conscious is their being the object of *actual* higher-order thoughts—here the idea is that what makes these states conscious is that one is able to learn in a certain way to have higher-order thoughts about them. In any case, there is the problem that, since actually we do not seem to acquire the concept of (nonphenomenal) visual sensing (if we acquire it at all) partly through learning to think spontaneously that we visually sense (since we do not learn to do this), it is unclear that our conscious visual experience is, in fact, of the sort that can enable one to acquire this concept in this way. But suppose we waive this objection. Even if we can learn to use the concept of visual sensing by learning to employ it in spontaneous first-person judgments, and even if one could learn to do this only if one had conscious visual experience, an argument much like one I gave in the last section shows us we should not adopt the thesis that our blindsighters' lack of conscious vision would be nothing but the absence of such an ability for learning.

Compare again our hypothetical subjects, Linda and Glenda. Then notice: on the assumption that this thesis is true, it follows that Glenda's conscious visual experience does not display her ability to acquire the concept of visual sensing by spontaneous first-person discrimination. For the proposal has it that all we have in mind in saying Linda lacks the conscious visual experience Glenda has, or all that is attributed to the one and withheld from the other in saying this, is just the ability to acquire this concept in this way. Now, is there any manifest feature in respect of which Linda and Glenda would have to differ, which is reasonably regarded as displaying the one's possession, and the other's lack, of the power to acquire the concept of visual sensing through first-person discrimination? We may well think that Linda would not be able to think that she *consciously* saw things, as Glenda would. But that is not a view we can reasonably hold if we adopt the proposal under consideration. For according to this proposal, for Linda to think she consciously saw, would be for her to attribute to herself nothing over and above the sort of visual discrimination she has, except the ability to learn what 'visual sensing' means from first-person discriminations. And if we do not deny the possibility of Linda and Glenda, there is no reason to deny the possibility that someone might believe that they both could engage in this form of learning. So we would not (on the view under consideration) deny that Linda would be able to believe this of herself. Now, if we cannot say that Linda and Glenda must differ even in *this* manifest feature—the ability to think they consciously see things—given the other similarities between them, there will not be *any* manifest difference between them that we can reasonably say displays the ability to acquire the concept of visual sensing from first-person discrimination, and its lack. Then, if we look for some necessary *hidden* difference between them, we run up against the problem that hidden differences will display one's ability to acquire a concept (or one's lack of it), only if they are tied to manifest differences that do. Since we could find no manifest differences of this sort, we will find no hidden ones either. But if there is no way Linda and Glenda would differ, which would display their respective lack and possession of the concept-learning ability in question, there is nothing Linda would lack for this at all.

The argument that emerges is this. Assume—as the proposal would have it—that Belinda's lack of visual consciousness is just her lack of a manifest talent for learning to think the higher-order thoughts called for in Rosenthal's theory of consciousness. Then a blindsighter and a consciously sighted person could not possibly both have this talent. But then also, if we do not deny that a Belinda-like blindsight is possible, we will be unable to find any feature someone like Linda, who would lack conscious sight entirely, would be missing that would display her lack of the talent in question. Then Linda would not lack this talent at all. And so we would reject the hypothesis that her lack of conscious vision would be nothing but her lack of this talent.

This is to reject the claim last introduced to see how one might try to save the idea that the absence of visual consciousness is the absence of a kind of manifest talent for discriminating—in "higher-order thought"—one's own discrimination. So again, we have found no acceptable version of this idea.

In this section, I have considered how a higher-order-thought theory of consciousness might try to account for phenomenal consciousness. What I have discovered are two basic arguments for regarding such an effort as futile. The first is that, if it is to avoid a trivializing circularity that would make of it no account at all, and avoid denying blindsight possibilities it should not deny, by appealing to nonphenomenal "visual quality," it will require us to deny what is evidently true: we just do not have the kinds of thoughts about our conscious visual experience the theory tells us makes it conscious. The second argument is that we could hope to account for phenomenal consciousness in terms of a nonphenomenal mentalness targeted by higher-order thought, only if we can rule out the possibility that one might lack conscious visual experience, but have all such a theory says there is to having it. But, if we leave open the possibility of reflective blindsight, there is no reasonable way to offer such an account. For such an account would have us reject possibilities closely related to that of reflective blindsight as earlier described, where no good reason exists to accept the one and reject the other, or else it would have us try to build on convictions about the connection of consciousness to concept acquisition, in ways that are ultimately self-defeating.

We have shifted attention from the talent for discriminating visual stimuli to the talent for discriminating one's own discrimination in higher-order thought: and this has still shown us no acceptable way to make conscious vision into a manifest discriminatory talent, while granting the reality of phenomenal consciousness. It has only acquainted us with yet more complicated ways of leaving this out of account. The neglect we have uncovered here does not appear to be due to some supposed lack of theoretical refinement in what some might disdain as the "folk psychological" notion of a thought about one's own mind. If we dress up the higher-order-thought story in higher-tech lingo, the problems remain, for we can just reformulate the reflective blindsighter story in the new jargon. For instance, one might suppose, with Johnson-Laird (1988a, 1988b), that consciousness involves a system's having within it a "model of itself" in which it represents its own representations, or, with Armstrong (1965), that consciousness is a matter of "scanning" one's own "internal states." If we adopt Johnson-Laird's vocabulary, then we may want to treat our talk of a spontaneous thought that one visually judges there is an X on the left as a crude layperson's way of describing a situation in which a representation of one's visual representation is formed in a specialized subsystem devoted to the self-modeling of the larger system one is. And if we talk Armstrong-ese, we may want to redescribe the situation in which one spontaneously thinks that one visually judges there is an X, as that in which one's internal scanner scans something into one's visual system. But in either case, we will run into the problem that these descriptions would apply to the reflective blindsighter, who does not consciously see an X. Again, one will try to respond to this by positing a distinctive nonphenomenal visual quality, but then I will have the same objections as before: I do not spontaneously represent myself as having that kind of visual state, and even if one did, there is no reason to think one could not do this and be in such a state without consciously seeing anything. And, even if one could have learned to form the relevant self-representations (or scan one's own visual sensing) only from conscious vision, and never from blindsight, then we still must not identify a lack of phenomenal consciousness with missing this ability to acquire certain forms of self-representation or inner scanning. For then the blindsighter would not display her inability through her lack of experience, and ultimately, we would be led to conclude that she lacks nothing for this ability at all.

Perhaps "inner scanning" of one's visual sensing, and "forming representations in a model of oneself," are meant to describe some mental process crucially unlike spontaneously thinking that one is in some kind of visual state. But we would have to know more about what this kind of scanning or self-modeling might be, and just what distinguishes it from higher-order thought, if we are to understand what it might mean to identify it with phenomenal consciousness. I will have something more to say about this in Chapter 6; in the meantime, though, we can conclude that we have seen enough to be dissatisfied with theories that give us no consciousness but one contrived from nonphenomenal sensory qualities and higher-order thoughts.

4.5 Consciously Seeing Is Not Just Thinking You Do

But it might seem I have still left a loophole for a higher-order-thought theory of phenomenal consciousness. I have admitted that the presence or absence of conscious vision may, for all I know, necessarily bring with it a difference in manifest talents for learning—I only said that where we can plausibly think it does, we cannot reasonably suppose that the absence of conscious sight is nothing more than the absence of that talent. However, there is one respect in which we might think the abilities of the blindsighted and the consciously sighted would inevitably differ—already encountered a couple of times—that I have not considered as a candidate for the crucial missing discriminatory talent with which an absence of conscious vision is to be identified.

Recall that I have not asked you to conceive of a blindsighter unable to tell the difference between the blindsight she has on the left, and the conscious vision she has on the right. So I have not asked you to suppose that she is spontaneously struck by the mistaken thought that she consciously sees an X (or something green, or a brighter patch of light) on her left. And I have not had you suppose that Belinda would do anything other than sincerely and flatly deny that she consciously saw anything on her left, if asked. So we might want to ask: Would it be possible for Belinda's blindsight of certain stimuli to make her think she consciously sees them? Earlier I argued that we should not deny this, if we were assuming certain proposals then under consideration for making the lack of conscious vision into the lack of a learning talent. But suppose we do not assume them; maybe then our answer should be "no." And then perhaps, in a last-ditch effort to find some way to account for phenomenal consciousness in terms of higher-order thought, we might try supposing that what makes conscious visual experience conscious is that it is a state of (nonphenomenal) visual sensing, about which one thinks (or perhaps, is *liable* to think), seemingly without inference, that it is a phenomenally conscious visual experience.

Perhaps in response we will say that, however strange it might seem, it could happen on some occasion that someone who only blindsees an X might falsely think that she consciously sees an X. But even so, we could still reasonably hold that conscious visual experience gives one a capacity to judge that one has it, which no nonconscious substitute would have. The plausibility of this idea, I believe, lies in the thought that one could not understand what is meant by 'consciously seeing' in the first place, without having had phenomenally conscious experience. And so, conscious states can enable one to form assertions, judgments, or beliefs that they are conscious, as nonconscious states simply cannot. On this view, the notion of a being who had never had conscious experience, but judged, asserted, believed that he (she, it) had, would be absurd. If this is correct, then however meager Connie's blurry conscious visual experience might be, inevitably it would have *some* capacity that no blindsight substitute could provide. It would be such as could enable one to begin to judge that one has conscious experience, and no nonconscious state would have this capacity, or would afford one this talent.

Here we face another possible variant on some consciousness empiricism with regard to the acquisition of concepts. This time it would be alleged that all that would inevitably separate Belinda from Connie is not Connie's ability to grasp the concepts of *light* or *color*, or of *visual sensing*, in a certain way, but rather Connie's ability to come by the concept of *phenomenal consciousness*. The claim would be that all we have in mind when we suppose Connie would have phenomenally conscious visual experience that Belinda would lack, or all we would attribute to Connie in saying she would have this, while Belinda would not, is the kind of left-field visual discrimination that enables her to acquire the concept of phenomenally conscious vision.

This would tell us that having a conscious visual experience of light such as Connie would have on her left is nothing but having what Belinda has when she blindsightedly discriminates light on her left, except that this state is also such as could enable one who is in it to have learned to judge that one *consciously* sees some light. I think that as soon as we spell this out, we will begin to sense that something is amiss, and it will not surprise us if no one has actually put forward a proposal of this kind. I believe an argument similar to those I made regarding acquisition of the concepts of light and visual sensing would, with suitable adjustments, work here as well, but I want to make my point here with different reasoning, specific to the case at hand.

If there would be a genuine difference between the likes of Connie and Belinda, if one of them would have some feature the other does not, then surely the difference between having and lacking this feature cannot consist *entirely* in whether or not one could have judged that she had this feature, under certain conditions. The point here is a general one. Two genuinely distinct features will not be distinct *solely* in virtue of an alleged difference between the thought that something has the one feature, and the thought that something has the other. We can appreciate this when we consider examples of trying to distinguish two features in this way, entirely by means of an alleged distinction between the beliefs that things have one or the other of those features. Imagine this conversation:

—How do you like my new ultra-shoes?

—I see your new shoes—but what makes them *ultra*-shoes?

—Well, being an ultra-shoe is a lot like being a shoe, in fact, it's *precisely* the same as being a shoe, save in this respect: ultra-shoes have the capacity to make the wearer believe they are ultra-shoes.

—What's so special about that? Any shoes can cause you to believe that you're wearing shoes.

—Of course, but ultra-shoes don't merely have *that* capacity. *They* cause you to believe not just that you're wearing shoes, but that you're wearing *ultra*-shoes. And plain old shoes can't do that.

—But there's still no difference, unless there's a difference between believing you're wearing shoes and believing you're wearing ultra-shoes. And what's the difference between those beliefs?

—I've already told you: to wear ultra-shoes is simply to wear shoes that make you believe they're ultra-shoes. And *that's* what I believe about my ultra-shoes that regular shoes are powerless to make me believe about them: that they're ultra-shoes.

I hope it is obvious that the proud owner of new "ultra-shoes" cannot be taken to have genuinely distinguished the property of being an ultra-shoe from that of being a shoe. Nor has he even shown how to think of them as two features. The failure is not due to any peculiarity of shoes, but rather to an absurdity in the way the speaker tries to individuate properties. One asserts first that the property of being F is distinct from that of being G. Second, one says, however, there is no property, distinct from being an F, which G's must have, save this: having a propensity (of some sort) to cause the belief that they are G's.

But this was just the sort of suggestion entertained regarding blindsight of light and conscious visual experience of light. That is, we first agreed that blindseeing light was distinct from consciously seeing light. Then it was proposed that there is no feature, distinct from that which one who blindsees light would have, that those who consciously see light must possess, save this: being in a state with the capacity to cause one to learn to judge that one consciously sees light. For I take it that this follows from saying that all we have in mind when we speak of Belinda's lack of conscious vision, or all there is to her lacking this, is her lack of a talent for learning to think that she consciously sees things on her left. But if the distinction between consciously seeing something and blindseeing it amounted to nothing but this, it would be just as fake as the distinction between shoes and ultra-shoes. There would be no genuine distinction of the sort for which we proposed the account.

So—even if we have here located a difference in manifest discriminatory talents that necessarily separates Connie from Belinda, and conscious sight from blindsight, we would entirely undermine our grasp of the distinction between these, were we to insist that when we draw it in the case of Belinda and Connie, we have in nothing in mind (or there is nothing to this difference) over and above the difference between having and lacking an ability to think one consciously sees.

4.6 THE CAPACITY TO USE VISUAL INFORMATION

The suggestion that all we have in mind when speaking of conscious vision, and contrasting it with blindsight, is some difference in manifest discriminatory talents—whether these discriminatory talents are directed "outward" or "inward"—has yielded only a collection of theoretical strategies for hiding phenomenal consciousness from ourselves. But perhaps this is simply because what we have in mind when we speak of conscious vision is some manifest talent other than a "discriminatory" one?

Recall that Dennett also mentioned that we might be speaking here of special "regulative," or "evaluative," talents. Let's concentrate on the "regulative" sort. What capacities, of the sort we could have warrant for attributing to ourselves without internal examination, might be meant here? Presumably, the idea would be that Connie, in virtue of her left-field visual experience of light, would have some talent or ability to regulate (or control, or affect) her behavior, or her other manifest features, which Belinda, who consciously sees no stimuli in that part of her visual field, would inevitably lack. And consciously seeing things there, is just having something that Connie and Belinda would share, plus this extra "regulative" talent that only Connie could have.

But what might this extra talent be? I assume the point is not just that Connie would have (or would exercise) an ability to regulate her condition in response to her consciously seeing light on the left, which Belinda would not have. That would undoubtedly be true; but that is just to say that Connie has a certain conscious visual experience, *and* an ability to make her condition contingent on her having it, while Belinda lacks that experience, and thus is unable to make her condition contingent on her possession of it. If that were all that was meant by saying that the difference between Connie and Belinda would be a difference in their regulative talents, then the claim would be a trivial one.

Perhaps the suggestion is something more like: Connie would be able to make use of visual information, as Belinda would not. So: Connie's having a conscious visual experience of light on her left is nothing but her being able to use visual information in a way in which Belinda could not. This suggestion would be in line with what one finds in a number of writings in contemporary philosophy and psychology, in which what is conscious is distinguished from what is not in terms of whether informational content is accessible to, or "flowing" to or from, certain hypothesized information-processing capacities, certain "modules," or "subsystems" (see Baars 1988; Dennett 1978; Johnson-Laird 1988a, 1988b; Shallice 1988). Such proposals might be taken to offer a way of making good the suggestion that what is missing when conscious vision is missing is nothing but a certain manifest talent, for one may hold that we can have some warrant for regarding things as having certain information-processing talents without having to open them up.

A crucial question here is, obviously, which modules or subsystems are the consciousness-making ones? A number of different suggestions have been made, but usually they involve some variation on the idea that the information-processing capacities crucial to making some states conscious are those specifically involved with either the production of speech, or the control of goal-directed behavior—especially that concerned with planning, or with nonroutine sequences of movement. Such proposals have, of course, been worked out much more elaborately than this indicates, but I think we can see it would be a mistake to say that the difference between having a conscious visual experience and lacking it is nothing but a difference between having and lacking certain capacities of this sort, even without delving into the details of various theories.

Recall again the kind of spontaneous blindsight capacity we contemplated at the beginning of stage two of our thought-experiment. How should this situation be described in information-processing terms? We should presumably want to begin by saying that the subject of spontaneous blindsight would have, as they say, encoded somehow in his visual system the information that there is an X on his left, and this triggers the thought he expresses by saying, "There's an X on my left." But now, how should we want to say that the flow or access of this information differs between this case and the case where one consciously sees a flashed X?

It would seem that in either case, the same visual information would be accessible to whatever subsystem we suppose is responsible for generating the person's meant verbal utterance. And this information would be available to be used by whatever subsystems we suppose are responsible for goal-directed behavior, or deliberative reasoning or planning. Both the person who consciously sees an X on the left, and the one who only blindsees an X there, would be able to decide, or choose, or plan to do things, based on whether or not there is an X on their left. For in supposing that one could verbally discriminate such a visual stimulus spontaneously, without consciously seeing it, we are supposing that one has "verbal access" to information about it, and one is able to use this information in whatever reasoning, deliberating, or planning one can do with information to which one has spontaneous verbal access. So the spontaneous blindsighter would be able to do with a certain piece of visual information whatever one can do with that information when it is given one by a conscious visual experience. The blindsighter would have (in Block's [1995] terms) a form of visual "access consciousness" where she lacks phenomenally conscious visual experience. For the information that there is an X on her left would be "poised for use as a premise in reasoning" and "rational control of action and speech" (Block 1995, 231), even though she lacked a phenomenally conscious visual experience of an X on her left.

One might say, "A blindsighter would lack a lot of *other* visual information and processing capacities with respect to this, which a normal consciously sighted person would not lack; the information that there is an X on her left is not the content of conscious visual experience, simply because there is *other* information concerning what stimuli are in that area that the relevant subsystems are not being fed, or to which they do not have access." Again, this move will seem unimpressive if we do not deny the possibility of premium blindsight. But also, once more, we needn't go this far. We may simply contrast again the person who has only some hazy limited conscious vision on her left, and the person who has no conscious vision on the left at all—Connie and Belinda. If their visual discriminatory powers are as we have described them, then it seems we should say that Belinda's language and control faculties would have access to the same visual information as would Connie's. Or again, Belinda would have "access consciousness" where she lacks phenomenal consciousness.

But suppose we theorized—as I have already mentioned Tye does—that our brains "mentally represent" in different ways—both "matrically" and "sententially." Though abilities to represent things in these ways would not seem to fit naturally under the category "regulative talents," might this not be a difference in the manner in which information is processed by which we could distinguish blindsight from conscious sight? The idea would be that what we have in mind when we say Belinda would lack conscious visual experience, or what feature we withhold from her but apply to ourselves, is the ability to encode information about left-field stimuli, not in a sentencelike way, but in a matrical form, in her visual system. This suggestion runs into problems similar to those we found in others. If we do not assume one such as Belinda is impossible, I do not think we have reason to find it impossible that a Belinda-like blindsighter could matrically represent the stimuli in her left field to which she responds. A believer in something like Tye's conception of mental representation will presumably not reject the idea that normally sighted individuals form or could form *nonconscious* matrical (or maplike) visual representations; it is not maintained that non-conscious matrical visual representation of any sort is strictly impossible. So even if we think (like Tye) that actual blindsighters differ from actual nor-mally sighted subjects in ways that suggest they lack matrical visual repre-sentations of the stimuli about which they can make visual judgments, there seems to be nothing ruling out the possibility of a hypothetical blindsighter of Belinda's type *having* such visual representations. And so Tye's idea that visual experience represents in the manner of a map or a matrix will not supply us with some essential feature, lacking which, Belinda would lack what Connie would have.[7]

Now, I have conceded that there may be certain kinds of learning from experience that could not take place without visual consciousness. So I sup-pose one might say that Belinda cannot use visual information as Connie can in this way: Belinda cannot use visual information about her left field to acquire certain concepts as Connie can. But we have seen the folly of trying to say that the difference between Belinda and Connie consists entirely in some such difference in learning capacity.

If we say that what we have in mind when we speak of the absence of a conscious visual experience of an X or of green—or all there is to lacking this feature—is nothing but the absence of certain capacities to use visual infor-mation, then we wind up denying the possibility that Belinda lacks con-scious visual experience that Connie has, when the two do not differ with respect to such capacities. And this either rules out forms of blindsight we must not rule out, if we are to recognize phenomenal consciousness, or else has us try to distinguish the occurrence of consciousness from its absence purely in terms of a difference in concept-learning capacities, in a way that we have already seen is futile. In this way, information-processing theories of consciousness neglect phenomenal consciousness.

The problem here is not eluded by refusing to couch the theory in terms that tell just what type of information access is necessary and sufficient for having a conscious visual experience of a certain type. If we maintain at least that a possessor of conscious visual experience must differ from a subject who lacks that kind of experience in respect of *some* manifest capacity to process visual information (though refusing to commit ourselves to any definite list of such capacities that would make the difference between con-scious sight and its absence), we still run into the problem of denying the possibility of subjects such as Connie and Belinda.

We might also try saying here that the sense in which two who differ in what conscious visual experience they have "must" differ in what they can do with visual information is not one that entails that their failing to differ in that way is strictly impossible—the theory, we may say, is not to be taken as committed to any claims about either the concept or the "real essence" of consciousness. And if we claim no more than that there is a lawlike relationship between having conscious visual experience and being able to do certain things with visual information, for which we do not claim any conceptual or metaphysical necessity, but which would be violated by the actual existence of two subjects such as Connie and Belinda were supposed to be, we do not neglect phenomenal consciousness. But then we face a problem similar to one plaguing higher-order-thought accounts of consciousness. It is unclear why, once the theory relinquishes all pretensions to conceptual or metaphysical necessity, we should regard its claims as providing the basis for an explanatory theory of phenomenal consciousness. For if one is offering an explanatory theory here, one is proposing that our possession of certain phenomenal features, our having visual experience with a certain phenomenal character, is in some sense *accounted for* or *explained by* the fact that all subjects with such experience differ from those without it with respect to some (or certain) capacities for using visual information. However, why should this fact (if it is one) seem explanatory of consciousness? And why not suppose that it is the possession of conscious experience that explains the possession of the capacities, and the lack of phenomenal features that does (or would counterfactually) account for a subject's lack of certain capacities? (So we might say, for instance, that an actual blindsighter [like D.B.] has no unprompted access to visual information about figures in his left field, and he has no access at all to "rich" visual information about these, *because he cannot consciously see them*; and that a normal subject would not have been able to access information about the movement and position of things in the relevant part of his visual field so as to control purposive movement, had he not consciously seen anything there.) The point is, it's not clear how information-processing accounts of consciousness can recognize phenomenal consciousness, while disclaiming any ambition to tell us what we have in mind (or should have in mind) when we speak of visual consciousness and its lack, or what being a conscious visual experience consists in. For then there is no evident way of seeing them as attempts at explaining our possession of conscious experience, rather than just as efforts to describe in information-processing terms the capacities our possession of conscious experience explains.

4.7 EVALUATIVE TALENTS

I have tried to find ways in which one might be tempted to think of a lack of conscious visual experience as nothing but a lack of discriminatory or regulative talent. But I have not had anything to say so far about the third sort of talent Dennett suggests in this regard—the "evaluative." Perhaps all we must have supposed was crucially absent in blindsight, so that conscious visual experience of some light or color or figure was missing, was a special capacity for *evaluation*. Perhaps if only *that* were added to the spontaneous reflective blindsighter's talents, her left-field conscious vision would be restored.

But what sort of evaluative talent is going to be a likely candidate here? A talent for evaluating what, and in what way? We might suggest that what we need to think of here is some talent for evaluating courses of action, deciding upon them, or planning. But we've already seen that the visual information that there is light to the left that is getting brighter would be just as available or accessible to be used by a blindsighter like Belinda in making decisions, planning, or deliberating, as to a person who had conscious left-field vision of the sort Connie would have. So that cannot be the sort of evaluative talent we have in mind.

We might seem to come closer to some ineradicable connection between conscious experience and what is in some sense an "evaluative" capacity, if we ask whether conscious color vision has a potential to affect us *emotionally* in some way that chromatic blindsight just could not. Colors that we see can strike us, for example, as soothing or exciting, jarring or calming. Now, someone who consciously sees colors may, as a matter of fact, be quite unmoved by them. And it seems that whether you have a blurry, amblyopic, but conscious, visual experience of green or blue or whatever on your left, or whether you have total left-field blindsight, could very well be something to which you are totally apathetic. But, perhaps even this small difference in what conscious color vision you have would inevitably involve some difference in your *potential* to be emotionally affected in a certain way. Recall the chromatic blindsighter, who can correctly visually judge what colors things are that he sees, but to whom the world looks no more colored than does a black-and-white movie. The idea would be that such a person would necessarily lack the capacity to be affected emotionally by color as those of us with conscious color vision can be. And any conscious color experience, even the most meager, has in some small measure an affective potential of this sort, which nothing else would. Then comes the suggestion: consciously seeing color is nothing but having what the blindsighter would have, *plus* the capacity to be emotionally affected by color.

But this cannot be right. For after all, what you ingest can affect you emotionally, but you needn't consciously taste what it is in your drink or food that alters your mood or feelings. And so it seems possible that the chromatic blindsighter's feelings or moods might be affected by color without his consciously seeing colors. One will want to say at this point that there would still be a crucial difference in the way colors affected the blindsighter and the way they affect us. One might say: in the case of such a blindsighter, the impact color has on him has nothing to do with the *evaluative attitudes*—desires, preferences, likes, and dislikes—he has toward colors, whereas conscious color experience gives one a capacity to be affected by colors, at least in part, by making one able to like certain colors, or to prefer some to others. However, this still does not seem quite right. For it seems possible still that a chromatic blindsighter could have color prefer- ences. He might prefer to wear blue rather than red, because he believes that this color "suits" him; he thinks of blue as a calming, conservative color, and this fits with his personality. We might even suppose that he enjoys blindsee- ing himself in this color. For we might imagine that as he stands before the mirror, he is quite satisfied at the thought which strikes him: "Here I am all in blue."

But still, we may want to interject, there is a sense in which he could not enjoy the way blue *looks* on him, if he has only blindsight for color. That, I think, is right. But it is true, only if we are thinking that being able to enjoy the way blue looks requires that something can look blue to you, in the sense of 'look' in which we said that visual stimuli of which you had only blind- sight would not look blue to you. So, to say that the blindsighter cannot enjoy the way blue looks on him, is to say that he is unable to enjoy its looking to him as if he is dressed in blue. That is, he is unable to enjoy having a conscious visual experience of blue, for the simple reason that you cannot enjoy having what you haven't got. But then, this shows us no more than that the consciously sighted have this talent that the blindsighted inevitably lack: the talent for having conscious visual experience. And that would be a rather trivial way to distinguish the two with regard to their evaluative talents.

However, we might take this further, and say that not only can a person who lacks conscious color experience not have satisfied desires or prefer- ences for having color experience, but also that whatever nonconscious states he has would not have the capacity for giving him such desires, which conscious experience would. Conscious experience has a potential to make one want to have (or not have) conscious experience, which what is not conscious does not. This seems plausible, but I think it would be a compli- cated affair to try to make this point in just the right way. For it seems we could say that the chromatic blindsighter wants to have the conscious color vision he lacks, and, in part, because of the character of what he does have.

For current purposes, I just want to make the following point. If con- scious visual experience enables one to have preferences, wants, or desires for having conscious visual experience, as what is not conscious cannot, this is *not* a difference in "evaluative talent" with which we can identify the difference between having and lacking such experience. For we cannot rightly say that to consciously see green is to have nothing but what the person who blindsees green has, *plus* a capacity for preferring (wanting, valuing) one's consciously seeing green. This would be just as absurd as saying that consciously seeing green is nothing over and above having what the person who blindsees green would have, *plus* a capacity for believing (thinking, judging) that one consciously sees green. If we cannot intelligibly distinguish between shoes and ultra-shoes by saying that ultra-shoes are just like shoes, except that they make you think they are ultra-shoes, we cannot do this by saying that ultra-shoes are just like shoes, except that they make you want to wear ultra-shoes. The point is again, that you cannot make a difference between features solely out of a difference in attitudes toward those very features.

4.8 Consciousness Neglect in Functionalism

Let's review what we have found about conscious experience and its relation to the sorts of talent with which Dennett suggested we identify it. We have been able to find no discriminatory, regulative, or evaluative talent of a manifest sort, of which we can truthfully and nontrivially say that, when we suppose that conscious visual experience of, for example, something green is absent, we have in mind nothing over and above some such missing talent, while leaving open the possibility of a blindsighter such as Belinda. For when we contrast Belinda's lack of conscious visual experience with Connie's possession of it, we find that Belinda's blindsight would give her the same manifest talents as Connie's conscious sight. Or, where it is plausible to suppose their talents would inevitably differ (as in the case of talents for thinking one consciously sees), then if it is claimed that all we mean by saying the one would consciously see and the other would not is that the second would lack this manifest talent the first possessed, the thesis ultimately undermines itself. One could, of course, respond to this situation by declaring that blindsight such as Belinda's is inconceivable—conceptually impossible—but that would be tantamount to denying the reality of phenomenal consciousness. So the attempt to identify Belinda's lack of visual consciousness with one or another of Dennett's talents has left us no recourse but consciousness neglect. The same points apply, should we switch from a conceptual or semantic mode to a metaphysical one. We have found no collection of discriminatory, regulative, or evaluative manifest talents such that we can truthfully and nontrivially say, that to lack the property of consciously seeing something (a grayish patch of light) is just to lack the property of having one or another of these manifest talents—or, if you like, that the essence of conscious vision is the possession of one or another of these talents. For again, either this leads us to say that Belinda-like blindsight is strictly impossible (and so to deny consciousness), or else it undermines itself in one or another of the ways earlier discussed.

Now, 'talents' has been construed here broadly. We may as well have said that we found no *disposition* to discriminate or regulate or evaluate, of a sort we can have warrant for attributing to ourselves without internal examination, which we can rightly and nontrivially identify with conscious visual experience. We might then wonder whether my negative finding here depends crucially on the proviso that the disposition be of a "discriminatory, regulative, or evaluative" sort. Is there perhaps some other manifest dispositional feature with which we should identify visual experience?

One might say that surely such a pair as Connie and Belinda would have to differ in their speech or in other manifest behavioral dispositions, in some way. After all, we never abandoned the assumption that Connie had an inclination to assent to the question of whether she consciously saw green on the left, which Belinda lacked, whereas Belinda had a disposition to deny that she consciously saw anything there, which Connie lacked. I am not asking you to suppose that Connie and Belinda would not differ in respect of such behavioral dispositions. However, I think that they *must* differ in such a respect, only if that is an essential part of their differing in the way already mentioned: Connie is inclined to think (believe, or judge) that she consciously sees green on her left, while Belinda is inclined to think (etc.) that she does not. And so, in allowing that perhaps Connie and Belinda would have to differ in their disposition to such thoughts, I have already included such differences in behavioral dispositions as would necessarily distinguish the two. But the point remains that we cannot make a conscious visual experience purely out of what Belinda has, plus a propensity, which only Connie would have, to think that one has such an experience. Analogous remarks would apply in the case of Belinda's and Connie's desires, preferences, or "evaluations." And we could make similar observations concerning whatever *conceptual* abilities I have allowed may be dependent on having conscious experience. If we cannot identify the absence of conscious visual experience with the absence of these abilities, we cannot identify it with the lack of whatever dispositions to manifest utterances or behavior we may suppose essential to them.

So it seems we are left with this result: a person such as Connie would have a conscious visual experience that such a one as Belinda lacked, though the only differences in manifest features they had or were disposed to have, were such as we cannot rightly and nontrivially identify (whether conceptually or metaphysically) with the difference between having and lacking that conscious experience, that phenomenal feature. This has negative consequences for the general view of the nature of mind (or of mental concepts) known as "functionalism." It emerges that the often-voiced complaint, that functionalism (at least in certain varieties) "leaves out" consciousness or the phenomenal character of experience, is a fair one.

Let's assume, with Block, that functionalism is the doctrine that "each type of mental state is a state consisting of a disposition to act in certain ways and to have certain mental states, given certain sensory inputs, and certain mental states" (Block 1978, 262). Now, if we assume further, that the types of mental states, acts, and sensory inputs with reference to which such dispositions are identified are types we can claim with warrant we instance without internal examination, then functionalism will say that to have a certain mental feature is just to be disposed to have certain other manifest features. We might call this *manifest functionalism*. And as we might say that for one to be in a state of being disposed to have such features is to have a state with a certain "functional role," on this view, having a certain *mental* feature is being in a state that has a certain *manifest functional role*.

We can now see how functionalism—whether this is put forth as a (conceptual) doctrine about what we mean by mental terms (as in Armstrong 1965, or Lewis 1972), or as a (metaphysical) doctrine about the "nature" of the mind (as in Putnam 1960, 1965)—*if* it tells us to specify a functional role only in terms of manifest features of inputs, outputs, and mediating states, seems to leave its adherents no choice but to neglect phenomenal consciousness. The style of theorizing about the mind articulated by Armstrong and Lewis is, I believe, a manifest functionalism about mental concepts. For their claim is that the meaning of our mentalistic terms is given by a theory we implicitly hold about the causal role each type of mental state plays vis-à-vis other mental states, sensory inputs, and behavioral outputs. Since this theory is presumably supposed to be the common property of all who use and understand everyday mentalistic language and have done so in the past, it would seem that it must identify the inputs, outputs, and mediating states in virtue of features that have been generally accessible to such people—features, that is, we can have warrant for claiming we have without internal examination. So the causal roles would be manifest ones. But—as it now appears—there is no disposition to manifest features, and hence no manifest causal role, of which we can rightly assert that what we mean by saying Connie would have a conscious visual experience Belinda would lack, is just that Connie would be in a state that fills *that role*, whereas in Belinda that role would go unfilled. For again, either Belinda's blindsight would take care of any such role just fine, or else, where it plausibly could not, our specification of this difference in roles cannot be used to state what we mean by saying one has an experience that the other does not without absurdity. (For in the case where we claim that by saying Belinda lacks conscious vision, we mean just that she lacks a state that can play a certain role in concept acquisition, we deprive her of anything by which she might display a failure to fill that role, and so ultimately we undermine the claim that visual consciousness is essential to filling that role [and with it, the claim about what we mean]. And in the case where we say what we mean is just that Belinda is not liable to think she consciously sees, we erase the distinction between blindsight and conscious vision—of which we are supposed to be giving an account—by making it as empty as that between shoes and ultra-shoes.)

Notice that it does not help here if we make use of the idea (prominent in Lewis's exposition) that what we mean when we say x has a certain kind of mental state (e.g., is in pain) is that x is in the state that, *in x's population,* plays a certain manifest causal role. For if the role in question is that which Belinda's blindseeing shares with Connie's visual experience, then this would rule out the possibility that the state Belinda is in is of a type that plays this role in a larger population to which she belongs—say, a population of blindsighters. But there is evidently no reason to declare this impossible, if Belinda as originally described is not deemed impossible. And requiring that the population be defined with reference to normal members of one's kind—one's species, say—would not help. For what we mean by saying Belinda lacks and Connie has a certain sort of conscious visual experience does not seem to rule out the possibility that Belinda belongs to a species whose normal members have the sort of blindsight capacity we have attributed to her. Nor would it appear to rule out the possibility that Connie's conscious visual experience, though it plays the manifest role in question, is not the kind of state that is responsible for filling this visual discriminatory (regulative, etc.) role in normal members of her species. So we cannot fix up a manifest role functionalism by having it hold that what we mean by saying Connie has a conscious visual experience Belinda lacks is that, whereas Connie is in a state that in normal members of her species plays the manifest functional role her blursight shares with Belinda's blindsight, Belinda is not in the type of state that in normal members of her species plays that role. For this would rule out possibilities we have no reason to rule out, if we do not deem Belinda and Connie as originally described impossible. What about the kinds of manifest roles we can plausibly maintain Belinda's state of blindseeing could *not* play, which Connie's visual experience could? Would functionalism tell us that what we mean by saying that Belinda would not consciously see the light on her left is that she would not be in the state that, in her population, enables one to learn in a certain way what 'light' or 'visual sensing' means, or to think one consciously sees? With or without the qualifying phrase "in her population"—this would, as we have seen, either make the alleged difference in learning undisplayable, and hence nonexistent, or render the distinction of which one is supposed to be giving an account (between blindsight and conscious sight) altogether bogus. Either way, the functionalist thesis is untenable.

But mightn't there be some overlooked ineradicable difference in manifest roles that blindsight and conscious sight could play that does not run up against this problem? Frank Jackson's "knowledge argument" has us consider the knowledge a neuroscientific expert on color vision who had never seen colors herself would inevitably lack, in her ignorance of (for example) what it is like to see red. It has sometimes been said in defense of functionalism that the knowledge such a person would be missing is purely a kind of *know-how* or *ability*: the ability to recognize and imagine red. Inspired by this, one might propose: all we mean by saying Belinda would lack conscious vision that Connie had is that Belinda's left-field visual capacity would not include the ability to recognize patches of light, or enable her to visualize them. But if by saying she cannot recognize them, we mean that she cannot spontaneously visually discriminate them, this is clearly wrong. And if we require more for recognition, namely, a sensory experience that has the *phenomenal character* of that which enables one to classify or judge that what one perceives is of a certain type, then we trivialize the thesis: what Belinda lacks in lacking left-field conscious visual experience is the ability to have conscious visual experience of a certain sort. Similarly, if by saying her left-field visual capacity would not enable her to visualize light patches or flashes we mean something like: it would not enable her to have experience with a phenomenal character like that of conscious visual experience, though of a sort subject to voluntary control, and uncaused by external light stimuli—and (perhaps typically) less "forceful and vivacious"—then again we introduce a trivializing circularity. Then the claim is that when we say she lacks conscious visual experience, part of what we mean is that she lacks a state that can enable her to have a second sort of state, such that the two are similar in a way that would entail that the first was a conscious experience. So, then, functionalism tells us that to say she lacks left-field conscious visual experience means, in part, that she lacks a certain kind of conscious experience. This is true enough, but it makes the functionalist account of visual consciousness trivial and viciously circular.

On the other hand, we could try to understand visualization in a way that dispenses with the requirement that it be like vision in *phenomenal character*, and think of its defining relation to vision by conceiving of the latter in ways that could apply where phenomenally conscious vision is lacking, as in blindsight, as we would if we said it is enough to be visualization if it shares with vision a maplike form of representation of certain classes of features. But then there will be no evident reason to think the capacity for "visualization," so understood, is *not* one that any blindsight could afford. Assuming (as this does) there could be mental representation of a nonphenomenal but in some sense "visual, imagistic" sort, why *couldn't* blindsight (like Belinda's) enable her to use it somehow? Thus, an attempt to save manifest functionalism with the claim that it is conceptually impossible for Belinda's blindsight to play the role Connie's visual experience would with regard to recognition and imagination, will, depending on how we interpret these terms, make it either trivial or unwarranted.

It will not save manifest functionalism from these problems, if we take it to be a metaphysical, and not a conceptual, doctrine—one that would say something like: (The property of) being a conscious visual experience is (the property of) being a state that fills a certain manifest functional role. Again, either the manifest role Connie's conscious vision plays would be played by Belinda's blindsight, or, where the roles would differ, this offers no basis for making functionalism acceptable (since we do not want to say, e.g., that being a conscious visual experience of a grayish patch of light differs from being the kind of visual sensing some blindsighter would enjoy, *only* in that something with the former property makes one think it has that property).

One might maintain that I have still overlooked some crucial manifest functional role that clearly could not possibly be played by a Belinda-like blindsight. But to be convincing, this rebuttal needs to offer us some manifest dispositional feature Connie would have but Belinda could not, not covered by the considerations I have raised, and I can only say that I am unaware of a likely contender. One might, for instance, try looking to something like Dretske's (1995) theory for a candidate. The suggestion would be that having conscious sensory experience consists in having an internal state that naturally functions to indicate certain things in one's environment—the function is natural, the story goes, because it was selected by evolution. But it is unclear what natural function of indication we are to suppose a blind-sighter like Belinda would have to lack, that Connie would not. Both subjects would, I suppose, on a theory like this, have internal states whose function it is to indicate the presence of light on their left. And if both are creatures of evolution, I see no reason to suppose they would not both be carrying out their *natural* functions in this regard. Both Belinda's blindsight and Connie's vision would be, we may suppose, abnormal or "unnatural" in some ways—but in neither case would the natural capacity to indicate light in their left fields be broken.

My complaint about functionalism here is not entirely novel, but I wish to distinguish it from others. My point is not that certain kinds of conscious experience could be completely absent, without this affecting in *any* way one's dispositions to have other kinds of mental states and behavior. And I have not claimed that the total way an experience with a certain phenomenal character affects one's dispositions to other mental states and behavior might just as well belong to an experience with a quite different phenomenal character. My argument does not, like those from "absent qualia" or "inverted spectra," invite us to contemplate a situation in which two persons are totally "functionally equivalent," but differ in the phenomenal character of their experience. My argument, roughly, is this. Hold constant all the manifest functional likenesses we cannot reasonably deny could obtain between subjects, one of whom had a given kind of conscious experience, the other of whom lacked it, without denying the reality of consciousness. Then there will be *experiential* differences such that the only *manifest functional* differences I can discover that we may plausibly think still cling ineliminably to them, are ones of which we cannot rightly say: that's all we mean by (or that's all there is to) the experiential difference. Thus I can find no acceptable interpretation of a manifest functionalist approach to mind that does not lead to the exclusion of phenomenal consciousness from consideration. If you can find none, and if you do not want to deny that we have phenomenally conscious experience, then you cannot find manifest functionalism an acceptable account of the minds we have.

4.9 Is Consciousness a Hidden Feature?

One may try to hold onto a form of functionalism in the face of this, by shifting from manifest functions to *hidden* ones—maintaining that the functional role filled by conscious sight that no blindsight could possibly fill is to be specified relative to hidden features of inputs, outputs, and mediating states, and that the difference between having and lacking conscious visual experience lies entirely in that between having and lacking a state playing the role so specified. This might seem odd—is it not clear that phenomenal features, and consciousness in general, are manifest features, and that our warrant for believing in their occurrence does not require us to engage in observation of what is hidden beneath our skins? How could such features be both manifest and hidden?

This isn't impossible. One and the same feature can be both manifest (relative to one way of describing or conceiving of it) and hidden (relative to another). Without internal examination, I can have warrant for believing that I have some (probably complex) feature, my possession of which explains my runny nose, headache, and fatigue. But there is another way of describing or conceiving of that very feature, needed to be able to give the explanation in question (in terms of viral infection). And the warrant for attributing such features described and conceived of in *that* way *would* require some such examination. Now, the criticisms of the last section would warn us off directly appropriating this model for explaining how phenomenal features could be both manifest and hidden; that is, they count against the suggestion that we conceive of its looking to us as if there is some green on the left simply as that feature our possession of which accounts for certain manifest phenomena—verbal utterances, finger-pointing, etc. For we said that it would be a mistake to suppose all we had in mind when we spoke of an absence of such phenomenally conscious experience was the lack of a kind of state that enables us to have a certain manifest discriminatory (or some other) talent—for making certain (silent or noisy) utterances, pointing fingers, and so on. That would not account for how we can conceive of Belinda and Connie differently. But perhaps some other story can be told to make sense of how, relative to our ordinary (and first-person) concepts of phenomenal features, they are manifest, while relative to some (yet to be discovered) theoretical conception of them, they can be hidden. And perhaps that theoretical conception of them will reveal them to be features of being such as to play this or that hidden function.

Putnam's erstwhile (1960, 1965) functionalist theorizing would illustrate a move of this kind. Abandoning any claim to provide a functionalist account of our *concepts* of the mental, he proposed that the nature of the mental (e.g., the nature of pain) will be found in a scientific theory specifying the functional role of our internal states relative to inputs, outputs, and one another, where the inputs at least are such as would be hidden from ordinary inspection. But this sort of maneuver would not save a functionalist theory of mind from the problem of consciousness neglect. For even actual blindsight subjects can have hidden inputs in common with consciously sighted subjects—since the cause of their deficit is way back in the visual cortex. So if we do not object to the metaphysical possibility of Belinda and Connie as previously described, we will not have grounds for saying it is metaphysically impossible that they should be alike in respect of hidden inputs (such as patterns of activity at the retinal level). And something similar goes for hidden outputs. If we have no objection to the possibility of our subjects' engaging in equally fine (or crude) spontaneous visual discriminations, we will have no objection to the possibility of their being correspondingly similar in respect of hidden outputs (such as the volleys of efferent neural impulses to their motoneurons).

So "hidden-function functionalists" (as we might call them) will need to suppose the as-yet-undiscovered hidden role that *is* phenomenal consciousness involves features of internal states "farther in," presumably states conceived of as "mediators" rather than as inputs or outputs to the system. Perhaps this is what Loar (1990) has in mind by speaking of phenomenal features as "physical-functional" features; Lycan (1990) seems to be after something similar. The thesis that consciousness is a hidden functional feature of some such sort does not, by the test I have proposed, inevitably commit one to consciousness neglect. However, I do think such theories face formidable challenges that should make us wary of them, among which I will mention three.

First, it is unclear why, if we are now to take something so deeply hidden to be essential to the possession of phenomenal consciousness of various forms, and we no longer offer a functionalist account of our *concepts* of phenomenal features, we should suppose that these features are, in any substantive sense, functional roles. Why not identify the conscious visual experience of a certain shade of green, say, with some hidden feature of the brain, but *without* claiming this feature is that of playing a certain role vis-à-vis certain types of input, output, and (hidden) internal states? Hidden-function functionalism would seem to be no less vulnerable to the charge of unduly ("chauvinistically") restricting just what kinds of insides a genuinely mental being could possibly have, than would be the view that types of conscious experience are identical with (hidden) physical (but not functional-role) types.

Second, either variety of physicalism faces the challenge posed by Chalmers's (1996) argument, centering on the claim that it is logically possible that there be creatures who are complete physical duplicates of ourselves, but whose existence is completely devoid of phenomenally conscious experience. This would be to say, it is *not* strictly impossible that something have all our physical (or physical-functional) features, while lacking our phenomenal ones. Though the possibility of such "zombies" goes well beyond what I have asked you to contemplate in connection with blindsight, acceptance of the reflections I have invited may well leave you thinking that nothing ultimately rules out the possibility of a world such as Chalmers describes.

Third, there seems to me to be a problem with justifying any attempt to flesh out the proposed sort of hidden physicalist identification (functionalist or otherwise) into a more substantial theory. How do we decide *which* hidden features are, as a matter of *metaphysical* necessity, phenomenal features? Evidence that various forms of conscious experience will not occur *in us*, if certain hidden kinds of brain activity do not take place, and that such experience will occur *in us* if those kinds of activity do, presumably would not sufficiently justify the conclusion that *in no possible world* might some being lack brain activity of just that sort, but talk noiselessly to itself, feel an itch, or see orange. We might then be inclined to settle the question of the physical absolute *sine qua non* of consciousness with maximal liberality. But it is unclear how we are to tell that we have not at some point overshot the mark in saying what is sufficient for consciousness, so as to include among the types of beings who allegedly *must* have phenomenally visual experience of, say, Connie's amblyopic sort, some in whom the relevant visual capacity—it is (metaphysically) possible—might be only a form of blindsight. We may say that there is a right answer to the question of how to state the hidden conditions of consciousness in a way that ranges over all possible worlds, and is neither too liberal nor too restrictive. But if God only knows what that answer is, and we have no idea of how to justify a claim to have found it ourselves, this does not help us much to understand the nature of consciousness.

So, while saying that consciousness is a hidden feature of our brains would not, by my standards, prevent us from recognizing the reality of phenomenal consciousness, we have, as I see it, no business saying this, if we have no satisfactory answer to the difficulties I have just named. And I do not have one. However, if you do, I would only ask that you recognize the need to say that the *hidden* feature you tell us is consciousness, and the *manifest* feature identifiable via the first-person method I have prescribed, are one and the same. Otherwise it will not be clear that you are talking about phenomenal consciousness.

4.10 SUMMARY

In this chapter my aim has been to uncover certain ways of thinking that can prevent our theories—despite the considerable intelligence and ingenuity that have gone into them—from taking phenomenal consciousness into account. To understand how sophisticated attempts to theorize about our minds can conceal perhaps their most important aspect, it is crucial first to develop a reasonably firm sense of what I mean by 'phenomenal consciousness.' I have explained that by this I mean, that feature we know with first-person warrant to be shared by silent speech, other imagery, and sensory experience, whose occurrence one altogether denies, if one maintains that certain absences of experience in certain circumstances are strictly impossible—these kinds of absences and circumstances being such as were described in my blindsight thought-experiment.

With this conception in hand, we can test whether a discussion of mind neglects consciousness by posing the following question. If we confine ourselves to the use of concepts employed or features attributed in it, does this allow us some reasonable way of leaving open the possibility of such forms of blindsight? I have argued that, by this test, certain theoretical approaches to the mind generally, and (ostensibly) to consciousness in particular, do neglect consciousness. I find that, far from clarifying what we mean when we contrast conscious vision with its lack in hypothetical cases, or what feature we attribute to ourselves and contemplate missing in such situations, such theories would offer us no acceptable alternative to the conclusion that there is nothing of a relevant sort that could allow for such absences—and so there is no phenomenal consciousness. If we try to interpret them in a way that would not lead to a denial of the relevant blindsight possibilities, we find that they would have us rule out closely related possibilities we evidently lack reason for treating differently. Or else they would lead to various false-hoods and self-undermining absurdities. For it is not true (for instance) that we continually and spontaneously attribute to our visual experience some "visual quality" such as our hypothetical blindsighters would enjoy. And, it would render absurd the difference between blindsight and conscious sight we want to recognize, to say that it would consist only in the latter's making one think one *consciously* sees—while an attempt to account for their differ-ence purely in terms of a difference in their potential contribution to the acquisition of concepts is ultimately self-defeating. And finally, would-be accounts of consciousness would effectively abandon any claim to that title, if we saved them from criticism either by trivializing their content, or by taking them to tell us only that certain visual abilities (or certain kinds of access to visual information) are found wherever conscious vision is.

My point of departure on this tour was Dennett's remarkable denial of a distinction between visual seeming and judging—a denial apparently at odds with a tolerance for the possibility of spontaneous blindsight, and hence incompatible with a recognition of consciousness. I found Dennett's apparent willingness elsewhere to admit this possibility puzzling, but lo-cated some clue to his position in his view that a lack of conscious vision is nothing but *some* missing talent or other, of the sort actual blindsighters lack—"discriminatory, regulative, evaluative, etc." I decided to pursue this vague thesis, suspecting I would find in it not a way of removing the initial appearance of neglect involved in the repudiation of "real seeming," but a rich source of further suggestions for ways in which to conceive of "con-sciousness" so as to suppress recognition of the genuine article. I was not disappointed, and I found ways of giving substance to Dennett's contention in the writing of other authors: Rosenthal's efforts to see consciousness as some sort of higher-order mentalness; kindred views based on the notion of consciousness as self-representation; proposed information-processing ac-counts of consciousness; and certain functionalist accounts of the nature of mind. My conclusion is that if one recognizes no "consciousness" but what such theories admit, one will neglect phenomenal consciousness.

I find that too often, attempts to theorize about consciousness have been unsatisfying, not only because they leave out phenomenal consciousness, but also because they are less than forthright about doing so. Either they pass it over in silence, or they leave the impression that, if they deny or decline to recognize something, it is only some curious, stubborn bit of philosophical detritus, attributable probably to Descartes' baneful influence—a "Cartesian intuition" about ourselves, or a conviction that the mind is some "ghostly" or "spooky" place in which "self-luminous" mental objects disport themselves. Part of what I have tried to do is to clarify what we can mean by 'conscious' in a way that does not depend on any such notions and the evasions they inspire. If we have no conscious experience, it is not Descartes' fault that we think we do. And if we need theorists to show us the error of our ways, they have not done their job if they try only to embarrass us with epithets.

But if I am right, and consciousness has been intellectually neglected by many talented and subtle thinkers, shouldn't this seem strangely puzzling? How could something so ordinary and ubiquitous in our lives be ignored? My claim will seem perhaps a little less audacious, if I say that I do not claim that those I criticize do not in any sense heed their own experience, both when they theorize about it, and in the course of otherwise living their lives. My point is just that we are sometimes attracted to ways of thinking that keep us from explicitly acknowledging, in philosophical and psychological theories, that it is conscious and has phenomenal character.

Now, some may think, faced with such theories, that the fact that they "leave something out"—what it's like for us to feel pain, the way colors look to us, how a trumpet sounds to us—is obvious. But it is surely fair to ask here for much more than an assertion of obviousness. And when we try to provide this, we find ourselves trying to navigate the labyrinth of consciousness neglect we have just partly explored. Its intricacy helps account, I suppose, for how the problem I've discussed can go unacknowledged, but I do not think this fully explains how consciousness can be both so ordinary and so elusive. One aspect of the explanation lies, I suspect, in the refusal of some to take seriously the kind of first-person approach that has made the neglect evident to us. In articulating and defending this approach, I have perhaps implicitly indicated—and rebutted—some of the philosophical assumptions that can help us conceal consciousness from ourselves. But I do not imagine that this has addressed by any means all that buttresses the theoretical attitude I have descried, all that may be called on to furnish argument that there has really been no *neglect* here at all. For it will perhaps be said we have good reason to think there just is nothing of the sort I claim to point out, to which we might have *paid attention*. In the next chapter, I address some reasons I think would likely be offered in defense of that claim.

Preventing Neglect

5.1 SEEKING RATIONALES FOR NEGLECT

Consciousness, I have argued, tends to get lost in certain writings one might have presumed were devoted to it. I hope you are willing to acknowledge you have experience that is conscious in this sense others have slighted—or, as I might now say more simply, without too much risk of misunderstanding: I hope you will admit that you are conscious. But if you will not, I hope I have at least aroused some desire to make plain this refusal, and the reasons for it, without reliance on the vague insinuations of "anti-Cartesian" rhetoric.

Some will undoubtedly want to take up this challenge. However, the writers I have mentioned do not discuss precisely the way of introducing the notion of consciousness I have employed. So I will have to try to anticipate potential strategies of rebuttal. I will try to imagine what might be said on behalf of what I call consciousness neglect, what reasons might be given for thinking there just is no feature, known with first-person warrant to be shared by the examples I have offered, that leaves open the possibility of the various forms of blindsight I have discussed. By searching out and arguing against rationales for consciousness neglect, I want to identify and remove some of its probable philosophical sources.

5.2 DOES NEUROSCIENCE SAY WE ARE NOT CONSCIOUS?

Our confidence that we are conscious may well seem unassailable. But perhaps this may be undermined by an attack on the notion that these diverse occurrences I have offered as paradigm cases of phenomenal consciousness—silent speech, imagery generally, sense-perception in various modalities—really exhibit a shared feature. My conviction that they do, one might suggest, merely reflects ignorance of the brain. Once we find out more about this, we will see that we are not (in my sense) conscious after all, for neuroscience will show us that we were mistaken in the way we grouped certain events together, calling them all 'conscious'; it will explode such "folk psychological" categories. Perhaps, in fact, we already know enough about the brain to anticipate this eventuality.

Patricia Churchland's (1988) discussion of consciousness suggests just such a line of argument. She observes that we are inclined to group under the term 'conscious' a rather heterogeneous collection. But, she invites us to suppose, perhaps there really is no feature these share on which to pin this term. Consider our use of the term 'fire.' It once would have been said, and accepted as a matter of common sense, that fireflies, the sun, and burning wood are all instances of fire. But now science has shown us this is a mistake. Perhaps similarly, science—in particular, neuroscience—will show us that we were mistaken in saying that these heterogeneous states to which I have made reference share the feature of being conscious. Then, it seems, we will have found that we do not have experience conscious in the sense explicated by reference to these paradigms, after all. Now—so the argument goes—it is much more likely than not that science will show us precisely this. Why? Because it is highly improbable that a sophisticated neuroscience will permit us to theoretically reduce sentences in which 'conscious,' with something like its current extension, figures, to sentences of the neuroscientific theory; the terms proper to this theory just won't classify things together in this way. But now, if "folk psychological" terms like 'conscious' cannot be matched, via intertheoretic reduction, with the terms of neuroscientific theory, then we should conclude that their extension is, after all, quite empty. Therefore, we do not have any conscious experience.

I won't spend a lot of time with this sort of strategy for vindicating consciousness neglect, since much of my answer is implicit already in my discussion of eliminative materialism in Chapter 2. There I said that we have no good reason for thinking that our warrant for applying mental predicates to ourselves generally depends on our ability to justify the faith that we will find a tight nomological match between these and those predicates which, through observing and theorizing about our brains, we discover apply to them. For no adequate argument has been given for holding that our warrant for using lay psychological terms should be assessed by regimenting them into a theory of what is described in wholly *other* terms, and then asking whether such a theory explains what is so described better than any rival. Thus I do not believe we face the eliminativist's dilemma of either showing how we can theoretically reduce the former to the latter, or else rejecting their use altogether. And I would apply this same point to 'conscious,' and whatever terms we use for speaking of the indefinitely vast variety of phenomenal features.

But setting this reduction issue aside, one still might think something could be done with the analogy Churchland would have us draw between 'consciousness' and 'fire.' Let's grant that we did alter what we took to be the extension of 'fire' under pressure from scientific theorizing. Mightn't the same thing happen with 'conscious'? It seems to me that if we try to follow through this analogy, it fails to motivate any substantive doubts about consciousness. The idea, presumably, is that we will find the neurophysiology of the kinds of states I want to call 'conscious' so diverse—just as what explains the light and heat of fireflies, the sun, and burning wood turned out to be so diverse—that we will not want to say they are all "conscious," just as we do not say the fireflies, the sun, and the wood are all "on fire." But now, if this analogy is to lead to the conclusion that silent speech, other imagery, and sense-perception do not share the feature of being conscious, we need to suppose analogously that when we wised up about fire, we came to believe fireflies, the sun, and wood did not share some feature, which we formerly thought they did. And what will that be? Presumably, it will have to be something like a shared (perhaps complex) feature in terms of which light and heat coming from each can be explained. But then, what is the analogue of this supposed to be, in the case of conscious experience? We will need to say that we will find that there is no shared feature of imagery and perception in terms of which . . . something or other . . . can be explained. But how do we fill in this gap? We cannot fill it with something like "the fact that they're all conscious"; this would be to admit there is a shared feature, and then to suppose it will be neurophysiologically inexplicable. Perhaps someone will propose that there are effects (analogues of light and heat) that typically result from (what we consider) phenomenally conscious experience (of whatever sort), but that we will find radically different neurophysiological explanations of these shared effects. It is not at all clear why we should suppose we have good evidence that there will be no unitary neurophysiological explanation to be had of the shared effects of conscious experiences. But even if this can be made plausible, it would still remain unclear why it would follow that there are no instances of consciousness. When we apply a certain predicate to a range of things typically involved in some roughly identified kinds of effect, it may turn out that there is no uniform scientific explanation of the occurrence of these effects in all the various cases. But would that necessarily show that the statements in which we applied a predicate of this sort were false? I suppose a reasonable case could be made that ". . . is a tree" is a predicate of this sort. If neurophilosophy shows us there are no episodes of consciousness, would "botanophilosophy" show us that there are no trees? Unless one accepts some general "reduction or death" ultimatum, I see no reason to assume that there must be a unified scientific theory of the effects typical to every class of things to which we can legitimately apply a common term.

Thus it would be misguided to base a reluctance to affirm that one is conscious on some fear that one will be refuted by brain science. Nothing we have reason to anticipate will be discovered through observing and theorizing about our brains justifies our denying or refusing to recognize that we have a large and fascinating variety of conscious experiences, and that we have a distinctively first-person knowledge of this. This is not to say that we should not try to find out all that we can about conscious experience and its forms by studying our brains. Nor would I deny that such study may contribute significantly and legitimately to reshaping and enriching the distinctions and assumptions we apply to our experience. But I see no reason to think neuroscience counsels us to say we are not conscious in the sense I have explained, nor does it discredit our claims to first-person knowledge of conscious experience, and ask us to dismiss or disdain these, and just look at our brains. We can, I think, pursue neuroscientific studies while also respecting and cultivating first-person knowledge of our experience. In my view, it is important that we do both, since much of the interest in what we find from studying the brain ultimately lies in what it has to tell us about forms of conscious experience of which we have first-person knowledge.

5.3 IS BELINDA A METAPHYSICAL MISTAKE?

In explaining what I mean by 'conscious' I have said that one would deny that we are conscious in this sense, if one denied that spontaneous, amblyopic, reflective blindsight is strictly possible. So one obvious strategy for defending oneself against the charge that one has neglected consciousness would be to argue for this denial of possibility. "Since one or more of the forms of blindsight with reference to which you have identified phenomenal consciousness are strictly impossible, there is no phenomenal consciousness, hence nothing to neglect."

But how might one go about defending this claim of impossibility? I suppose one might say that my descriptions of the hypothetical blindsighter simply seemed unintelligible on the face of it. One might say to me: "I made a sincere effort to consider my own experience, and the hypothetical deficits in visual consciousness you described, adopting the first-person approach you recommended, but I just can't make any sense out of these descriptions. It just doesn't seem consistent or coherent to say Belinda spontaneously judges that there was a patch of light, darker or lighter, on her left, on account of visual stimulation by it, but it didn't look to her as if there was one there. You may as well have asked me to conceive of a round square or a male vixen." I have now done all I intend to do by way of making the situations I described seem intelligible. If they do not seem intelligible to you, whether because they appear inconsistent or for some other reason, I will simply have to admit that I have not convinced you. But there will be many of us, I trust, to whom the blindsight scenarios do seem intelligible. So the question is whether, given this, we can find reason for thinking they are strictly impossible. I assume that, if these scenarios at least seemed intelligible, coherent, and consistent to you, then you would not have warrant for adopting the belief that they are, after all, strictly impossible, unless you have found or have been given some reason for reaching this conclusion. *Is* there any good reason for thinking Belinda-like blindsight is strictly impossible?

These days, in philosophy, much is made of the notion of metaphysical possibility, and we have been warned off holding that just because a certain description of a situation seems intelligible and consistent to us (and because it thus seems possible to us that such a situation obtain), it does not follow that it *is* possible in the metaphysical sense: it does not follow that in some possible world, that description holds true. So, for example, we are told that it may seem possible to us that water is not H_2O, but really this is *not* possible. Now, perhaps one will suggest that we are liable to some similar modal error or illusion regarding consciousness. And one might argue that this accounts for our failure to acknowledge, as we should, that there is no possible world in which someone could (for example) spontaneously think that she visually judged this or that, about what she did not consciously see, or that her language or control or planning systems could have access to visual information about things on her left without their looking any way to her. Conscious vision just is a talent for spontaneous visual judgment (or access of such-and-such operations to visual information, etc.), the way water just is H_2O.

Thus I imagine someone might draw an analogy between the case of consciousness and the case of water, and appeal to certain views distinguishing merely apparent and real possibility in the latter case, to argue that, while Belinda-like blindsight may not seem impossible to us—indeed, it may seem *possible* to us—really, metaphysically, it is not possible. But now, exactly how might this argument go? First, let's be clear about what is claimed regarding water. It is admitted that it might *seem* possible to us that water is not H_2O. But we should not believe that it *is* possible that water is not H_2O. It is a necessary truth that water is H_2O; the property of being water is none other than the property of being H_2O. It may seem possible to us that they are distinct, because our ordinary *notion* or *concept* of water is distinct from the scientific concept of H_2O. And our ordinary notion or concept of water is something like our usual nonprofessional means of identifying instances of the property of being water, that is, its appearing certain ways under the sorts of conditions in which we are ordinarily concerned with water—when we see it in oceans, lakes, rivers; when we drink it, clean with it, cook with it, swim in it. So, then, the reason it seems possible to us that water might not be H_2O, is that we might identify something by the means we ordinarily have for identifying something as water, even though it is *not* H_2O, but has some *other* chemical structure ("XYZ"). This does not show that it is possible that water is not H_2O, but only perhaps that it is possible that we might have evidence for denying that water is H_2O. Or perhaps we should say it shows only that the denial that water is H_2O may be consistent with what we happen to know about water at a given time, or consistent with what we happen to have warrant for believing about water. In one or another of these ways, we might say it is "epistemically possible" that water not be H_2O, but it is not "metaphysically possible."

So much for water—now, how might we tell a similar story in the case of consciousness? The account, I take it, would go something like this. Sure, it *seems* to us possible that Connie and Belinda exhibit equivalent talents for visual discrimination as earlier described, even though the former consciously sees where the latter does not, because our concept of visual consciousness is not the same as our notion of the visual discriminatory talent (or higher-order mentalness, or information access) that visual consciousness is. For our concept of consciousness is our means of identifying instances of consciousness. And this way of identifying occurrences of consciousness might not coincide with instances of the property of consciousness. Though we may think we are conceiving of a situation in which Connie has, but Belinda lacks, conscious vision, the most we can really conceive of is a situation in which Connie identifies in our ordinary first-person way instances of the same property that constitutes both her and Belinda's having conscious visual experience, while Belinda, for some reason, fails or is unable to judge that her experience is conscious in this way. All that really could be missing in Belinda's case is the way of judging her experience is conscious, which we and Connie employ—our ordinary concept of consciousness—*not* consciousness (the property) itself. We confuse the genuine possibility that this way of identifying consciousness is absent, with the spurious possibility that consciousness is absent. For that reason, it seems to us that Belinda may lack conscious vision, and that is why she does not seem impossible to us. But she is impossible.

Here we have some remarks about water and necessity, and an analogy with the case of consciousness that includes the claim that Belinda-like blindsight is impossible. But can we find in this a reason for believing this denial of possibility? First, let's be clear about just where the controversy lies. If Belinda seems possible to us, we can grant that our concept of visual consciousness differs from our concept of the collection of visual talents we attributed to Belinda. And we can allow that, in considering Belinda's situation, we supposed that there was someone with those talents, who was indeed missing some aspect of "the ordinary first-person way of identifying conscious visual experience" that someone with Connie-like left-field visual experience would have: in some sense, Connie identifies her left-field conscious experience in a way that Belinda does not use in thinking of her left-field visual capacities or their exercise. So far, no controversy. But we were also supposing that Belinda lacked conscious visual experience of anything to her left. Now we are imagining someone makes the following assertion: "When *that* is added, we have something that only seems, but isn't really, possible. What's really possible is (a) that someone with the discriminatory powers attributed to Belinda might have conscious visual experience, but fail in some way to think she had it. What's not possible is (b) that someone might have those discriminatory powers, and not have conscious visual experience of anything on her left. If (b) seems possible to you, you're only misdescribing or misreporting (a)." The controversy is, whether we have any reason to accept that assertion.

Now this should be clear: merely to assert the view in quotes is not to offer any reason for us to adopt the denial of possibility included in it. In particular, it does not give us any reason to deny that possibility, if someone merely offers a "rephrasal" or "restatement" of our "modal intuitions" here—that is, what is reported by saying, "It seems possible to me there could be someone with Belinda's visual discriminatory powers who lacked a certain visual experience." One may *claim* that reporting one's modal intuitions in this way would put them at odds with genuine metaphysical possibility, so that one's attitudes can be brought into line with this, only if one agrees to *redescribe* what possible visual subject one is contemplating, in a fashion consistent with the assumption that she does have conscious visual experience of what is in her left field. But unless we are given a reason for thinking our claims about what we are conceiving of, or about what seems possible to us, need such rephrasal, we will have no reason for thinking that Belinda-style blindsight is strictly impossible.

The question, then, is whether the analogy with water gives us any reason for thinking this. Let's grant that 'water' is to be interpreted so as to make the claim, "It is impossible that some water is not H_2O," come out true. Now, if we accept the analogy, we will accept an analogous interpretation of 'conscious'—one according to which it is impossible that someone have Belinda's talents, but lack conscious left-field vision. So the analogy exhibits a proposed understanding of 'conscious' different from the one I am urging. But while we may, I suppose, accept such an interpretation of 'conscious' if we choose, *must* we? The suggested analogy seems to leave us with a choice: either (a) accept the analogy, and with it an interpretation of 'conscious' that rules out the earlier discussed forms of blindsight; or else (b) reject the analogy and stick with an interpretation of 'conscious' that leaves open this possibility. But merely by making the analogy, one does not offer us any reason for thinking that choice (b) is not available; one simply manifests one's choice of (a). So far, then, we have found no reason to think Belinda is impossible, just an alternative way of interpreting 'conscious' that rules out her possibility.

Now, maybe someone will say that we do have a reason to think that the interpretation of 'conscious' that opts out of the analogy is simply unavailable, and that is this: the sort of interpretation of 'water' that would be like that I claim to give to 'conscious' is not available. Something like (b) is just not an option for 'water.' And (the suggestion runs), if it is not available for 'water,' then it is not available for 'conscious.' However, an immediate problem with this maneuver is that the initial premise is false. For consider what would constitute an alternative interpretation of 'water,' that differed from that given a moment ago in the way my interpretation of 'conscious' would differ from that suggested by the water/consciousness analogy. Presumably, this would be a way of understanding 'water' such that it applied to the stuff that comes out of the tap, the stuff found in lakes, rivers, and seas, which we drink, and use to clean and cook, *and* which makes the claim, "It is possible that not all water is H_2O," come out *true*. Is such an interpretation of 'water' available? Yes, it is. We may well grant that our actual use of the term 'water' is such that, on a distant Earth-like planet, something that behaved on a macro-scale and to ordinary appearances as does our H_2O, despite its quite different chemical structure, could not possibly be water. Still, we easily *could* interpret 'water' to apply to whatever behaved on a macro-scale, to ordinary appearances, and for practical purposes, as does H_2O, regardless of whether it had that microstructure. Such a use of the term is available for us to stipulate if we wish. And once we adopted it, we could with full justification state many truths employing that term understood in that way. It would be true, in this sense of 'water,' that hot coffee is made with water, I bathed in water last night, not much water has fallen on West Texas this year, and so on.

Thus, even if we thought it would cast doubt on the availability of my way of understanding 'conscious' if an analogous interpretation of 'water' were unavailable, this would give us no argument against saying we are conscious in my sense. For to the extent that we can say what the appropriately analogous interpretation would need to look like, it seems that it *is* available.

There is, however, a certain disanalogy between the two cases worth noting. One might reformulate the point I have just made by saying that we can interpret 'water' so that having what we might call an adequately "watery" appearance in ordinary circumstances in which we use water is sufficient for something to be water (regardless of whether it is H_2O). However, there is nothing we can say stands to those features of experience from which I want to distinguish consciousness (being a discriminatory state, a mental state targeted by a higher-order thought, etc.) just as an adequately watery appearance stands to the property of being H_2O. There is no "appearance" of my visual experience, whereby I judge that it is, for example, a discriminatory state. If some grass looks green to me, we may say it appears some way to me. But its looking this way—its appearing this way—is not itself something that also appears to me. There is no sense in which the grass appears to me, in which my visual experience also appears to me. (Or so I shall argue, in the next chapter). Therefore, when we conceive of being spontaneous, reflective blindsighters of the sort I have described, we should not say what we are supposing is that our visual experience fails to appear to us, we should not say that what we suppose missing is the "appearance of conscious visual experience" (for there is no such thing), but rather simply conscious visual experience itself.

Once we recognize this point, we come upon a new problem for someone who denies the possibility of the forms of blindsight I have described. It becomes very difficult to see how that person can explain, in a manner that would help make the case for denying their possibility, why it seems possible to some that one could possess these forms of blindsight. In the water example, we are offered an account of why what it is said is not possible (i.e., that some water is not H_2O) nonetheless *seems* possible, which is supposed to help support the claim that this is not possible. The account is that it seems possible to us because we confuse (or fail to distinguish) the superficial appearances whereby we judge that something is water with the property of being water, and so mistakenly think of a situation in which some non-H_2O has that appearance, for one in which some non-H_2O is *water*. But a similar account does not seem available in the consciousness case. For one cannot say that we are confusing the "superficial appearance" of conscious experience with the property of consciousness (its "real essence"), as one would perhaps say we might confuse the superficial appearance of water with the property of being water. Experience has no appearance, "superficial" or otherwise, in the relevant sense.

The challenge here is really more general than that of how to explain why Belinda seems possible to some. For suppose I took the following attitude: "I find the description of Belinda intelligible and free of inconsistencies, but I'm not sure this is enough for me to commit myself to the belief that she is, as described, possible in some strict sense (metaphysical or logical), so I hold back from saying she seems possible to me. But I will say this: she doesn't seem strictly impossible to me." The denier of Belinda's possibility would still have a problem of how to explain my failure to grasp the necessity that someone of Belinda's talents have the sort of visual experience we attributed to Connie—why it does not seem impossible to me that Belinda could exercise these talents without its looking to her as if there is a blurry patch of light on her left—and how to explain this in a way that helps make the case for the denial of possibility. My concern here is not just that there is no reasonable account available that establishes the truth of this denial— though that does seems true to me; the difficulty is in even finding a credible account that the deniers of Belinda's possibility can maintain contributes to their case.

Suppose we take as our model the type of account suggested in other cases, where some will say it seems possible to them that some feature F may occur without G, even though (it is said) any occurrence of F is an occurrence of G, by metaphysical necessity. It might seem possible to us that mean molecular motion may vary without any variation in something's heat—or without its having any heat at all (or, at any rate, it may not seem impossible to us). But (so the story goes) that is only because our concept of heat—our ordinary understanding of 'heat'—is that of something that can produce a certain kind of *feeling* (a "heat sensation"), and implicitly (but falsely) we suppose that being able to make us feel that way is necessary to something's having heat. So when we consider a hypothetical situation in which something has whatever mean molecular motion you like without feeling hot to us (maybe it would make us feel some other way entirely), we are misled into thinking it possible that heat itself has fled, while molecular motion stays (or at any rate, we are led into not thinking it is impossible). To apply this to the case of visual experience, we would say that it seems possible to us (or does not seem impossible to us) that someone might have the kind of visual capacities we attributed to our blindsighter in Chapter 3—call this "F"—without having conscious visual experience of her left field (without having G). And this is to be explained as follows. There is some feature H, which we (implicitly, mistakenly) presume is essential to the occurrence of G, and then, considering a situation in which F occurs without H, we are liable to think that it is possible that F may occur without G (conscious visual experience). Or, at any rate, we are liable not to find this impossible. To fill out this story, one needs a credible candidate for H. But can such a candidate be found? What H can those who deny the possibility of Belinda defensibly say we have supposed her to lack, which we (mistakenly, they say) deem essential to having that experience?

I assume they do not want to say here something like: "the superficial appearance visual experience presents to the person that has it"—for again I assume that visual appearance does not itself *appear* any way at all—unless, by saying experience "appears" some way to the person who has it, we mean that he or she *thinks* something about it. This invites the suggestion that some kind of self-directed thought is indeed what should fill the "H" role. But then we need to ask: Did we, in conceiving of our hypothetical blindsighters, suppose they lacked some kind of *thought* about themselves, which we assumed essential to conscious sight?

I, at any rate, assumed that Belinda did not think that she consciously saw anything on her left. If you want to explain how it could seem possible to me that she might indeed not consciously see on her left, might you then say that I am (falsely) supposing that her having such a thought is essential to conscious vision, and then confusing the possibility that she might lack such a thought with the possibility that she might lack visual experience? Maybe that thought is the H we seek. But this won't work. I deny that having such a thought *is* essential to conscious vision, as I understand it, for I believe people and animals can consciously see without thinking that they do. And I even believe that philosophers can consciously see while denying that (in my sense) they do. But what if you say you mean something other than what I do by 'conscious,' when you describe the thought whose absence, you contend, I confuse with an absence of experience? Then, while I will agree that I also suppose Belinda to be absent the thought that she consciously saw on the left in this other sense, I will also want to say that I did not suppose her to think she *did* consciously see in this sense on her right either. So it also won't be correct to say that I regard *that* thought as essential to conscious vision. Of course, it won't help here to suggest that I suppose her to lack the thought that she visually judges about things on her left: I explicitly attributed that thought to her in making her "reflective." But what if one distinguishes between the thought that one visually *judges* and the thought that one visually *senses*? If, by saying someone "visually senses" light on her left, you mean it looks to her like there is light there, I will agree that she does not have this thought, but this just sends us back to the problems contained in the first suggestion, for by saying it looks some way to her, I mean she has a conscious visual experience. And no, I do *not* regard that thought as essential to having such experience. If by "visual sensing," you mean something for which phenomenally conscious vision is not necessary, I would say that I do not regard the thought that one visually senses in *that* sense as essential to conscious vision either, since I do not suppose Belinda to have it when she does consciously see, and I believe I commonly lack that thought myself.[1]

I see no prospects, then, for explaining the appearance of contingency here (or the nonappearance of necessity) in the link between Belinda's visual talents and visual experience, by saying that there is some thought I suppose Belinda lacking, which I falsely deem essential to conscious vision, so that I mistake the absence of *that* for the absence of experience. Perhaps then someone will try this strategy: "It's not that there's some feature H which your concept of *visual consciousness* associates with it, that you wrongly believe *essential* to it; rather, there's some feature H, that your concept of the *left-field visual capacities* you attribute to Belinda associates with *these*, which you wrongly consider *sufficient* for them. So when you conceive of a situation in which H is present without conscious vision, you want to say you're conceiving of one in which certain visual discriminatory capacities might be exercised without conscious vision. And that's a mistake, because H is insufficient for having those capacities." But I have not been thinking of these capacities in terms of some features associated with them, but insufficient to guarantee them. I am thinking, for example, of a case where a subject really does accurately judge that there is a patch of light on her left, that it is growing or shrinking, and getting lighter or darker, on account of visual stimulation—not of a case with features making it merely resemble or appear to be such visual discrimination.

It seems, then, that someone who says Belinda's blindsight is metaphysically impossible should abandon the approach of trying to explain my "failure" to appreciate this, by finding some feature that my conception of conscious vision or of visual discrimination wrongly links to these. But why isn't it enough simply to say that my concept of conscious vision and my concept of the kinds of feats I have attributed to my "blindsighters" are different, and leave it at that? Saying I have here two different concepts by itself would hardly begin to explain what prevents me from grasping the (alleged) necessity. I may grant that it is possible that someone's concept of F differs from his concept of G, even when, necessarily, G occurs when F does. And I may grant that my concept of the sorts of left-field visual capacities attributed to Belinda is distinct from my concept of consciously seeing light on one's left. But still, perhaps: it just does not seem to me that the necessity (if F, then G) holds, if we assume F = the sorts of left-field visual capacities attributed to Belinda, and G = consciously seeing light on one's left. And it seems possible to me that one can have this F without this G. Noting that there are two concepts here does not explain why in this case I do not believe F and G to be related by necessity in the suggested way, much less why I believe them *not* to be so related. And it won't remedy this to say that I must have falsely inferred a lack of necessity here from a distinctness in concepts; I may sincerely deny that such an inference is valid, but still not affirm, or even deny, the (supposed) necessity. So, then, why is the (alleged) impossibility of Belinda unclear to me?[2]

One might suggest (following some remarks made by Loar [1990] in a different but related context) that my difficulty is explained by a difference in the nature of the concepts I am using. On the one hand, I have a *recognitional* concept that is my ordinary pretheoretical way of thinking about my own visual experience, "involving," as Loar says, "the ability to classify together certain states in the having of them" (ibid., 97). On the other, I have a more discursive concept of talents for visual judgment and the like. Possession of the first concept includes the ability to discriminate the character of my own experience—to tell that this one differs from or is similar to that one, and so on—but it does not (as the second concept does) give me the wherewithal to say under what possible circumstances the property it picks out is, or is not, instantiated. Having that recognitional concept does not, as we might say, give me the information I need to answer this question: in which "possible worlds" are various statements employing that concept true? So, I may employ this recognitional concept in thinking about a certain kind of visual experience without its seeming to me there is any essential connection between what it allows me to pick out and what is described in ways manifesting my possession of the other, discursive concepts: thinking with recognitional concepts does not put you in a position to understand and assess connections of that kind.

But this does not seem to me to be a plausible line to take, because it makes my concept of phenomenal features too cognitively primitive. It is not the case that the concept I use in thinking of visual experience in connection with the Chapter 3 thought-experiments gives me *no* competence to assess the presence or lack of necessary connections between what it picks out and what is described in other terms (assuming we have such competence at all). Suppose someone proposed that there is nothing essential to what I am thinking of when I speak of phenomenally conscious vision beyond what any phototropic organism possesses. If I balk at this, and reply that it is at least possible that a sunflower, say, has no conscious visual experience, why can't this person object that since I am thinking about the phenomenal character of visual experience employing my merely recognitional concepts, I have no business speaking out on the possibility that something with a simple phototropic response may lack visual experience? Perhaps he will insist that it is metaphysically impossible that things might not look any way at all to the sunflower. If this is absurd, it indicates that the concept I have of visual consciousness and I use in first-person thought does include some ability to assess relations of necessity and possibility. So one cannot reasonably explain my supposed failure to understand that someone like Belinda could not possibly fail to have visual experience of a patch of light, by saying that in thinking about visual experience, I am employing a merely recognitional concept unsuited for the business of thinking about what is possible and what is not.

I will give up trying to find ways for someone who denies the possibility of the forms of blindsight I discussed to account for how they could seem possible to me (or not seem impossible to me), and I will just say that I find a notable lack of suitable suggestions. I am not saying that there is no explanation of my not apprehending the alleged impossibility. After all, we might explain it somewhat along these lines. On reflection, the description I have given of Belinda seems intelligible to me and without inconsistency, and I cannot find any good reason to think it describes a strictly impossible situation, so I do not believe it is impossible, and maybe even regard this as giving me reason to believe it is possible. But *that* explanation, as it stands, does not help at all to make the case for impossibility. Of course, it might contribute to that case, if one could find a good reason why I should believe the situation impossible, and then one could explain my failure to appreciate the metaphysical impossibility of Belinda by explaining why I failed to appreciate this reason. But this just sends us back to the problem that one has made this strong claim of impossibility, in the face of appearances to the contrary, but has given us no good reason to accept it.

I conclude that the notion of metaphysical necessity and modal illusion that has emerged in connection with contrasts between ordinary and scientific concepts of heat, water, gold, and so on, does not provide a sound basis on which to argue for the impossibility of the absences of experience I have described, and thus against the reality of a consciousness that would admit of such absences. It seems that analogies offered to the interpretation given certain "natural kind terms" will do no more than display a different understanding of 'conscious' than that I exhibited in previous chapters; they will not show that my way of understanding this term is not available. And that, it seems, is what is called for.[3]

But suppose at this point someone who wants to say Belinda is a modal illusion complains to me:

> You say I haven't shown it's *impossible* for there to be such a one as Belinda. But *you* haven't shown it's *possible* either. And you need to do so. For you say you know you're phenomenally conscious, in a sense in which one would deny being conscious, if one maintained the impossibility of certain forms of blindsight. So if these aren't possible, you aren't conscious, and a fortiori don't know you are. Therefore you know you're conscious only if these are possible. And then, you know you're conscious, only if you know that they're possible. And to know that, you need more than a lack of reason to believe they're not possible. So you don't have any right to claim to know you're phenomenally conscious.

I would question the move from: "If someone maintained the strict impossibility of certain forms of blindsight, then that person would deny you are conscious," to "If these aren't possible, then you don't know you're conscious." For we may rationally accept the first, while withholding judgment on the second. We may hold the first, while we are unwilling to commit to the second, because we do not know whether there really are modal truths of the appropriately strict sort to be had, regarding these forms of blindsight. That is, we may not know whether the claim that they are not possible even has a definite truth-value, and so do not want to commit ourselves to saying it is true that if they are not possible, then you do not know you are conscious. It is difficult to reach a truly satisfactory understanding of the notion of possibility at issue here; and it is not clear just what warrants us in making such claims of necessity and possibility in this or that instance, and where our grounds are relatively firm and where they are relatively weak or nonexistent. So it is not too hard to entertain doubts about the strength of our warrant for affirming or denying that there are certain necessities and possibilities. Some are even dubious about the very idea of necessity and possibility. But whatever the merit of such doubts, they do not, I believe, threaten our knowledge that we have phenomenally conscious experience. We can know we are conscious, while remaining agnostic about whether there is some fact of the matter regarding the possibility of certain styles of blindsight, and still maintain that someone who boldly held them to be strictly impossible would deny consciousness.

My basic contention may be put like this. Suppose one is prepared to claim that, in either a metaphysical or a logical or conceptual sense, something is impossible, when that claim is incompatible with recognizing the reality of phenomenal consciousness. Or one makes assertions about what is meant by a term, or about what properties are identical, that can be fairly interpreted to commit one to some such modal claim. Then those of us to whom such claims are not evident, and who believe we have first-person warrant for our belief that we have conscious experience, should not adopt these claims and relinquish our beliefs, until we find or are given reasons to do so. And my search for such reasons has turned up no good ones.

However, I should add that, on the basis of what I have said, a good case can be made not just for the conclusion that we *lack* warrant for thinking it impossible that the forms of blindsight I have discussed could occur, but also for the stronger result that we have *more* warrant for thinking these *are* (in the relevant sense) possible than for thinking they are not. For I believe that if, on careful consideration, a description of a situation seems intelligible, coherent, and internally consistent to us, and so, if in that way the situation as described "seems possible" to us, and further, an examination of relevant sources of reasons to think it is, in some strict (logical or metaphysical) sense, impossible, finds none that withstands criticism, then we have more warrant for thinking it is in this way possible, than for thinking it is not. And the more searching the examination that yields no reason to defeat the appearance of possibility, and the less remote the hypothetical situation from what we take to be actually the case, the more warrant we have for thinking it is possible. So, if you want to hear not only why the claim that Belinda is *not* possible *lacks* warrant, but also why the claim that she *is* possible *has* warrant, then by this standard, I believe that I have given you (and will in the next section give you more of) what you want.

5.4 THE WARRANTABILITY OF MISSING-EXPERIENCE REPORTS

I would like now to explore a potential source of reasons for thinking there is nothing for "consciousness neglect" to neglect, latent in some remarks of Dennett's that were alluded to in the last chapter. Recall that Dennett led my list of those who, though having apparently directed considerable intellectual energies toward "consciousness," are neglectful of what I have called phenomenal consciousness. In Dennett's case, this is no mere oversight; he has devoted much effort and many pages to trying to persuade us to doubt and disown any impression that he is missing something. So we should be able to find in his discussions some defense against this criticism.

When one prunes away his polemical attacks on the mind as a "theatre," "inner presentations," and "inner lights"—metaphorical inroads to consciousness to which I have no allegiance—one finds a central strategy by which he tries to instill in his readers doubts about the notion of consciousness he ultimately wants us to spurn. We are invited to apply this ostensible notion in ways that appear to set up certain epistemic predicaments. In these situations, though we are apparently able to entertain both the hypothesis that a person *has* a given sort of conscious experience, and the hypothesis that he *lacks* it, that person is supposed to be in no position to choose between these rival accounts, and determine which is correct. And, in some of these situations at least, Dennett claims no one else could justifiably make this choice either. His discussion of "metacontrast" experiments provides a fairly simple example of the pattern. The image of a disk is flashed before a subject very rapidly. Though the subject reports seeing it when flashed by itself, when instead it is immediately followed by a donut-shaped image, whose hole matches the boundaries of the disk, the subject denies having seen the disk. Here is the dilemma: did he briefly have a conscious visual experience of the disk, which he cannot remember on account of the second stimulus, or did this second stimulus prevent him from having such an experience at all?[4] Dennett invites us to feel a sense of futility at trying to make a principled choice here. Neither the subject himself nor his observers are supposed to be in a position to know which answer is correct—and, I take it, Dennett thinks neither could even correctly claim to have more warrant for believing one than for believing the other. And the undecidability of this question is somehow supposed to lead us to think the very notion of an intelligible choice here is a mistake: we do not have conscious experience in a sense that would make such a choice intelligible.

A similar sort of reasoning surfaces in Dennett's discussion of a kind of spontaneous blindsight, mentioned earlier. Remember, Dennett concedes he can imagine he might be able to make rather crude spontaneous discriminations of visual stimuli without consciously seeing them. But he suggests that if he had conscious visual experience of them, he would also have to be able to make much richer ones, of a sort he could not possibly make only with some sort of blindsight. He then seeks to disabuse us of the idea that even fancy and subtle unprompted discriminations of visual stimuli might possibly be made by a person who did not consciously see anything. He says that he can imagine making such discriminations, and wanting to say that he does not consciously see anything. But, he adds, if this were his situation, he should also consider that, in addition to this denial of visual consciousness to which he felt impelled, there would be another hypothesis to take into account: that he is subject to some kind of "delusion" (a "hysterical linguistic amnesia," Dennett suggests): he *does* consciously see but is somehow disinclined to report that he is. And he should also, he thinks, admit this further point: that he would have no grounds for choosing ("from the inside," as he puts it) the first of these hypotheses—the denial of conscious vision—over the second.[5] And once we agree that he (or any of us) would be in this hypothetical epistemic predicament, we are apparently to conclude from this (in some way Dennett does not make clear) that we really are not conscious in the sense that leaves open the possibility that his denial of conscious sight could, in such circumstances, be true. So the sort of occurrence we might think Dennett neglects, simply is not there to be neglected.

A question that looms large over this sort of argument is: Just what entitles us to move from the claim that some putative facts about conscious experience are *unknowable*, to the claim that there are *never any* facts about conscious experience? For example, just how are we to move from the saying that we cannot know whether the metacontrast subject had a split-second disk experience, to the conclusion that we do not ever have, for longer duration, the kind of experience no one knows if he briefly had? It seems to me that Dennett's arguments are supposed to secure this link via some such claim as this: the truth of one or more of the apparently available options for saying what experience someone had in certain circumstances is somehow inconceivable, since grounds for believing it to be true would be entirely lacking. And I take it that the relevant sense of inconceivability here is the kind that would entail strict impossibility. The idea appears to be, roughly: since we would not be able to know of such experiential absences, there could not be any such absences, and since there could not be any, we do not have conscious experience in any sense that would leave open their possibility. At least, I have a hard time seeing how Dennett wants to reach the negative conclusion he needs from the unknowability of putative experiential absences, if not in some such way.

Does this sort of argument give us reason to doubt we are phenomenally conscious? I have not made affirmation that we are conscious hinge on leaving open the possibility of premium blindsight. Perhaps there is some reason for thinking that this is strictly impossible, which does not rule out the forms of blindsight I did tie to acknowledgment of consciousness. Also, I have not said that if we have conscious experience, there is some fact of the matter concerning whether or not the subject of the metacontrast experiment had a momentary experience of a disk before he saw the donut. Maybe we can admit the nonexistence of such a fact, without denying consciousness. However, it seems, on the face of it, plausible to suppose there would be such a fact, given our acceptance of the notion of phenomenal consciousness. So the argument that there could be no such fact at least appears to require us to reject this notion. And, since Dennett's view would also apparently ask us to rule out the possibility of the extremely "subpremium" (amblyopic, but spontaneous and reflective) blindsight we contemplated in Chapter 3—the kind we supposed Belinda to have in Chapter 4—it seems we should at least consider whether his style of argument against super-duper blindsight would count against the possibility of subjects like Belinda, and so justify the conclusion that we are not phenomenally conscious. Also, Dennett is not the only philosopher who defends his view of mind against thought-experiments that ask us to conceive of diminishments in consciousness that leave one's behavior intact, by contending that one would not be able to *know* experience was "shrinking" under these conditions (see Shoemaker 1994). This sort of thinking clearly has some allure.

So let's consider: can a sound argument of roughly Dennett's sort yield the result that phenomenal consciousness is not real? We need to be clear about the argument's premises. They include not only the thesis that certain claims about the presence or absence of experience are, in certain circumstances, unwarrantable, but also the premise that such claims could *possibly be true* under these conditions, only if they were then warrantable. In other words, where these claims are concerned, the rule "possible, only if warrantable" holds. For the argument seems to be that, since a certain kind of claim about experience made in certain conditions—for example, denials of visual experience, made under the (real) conditions of the metacontrast experiments, or the (imaginary) ones of our "blindsight" scenarios—would be, in those circumstances, unjustifiable, or unwarrantable, it could *not*, in such circumstances, (conceivably) be true.

Let's focus first on this "possible, only if warrantable" assumption. Its truth is far from obvious. There seems to be nothing manifestly absurd about the possibility of situations in which certain true beliefs are unwarrantable—the situation may be such as to prevent anyone from getting the warrant needed for the belief. Perhaps the metacontrast case is an instance of just such a situation. This crucial premise calls for some kind of support, then. Where should we seek it out? Here is a candidate: *no* statement is *meaningful* unless there is a way of knowing it is true, or of "verifying" it, so the prospect that some claim about experience may be true in the absence of any way of knowing it to be so, is literally inconceivable. But making a case for a general verificationist theory of meaning is a doubtful undertaking in its own right—to say the least. After all the powerful objections such theories have encountered, few are likely to find this a promising line. It should be noted Dennett does not want to say that warrantability follows from possibility quite generally, but only specifically in the case where assertions about consciousness are at issue—he embraces a *selective* sort of verificationism. And, even if we *were* interested in endorsing a general verificationism, we would still have the question of why cases like Dennett's metacontrast example do not show us the falsity of this view. Why should we assume the verificationism, and infer from this the impossibility that there is a fact of the matter about the subject's disk experience, rather than believe it is not impossible that there is such a fact, and infer the falsity of a consciousness-specific (and thus also *general*) verificationism? Some way or another, we must face the issue of just why we should be verificationists about consciousness, in the way required for this argument. If this "possible, only if warrantable" premise we are asked to accept is supposed to yield such a counterintuitive result (consciousness is not real), we may fairly suspend judgment on it, until we can be explicit about why we should accept it.

What we want to know is what might support this sort of thesis: it is possible that such and such a missing experience claim is true under such and such conditions, only if someone could have more warrant for that claim than for its contrary, under those conditions. A natural way to proceed here would be first to consider the conditions in question, and then to ask whether we can think of any way someone could have warrant for making the claim at issue, if those conditions obtained. Then, if we say yes—the claim *is* warrantable in those circumstances—we will say claims are possibly true in those circumstances, only if they are warrantable in those circumstances. On the other hand, if we say no—we cannot come up with any way someone could have warrant for the claim at issue under the circumstances—then we will not have found a reason to accept the "possible, only if warrantable" thesis in question.

So we have here a procedure that, it seems, could potentially generate support for some "possible, only if warrantable" premise about missing-experience claims. But clearly its doing so would provide no help to the argument against consciousness. Consider the metacontrast case. If we are inclined to Dennett's way of thinking about the evidence here, we will conclude that, in the circumstances of the experiment (duration of stimulus, response to stimulus when given alone, etc.), the subject's denial of a past disk experience is not warrantable (for under those conditions neither he nor anyone else could justifiably elect to believe the denial—or its negation, for that matter). However interesting that may be in itself, it gives us no reason at all to think that the subject's denial, if possibly true in the relevant circumstances, is warrantable in those circumstances. But what if, on the other hand, we consider the situation, and determine that the circumstances of the subject's denial would, after all, make warrant available for someone to decide the denial was true (so he did *not* have a disk experience; it did *not* look to her as if there was a light on her left)? Though showing that the missing-experience claim was warrantable would show the "possible, only if warrantable" conditional was true, it would obviously rob us of the unwarrantability premise, without which the argument against consciousness fails. So, there *is* a way of finding support for the "possibility-knowability" link Dennett's style of argument needs. But success in establishing the link in this way would guarantee failure for its use in the argument against consciousness.

There is another way one might try to establish the needed premise, which would not have this problem. Again, one might determine that under the circumstances in question, the relevant missing-experience claim would not be warrantable. Then, by some sort of independent test, one would determine that it is impossible for the claim to be true under these circumstances. Then one could reason: since both the antecedent and the consequent of the conditional "possible, only if warrantable" are false, the conditional as a whole is true. But this way of establishing "possible, only if warrantable" would make another sort of problem for the argument against consciousness in which it is supposed to figure. If we supported the premise in this way, we would have already established (somehow) the very claim of impossibility we are supposed to prove by means of the argument in which that premise is to figure. And if we had already established that, we would have no use for the proposed form of argument against consciousness. Of course, that is not to say we *do* have an independent way of establishing it is impossible that the subject's denial of the disk experience, or Belinda's denial of left-field conscious vision, might be true. The point is, supposing there may be one does not give us any prospects of establishing the link between possibility and warrantability in a way that would make the argument against consciousness that appeals to it persuasive.

We need to find some source of support for the crucial "possible, only if warrantable" premise, if we are to use it to mount the proposed type of argument against consciousness. But I cannot locate a prospective source that is not guaranteed either to be quite useless to that end, or to subvert it totally. Maybe someone will say there is some other promising way to argue for the premise in question that does not run into this difficulty. Until we find out what that is, though, we will not be able to get this defense of consciousness neglect off the ground.

But what about the argument's other crucial premise—the one that says certain claims about experience would not be warrantable? Is at least *that* part of the argument against consciousness acceptable? To address this, let's first consider again how the premise would apply in the case of Belinda-like blindsight. I take it the claim would be that if, like Belinda, I had the powers of discrimination in my left visual field that a severely legally blind person would have, *and* I also sincerely deny consciously seeing anything there, then I could have ("from the inside") no more warrant for this denial than for the contrary claim: that I *do* consciously see things there (albeit poorly). According to this alternative hypothesis, my denial manifests some kind of pathological dissociation of vision and verbal judgment (Dennett's diagnosis: "hysterical linguistic amnesia"). Before considering whether anyone fitting Belinda's description would indeed be in this epistemic predicament, we need to clarify several points about its alleged character.

First, what is meant by "from the inside" here? I take it that Dennett is after the idea that there is not, from the distinctive perspective of the subject in such a scenario—from the "first-person perspective"—any way of knowing that one lacks conscious experience on the left, in these circumstances. That is to say, one has no more warrant of the type ordinarily had only for first-person beliefs about attitudes and experience—in my terms, no more first-person warrant—for denying that one consciously sees anything to the left, than one has for the contrary proposition. Second, I take it that Dennett would not want us to think that though the putative blindsighter would not be in a position to say that she did not consciously see on her left, someone else observing her (perhaps with the aid of brain-imaging technology) would be. For I take it that the argument turns on the claim that *no one* could find grounds for saying she lacks any conscious visual experience of her left field—either because that claim is no better justified than its contrary, or because it is less so. So the unwarrantability claim is supposed to apply to both the first- and the third-person points of view. Some have argued against Dennett's claim that various ostensible experiential facts would be unknowable, by speculating about how advances in neuroscience could give us ways of resolving the issues he raises (Block 1993; Flanagan 1992). Such objections are, I think, well taken; but I will confine my discussion to the question of whether the unwarrantability claim is true even where first-person knowledge, with the manifest, not hidden, resources available to it, is concerned.

Third, it seems to me that Dennett's notion of the alternative to thinking the blindsighter's denials are correct—the hypothesis of "hysterical linguistic amnesia"—does not give us a helpful way of posing the question of what she would have warrant for believing. Consider first the "hysterical" part of the hypothesis. Belinda, we may suppose, would exhibit none of what I take to be required signs of the hysterical blindness to which Dennett alludes here: she has no discernible motivation for making people believe she has lost visual consciousness on her left even if it is not true, and she does not evince such motivation (as the hysterically blind do) by, for example, making visual discriminations whose accuracy falls below chance performance, or by going out of her way to collide with furniture. If we want a story telling us how we might plausibly suppose Belinda has as much warrant for thinking that her denials of visual consciousness are mistaken as for thinking they are true, hysterical blindness is not a good model—for there would be nothing much to say for the view that her denials are "hysterical." And there are troubles with thinking of her mistake as revealing "linguistic amnesia." Belinda has not forgotten the *word* she is to apply in the case at hand—'conscious.' Is the suggestion that she somehow forgets what she *means* by 'conscious' just when it comes to her left-field vision? Selective linguistic amnesia of this sort is hard to grasp: she presumably knows what she means when she says, "I do consciously see on my right . . ."—does she somehow forget what she meant as she finishes the sentence by saying, ". . . but not on my left"? I assume if a sentence you utter reveals a failure to understand a word it contains, it would be absurd to suppose you failed to understand only during the part of the utterance that reveals the failure.

What it may appear we should consider here is the suggestion that Belinda suffers from a peculiarly selective *failure of recognition*: she can judge visually that there is light on her left, even tell that she does this, but somehow on account of a mental block or a failed connection in her brain cannot notice her blurry visual experience of something on her left. While this seems intelligible, notice that it is not the way Dennett wants us to think of this. For on his view, all there is for her to lack is just some power of visual judgment ("visual seeming" is nothing else); so if she can tell she has that, there is nothing else for her to fail to notice or recognize. This perhaps explains why Dennett feels driven to speak of "linguistic amnesia" rather than of some kind of agnosia or neglect here: since in the end he wants us to think there is no deficit for her to neglect, he needs to say that she forgets that all she has in mind when she speaks of 'visual consciousness' and the like is this talent for judgment—she has become generally confused about what she means by 'conscious.' But Dennett is getting a bit ahead of himself by suggesting that the alternative to believing the blindsighter's denial, which would be at least as warranted, is the hypothesis that she does not understand what she means by 'consciously see,' 'looks,' etc. For that really is the conclusion at which we are supposed to arrive, by means of the claim that she would have no more warrant for the "hypothesis," "It doesn't look to me as if anything's on my left" than she would for the "hypothesis," "It looks to me as if there's something on my left." Thus it seems to me we will have a clearer view of the kind of situation we need to consider to assess the argument Dennett suggests, if we think of her alternatives in this way, and leave "hysterial linguistic amnesia" to the side.

Now, then, just what *are* we to think of Belinda's epistemic situation? Should we say that someone with the discriminatory powers with which Belinda was supposed to be endowed, who denied consciously seeing anything to her left, would have no more warrant for this denial than for its contrary? I have to say that this is not how *I* size up the situation. That is, it seems to me that if you were such as I have described Belinda as being, and not only did you have her spontaneous if severely limited powers to discriminate visual stimuli on the left, but *lacked any conscious visual experience of them, and believed you lacked this*, well then, that would indeed put you in a position to know that your denial was correct. At any rate, it would put you in a position to have more first-person warrant for the denial than for its opposite. In such a situation, it would *not* be the epistemically responsible thing to do to suspend judgment about your visual experience, or to endorse the view that your inclination to deny things look any way at all to you on the left is only the symptom of some kind of pathology.

Someone might say I have no right to take into consideration the putative absence of visual experience in assessing the subject's epistemic situation. But why not? It might be right to say that part of what puts the subject in a distinctive epistemic situation where judgments about her own lack or possession of experience are concerned is the fact that she is the one who has it or lacks it. In other words, part of what gives her a first-person warrant for her belief that she does not consciously see anything on her left (and is not pathologically dissociated) is the fact that she does not consciously see anything on her left. If you insist on leaving *that* fact out of consideration as irrelevant to determining what she has warrant for believing or not, then you may get the result that she would not know "from the inside" that she lacked the experience—but only because you excluded from consideration precisely what was essential to her knowing that in this way.

So our decision about whether Dennett would be right, if he said Belinda would not be able to know she was a blindsighter, can depend on whether or not we think that the lack of conscious experience plays a role in giving one first-person warrant for thinking one lacks it. For if it does, we may reject the claim that Belinda's denial of experience would be unwarrantable, because we think her lack of experience itself would, in the circumstances, give her warrant for her denial—would enable her to know "from the inside" that she did not consciously see something. Denials of conscious vision are not infallible or incorrigible (as hysterical blindness shows). But that is consistent with holding that if Belinda lacked conscious left-field vision, and thought she did, then, even though she had the spontaneous discriminatory talents we have described, she could tell that she lacked this experience.

So, there is a way of looking at the epistemic situation of our hypothetical blindsighter that is rather different from the one Dennett suggests. And unless we can find reason to adopt an epistemology that would yield Dennett's view that she would lack warrant for her denial of experience, we do not have reason enough to accept that assessment. In that case, we don't have any business saying that the blindsighter's denial is unwarrantable.

We may worry, however, that by invoking this notion that having or missing an experience can (together with other conditions) give you warrant for thinking you do, we drag up many large-scale, highly controversial epistemological issues about the nature of knowledge, warrant, and justification, so that I do not move the debate very far along until I grapple with these—which would take another book, or several. Plus, it is not very satisfying to be left merely with two divergent intuitive responses to the question of what Belinda would have most warrant to believe, given that her situation is as described. This is not such bad news for me, for still, assessment of our hypothetical blindsighter's epistemic status can hardly be taken for granted, and attempts to defend the assessment called for in the argument against consciousness may simply stall it interminably in other, larger controversies.

However, we will have a still stronger case against epistemically motivated attacks on consciousness like Dennett's, if we have grounds for thinking our blindsighter could have more first-person warrant for her belief that she lacks it than for its contrary, which did not simply assume that having or missing an experience can make a difference to the warrant for one's beliefs about it. And we do have grounds for thinking this, even without drawing on a general theory of warrant or justification, but looking just to our discussion of first-person warrant in Chapters 1 and 2.

First consider: does one ever have more warrant for denying that one had a certain experience than for believing one had it, even though the evidence available to others indicates one had it? We earlier said that we sometimes have what I called solitary self-knowledge regarding what we are thinking or experiencing, and that if this is so, we sometimes have warrant for first-person belief available when that kind ordinarily needed for third-person beliefs is not. So we have a kind of warrant—first-person warrant—for claims about experience that is of the right sort to give us at least part of what we need in order to have warrant for a belief about our own experience, even where the kind of evidence ordinarily available to others counts against it: namely, a source of warrant distinct in kind from that ordinarily available to warrant third-person beliefs about experience. The question, then, is: Can one still have more warrant of this sort for a belief about one's experience (or lack of it) than for its contrary, even in the face of third-person evidence supporting that contrary belief? Can one have solitary self-knowledge at odds with manifest third-person evidence?

To answer this question, ask yourself whether you can do the following and know that you did. Think of a number between one and one hundred, and lie convincingly to someone about what number you then thought of. Do you believe there are circumstances in which you can do this and know you did it? If you say yes, you believe you can intentionally mislead others into believing you thought something you know you did not think. If you say no merely because you believe you are too averse to lying to do this, but you think there is a way of acting that someone who knew what you knew could engage in, which would meet with success, then that is enough for my point. Either way, you would grant that you can know (and have first-person warrant for believing) you did not have an experience, even if there were contraindicating evidence of the sort ordinarily available to others. One may observe that in this "thinking of a number" example, the evidence available to others (saying, for instance, "The number I thought of was sixty-seven; it really was"), which points to the contrary of the belief for which one has first-person warrant (actually I was thinking of twenty-three), is unusually simple and isolated. And it may seem worrisome that the fact in question—what number one just thought of—may appear rather arbitrary and trivial. But it is not difficult to think of decently realistic cases where the relevant third-person evidence is more complex and the thought more significant.

So we might suppose that when Bob is sitting with Irene, his gaze lingers an extra moment or two on her face—he is noticing wrinkles around, and circles under, her eyes, and he thinks (while saying nothing aloud) that they once were not there, and imagines how she will look when she is very old. Noticing his gaze, Irene asks, "What are you thinking?" Not wanting to say what was really on his mind, Bob, quickly improvising, says, "I was just thinking . . . maybe we should get away this weekend somewhere . . . by ourselves." She has every reason to believe this is what he was thinking, for he pursues the idea further, as he talks, with apparent enthusiasm, perhaps even convincing himself it really is a good idea. And perhaps all that Bob does or is disposed to do for the rest of his life speaks in favor of the assumption that he had the thought he said he had prior to Irene's query; and maybe what was alleged to have happened then will come to seem important, so that Bob's professed thought will seem to be key to explaining much that came afterwards in the lives of Bob and Irene. All the same, Bob knows he was then thinking something else entirely.

The point is, there is no general obstacle, in principle, to your having more warrant for believing that you lack a given sort of experience than for the contrary belief, even when ordinary third-person evidence points to just the opposite conclusion. Now, then, what does this tell us about how the blindsighter might stand with respect to knowledge of her missing visual experience?

Notice that in both cases (Bob's and Belinda's) we have a subject who lacks a certain experience, and, if he or she has first-person warrant for the belief that this is so, has it in spite of the fact that evidence available to others' observation is of the kind that supports the contrary belief. Now Bob, I am assuming we agree, *does* have first-person warrant for his belief that he did not think a certain thought. What we want to know is if Belinda could have, for her corresponding belief, the same sort of warrant. So we might ask ourselves whether there is anything reasonably considered generally essential to having first-person warrant for a belief that one lacks a certain experience, when that belief is at odds with third-person evidence, that is of the following sort. While it *would* pertain to someone in Bob's situation, and give him warrant for the belief he lacks a certain thought, it *could not* pertain to someone in Belinda's situation, and give her warrant for the belief that she lacks a certain visual experience. If we can find nothing like that, nothing essential to having self-knowledge at odds with manifest third-person evidence, that distinguishes Bob's situation from Belinda's, then we should conclude that someone with Belinda-like blindsight could indeed have first-person warrant for her denial that she consciously sees anything to her left. For she would lack nothing she needs, generally essential to knowing one did not experience what others have evidence for thinking one did.

So—would Bob and Belinda differ in any way essential to having self-knowledge at odds with manifest third-person evidence? Well, Bob's knowledge is about his not having a certain *thought* and Belinda's is about her not having a certain *visual experience*. Is that a reason to say Belinda would lack something she needs for self-knowledge, which Bob has? It might be, if it were true that we can have solitary self-knowledge about what we think, but not about what we see or how things look to us. But that is not true. Perhaps, then, there is something about the nature of the third-person evidence that would warrant others' belief that Bob had the thought he knew he did not, that leaves Bob secure in this knowledge, but isn't true of the evidence others would have that might lead them to think Belinda consciously sees light flashes on her left. This presumably would be something that made the evidence that Bob had the thought he lyingly says he had notably weaker than the evidence that Belinda saw what she says she did not. But I do not see any reason to assess the relative strength of the evidence in that way. Bob, we may suppose, is usually pretty honest, and his relevant behavior seems quite genuine: the contraindicating evidence is not so weak. And Belinda generally shows herself by available standards to be a quite competent and believable reporter of her right-field visual experience, as well as her thoughts, olfactory experience, and so on. So even though she discriminates left-field stimuli with a kind of spontaneity indicative of conscious vision, it is arguable on these grounds that Belinda's observers would have more warrant to believe her denial of visual consciousness than its contrary—even before they haul out any brain scanners or neuropsychological theory. So it seems the contraindicating evidence is, if anything, actually *weaker* in Belinda's case than in Bob's (and so less strongly at odds with what first-person warrant she might have), all things considered.

There is a further notable difference between the two circumstances. In Bob's case, the behavior furnishing the contraindicating evidence is *intentionally performed* by him, precisely *because* it is contraindicating. Might we reasonably hold that this intent to give out misinformation is essential to having self-knowledge somehow at variance with the face one presents to the world? If so, then we might take its absence in Belinda's case to show that she lacks warrant for her denial of left-field experience—for Belinda, unlike Bob, was not trying to mislead anyone. But this would be a bad move, for two reasons. First, even though we did not suppose Belinda intentionally manifests her left-field discriminatory powers because they would indicate she had the experience she believed she lacked, we can readily enough suppose she does this. If adding that to the story will enable her to know she is blindsighted, it is an easy condition to add—maybe Belinda wants people to think she is like Connie. Second, though, the evident absurdity of thinking that this change in Belinda's scenario dramatically alters her epistemic situation, shows that an intent to engage in evidentially misleading behavior really is *not*, in general, an essential part of having first-person warrant for the belief that one lacks an experience when this is at odds with third-person evidence. So here again, it seems there is nothing Bob has, making him a self-knower, that Belinda needs for being one, but lacks.

But here is a worry. How does Belinda's situation compare with that of the metacontrast subject? It seems pretty plausible to say *he* at least would be in a genuine epistemic predicament: he has no more warrant for his denial that he consciously saw a disk before the ring than for the contrary assertion—and this remains so, even if we grant that he did not see the disk. But then, is Belinda's situation relevantly different? She (supposedly) lacks the experience and thinks she does. If the subject of the disk-donut experiment is epistemically forlorn, then (seemingly) so would be Belinda. It then seems there must indeed be some relevant difference between her situation and Bob's that makes him a self-knower, but not her. This also may seem to raise a problem for my earlier suggestion that part of what would give Belinda first-person warrant for her denial that she consciously sees light in her left visual field is the fact that she does not. Why is it not enough for the meta-contrast subject simply to lack the conscious visual experience of the disk, and deny that he had it, in order to have more warrant for his denial than for the claim that he had a brief flicker of a disk experience prior to seeing the donut?

If we look more closely, we will find that the metacontrast subject *is* relevantly different from our hypothetical blindsighter: Belinda's lack of visual experience could better situate her for self-knowledge; and we should not think that she must lack something she needs in order to have the kind of self-knowledge Bob has. Note first: I never suggested that if one lacked a given sort of conscious experience, and sincerely judged one did, that *by itself* would necessarily be enough to give one more warrant for this judg-ment than for the opposing claim, regardless of what other conditions held. So the question we need to pose here is whether there are conditions peculiar to the metacontrast subject's case that would make it reasonable to think he is worse off, warrant-wise, with respect to his missing-experience claim than Belinda would be with regard to hers.

These peculiarities of the situation seem relevant. First, the time during which the experience in question is alleged to have occurred is brief (30 milliseconds). And so, when the subject is asked whether or not he saw the disk, the event at issue, if it occurred, is no longer in progress, and the judg-ment that it did not occur is based entirely on his lack of memory of it. Second, the experience that is alleged to have occurred would be continuous with its successor in the following way: the boundaries of what appears at each moment are shared to such an extent that an image of what appears at t_1—the disk—would be entirely contained in an image of what appears at t_2—the ring. This being the case, the first experience contrasts much less strongly with its successor than it would if it were otherwise.

Now, we clearly do not remember all that we experience—in fact, we remember rather little of it. So a lack of the memory of a particular experi-ence is clearly a fallible indicator that it did not occur. Also, we are, I think it is fair to say, less likely to remember a particular episode of experience, and to distinguish it from others—it is more likely to join the vast ocean of (literally) unmemorable experience—the less it *contrasts* with the experience that immediately follows it. It is an open question just what types of contrast make this a truism, but I think that the kind of contrast notably absent in the disk-ring experiment, where the one figure slips smoothly and instantly into the other, is plausibly one of the sort needed to make experiences stand out for us sufficiently to be remembered and distinguished from others. This leads us to the following observation concerning the subject's denial that he saw a disk: it is a judgment of nonoccurrence wholly based on lack of memory, where the type of occurrence in question is of a kind especially likely to evade memory.

This, I submit, is why the subject himself has good reason to question whether he has more warrant for saying that he saw no disk than for saying that he did see one. But these reasons for thinking one is in a genuine epistemic dilemma do not apply to our hypothetical blindsighter. Her denials are not based wholly on a lack of memory of conscious vision—she thinks she does not consciously see anything to her left at the moment. And the reason we have for suspecting the metacontrast subject may be oblivious to his disk experience—that it slips too quickly and uncontrastingly into what follows it to be memorable—cannot reasonably motivate a suspicion that the blindsighter is continually oblivious to all her left-field conscious visual experience.

So, granting that the disk-donut subject lacks warrant for his missing-experience claim gives us no reason to think Belinda would lack warrant for hers, nor for doubting that her lack of experience itself would play a role in what gives hers first-person warrant. For there are differences between the two cases that make his judgment doubtful that do not apply to hers. Once again, we have found no reason to think there is anything Belinda would need, essential to having solitary first-person knowledge at odds with third-person evidence, that Bob has that gives him his—they do not relevantly differ. We could keep looking for relevant differences indefinitely, I suppose, but I take the survey thus far to be enough to support the view that—contra Dennett's suggestion—our blindsighter would know she was one.

I conclude that there is not much to be said for an argument against the reality of consciousness of the sort I believe Dennett would have us consider, that would derive the impossibility of the blindsighters I have discussed from the unwarrantability of their denial of conscious vision. Not only would this rely on a "possible, only if warrantable" premise lacking any evident means of support compatible with the argument's aim, but also, there is reason to reject the other premise: that our blindsighter would have no more warrant for thinking she lacked conscious vision of things on her left, than for thinking she had it.

But is this to say that in some *other* case—perhaps in the metacontrast case—where the "unwarrantability premise" is more defensible, nothing stands in the way of an argument against consciousness of this sort, other than the weakness of the possibility-warrantability link? The weakness of that link should not be underestimated, but in any case, it would not necessarily be smooth sailing for this kind of argument, even if we lay those worries aside, and even if we grant the unwarrantability claim. In the unlikely event that we could adequately justify (for example) the thesis that the denial of the disk experience could be possibly true in the relevant circumstances only if it were warrantable in them, without undermining the unwarrantability premise, and even if we could sufficiently answer those (like Block and Flanagan) who purport to tell us how there could be warrant for the subject's denial of experience (whether from a first- or a third-person point of view), there would still be this problem. Suppose we were firmly convinced that there really are no facts to be known about the occurrence of conscious visual experiences, whose extreme brevity and relation to other experiences would make people who had them unable to form the spontaneous belief that they had them. We would still need to address the question: Is this incompatible with thinking we have phenomenally conscious visual experience? It is hardly clear that one could not hold that there is no fact of the matter to be had about fleeting, subjectively undetectable experiences, while leaving open the possibility of the forms of blindsight earlier discussed—my proposed measure of realism about consciousness. The same could be said regarding other would-be motivators of epistemic quandaries about what conscious experience happened when. Have we reached the point of being convinced that the question of whether someone had a given experience at a given time is really unresolvable in principle, and that this implies that there just is no correct answer to the question? Then we still have to ask whether the reality of conscious experience is really threatened by that kind of indeterminacy.

I have said what I have to say about the acceptability of assumptions needed to try to undermine belief in the reality of consciousness by appeal to various special epistemic predicaments to which it purportedly gives rise. But in all this detail, I fear I have not explicitly taken due account of what may be a source of such an argument's intuitive appeal. Perhaps part of what may make this kind of argument look persuasive is acceptance of some ill-articulated background assumption inculcated partly by common sense, partly by philosophical tradition, to the effect that if you have conscious experience, you must be in a position to know what experience you have, come what may—for experience unfailingly makes itself known to the experiencer: it is "self-intimating." But then, directed to cases—like the metacontrast experiment—in which we believe a person may have lacked a given conscious experience, though no one can justifiably decide the question of whether he did or not, we may be struck with a sense of paradox so violent as to make us believe the only solution lies in some extreme reaction against consciousness—a reaction whose evidently "radical" character can have an allure of its own—we must junk the very notion of consciousness altogether.

A better response would be to consider the possibility that, even if conscious experience is, in some sense, itself involved in the special warrant had for first-person beliefs about it, the nature of this involvement is no simple affair; we are easily misled by vague and sweeping formulations about it. And, if we examine carefully the cases that seem to generate puzzles, we will find that either (as in the blindsight case) we would not be as epistemically helpless as some would suggest, or else, where we would be at a loss to form a warranted belief about our possession or lack of experience (as perhaps with metacontrast), this is explicable in ways that preserve the belief that we are conscious, and that our being so is part of how we know we are.

It would indeed be hasty and uncritical for us to think the link between consciousness and first-person knowledge is so tight as to rule out the possibility that a person might have conscious vision when he sincerely denies it—though it may take examination of some rather exotic cases (metacontrast, hysterical blindness) to make that clear. But belief in the reality of consciousness can survive such refinements. I should think so, at any rate, for the way I have approached the debate seems to require me to acknowledge that there could be such a dissociation between thought and experience, even leaving psychological experiments and case studies aside. For I suppose I would have to say that philosophers can present us with what we should regard as a case of false consciousness denial. Though Dennett apparently would deny ever having phenomenally conscious visual experience, I think he, like the rest of us, does. And this sort of denial is not the result of emotional trauma, neurosurgery, or brain lesions, but of philosophy. That this activity is more likely to cause a false denial of conscious vision than its actual loss is plain enough: philosophy may be unwholesome, but you don't literally go blind from it. And though it may engender a kind of alienation of thought from experience, we must not avoid it on that account, for I think the only good way to prevent or remedy such ill effects from philosophy is: more philosophy.

5.5 FEAR OF SKEPTICISM

I assumed in the course of discussing Dennett's epistemic predicaments that these were supposed to inspire a retreat from phenomenal consciousness by showing that the scenarios its acceptance invites us to consider are not possible. But maybe someone will suggest that such dilemmas can be used to show, not the impossibility of Belinda's form of blindsight, but rather that we could not know that such lack of consciousness occurred when it did, and consequently, that we cannot know that it does *not* occur in our case: therefore, we do not know that we are phenomenally conscious. So, the problem is not that the notion of consciousness is somehow incoherent; it is just that we do not know that it applies to us. And that seems bad enough.

If someone offered such an argument, I would object first, as before, by questioning its starting point—the assumption that the blindsighter could not know of her own condition. But let's consider how the argument might proceed if we waive this objection. One would, I think, need to argue somewhat as follows. (1) If Belinda could not know she *doesn't* consciously see the patch of light to her left, then a legally blind consciously sighted person doesn't know that he *does* consciously see such things. (2) But surely the latter has as much warrant for thinking he consciously sees as we do. (3) Therefore, we do not know we consciously see, either. But this line of argument is unconvincing, if for no other reason than the weakness of (1). For even if the hypothetical blindsighter's sincere denials leave us (and her) unable to settle the question of whether she does or does not have conscious vision, this worry does not arise where the *consciously* sighted person is concerned. He does not deny that he is visually conscious—so where he is concerned, there is every reason to believe, and no reason to doubt, that he has conscious sight.

Or is there? If we do not deny that it is possible that those who do not consciously perceive certain stimuli may nonetheless respond as well to them as others who do, someone will want to ask: "Well, then, do I really know that others *ever* have conscious experience, if they may lack it, while behaving as if they had it?" Such skeptical reflections can effect a sort of intellectual paralysis. It can seem so troubling to us that our thoughts about consciousness take this turn, we may find them obsessively stuck here. I want now to indicate why I think we oughtn't to be so intimidated by skeptical thoughts.

First, consider how they might naturally arise in the course of our discussion. Our hypothetical blindsighter correctly denies she has certain conscious visual experiences. But it seems a short jump from here to ask: mightn't there be a similar blindsighter who falsely asserts that she *does* consciously see? And this may lead us to greater boldness still: mightn't there be a person whose visual response was just as good as that of any consciously sighted person, and who went around saying just as we do, "Of course I consciously see," but who had *no* visual consciousness—or maybe no conscious experience of any sort—whatsoever? That is, mightn't there be an entity shaped more or less the way we are, that behaved more or less the way we do, whose movements were as internally generated as our own (not some sort of elaborate puppet), but that is, as they say, a mere zombie, having no conscious experience at all? And if this is possible, why not also allow that it is possible that such a being could be internally, physically, type-identical to a conscious human being, without having any conscious experience? But if that is allowed, how do I know that I am not the sole conscious person in the world, surrounded by nonconscious zombies?

Thus we wander into the unhappy land of other-minds skepticism. The line of thought just sketched does not lead us to the point of saying we do not know that *anyone* has conscious experience—so far it is unchallenged that we know this, at least in the first-person case. But I suspect that if we are led inevitably into this much skepticism, that will be enough to cause many to want to shrink from the very notion of consciousness, and make its neglect seem benign. And further, our distaste for, or boredom with, this particular epistemological entrée, together with visceral suspicions of "Cartesian" claims that self-knowledge depends on nothing outside oneself, may tempt us to reflect: "Since I can't know others have conscious experience, can I really know that I have it? Maybe, if I don't know others are conscious, I don't know *anyone* is, including myself."

I want to say a few words about such reflections, because I have a hunch that they can, even if not articulated, make us less critical of consciousness neglect than we should be. I suspect these skeptical worries help explain a lot of the unease people sometimes feel around the subject of consciousness, and thus why perhaps they *want* to neglect it.

The train of thought we are concerned with goes like this: (1) I don't know that others are conscious; (2) if that is so, then I don't know I'm conscious, either; therefore (3) I don't know anyone is conscious. Now, I assume that an acceptance of the initial skeptical premise (1) depends on the belief that we do not know that totally nonconscious humanoids—"zombies"— are impossible. I have not appealed to such a notion in explaining what I mean by 'conscious,' so it might seem open to me to refute skepticism by arguing against the possibility of zombies. But again, I cannot think of any conclusive reason to hold that they are not possible; and I confess that they seem possible to me, too.[6] However, I do not think this leaves me without resources for rejecting premise (1).

I will return to this in a moment, but first I want to focus on premise (2) above, the bridge to a universal skepticism about consciousness. The question of the truth or falsity of (2) is the issue I earlier labeled, in Chapter 1, that of whether or not self-knowledge is in some sense *dependent* on knowledge of others. The little anticonsciousness argument I just sketched needs some such dependence assumption—it needs to assume that knowing one is conscious in some way depends on or presupposes knowing that others are. The first point is that this is not at all obvious—it is not clear initially why I should not be able to know that I am conscious, though I am hopelessly condemned to ignorance with regard to others. So if I could not be in this situation, it needs to be explained why. And second, some ways of making out and interpreting this dependence thesis, far from landing us in a universal skepticism about consciousness, would actually lend themselves to an argument against even other-minds skepticism. For, faced with the initial skeptical argument from the point that others might (for all one knows) be zombies, one might reason in the following manner. I can't show it's *impossible* that these other bodies I observe are the bodies of zombies, but I do have more warrant for thinking they aren't, than for thinking they are. For I have more warrant for thinking *I* am conscious than for thinking I'm a zombie—until (1) is established, that is not under challenge. And I am convinced by philosophical argument that I have more warrant for thinking *I'm* conscious than that I'm not, only if I have more warrant for thinking *others* are conscious than for thinking they're not. *Therefore*, I have more warrant for thinking others are conscious, than for counting them zombies.

Now, as I said, there may be some version of the dependence thesis, and some rationales for this, that would not permit such an antiskeptical argument. For example, some eliminative materialist might say, "Knowing I'm conscious depends on knowing others are conscious, because I don't know I'm conscious, unless I can show how this notion of consciousness is indispensable to that general theory of human bodily movement which explains this better than all conceivable rivals." If one assumes this view, then one cannot argue against consciousness skepticism in the manner suggested a moment ago. However, other kinds of dependence thesis would not have this feature. I might hold some vaguely Wittgensteinian view that I would not be able to think about how things appear to me (and hence I would not be able to think my experience had "phenomenal character"), unless I were able successfully to identify how things appeared to others. For what constitutes following the norms I follow in thinking and speaking (about anything) is not (perhaps could not be) essentially solitary, confined solely to the first-person case. Maybe something along these lines is true. But if it is, then the reason why the dependence thesis, premise (2), is true, is consistent with thinking I am conscious in the sense I have been concerned to elucidate, and permits me to argue against skepticism with regard to others' being conscious.

So my first point about arguing from other minds to universal skepticism about consciousness is this. This argument requires us to adopt some sort of dependence thesis. But some versions of this view would give us the materials to undermine the initial skeptical premise of the argument against consciousness. And I see no reason to endorse a version of the dependence thesis that would allow that argument to go through. But what if I am unconvinced by *any* version of the dependence thesis? That may leave me confident that I am conscious, but aren't I still helpless before the old skeptical doubts about other minds? No, for if my knowledge that I am conscious is *not* dependent on my knowledge that others are, I might reasonably argue as follows.

First I might observe: If someone were to use the same way of forming third-person beliefs about me and my possession of conscious experience as I use to form beliefs about others and their experience, then they would come to what I know to be, by and large, correct views about me. So my way of forming beliefs about others' conscious experience repeatedly proves itself accurate when applied to *me*. Then I might ask: Do I have reason to think that others differ from me in some way that would be deeply detrimental to the accuracy of my way of forming third-person beliefs about conscious experience, when it is applied to *them*? Perhaps, to be more careful, I should ask: Do I have reason to think other bodies, which I believe to be the bodies of other persons, differ from mine in some way that makes my manner of forming third-person beliefs about experience fundamentally faulty when directed toward them? For in speaking of "others," I may be taken to imply already that I speak of persons, which may (arguably) imply that they are conscious, and so beg the question. So, do I have reason to think other bodies differ relevantly from mine? I would, if I found the following. When my way of forming third-person beliefs about experience is directed on other bodies, it gives rise to a picture of someone's experience notably less logically and explanatorily coherent than the story about me that emerges when this manner of belief formation is turned my way. However, I do not find this difference at all. But how about this: I would have reason to think that other bodies relevantly differed from my own, if this were true: forming beliefs about other minds in this way does not enable me to anticipate in my own thought and actions how other bodies will move and what utterances they will make, nearly as accurately as it would if another used it to form beliefs by perceiving my body. But again, this is not at all what I find, but the reverse.

Well, then, suppose I had reason to believe there is something in me—in my body—some anatomical structure undergoing certain kinds of change, without which I would not have the various forms of conscious experience I do, and that this is entirely missing in other bodies. Would I then have some reason to think other bodies differed relevantly from my own? Yes, I suppose I would, but I clearly do *not* have that sort of reason to think this. For first, though I do have reason to think there is something in my body of the required sort—my brain—my actual grounds for thinking that I have a brain and that it has this sort of role in relation to my capacity for experience cannot give me reason to think the other bodies at issue here do not have the anatomical wherewithal for consciousness. For these grounds assume that other skulls *do* have contents similar to my own, whose structure and activity *is* productive of conscious experience. Perhaps I could, in principle, gather enough evidence by self-examination alone to determine that I have a certain kind of organ in my head and that its structure and activity relates to my capacity for experience in the ways I have been taught. But the evidence that I am a member of the same species as these creatures whose "other bodies" these are, and hence am broadly anatomically quite similar to them, is so overwhelming that it would obviously be not only impractical, but an enormous waste of time, for me to go around looking in other heads for reasons to think there is some relevant, radical difference between what is in them and what is in my own head. I would have to find some pretty remarkable pervasive structural and compositional differences before I could say that this gave me reason to think other bodies differed from my own in some way that upset the basic accuracy of my way of forming beliefs about others' experience. For not just any notable difference I find will provide this. Since the way I form beliefs about others' experiences gives them experiential histories and talents different from my own in significant respects, trust in its accuracy would lead me to expect that other brains will indeed differ from my own in significant ways. So I would need to discover quite enormous differences between what is inside other bodies and what is in my own, before I could say I had any evidence at all that other bodies differed from mine in ways that radically and adversely affected the accuracy of my way of coming to believe other people had experience. And of course, I am not going to find that.

Thus I might argue that I have no reason to think other bodies differ from my own in ways that affect the accuracy of my way of forming third-person beliefs about experience when directed at them. But do I have some reason to think other bodies do *not* differ relevantly from my own in this way? Yes, the same reflections by which I have discovered I have no reason to think they do relevantly differ shows me this. For when comparing what comes from forming beliefs about others' experiences in the way I do with what would come from this way of forming beliefs when directed at me, I find the results are roughly equally coherent, and would enable one to anticipate another's movement and utterance roughly equally well. And there is good evidence that other bodies are those of creatures belonging to the same species as I do, and have in them whatever I have in mine that is needed for me to have conscious experience. Taken together, that gives me some reason to think other bodies do not differ from mine in any way that would make my way of forming third-person beliefs pretty accurate when used on me, but radically mistaken when used on others.

So here is the situation: my way of forming third-person beliefs about conscious experience shows itself to be accurate on numerous occasions when applied to me; I have no reason to believe other bodies differ from mine in any way that would adversely and fundamentally affect the accuracy of beliefs formed in that manner, and considerable reason to believe they do not differ from mine in any such way. Altogether, that sounds to me like a pretty good reason to conclude that this way of forming beliefs is accurate when I apply it to others. This does not prove to me that it is not possible that I am surrounded by zombies, but why should I insist on such proof? Surely it is enough for me if my belief that I live amongst other conscious beings is more warranted than the claim that I do not.

Clearly, in these remarks I only begin to address questions about how one knows other minds. A thorough job would require a more searching examination of the way (if there is one) in which self-knowledge is dependent on knowledge of others. And I would need to consider how, if the dependence of self-knowledge on knowledge of others fails to answer skepticism regarding third-person beliefs about consciousness, the second suggested strategy for doing this would fare when faced with the sorts of criticism made of other answers to the "problem of other minds"—most notably, those directed at the "argument from analogy." My point is, whether self-knowledge is dependent on knowledge of others or not, there is much to say to defend consciousness against skeptical worries. We have no call to think that if we are friendly to consciousness, we will inevitably be struck dumb by some kind of obviously unanswerable other-minds skepticism. And so we should not take this as a pretext for some universal skepticism about consciousness, or for its neglect. Though the door is not easily or conclusively closed on "other-minds" questions (and why should it be?), we need not let philosophical skepticism of this kind panic us into abandoning consciousness.

In any case, we should be at least as easy on ourselves here as we are where philosophical skepticism about the "existence of the external world" is concerned. We may not be entirely sure what to say about this, but we do not any longer let this pressure us into some phenomenalist doctrine that when we talk about tables and trees we are really speaking only of our sense-experiences, or else into the thought that strict intellectual scruples demand we suspend belief in the existence of material objects. Similarly, we should not let the bogey of other-minds skepticism scare us into thinking that all we have in mind when we say we see consciously is that we are able to make certain kinds of discriminations of visual stimuli, or into the illusion that there is something admirably fastidious, hard-headed, or principled about neglecting consciousness.

5.6 SUMMARY

In the last chapter, I pointed out ways in which phenomenal consciousness has been subject to neglect. Here, I have tried to explore and examine some reasons why such neglect may appear attractive. First, I looked into how one may find these in worries about the heterogeneity of episodes of consciousness. The idea was that neuroscience will somehow take from us the right to group under a single heading the various phenomena I treat as paradigms. These qualms about consciousness were seen to stem from a general view about the kind of justification we need for the claims we make about our attitudes and experience—including the claim that we have conscious experience. I have argued that we needn't let our respect for neuroscience make us consciousness-shy in this way; for the epistemology implicit in such an argument has no call on our allegiance.

I then asked whether we can see reason to say that while the forms of blindsight to which I appeal in explaining what I mean by 'conscious' do not *seem* to be impossible, really they are, by applying to this case the diagnosis of modal error we find in current views about necessity and natural kinds. But I could discover in such a maneuver nothing more than an interpretation of 'conscious' incompatible with my own, not a reason for thinking mine unavailable. And there is a notable disanalogy between the standard cases to which we are treated in discussions of natural kinds, and the case of consciousness—namely, the lack of anything in the latter case that might be cast in the role of the "superficial appearances" with which the underlying property can be confused. A search for some other way in which one who made an accusation of modal oversight or error might reasonably try to explain the source of the alleged mistake discovered no good candidates. So it is not just that recent doctrines about necessity and natural kinds furnish no reason to think our belief that we are phenomenally conscious rests on some failure to appreciate metaphysical necessities. Also, someone who would say this evidently has no adequate resources for explaining, in a way helpful to the case that the alleged necessities obtain, why they are so unevident to some of us who consider the matter, or why we believe that they do not obtain at all.

Next, I examined a strategy for legitimizing a refusal to say we are conscious found in Dennett's writings. This strategy tries to show that if we believe we are phenomenally conscious, we will be led to admit something that allegedly just cannot be—that there are certain types of case, real and hypothetical, in which we cannot with warrant say whether or not a given episode of consciousness took place. Against this, I have argued that the premise that impossibility follows from unwarrantability either rests on no grounds compatible with the aims of the argument in which it is to figure, or else is simply groundless. What's more, we have reason to think the alleged epistemic dilemmas are not genuine in the cases that matter for recognition of consciousness.

I noted finally that worries about knowledge may pressure us into consciousness neglect in another way, by raising the specter of other-minds skepticism. But there are resources available for a response to such doubts, whether first-person knowledge of experience depends on third-person knowledge or not. And if a successful response to such skepticism is not assured, then I think we can at least say that our situation here is no worse than it is when other forms of philosophical skepticism come into play, where we do not allow them to terrorize us into intellectual withdrawal.

At this point I have articulated, defended, and employed a first-person approach to identifying phenomenal consciousness and to thinking about phenomenal features generally. I have also identified theoretical perspectives that would frustrate the recognition of these features in our philosophy and psychology, and argued that we should not let these hinder us. Now I believe we are ready to deepen and broaden our investigations into the phenomenal character of experience, again making critical use of our first-person knowledge. In the next three chapters, we will be dealing, in one way or another, with these two interconnected themes: the relation of the phenomenal character of experience to its intentionality, and the richness of this character— how much it varies, and in what ways. Then we will be in a position to start to think about why consciousness matters to us.

CHAPTER 6

Consciousness and Self-Reflection

6.1 CONSCIOUSNESS AS SELF-DIRECTEDNESS

Some people will want to think of consciousness as the mind's somehow bending or doubling back onto itself. They will want to say that it somehow consists in one's "thinking of," or "representing," or "perceiving" one's own mind—some kind of self-directed, inward-pointing intentionality.[1] I have already had some occasion to criticize such a conception of consciousness, focusing on Rosenthal's account of conscious states as mental states one seemingly noninferentially thinks that one is in. Now I want to broaden and deepen this critique. For though this and kindred views can seriously mislead us about consciousness—even induce a kind of theoretical blindness to it—we seem perennially susceptible to them, so it's worth trying to be as thorough as we can in extricating ourselves from the errors they embody. Though some will think it clear from the start that such accounts conflate consciousness with self-consciousness, it is not enough to say that we need to distinguish these or risk misunderstanding them both.[2] We need to explain why it would be a mistake to think of consciousness as a kind of self-directedness of the mind, while trying to understand why we might, nonetheless, feel drawn to some such conception.

My explicit advocacy of a first-person approach to understanding consciousness makes this especially incumbent upon me. Though I recommend this first-person approach, it can tend to subvert the very project for which I've enlisted it. For when we reflect on our own experience, reflection and consciousness are known together in a way that promotes their confusion, and makes the prospect of teasing them cleanly apart in thought sometimes seem doubtful, if not hopeless. But if neglecting their distinctness can make one misconceive of consciousness, or even miss it altogether, we need to face this task: we need somehow through self-consciousness to undo the tricks it plays on us.

I have so far given only a vague characterization of the sorts of views I want to criticize. I will now try to identify my target less vaguely, but for this I need to be clearer about the notion of intentionality or "directedness" than I have been. It's worth taking a little while to explain what I take intentionality to be, since the discussion here will initiate a more general effort to clarify the relationship between consciousness and intentionality.

6.2 Intentionality and Mentally Self-Directed Features

In explaining what I mean by 'intentionality,' I am not going to offer or subscribe to some analysis of the notion. Rather, I will just state some conditions sufficient for a feature's being an intentional feature adequate for my purposes here. And I will introduce and explain my statement of these conditions by reference to examples of certain of our intentional features. So I recognize no requirement that my explanation be somehow purified of intentionalistic terms. I am not trying to provide what one would like to call a theory of intentionality. I want simply to say enough to permit me such use as I need to make of this notion, without requiring too many initial assumptions about the philosophical questions and disputes surrounding it.

Philosophers often have explained what they mean by 'intentionality' by speaking of the directedness of thought and language *toward* something, or of their having the feature of being *about* things—these things being the "objects" of thought or reference, the objects of intentionality's directedness. I do not entirely oppose these ways of talking about intentionality; I have indulged in them myself. But these suggestive prepositions and this figurative talk of "direction" do not adequately frame the discussion, unless we try to press further, and answer certain questions about them. It seems we are obliged to say something about what kind of "directedness" or "aboutness" is at issue here, and to say what sorts of things we're to suppose that thought and language (and whatever else has intentionality) are directed toward, or about. And this inevitably sends us hurtling into a notorious thicket of puzzles, some as old as Parmenides (such as how to distinguish thinking of what does not exist from not thinking at all). I do not think it would be helpful at this stage to become entangled in these issues or to commit myself to some particular way of looking at them.

Similarly, I would prefer not to try to indicate what I mean by 'intentionality' by appeal to the notion of "informational" or "mental" (or just "intentional") content. We may fairly readily speak of what one thinks as the content of one's thought, but speaking of what we perceive does not so clearly lead us to a univocal notion of the content of perception, even though it seems both thought and perception are supposed to be somehow paradigmatic of intentionality. And we may be led to wonder how the content of an attitude is distinguishable from its object—for example, are particular things I think about constituents of thought's content? If so, how can we think different thoughts about the same object, or think of what does not exist? And, if thought and perception do all have content in the same sense, we may wonder if they all have the same sort of content—is having content always a matter of possessing concepts? And what is the relation between the content of mental states and the meaning, sense, or content of the sentences we use in saying what we think, and perceive? My concern here is that we possess little pretheoretical notion of what "content" is supposed to be that is clearly broad enough to give us a useful means of characterizing intentionality, and the notion of content is so much shaped by its use in theories devoted to obscure issues we oughtn't to prejudge, that it does not serve as a helpful starting point.

So let's try a different way of getting a foothold. I propose to explain what I mean by 'intentionality' by calling attention to the way in which one may be assessed by means of contrasts between *truth* and *falsity*, and *accuracy* and *inaccuracy*. The conception of intentionality I want to work with revolves around this idea: *many of our intentional features are ones with respect to which we are assessable for truth or accuracy.*

Let me explain what I mean by saying that we are assessed for truth and accuracy with respect to certain features. For example, if today is Monday, and I believe that today is Monday, the following is the case: *what I believe is true*; and if today is not Monday: *what I believe is false*. To assert that either of these is the case is, as I will put it, to assess me for truth with respect to this feature: believing that today is Monday. By putting things this way, I do not intend to advance the view that in having a belief I have some kind of relational feature: a relation between myself and an entity indicated by the phrase "what I believe." Whether or not this is a good way to look at these matters is not my concern now. As far as I am presently concerned, we might redescribe the example in a way that does not so directly suggest this relational view, by saying: if today is Monday, then *I believe truly*; if today is not Monday, then *I believe falsely*. To say I believe truly that today is Monday, or to say I believe falsely that today is Monday, is again to assess me for truth with respect to the feature—believing that today is Monday (provided, of course, that by "believe truly" one does not mean something like "genuinely believe," or "believe strongly"). We may be similarly assessed for truth with respect to our possession of many other "belieflike" attitudes, where the nature and strength of our commitment differs from that in the case of belief. So we can say that what someone is *supposing*, or *hypothesizing*, or *considering*, is true, or that it is false.

We might also say that one *sees* or *hears* something *accurately* or *inaccurately* (and, with a little oddness, that one so smells, or tastes, or feels something). And so, as the contrast between truth and falsity applies to one with respect to one's beliefs and similar attitudes, the distinction between accuracy and inaccuracy applies to one with regard to perception. But we cannot contrast accurately and inaccurately perceiving in a way precisely analogous to that used to contrast truly and falsely believing. To say that someone sees (or hears, or in general perceives) something, is already to imply that one's vision (hearing, etc.) is somehow accurate. So we cannot describe a case in which someone sees inaccurately in a manner parallel to that we used with false belief, by saying, for example, "She sees that the bottom line is longer than the top line; but it is not, so she sees inaccurately." And if a schizophrenic has a hallucination of a man standing outside of his window, we cannot say: "He inaccurately sees that a man is standing outside his window," as one might say: "He falsely believes that there is a man standing outside of his window." Nor is it even quite right here to say: "He inaccurately sees a man standing outside his window." In order to describe such cases, we should have to say something like: "It looks to her as if the bottom line is longer, but *she sees inaccurately*," or "*. . . her vision is inaccurate*," or "*. . . the way it looks to her is inaccurate.*"" And again, "It looks to him as if there's a man standing outside his window, but he sees inaccurately," or "*. . . his vision is inaccurate*," or "*. . . the way it looks to him is inaccurate.*" (Though in the case of hallucination, this sounds a little funny, because 'inaccuracy' may suggest only a minor failing; but, although it is quite an understatement to say the way it looks to the hallucinator is inaccurate, it is not false.) We could contrast such negative assessments of the accuracy of vision with: "She sees accurately"; "Her vision is accurate"; "The way it looks to him is accurate."

These examples illustrate what I mean by saying one is assessed for accuracy with respect to certain features—in this case: its looking a certain way to one. And I think we can in a similar way be assessed for accuracy with respect to other sense-modalities: the way it sounds, smells, tastes, and feels to one may be said to be accurate, or it may be said to be inaccurate. Or one might say, in any of these cases, that the way it appears to one is accurate or that it is inaccurate. (Though admittedly, how we spell this out for each modality is neither obvious nor straightforwardly the same.) The form of assessments for truth and accuracy in my examples suggests the following general statement. Provided that you mean by your utterance of "true," "false," "accurate," etc., what was meant by these terms in the examples of belief and perception just given, you assess x for truth or accuracy with respect to some feature, if you make some statement of the form:

"What x F's is true"; or
"What x F's is false"; or
"x F's truly"; or
"x F's falsely"; or
"x F's accurately"; or
"x F's inaccurately"; or
"The way it F's to x is accurate"; or
"The way it F's to x is inaccurate."

Now, although I have illustrated this notion of being assessed for truth or accuracy with examples of features that are intentional, it does not seem that it's quite enough for a feature to be an intentional feature, that it is one with respect to which its possessor is assessed for truth or accuracy. Suppose x makes some type of utterance. We might say, where x utters "u," that what x utters is true (or it is false). But uttering "u" is not an intentional feature. This seems to be because, even though x may be assessed for truth with respect to uttering "u," it is not, in some sense, *in virtue of* having *this* feature that x is *assessable* for truth. It is not in virtue of my uttering "Today is

Monday" that I am assessable for truth in this manner: what I utter is true. For it seems that I might have made this type of utterance, and meant nothing by it, and an utterance of this type might have had no meaning in any language. And in that case, uttering "Today is Monday" would not be a feature with respect to which its possessor was assessable for truth. So it appears there must be some other feature in virtue of which I am assessable for truth when I make such an utterance—something that makes me assessable for truth with respect to such an utterance, beyond the fact that I made it. And what would this be? We might reasonably say something like: it is in virtue of my *meaning* or *asserting* that today is Monday by uttering "Today is Monday," that I can be so assessed, or, this is so, in virtue of the fact that "Today is Monday" means in English that today is Monday.

This illustrates the point that features with respect to which one is assessed for truth or accuracy are apparently not necessarily intentional features. My making a certain utterance by itself is not an intentional feature—for there must also obtain some condition that, as we might want to say, *supplies it with an interpretation*, before it is a feature with respect to which its possessor can be assessed for truth. But the contrast just illustrated suggests a way to say what *is* sufficient for being an intentional feature. We might say: it is enough for a feature to be intentional, that it is one—not just with respect to which, but *in virtue of which*, its possessor is assessable for truth or accuracy.

Again, to illustrate: my believing that Los Angeles is south of San Francisco is an intentional feature, because all that need be added to my possession of this feature, for a correlative assessment for truth to follow as a consequence, is: Los Angeles is south of San Francisco. For then it follows that what I believe is true. The added condition is not one whose fulfillment furnishes my believing with an interpretation—it does not make this feature one with respect to which I am assessable for truth, as it otherwise would not have been. Believing that something is the case does not need to have anything added to it to give it that status. To believe that something is so is already to be assessable for truth. The added condition that yields that assessment for truth in this case does not make me assessable for truth with respect to a certain feature; it just makes what I believe true. Once what I believe is determined, no condition need obtain that supplies it with an interpretation, for it to follow that what I believe is true. (We might say that the attribution of beliefs to me *is* an interpretation, not the attribution of features to be interpreted.) Thus, my believing that Los Angeles is south of San Francisco is a feature in virtue of which I am assessable for truth.

Likewise, its looking to me as if there is something X-shaped in a certain place is an intentional feature. For if we add to my possession of this feature the fact that there is nothing X-shaped so located, then we have the consequence: the way it looks to me is inaccurate. And the fact that there is nothing X-shaped so located does not yield this consequence by furnishing an interpretation of the way it looks to me, that is, it does not make its looking this way to me a feature in respect of which I am assessable for accuracy—this feature is already that; rather, it fulfills a condition that makes the way it looks to me inaccurate.

So we have the following characterization of what is sufficient for some feature to be an intentional feature: it is enough for a feature to be intentional, that it is a feature in virtue of which (and not merely with respect to which) its possessor is assessable for truth or accuracy. And a feature is one in virtue of which its possessor is assessable for truth or accuracy just in case: from the possession of that feature it follows that there is some condition, the satisfaction of which, together with one's possession of that feature, entails some correlative assessment for truth or accuracy, though that condition need not include anything we can rightfully count as an interpretation of that feature. To put this a bit more precisely, we might say that a statement S of the form "... x ... F ..." is the attribution to x of an intentional feature, when the following holds. If S is true, then it follows that there is some condition C, such that, *first*, if S is true and C obtains, then either: what x F's is true (or false); or x F's truly (or falsely); or x F's accurately (or inaccurately); or the way it F's to x is accurate (or inaccurate). And *second*, it is not the case that C's obtaining furnishes the feature attributed to x in S with an interpretation.

Now, I have not said what it is for the possession of a feature to need an interpreting condition before an assessment of its possessor for truth follows, beyond what is provided by comparing the case of linguistic utterance with that of meaning, assertion, belief, and vision. But I believe the sort of contrast this provides is adequate for my purposes. To grasp the notion of an intentional feature, it is enough to see that it is sufficient for a feature to be intentional that it be one of a certain kind with respect to which its possessor is assessable for truth or accuracy. Even if we cannot say in general terms just what kind this is, we can have some understanding of this by means of the contrast between, on the one hand, the feature of *uttering* a certain concatenation of sounds, and on the other, the features of *meaning* something, *believing* something, and its *looking* to one a certain way. And this gives us also some grasp of a distinction between, on the one hand, *interpreting conditions*—conditions whose fulfillment, when added to the possession of a feature, make its possessor assessable for truth or accuracy with respect to that feature, as would not be the case without their addition—and, on the other, *conditions of truth or accuracy*—conditions whose fulfillment, when added to possession of a feature with respect to which its possessor is already assessable for truth or accuracy, yield a correlative assessment for truth or accuracy as a consequence.

This entrée to the notion of intentionality fits with the idea that intentional features are those in virtue of which one has states of mind "directed at" or "about" things. For, presumably, what would make one's thought or experience true or accurate—what would satisfy their conditions of truth or accuracy—is what these are about or directed at. But this account is clearly limited by the fact that not all we want to count as intentional in the relevant sense are features in virtue of which one is assessable for truth or accuracy. Desire, intention, and various emotions provide obvious examples. We could perhaps include these by saying a feature is intentional *either* if it is a feature in virtue of which one who has it is assessable for truth or accuracy, *or* if it is such that, if one has it, one has some feature in virtue of which one is assessable for truth or accuracy. (For any who desire, intend, or have emotion will also be thinkers or perceivers, it seems.) Another way of broadening the account would be to expand the list of that for which the possessor of intentional features is assessable—to include not just truth and accuracy, but also the *satisfaction* or *fulfillment* of desires or intentions. (And we might then group all these together, so as to speak generally, in something like Searle's [1983] manner, of our attitudes' having "conditions of satisfaction.") Or, perhaps we will want a more unified account than either of these options immediately provides.

But I am not going to pursue these concerns now. For now I want to return to the issue that led me to try to characterize intentionality, the attempt to characterize views that take consciousness to be a kind of directedness of the mind toward itself. We might now say that an intentional feature is one whereby a mind is directed toward itself, that it is, as I will say, a "mentally self-directed" or "mentally self-reflexive" feature, if it is *an intentional feature with conditions of truth or accuracy that concern its possessor's state of mind.* This is, in other words, an intentional feature having conditions of truth or accuracy that require its possessor to have a certain mental feature—for example, a certain attitude or experience. Thus, if I think that something looks red to me, or I think that I am speaking silently to myself, or I think that I want to finish this writing, then I have mentally self-directed features. We might put this a little more precisely by saying that a statement S of the form ". . . x . . . F . . ." is the attribution to x of a mentally self-reflexive feature, when first, if S is true, there is some mental feature M, such that: if S is true and x has M, then what x F's is true (or x F's accurately, or the way it F's to x is accurate). And second, x's having M does not furnish the feature attributed to x in S with an interpretation. By this account, x's thinking that something looks red to x qualifies as a mentally self-directed or self-reflexive feature, for if I think something looks red to me, then there is a mental feature—its looking red to me—such that, if I have it, then what I think is true. But its looking red to me does not furnish my thinking that it does with an interpretation. By contrast, my merely uttering a certain sound would not, by this standard, qualify as a mentally self-directed or self-reflexive feature—even if what I mean by this sound is that it looks to me as if something is red, and we take meaning something by a sound to be a mental feature. For without the addition of that interpreting condition, no correlative assessment for truth will follow.

It is with reference to this notion of what makes a feature mentally self-reflexive that I would explain what I mean when I speak of views that try to make consciousness into some kind of directedness of the mind toward itself, or inward-pointing intentionality. To make consciousness into a directedness of the mind toward itself would be to imply that it is either necessary, or necessary and (nontrivially) sufficient, for a conscious experience of a certain kind to occur (or for a certain state to be conscious), that its occurrence satisfy the conditions of truth or accuracy of some mentally self-reflexive feature belonging to the one who has that experience (or is in that state). This is how I will understand the view, put more roughly by saying that what makes a conscious state conscious is its having a certain kind of intentionality directed at it—its being, for example, "thought about," "represented," or "perceived," by the one to whom it belongs. I will argue that this is not so, if by 'conscious experience' we mean phenomenally conscious experience.

6.3 THE "CONSCIOUS-OF" TRAP

One way in which we are sometimes led to concede more plausibility to the notion that consciousness is a kind of self-directedness than it really deserves, comes from an insufficiently critical interchange of the terms 'conscious' and 'conscious of.' We can see an example of this in the following passage, in which Rosenthal sketches and motivates his proposed "higher-order-thought" account of consciousness.

> Conscious states are simply mental states we are conscious of being in. And, in general, our being conscious of something is just a matter of our having a thought of some sort about it. Accordingly, it is natural to identify a mental state's being conscious with one's having a roughly contemporaneous thought that one is in that mental state. (1986, 465)

I have already said (in Chapter 4) something about why I think it would be wrong to make the sort of identification Rosenthal says is natural. Being in a potentially nonconscious type of mental state, plus having an "unmediated" thought about it, cannot rightly be identified with having conscious sensory experience. In a little while, I will say something about a problem with this kind of account so far left unexamined—the assumption that every conscious state must be accompanied by some sort of thought about it. But right now I want to focus on something in the passage just quoted, supposed to provide some initial intuitive underpinning for Rosenthal's account, that I think leads his and other theories of consciousness astray.

When Rosenthal says conscious states are mental states one is conscious of being in, this may sound harmlessly truistic. For it may seem at least vaguely plausible to us to say that conscious thoughts are thoughts we are conscious (or aware) of, and that conscious perception is perception we are conscious (aware) of, and so on. But it is not at all clear that this remark is platitudinous when we construe it as Rosenthal suggests. And we should note that there are other ways to interpret it.

If there is a sense in which we want to say that our conscious states are ones we are "conscious of" being in, we should pause to consider what we mean by this, before rushing to infer from it that having a conscious experience must always involve the roughly contemporaneous occurrence of some sort of thought about it. Sometimes when one says one is "conscious of" something, one does report the occurrence of some sort of thought about it. But this phrase is clearly not to be so interpreted in *every* context. We sometimes say one is "conscious of" something, not to report that a thought about it occurred, but rather to assert that one has a certain kind of knowledge. Someone might be said to be conscious of a decline in standards of education over the years, where this does not mean: the thought occurs to her right now that there has been such a decline, but rather something more like: she knows that there has been. And she might be said to be conscious of something in this sense—even her own mental states—at such time as she possesses *no* state that is conscious in the sense with which we are presently concerned, as we might reasonably suppose is the case during at least part of the time she is asleep. She might, in such circumstances, be said to be conscious of, for instance, her desire to see this trend reversed, and her belief that this is hopeless.

It may be that we want to say that whenever one has a phenomenally conscious experience, one is invariably "conscious of" it, in this sense. So you may think that if something looks red to you, and this is conscious, it is invariably also true that you are conscious of something's looking red to you, that is: you know that it does. But this does not show that my experience must be accompanied by the occurrence of a thought about it, to be an episode of consciousness. And further, it is then quite misleading, if not downright false, to say a conscious state is simply a state one is conscious of being in. For this suggests, if it does not imply, that if one is in this sense conscious of being in a mental state, that is sufficient for its being phenomenally conscious. But that is false. For again, we might suppose that there are times at which one has no phenomenally conscious experience at all, such as when one is sleeping without dreaming, during which one may rightly be said to be in certain mental states and know that one is in them.

So there is a natural enough way of interpreting the claim that we are conscious of our conscious states that offers no support to Rosenthal's notion that conscious states are always accompanied by the occurrence of a thought of some sort about them. If we think that we are "conscious of" every phenomenally conscious experience we have because by saying this we mean we know what experiences we're having when we have them, we are committed at most to the idea that some kind of directedness toward our own experience is necessary for its being conscious, not that this is sufficient. And it is not clear that we would be committed to even this much, for it may be that we want to say only that *typically*, if one has a certain kind of conscious experience, one knows that one does (one is conscious *of* it)—not that this is *necessarily* so. Or we may want to say only that if *we* have a certain conscious experience, we know that we do, though perhaps this does not hold for other creatures—who have conscious experience of some sort, but are incapable of forming any attitudes toward it.

One might allow that conscious experience is experience one is conscious of, while questioning the sorts of implications Rosenthal reads into it, in yet another way. For though one might have supposed that if we say we are conscious *of* our experience, we must be attributing to ourselves some kind of mentally self-reflexive feature, this is not obviously the correct way to look at these matters. We might well challenge the assumption that, wherever we say we are, for example, conscious of thinking, or feeling, or seeing something, this phrase "conscious of . . ." expresses an intentional feature, whose conditions of truth or accuracy are indicated by what the "of" governs—our thinking, or seeing, or feeling. For we do not have to assume that the "of" in "conscious of . . ." is *always* the "of" of intentionality. That we do clearly sometimes use "conscious of" in this way does not settle the matter. Clearly the "of" in "thought of" is often the "of" of intentionality, but we would not suppose that by "a thought of some merit" we must mean something like: a thought about ("directed at") some type of merit.

Thus we might say that if there is a sense in which being conscious of one's own experience and its being conscious amount to the same thing, here the "of" is *not* best taken as introducing the "object" toward which some thought or other attitude is directed, or the condition of truth or accuracy of an intentional feature. So, in saying I was at a certain time, for example, conscious of thinking that I had not turned off the burner, I say only that I had a certain kind of conscious state: a thought that I had not turned off the burner. But this is not to say that, contemporaneous with my thought about the burner, I was thinking about my thinking about having left the burner on. For, I suggest, "I was conscious of thinking that p" could be taken to mean something like—I was (in a) conscious (state) of (the kind:) thinking that p. So, on this interpretation, instead of introducing some "object" toward which the sentence as a whole says I have some attitude, the "of" serves to introduces a phrase that indicates in what *way* I am conscious, that is, what variety of conscious experience I have. We might say that when I assert, "I am conscious *of thinking that I left the burner on*," the italicized portion renders determinate the determinable consciousness, in somewhat the way we might render determinate the determinable color when we say, of a piece of clothing, "It's the color *of a ripe banana.'*

I am not saying it is clear we should say we are conscious *of* every conscious experience we have, but should interpret this in a way that makes this "of' other than the "of' of intentionality. Nor am I advocating the interpretation according to which we always know what experience we have when we have it. Rather, the point is that both of these alternatives are at least as superficially plausible as Rosenthal's suggestion that to say you are conscious of some mental state you are in is always to say you have a contemporaneous *thought* of some sort *about* it. And neither alternative makes as strong a connection between consciousness and mentally self-reflexive features as Rosenthal wants; one of the alternatives draws no such connection at all.

So in my view, Rosenthal's remarks illustrate a pitfall to which discussions of consciousness are liable, which I call the "conscious-of" trap; it is responsible, I believe, for a lot of false starts in discussions of consciousness. (Lycan [1996], too, leans on this move from "conscious" to "conscious of"; see also Brentano [(1874) 1973] and Sartre [(1943) 1953].[3]) Some vague and faintly plausible claim to the effect that conscious experience is experience we are conscious of (or "aware of") is assumed or asserted, and then a dubious construction on this is slipped in unexamined, taking the object of the preposition "of" to indicate what some mental event is "directed toward," and taking the claim as a statement of necessary, or necessary and sufficient, conditions. In this way, we are hustled (or hustle ourselves) into supposing there is something obvious or intuitively compelling about the notion that consciousness is some sort of higher-order mental-ness, or self-representation, or "inner scanning." But when we slow down here, and examine the use of this phrase "conscious of," the appearance of intuitive support for such views evaporates. Whatever pretheoretical inclination some of us might have to say that conscious perception (or thinking) is perception (thinking) one is conscious of, it is initially so unclear just what we should take ourselves to mean by that, and what, if anything, makes it sound right to us, that it would be fair to say this "intuition" is useless as a source of support for views about the connection between consciousness and mental self-reflexivity.

6.4 UNREFLECTED-ON EXPERIENCE

I earlier argued against ways of identifying consciousness with a kind of mentally self-reflexive feature, and lately I have been bolstering this, by trying to account for how we might, nonetheless, be misled into accepting such views by an insufficiently critical reliance on certain ways of speaking. But I have not so far considered a way of arguing against them that might have seemed simpler than the route I chose. If the proposal is that we identify an experience's being conscious with one's having some sort of thought about it, it would be enough to show the folly of this that we show there are conscious experiences that are not, as a matter of fact, accompanied by the occurrence of any sort of thought about them. So we should now consider: Is our conscious experience continually shadowed by some kind of thought about it? Or is there sometimes conscious experience that, as we might put it, is *unreflected on* at the time we have it?

It may seem that, so long as we rely on a first-person approach, our very inquiry will inevitably spoil whatever it touches as a potential example of unreflected-on conscious experience, by insuring that it is indeed reflected on. The seeming paradox in trying to find, through reflection, unreflected-on instances of consciousness, helps us yet a little more to understand why one might think that some kind of self-directedness is essential to consciousness. We may think self-directed thought invariably clings to conscious experience, because we consider the issue of whether we have experience unaccompanied by such thought in a way that guarantees a negative answer. That is, we pose the question of what happens when we have conscious experience, and then, turning our attention to some example, either of our own current sense-experience, or of some thought or imagery we contrive on the spot for the purpose of illustration, we ask whether some thought about this experience occurs to us along with it. Thinking of this experience, we find, with undeniable inevitability, that—lo and behold!—it *is* thought about.

However, we *can* rely on our first-person knowledge to reveal episodes of consciousness not consciously reflected on at the time of their occurrence. Consider again silent speech. I do a lot of silent talking to myself in the course of an ordinary day. But often, even typically, when I do this, I am not *attending to*, or *taking note of*, this occurrence as it happens. Usually I am paying attention to, and consciously *thinking about*, only whatever it is that I am silently *talking about*. Though, for example, I am speaking silently to myself as I read something, I am not (consciously) thinking about my silent speech all the while—I am too busy concentrating on what I am reading about. This is not to say I do not *know* that I am thinking, as it is happening—I do know. But the kind of knowledge I then have of my own experience does not require that a thought of some sort occur to me about my experience as I am having it.

I do *sometimes* think about such occurrences; I am perhaps especially prone to do this, having spent an inordinate amount of time thinking about how this sort of event figures in questions about consciousness. So sometimes, while talking noiselessly to myself—perhaps in the course of composing a grocery list, or sorting through some personal troubles—I "catch myself" in the midst of doing it; it suddenly occurs to me: *that's* silent speech. I then perhaps speak silently to myself a little more, all the while marveling yet again at what a mundane but amazing phenomenon this is. Or again, in the midst of adding and subtracting figures while balancing my checkbook, I may be saying to myself something like, "Three from seven is four," and so on—in any case, I am engaged in conscious thought. However, I am typically not thinking *about my thinking*—I am thinking only of the arithmetic problem I am solving. I am immersed in the task at hand, and heedless of the occurrence of thought involved in carrying it out.

The point here is that taking note of, or attending to, one's experience constitutes a special sort of experience. We may want to say that when we attend to (or pay attention to, or take note of) our own experience, we are consciously thinking about it; or even: the conscious thought then occurs to us that we are having a certain sort of experience. I hope that this sort of self-directed thought at least sometimes occurs to the reader; the success of my earlier discussion depends on it. But this sudden turn of mind does not occur to me just whenever there is *any* episode of consciousness in my life. Nor, I imagine, does it thus occur to the reader. So one is not, as one speaks silently to oneself, continually consciously thinking about this occurring; and when one *does* have such a conscious self-directed thought, one knows that one had *already* been silently talking to oneself, and that this self-reflection is something new, a subtle change from what had been happening.

But what about conscious sense-perception—is it ever unreflected on? I suppose that in fairly ordinary circumstances, one could be said sometimes to attend to and consciously think about one's own current conscious sense-experience; for example, in answering the optometrist's question, "Which figure looks clearer to you?"—or when your friend asks, "Does the soup taste too salty to you?" But consider the sort of perception we have when engaged in activity that requires more coordinated movement than what is sufficient *merely* to perceive—the sort one typically has of one's own body and surroundings when going somewhere, whether by walking, riding, driving, or swimming; when grasping and moving things, whether in, say, building, cleaning, repairing, or cooking something; and in the course of all manner of movement involved in human contact—shaking hands, conversing, dancing, punching someone in the eye. It would be an odd sort of life, difficult to imagine, in which one without pause consciously thought about one's *perceiving* as one went about such activities. Often, if one is doing these things, and one is, properly speaking, consciously thinking about anything at all, it is about that which one perceives, *not* about one's perceiving—or else about something entirely apart from either of these. But this does not mean that, during such time, one lacks conscious perception.

One might resist this, by suggesting that the cases of self-reflection to which I draw the reader's attention (in which one suddenly takes note of or attends to one's own experience as one often does not) only manifest a specially *heightened* or *intensified* form of self-consciousness. But, one might say, in cases where this is absent, still there is always some kind of conscious self-directed thought—only it is somehow "peripherally," or less "intensely" or "acutely," conscious. A problem here is that the occurrence or nonoccurrence of something as ephemeral as a thought about one's own experience can be a less-than-clear-cut affair; one may on a given occasion be hard pressed to say that something of this sort definitely did or did not happen. We may not be entirely sure just what constitutes a shift from thinking about the *things that look* (sound, etc.) some way to us, to thinking also about *their looking* (sounding, etc.) the way they do, and it may not be so clear what the difference is between consciously thinking only about something other than one's own thinking, and consciously thinking about one's own thinking itself, as it occurs. We might want to say we are consciously thinking about our own experience when we are explicitly talking about things looking (sounding, etc.) some way to us, or when we verbally report that we are thinking something as we are thinking it ("I'm visualizing ['picturing'] her sitting on a horse"; "I think you've got a piece of food on your front tooth"). But even there, it is not clear one is thinking about one's thinking. (When I said, "I think you've got a piece of food on your front tooth," wasn't I thinking just about the food on your tooth?) Further, it seems that we may also consciously think about our experience without talking about it.

Nevertheless, I am fairly confident that there are, often enough in my life, times during which I consciously think or perceive, when there is nothing going on that I can recognize as a faint or more attenuated form, or lower degree of, something I can, in other instances, recognize as consciously thinking about my perceiving or thinking. It may be right to say that my conscious experience is always "available" for me to attend to, or it is "potentially attended to" in a way that no nonconscious mental state of mine ever is. It may even be right to say that as long as my experience is conscious, it is at least on the "periphery" or "margin" of my attention. But in whatever sense this may be true, it is not so in any sense that entails that my experience is such that I am always in some way *thinking about* it, or *representing* it to myself.

In any case, even those who are attracted to thinking of consciousness as consisting in, or requiring, some kind of mentally self-reflexive intentionality, will likely concede fairly readily that we have plenty of conscious experience without the occurrence of contemporaneous *conscious* thought about it. Rosenthal, for one, thinks he must concede this, for he believes that if one held that every conscious state is the object of a conscious thought, then (since any such thought will also be a conscious state) one would land in the absurdity that every conscious state gives rise to an infinite regress of higher-order thoughts. However, I am not convinced of the need to concede this, since I am not sure one cannot avoid the regress by proposing that higher-order thoughts come with every conscious experience, and are in every case conscious, but in some cases this is just because the state of having such thoughts is identical with the state they are thoughts about. So, on this view, if I consciously think I left the burner on, I must have a conscious thought that I think I left the burner on. But (one might say) this latter is conscious just because the state of having this second-order thought is identical with the occurrence of first-order thought it is about—and *not* because I have a (third-order) conscious thought that I think that I think I left the burner on. But I am not going to spend time examining this way of avoiding a regress, since I believe the proposal, even if coherent, is false. For we often have ground-floor, first-order conscious thought and perception without any contemporaneous occurrence of conscious thought about them.

Rosenthal is confident this makes no problem for the thesis that all conscious states have concurrent higher-order thoughts trained upon them, because he can just say that in cases where *conscious* thoughts of this sort are lacking, appropriate *nonconscious* higher-order thoughts *do* occur (1986, 465). Of course, Rosenthal can *say* this. But the question remains: Do we have any warrant for thinking what he says here is true? That is, why should we believe that occurrences of nonconscious higher-order thought—whatever these are supposed to be—constantly tag alongside our conscious experience, whenever we are not consciously thinking about it? We have, as near as I can tell, no warrant for believing this.

We may think otherwise, if we suppose, like Rosenthal, that cases of conscious experience not consciously reflected on provide counterexamples to his thesis only on the assumption that all mental states are conscious states. But my objection does not assume this. The point is not: "We have no *conscious* higher-order thoughts in some cases, and there are no nonconscious mental states, so we have in these cases no higher-order thoughts." The objection is: "In many specific instances, we simply lack warrant for claiming we have either conscious or nonconscious thoughts of the required sort." Perhaps someone will think that, whenever there are conscious states untargeted by conscious thoughts, we do have warrant for postulating occurrences of the nonconscious higher-order thought about them, because doing this explains something about the conscious states that would otherwise be left unexplained. But just what does it explain? The fact that they are conscious? There is no reason to think postulating a nonconscious thought about these states explains their being conscious, unless you presuppose that their being conscious requires that one have thoughts of some sort about them. But that begs the very question at issue. One might try holding (as Rosenthal [1993] does) that the postulated episodes of nonconscious thought are needed to explain our ability to report our conscious mental states. But they are not. One can have an ability to think about (and thus report on) some state at a given time, even though one is not exercising that ability—consciously *or* "unconsciously"—*at that time.*[4]

This leaves us with the following argument. First, often where we have experience not simultaneously consciously reflected on, there is no warrant for saying that there occur to us *any* contemporaneous thoughts about it—even nonconscious ones. Second, it is not necessary, for such experience to be conscious, that it be *subsequently* reflected on. For if that were so, we would need to say that, when we recall experience unreflected on at the time of its occurrence, we recall having had nonconscious states, which, through now being recalled, are retroactively *made* conscious. But this is wrong; we recall having had conscious experience. (One might here introduce skepticism about memory, but that is another matter.) It follows, then, that we should say we sometimes have experience that is conscious, though no occurrence of reflection on it—conscious or nonconscious, concurrent or subsequent—is essential to its being conscious.

So not only should we not identify consciousness with some sort of higher-order-thought property (as I argued already in Chapter 4), we also should not suppose that the latter is somehow essential to the former.

6.5 UNREFLECTIVE PERCEIVERS

However, one may agree with what I have said so far, but hold that, even so, we still do, at the time we have conscious experience, always represent it to ourselves in some way, because we always then *believe* that we have it. For I myself agree that having a belief that p requires no more than that one be disposed to assert or judge sincerely that p, should the question arise. And, if one recalls that one had an unreflected-on experience, it seems plausible to say one acquired, along with the experience, and had, however fleetingly, such a disposition with regard to it, and thus one had at the time of the experience a belief about it. Thus I cannot argue, by reference only to actual examples drawn from first-person knowledge, that such dispositional first-person belief is inessential to having conscious experience. For any experience I point to will at least be such as I am, and was, *able* to reflect upon.

But this does not indicate any essential connection between consciousness and mental self-directedness. I cannot find experience of my own in the absence of belief about it, only because I cannot identify an example of my own experience I was unable to think about, since in identifying it I demonstrate I was so able. But this does not entail that it is impossible that one *have* episodes of consciousness without believing that one does. If it seems difficult to suppose that you might yourself have had experience you were never even able to think of or recall, you might ask whether it is conceivable that a creature could have conscious experience, and yet lack *any* ability to think about it. It seems possible that beings having, for example, conscious vision or hearing might never contemporaneously think about their own experience, but might remain for their entire lives in the sort of unreflective condition we often are in, and further, that they might never think about their past sense-experience. And this would not be because they just happen never to exercise their capacity to think about their own experience, but because they have no such capacity. And so, they have no beliefs about their own experience.

If you hesitate to say this is possible, consider the following. First, forget for a moment about whether or not unreflective creatures (as I'll call them) have conscious vision and hearing. We can admit at least that it is possible for an entity to have sense-perception of some sort, without being able to form beliefs about its own perception. It seems reasonable to assume that an entity could conceivably see, hear, smell, and feel warmth or pain, without ever *believing* that it sees, hears, etc. This seems reasonable because it seems that to have beliefs about such psychological states at all, one needs to have beliefs about them of the sort we might say shows that one "has concepts of" various types of these—that one possesses certain psychological concepts.

Consider seeing and hearing. A creature could see or hear things without necessarily having what it takes to think that it, or some other being, sees or hears things. For one may see or hear without, as we might say, having, or grasping, or understanding the concepts of seeing and hearing. For this, one needs, for example, to believe that some of the kinds of things one *sees*, one does not *hear*, and conversely. For instance, one sees colors, but one does not hear them. Though there may be a way of understanding someone who said that the blast of a trumpet "sounded red" to him, it is also the case that often, typically at any rate, one does not, even in a metaphorical way, hear what color colored things have. This book on my desk looks red to me, but its color does not *sound* any way to me at all. And though you might be said to see someone honking her horn, or singing, you do not see the horn's noise, or the song sung—you do not see these sounds. But, a creature might see colors and hear sounds, and yet lack belief in such truisms, not because it believes their negations are true, but rather because it is incapable of forming a belief one way or the other about such questions. But if one lacks such beliefs, one does not have the concepts of seeing or hearing, and so, even though one sees and hears, one lacks the belief that one sees and hears.

Similarly, we might point out that having such concepts requires that one have beliefs that are sensitive to the way in which one's and other's seeing and hearing may vary with perspective. One has the concept of and can think about seeing, only if one believes that, though one sees the same thing as another, one may see part of it another doesn't see, as another may see part of it that one doesn't see. But a creature may see things, and, of course, see them from some perspective, though it neither believes nor disbelieves that such variations in perspective may or do occur. But if one does not understand that seeing allows for such variations in perspective, one does not grasp the concept of seeing.

And finally, if one is to have beliefs about seeing or hearing, one needs to understand how the contrast between appearance and reality applies to them. That is, one needs to believe in some cases, or at least be able to form the belief, that something someone sees or hears is *not* the way it appears or looks or sounds to him. However, one could see or hear things, without being able to form such beliefs.

I do not mean to suggest that it is a simple or straightforward matter what the possession of psychological concepts requires. And it is not easy to state explicitly what one counts as evidence that a creature has psychological concepts. But I think it will be hard to deny—whether for the reasons I have briefly noted, or for similar ones—that more is needed for *having* or *understanding* psychological concepts than what is sufficient for *instantiating* them. And if one cannot have beliefs about one's mind without having such concepts, this implies that it is possible to have a mind, without having beliefs about one's mind.

Now, not only can we thus conceive of someone or something possessing only a ground-floor mental life, without self-reflection; we would also find it quite plausible to say that this is actually the situation in which many animals, including some of our own species, find themselves. One important reason this seems plausible is that it is hard to see how second- (not to mention third- and fourth-) tier mentality can reveal itself, if not in the use of language, and we would want to attribute, for instance, the capacities to see and hear things to many creatures that either do not speak at all, or do not use language in ways manifesting powers of higher-order thought. But I do not want now to enter into disputes about just what would be sufficient grounds for attributing self-reflexive belief to some creature, and whether language would be essential here. Without settling these issues, we can at least consider some plausible candidate for unreflective status, and what we are required to maintain about such a subject, if we assume that possession of beliefs about one's own mind is essential for consciousness.

Consider a typical one-year-old child—presumably a good candidate for the category of mental but unreflective beings. We may indeed plausibly think that most one-year-olds see, hear, and want things, and feel warmth, and pain, but that they do not yet have the wherewithal to form beliefs about their seeing, hearing, etc. But now notice what we have to say, if we also hold that a certain kind of self-reflexive belief is essential to consciousness. On this assumption, if we think one-year-olds lack such self-directed belief, we must think they completely lack consciousness. So, for example, we commit ourselves to the claim that when one-year-olds, with eyes wide open, encounter shaped or colored things, they have no more conscious vision of them than we earlier imagined ourselves to have of the flashed X's and O's in our left visual fields, in connection with our blindsight thought-experiment. If we assume that beliefs about one's mind are necessary for consciousness, and that young children lack this cognitive capacity, we are driven to think that their eyes help them navigate the world only by means of a subtle and elaborate—premium-quality—form of blindsight. We are asked to accept not just that this is a reasonable hypothesis (which is already odd). We are supposed to accept also that, if young children are incapable of thinking about their own states of mind, they *must* have no conscious vision at all.

The absurdity of this becomes more evident when we ask ourselves how we are supposed to travel this developmental road—from blindsight at birth to the age of visual consciousness. I earlier criticized a claim that studies of the process by which young children learn to use everyday psychological concepts show that we lack first-person knowledge of our attitudes. But what does seem clear from such research is that learning to form beliefs about one's own mind is a complex and gradual affair, and not just a matter of the child's one day simply turning attention "inward." But what conclusion are we to draw from this if we assume children are blindsighted until they can form beliefs about their visual perception? We will not want to say that one night little Jimmy goes to bed blindsighted, and the next morning he wakes up with phenomenally conscious vision; he does not on some particular night suddenly acquire the ability to form beliefs about his vision. But how could he so gradually shift from blindsight to conscious sight? How could things only gradually begin to look some way to him over a period of months? One does not have to think the timing of experience can be precisely given to have difficulty with this. (It will not be right to think of visual experience as "fading in" over the months—for the experience one has at the beginning of a fade is just as much a conscious experience as that one has at the end. To say things gradually look more definite or detailed is not to say they only gradually look some way at all.)

We might try to save this picture by saying that the child is consciously sighted from the start—but only because he is *able to learn* to form beliefs about his sight. He is phenomenally conscious because he can grow up to be a mature wielder of psychological concepts. But then, what are we to say of a child born with developmental problems severe enough to preclude his ever maturing into a wielder of psychological concepts? Presumably a severely mentally retarded autistic child would fall into this category. Is the doctor who delivers this sad diagnosis to the child's parents to tell them, "And of course, it follows from this that your child will be blindsighted all his life"?

Children can be severely enough mentally disabled that there would be good grounds for concluding they were unable to learn to form beliefs about their own minds, including beliefs about their own vision. But it would be absurd to maintain that such a conclusion would commit us to holding that such children were blindsighters. However, we would have to maintain that, if we said the ability to learn to form beliefs about one's seeing were essential to conscious sight.[5]

An obvious way to try to escape this argument would be to set the requirements for what it takes to form beliefs about one's experience and apply psychological concepts to oneself so low that there would be no question but that such a child could meet them. So one would say that the kind of mental disabilities to which I am referring really would not cast serious doubt on children's abilities to reflect on their own minds. But in that case, we are, in effect, urging a distinction between two kinds of self-reflectiveness. One kind, we might say, is cognitively richer—this is the kind of reflectiveness that developmental studies show children gradually emerging into—and only here, perhaps, is talk of belief about one's experience, and possession of general concepts of seeing, hearing, and so on, appropriate. The other, more primitive kind of reflectiveness—had by small children of all kinds, and even many nonhuman animals—precedes the formation of such beliefs, and demands only the ability to attend to similarities and differences among one's sensory states. So the small child "thinks" (if that is the right word) of two of her feelings: *this* is like *that*. (Though we shouldn't say she thought of them both as feelings, rather than as hearings, imaginings, etc.) We might get some idea of this by considering our (adult) ability to recognize similarities and differences among our own experiences, when we are unable to classify in general terms the respects in which they are similar or different.

I assume that it is clear enough now that there is a kind of reflectiveness inessential to phenomenal consciousness, so that creatures do not need to believe that something looks some way to them for it to look any way to them at all (nor do they need to be able to learn to form such beliefs about themselves). But what can we say about this idea that there is a primitive, lower-grade sort of "thought" about one's sensory states, that precedes one's emergence into full-blown reflectiveness, and is essential to having conscious experience?

If attending to one's own experience is our paradigm of this, we should first recall what we said earlier about this sort of attention to experience being only occasional, and the lack of warrant for positing its nonconscious occurrence. Given that, we ought not to hold that every conscious experience must be accompanied by a concurrent or retrospective thought about it—even one of a conceptually primitive sort. But beyond this, I would say that we would be unjustified even in holding that the *ability* to engage in some lower-grade sort of higher-order thought about one's sensory states is necessary to having conscious sense-experience, until we can meet a couple of conditions. First, we would need to explain what differentiates this less-demanding sort of thought from the cognitively richer kind that is not essential to consciousness, in a way that leaves such "thought" still, nonetheless, a bonafide mentally self-reflexive feature, in virtue of which one is assessable for truth or accuracy. Second, we would need to say why we should believe that phenomenally conscious creatures who have not yet or will never become reflective in the demanding sense, do, in this other sense, think about their experience.

To meet these conditions, it will not be enough to point to our ability to distinguish and compare our own adult experiences in ways we are helpless to classify verbally. For this activity takes place in the context of our having already acquired the ability to form beliefs manifesting a high-grade understanding of a distinction between the way things appear to us and the way they are, and the ability to classify various sensory-modalities. Is inarticulately comparing our experiences in thought really something we can do prior to having the sort of understanding of experience, or of feeling, sounding, looking, and so on, that is acquired only gradually, and that some conscious beings do not acquire at all? Is it really separable from the demanding sort of reflectiveness? About some feeling I have, I think to myself: There's *that* again. But could I pick out my feelings and compare them in thought in this way without having the sort of understanding of what a feeling is that is indicated by beliefs like: people feel, rocks don't; feeling isn't the same as imagining; feeling pain and crying are not the same; feeling pain can make you cry? It is certainly not obvious.

So, then, just what are our grounds for holding that phenomenally conscious beings who are unreflective (in the demanding sense) are in some undemanding way able to think about their experiences so as to compare and contrast them? We need to beware here of loading some kind of mentally self-reflexive intentionality into all sensory perception, by making the requirements for thinking about one's own experience much too undemanding. If primitive thinking about one's own experience is thinking at all (or some kind of "mental representation"), it is a kind of mentally self-reflexive intentionality. But then it is thinking something *true* or *false* about one's own experience, or thinking *accurately* or *inaccurately* about one's experience. Presumably, though, more is required for this than just the ability to respond discriminatively somehow to differences in one's own sensory states. We cannot conclude that the rat thinks about how the buzzer sounds to it (or thinks that it sounds to it now just as it sounded to it a moment earlier, or thinks that it is sounding to it *that way* again), just because we train the rat to press a bar when it hears a sound. So we cannot say it is clear that small children and animals can think about their own sensory states (or "have concepts of their sensations") because they can distinguish them, if by this we mean just that they can respond somehow, in other experience and behavior, to differences in their sensory states. What has to be explained is why we should suppose that they can distinguish their experiences in some way that involves their thinking something true or false about their experiences.[6]

For this, it also won't be satisfactory to say that when they are in pain, the feeling of pain "occupies the center of their attention," which is to say that they *attend to* it, and then infer from this that they are *thinking of* it. For while we will probably want to say that children and animals can attend to the way they feel, or to how things look to them, in something like the way we do when we think about our experiences, it is not clear that whatever or whoever attends in this way to experience thereby *thinks something true or false about it*. That is, even though when we (mature psychological-concept users) attend to our experience, it is correct to say we are thinking about it—since when *we* attend to it, we do, because of our learning, have some thought about it—not every creature that attends to how it feels will thereby have some thought about it. Perhaps what we should say is that such attending is merely necessary to *acquiring the ability* to think about your experience.

There may be problems about our knowing just what kind of conscious experience a one-year-old, or any unreflective creature, possesses, because of difficulties in reflective creatures such as ourselves "knowing what it's like" to be one of these. But that does not prevent us from recognizing it would be a mistake to hold that among the consequences of saying that some children lack the capacity to learn to form beliefs about their own minds is this: they have no conscious vision of color and shape, but only some sort of spontaneous-blindsight capacity to respond to these. So if we want to say that some kind of mentally self-reflexive intentionality is essential to conscious vision, then we had better have either a powerful argument showing we are confused to find self-reflexive beliefs inessential to children's having visual experience, or else a good story to tell distinguishing the kind of reflectiveness such children would lack from some other, more primitive kind of reflectiveness they supposedly would have. In the absence of the first, we should regard it as an error to think that mentally self-reflexive belief is necessary to phenomenal consciousness. And until we have the second, we have no justification for saying that any form of mentally self-reflexive thought is essential to it.[7]

6.6 THE ABSENCE OF INNER PERCEPTION

I have found no acceptable way of making thought or belief about, or representation of, one's own experience essential to, or constitutive of, its being conscious. But I have not yet directly addressed the suggestion that what makes conscious states conscious is, in some sense, their being *perceived* by the person whose states they are. Maybe the directedness of mind to itself that consciousness is, or requires, consists in its perceiving itself, in some special way I have not yet considered. I have not yet directly taken on what I labeled, back in Chapter 1, the "perceptual model" of consciousness.

This picture receives a certain amount of support from the ease with which we find ourselves talking about imagery experience in terms that suggest it. We want to say that we "see" things in our imaginations, or with our "mind's eye," or that we "hear" ourselves talking to ourselves or humming a tune "in our heads," in a way not even the finest ear can detect. In fact, it is difficult to know how one could initially call attention to such phenomena as these, if not by speaking in some such fashion. Clearly such occurrences are in some way similar to seeing and hearing, and this similarity makes our scare-quote talk of them comprehensible. Saying just what this similarity consists in is a difficult matter. Right now I am concerned just to try to correct some ways of understanding this similarity that erroneously lead us into thinking of consciousness as a quasi-perceptual kind of self-directedness.

Here is one way of fleshing out the suggestion that we stand in a relation to our own conscious experience similar to that we do to things we perceive with our senses. In the case of sense-perception, we are so constituted that things in our environment regularly cause us to form judgments about them, though the occurrence of this process, even when it issues in true judgments, does not require that we know or be able to say how it occurs—which is why this process seems so "direct" or "immediate" to us. And similarly, we are so constituted that some of our own mental states—those which constitute conscious experience—regularly cause us to form judgments about them, though the occurrence of this process, even when issuing in true judgments, does not require we know or are able to say how it occurs. And this, again, seems to give us a peculiarly "direct" or "immediate" sort of contact.

But now, if this is all we have in mind when we compare our relation to our own experience with our perception of things seen, heard, etc., then the claim that what makes our conscious states conscious is our perceiving them simply amounts to the proposal we have already considered at length and found wanting: that consciousness is to be understood in terms of some kind of self-directed thought. I do not deny that we have thoughts about our own experience, the occurrence of which does not depend on our ability to state reasons for holding they are true. And someone may want to draw an analogy between our having such thoughts, and the thoughts we form about the things we see, hear, and so on. But even if we grant some such analogy, the point remains that having such self-reflexive thoughts is neither a necessary nor a nontrivially sufficient condition of having certain conscious experiences.

Is there, then, something more to perceptual intentionality, distinct from perceptual judgments, to which we can assimilate consciousness? There is another aspect of perception, distinguishable from perceptual judgment, brought to our attention by the discussion of blindsight. I have said that in vision, for example, there is, distinct from judgments we form about stimuli, the way they *look* to us, where their looking some way to us was what we supposed missing when we considered various possible forms of blindsight. We could extend this sort of point to other sensory modalities, distinguishing similarly, for example, between our making judgments about and triggered by aural stimuli, and there being some way these sound to us. And we might generalize this by speaking of things we perceive appearing to us, in a sense to be distinguished from our making judgments about them. But we might say also that its appearing to me as if something is so, in this sense, is still an intentional feature, for this is a feature in virtue of which I am assessable for accuracy: the way it appears to me may be accurate, or it may be inaccurate. Here is where the account of consciousness as self-directedness comes in. Just as things we see are both visually judged by us to be a certain way, and visually appear to us a certain way, and to say this is in either case to attribute intentional features to us, so our visual experience itself also is judged by us to be a certain way, and appears to us a certain way, and to say this is in either case to attribute intentional features to us. However, in the last two cases, the intentional features are mentally self-reflexive features, and the kind of appearing is "inner" rather than "outer." The suggestion is that, in this sense, all conscious experience innerly appears to the person who has it in this way—even when one does not *make judgments about* or *attend to* one's conscious experience. And maybe even, for an experience to be conscious is just for it to present an inner appearance, for it to be an object of inner sense.

Perhaps something like this is what might be meant by thinking of consciousness as a kind of perception of one's own states of mind. The problem I have with this suggestion is that, as far as I can tell, there is no sense in which my experience "appears" some way to me, in which its appearing this way to me is a self-reflexive intentional feature distinct from my thinking or judging it to be some way.

This will emerge, I believe, if we examine some of the ways in which "inner appearances" (if there are any) would be different from acknowledged cases of sensory (so-called outer) appearance. In the latter cases, I understand what it means to say that something *inaccurately* appears to me, and to say that something appears to me *accurately*, partly by thinking of situations in which something is not as it appears to be, and contrasting these with situations in which something is as it appears to be. For example, I can contrast cases in which something is *not* the way it looks to me, and ones in which it *is* the way it looks to me, and say that in the former case, the way it looks to me is inaccurate, and in the latter, it is accurate. And since I understand this, I can understand something's appearing or looking some way as an *intentional feature*. Furthermore, I can understand this notion of sensory appearance, and its being accurate or inaccurate, as something distinct from perceptual judgments, and their truth or falsity. I may make a judgment triggered by and about a sensory stimulus, like the X in our blindsight story, without this X appearing to me, without its looking to me as if there is an X there. Also, when it *does* look to me as if there is an X there, in this sense, I may judge that there is not an X there. And the way it appears to me may be inaccurate, and my judgment true; or my judgment may be false, and the way it appears to me accurate.

But when I try to make analogous points, substituting my perceptual experience for things perceived, I run into at least this problem. I find that I do not know how to conceive of a case I could describe as one in which my experience appeared to me as other than it was—one in which my experience appeared inaccurately to me somehow. Or I should say, I *might* be able to conceive of a case so described, if by describing it in this way, I am not required to mean something other than what I might mean by saying that I *falsely thought* or *judged* that it was a certain way. So, for example, I might suppose that on some occasion it inaccurately appeared to me that something sounded like a police siren to me—but only if I interpret this to mean: I judged that it sounded like a police siren to me, but really it did not (really it sounded to me more like a car alarm). However, if I am forbidden to interpret the claim that my own experiences appear to me inaccurately in this way, where inaccurate appearings are just false judgments, I do not know how to conceive of the possibility that my experience appears to me inaccurately.

Someone might say:

> You think your inability to think of such a situation is a problem for the doctrine of inner appearance. But it's not. This situation *is* impossible; experiences can't appear inaccurately to the person who has them. However, this doesn't provide an obstacle to our recognizing this special kind of self-reflexive appearing; for this is simply a marvelous property it possesses: that which appears in this way—one's experience—always *is* as it *appears* to be—and that is to say, inner appearances (unlike outer ones) are necessarily accurate.

I admit that pointing to the impossibility of inaccurate appearances of experience is not quite enough to show that experience does not appear to us at all, accurately or inaccurately. For someone may suggest, as above, that the sentence, "The way her visual experience appeared to her was inaccurate," is necessarily false, because appearances of experience are necessarily accurate. And it is not obvious that the notion of a kind of appearance that is necessarily accurate is unintelligible. We might compare the situation here with that of the alleged infallibility of first-person judgments about current experience. It seems to me that even if first-person judgments about current experience could not possibly be false, it does not follow that it is senseless to say that someone's first-person judgment about current experience was false. We would not understand the notion of judgment if we could not conceive that it is not the case that p, though x judges that p, for at least some values of x and p. But it is not clear that there is anything unintelligible about the proposal that certain kinds of first-person judgments about experience (e.g., that I feel pain now) are true, whenever they are made. Perhaps the same may be said regarding the "invariably inaccurate appearances of experience."

However, we need to distinguish here two different reasons it might be impossible for our experience to appear to us inaccurately. One, we might say, would be similar to the (alleged) case of infallible first-person judgment. In this case, let's say (for the sake of argument) it is impossible that certain types of first-person judgment about experience be false, for it is necessarily so that first-person judgment about such things is true. But we might contrast this with another case. We might say that though pictures can represent things inaccurately, it is impossible that a picture be an inaccurate picture *of itself*. But we would say this, not because every picture is a perfectly accurate picture of itself, but because a picture is never just a picture *of itself* at all. (Some pictures do, in a way, *contain* a picture of themselves, but that is something else.) Now, I am suggesting that it is in the second way we are to see the point that experience cannot, in the relevant sense, appear inaccurately to the person who has it. It is not that experience presents an unfailingly accurate appearance of itself to the person who has it; rather, it does not, in the relevant sense, appear to the one who has it at all. So it cannot appear either inaccurately *or* accurately.

We can confirm this in the following way. I will assume that there are differences in the phenomenal character of experience that are differences in how something looks to us. There are phenomenal differences in the way things look to us. So, for example, the difference between the way two colors look to you, or the difference between the way two shapes look to you, is a difference in the phenomenal character of your experience, or in your phenomenal features. Now, according to the "inner-appearance" view, there is a manner in which its looking a certain way to us *appears* to us, that is to be distinguished from *judgment* about how it looks to us, in something like the way visual judgment is to be distinguished from visual appearance. And these "appearances of visual appearance" are made accurate by the way things visually appear to us—by their looking to us some way or another. Now, I take it that differences in these alleged appearances of visual experience are also supposed to be differences in the phenomenal character of our experience. Otherwise I do not know how to take the suggestion that these inner appearances are distinguishable from first-person judgments about experience in a way like that by which we distinguish visual judgment from visual experience. For I make this latter distinction by reference to real or imagined variation in the phenomenal character of visual appearance independent of variation in visual judgment. And if someone says that differences in the relevant inner appearances are other than differences in the phenomenal character of experience, I have to say it is unclear what such nonphenomenal "appearances" or "sensings" of appearances are supposed to be, and what is supposed to warrant the claim that they coincide with, and are appearances or sensings "of," conscious experience.

So now, if our visual experience does "innerly appear" to us, and the way this appears is distinct from the way things look to us, then there will be differences in the phenomenal character of the appearance of our visual experience, distinct from those which are differences in the way things look to us. If we are warranted in thinking there are indeed such distinct differences in phenomenal character, then we should be able to find, in actual or conceivable cases, independent variation of the two sorts of difference. So what we need is some warrant for thinking there is (or could be) some phenomenal difference in the way things look to us, while the phenomenal character of the appearance of our visual experience remains constant, or a variation in the phenomenal character of appearance of our experience, while phenomenal differences in the way things look to us hold constant.

I myself search in vain for independent variation of this sort. I cannot find any experience at all (real or hypothetical) that exhibits the kind of variation and constancy sought here. I find no kinds of phenomenal difference I can describe as differences in *the way my visual experience "appears"* to me that could vary, while phenomenal differences in *the way things look* to me did not. Nor can I find differences of the former sort that could hold constant while the latter varied. I *could* find such independent variation, if phenomenal differences in the way things look to me exhibited something analogous to the shape or color constancy through variation in visual appearances I discover in the case of things seen. But they do not. That is, I cannot say that the way things *look* to me remains *constant* while the *appearance* of its looking to me that way *varies*, as I can say that the shape and color of a chair remain constant while its appearance to me changes with a shift in perspective. Nor can I say phenomenal differences in the way things look to me are constant while the "appearance of the visual appearance" changes, as I can say the way some noise sounds to me changes as my distance from it does, though the noise does not change—or, as I can say, that the way my body feels to me changes as I shift my attention from my surroundings to my body, and from one part of my body to another. There is nothing I might figuratively describe as "viewing" my visual experience from different "angles" or "distances," and nothing I can call shifting my attention around on it, so that its "appearance" to me changes, while there is no phenomenal difference in how things look to me. Likewise, it seems futile to search here for some analogue to a variation in perceived objects while their sensory appearance is unchanged. Something may move so slowly that it looks still to me, and phenomenal differences in the way things look to me may occur, without my judging them different; but can I say that these differences occur while they do not, in another sense, appear different to me? That is, is there anything I could describe as a phenomenal difference in how things looked to me occurring, without a phenomenal difference in the appearance of the visual experience?

If you have no more success than I do in trying to discover some independent variation of phenomenal character, in (a) the way things look to you, and (b) the way its looking that way appears to you, then I think you should conclude that you have no warrant for thinking that there are differences in the phenomenal character of the "inner appearance" of visual experience *distinct from* phenomenal differences in how things look to you. There are no phenomenal differences of the (b) sort, distinguishable from those of the (a) sort. Well, then, should we say that there are inner appearances, but differences in their phenomenal character are identical to phenomenal differences in how things look to you? Then, since the way your experience "appears" to you is none other than a way something looks to you, we would need to say that your visual experience looks some way to you. But this is absurd. The stop sign looks red to me, but its looking red to me now does not look any way to me at all. (No more than does something's smelling some way to me—my "smell experience"—smell some way to me.) So if putative phenomenal differences in the appearance of visual experience cannot be *distinguished* from those in how things look to us, neither can they be *identified* with these. Then our only reasonable conclusion is that there just are no such differences in the appearance of experience: our visual experience is not something that appears to us—it *is* appearance.

Thus the reason it is impossible for your experience to appear inaccurately to you is not that it always appears accurately to you, but that it simply does not appear to you—accurately or inaccurately—at all. Thus, there is no mentally self-reflexive intentionality made accurate by one's experience, other than first-person thought or judgment. There are no "inner appearances."

This, then, is why I cannot accept the suggestion that we account for consciousness in terms of some self-reflexive intentional feature, by assimilating the relation we bear to our own experience, to that we bear to what we perceive with our senses, suggested by talk of "inner sense" and "introspection." For this proposal either (1) comes to the claim that consciousness consists in having a certain kind of self-directed thought, or judgment, or (2) rests on the notion that our own experience *appears* to us, where its appearing to us some way is an intentional feature we have, distinct from self-directed thought or judgment, as visual appearance is distinct from visual judgment. If the proposal is (1), then it is vulnerable to the criticisms we have already considered in previous sections. But if we try to develop the suggestion along the lines of (2), then we cannot accept it, unless we can distinguish the purported "inner" appearances of experience from sensory ("outer") appearances, and from self-directed thoughts about experience. And I cannot. I conclude that consciousness is neither a quasi-sensory appearing of, nor a quasi-sensory judgment about, what is "in" one's mind. If by saying that what makes conscious states conscious is their being inwardly perceived or sensed by the one to whom they belong, one means to make consciousness into a mental self-directedness in this way, then this is a mistake, and consciousness is not "inner perception."

6.7 SUMMARY

I have been examining the notion that consciousness is or essentially involves a kind of directedness of the mind to itself, because I think that this notion, or certain forms of it at least, can do much to impede or mislead our efforts to understand consciousness. I introduced the idea I wanted to criticize first in rather vague terms, because I think that it often appeals to us in an inchoate form, and admits of development in somewhat different directions. I have tried also, though, to formulate the sort of view I have in mind here with enough precision to make a reasonable assessment possible. The claim on which I have focused my criticism has been this: that it is either a necessary, or a necessary and nontrivially sufficient, condition of x's having a conscious experience (or of some state of x's being a conscious state), that it be such that its occurrence (x's having it) fulfills the conditions of truth or accuracy of some self-reflexive mental feature belonging to x. Such a claim would seem to me to be implied or suggested by views holding that what makes a state conscious, or is essential to its being so, is that one have a certain sort of thought about it, or represent it in some way, or, in some sense, perceive it. Maybe someone will gladly embrace some statement of that sort, or else endorse the even vaguer claim that consciousness is or requires a directedness of the mind to itself, but disavow any commitment to the claim I have targeted. But then I hope at least that my remarks have encouraged some useful clarification of just what view one does mean to assert about the connection between consciousness and "higher-order thought," or "self-representation," or "self-monitoring," or "internal scanning," or the like. My point is that the claim that some kind of self-reflection or self-directedness of mind is essential to or constitutive of consciousness does not hold up, on any construction I can devise for it, if we take 'consciousness' here to mean phenomenal consciousness.

I have argued this in part by trying to show how to understand what may appear to bolster theories that weld self-directedness to consciousness, in a way that reveals the actual absence of such support. So I indicated the potential pitfalls of relying uncritically on assumptions about what we mean by saying we are conscious *of* our conscious experience—of our thinking, perceiving, and so on—to support large claims about the nature of consciousness. And I have tried to explain how a first-person approach to understanding consciousness, though natural and desirable, can mislead us into assuming a tighter connection between consciousness and self-reflection than there is. For we tend to find self-reflection where we find conscious experience, because we tend to "look for" conscious experiences just by thinking about—reflecting on—our current ones.

I have argued that phenomenal consciousness and the self-directedness of mind nevertheless *are* distinguishable: first, by drawing on the kinds of thought-experiments described in Chapter 3; second (in this chapter), by appeal to our memory of unreflected-on experience and our knowledge of the change in experience wrought when one attends to it; third, by considering that it takes more to represent one's own mind than it does to have one (and in particular, more than one needs if one is to have conscious vision, and not mere blindsight); and finally, by showing that the notion that there are "inner appearances of experience," analogous to sensory appearances, is fatally confused—for we can neither distinguish any such "inner" appearances from, nor identify them with, "outer" sensory ones.

I should emphasize that I am rejecting specifically the idea that a representation of one's own *mental* states is essential to consciousness. It may be, for all I have said here, that there is some way in which one needs intentional features whose conditions of truth or accuracy require that one have certain features of *some* sort, if one is to have conscious experience. Perhaps one has to have perception that is in some way "directed at oneself" in order to have conscious experience at all. One might imagine someone claiming, for example, that a capacity to perceive one's own body is somehow essential to being an entity that could rightly be said to have conscious experience. Maybe, in that sense, consciousness is inseparable from self-consciousness. Of course, if that is true, it is not obvious—but in any case, that is not the sort of view I've been concerned to contest. What I have denied is that representing one's own *mind* to oneself is necessary or (nontrivially) sufficient for being phenomenally conscious.

Visual Experience: Intentionality and Richness

7.1 CAN WE TAKE THE INTENTIONAL OUT OF THE PHENOMENAL?

If consciousness is *not* essentially some way in which the mind is directed at itself, then just what does it have to do with directedness, or intentionality? Some may be willing to distinguish being phenomenally conscious from having a self-representing mind, because they want to dissociate phenomenal features from intentional ones entirely. The phenomenal character of experience, some might say, is its "raw feel"—to have phenomenal experience is merely to have "sensations" of one sort or another; to have a mind with intentionality, or to have "mental representations"—*that* is something else altogether.

This way of thinking is encouraged by a tendency in philosophy to taxonomize the mental from the start into "sensations" on the one hand, and "propositional attitudes" on the other, the former being the kingdom of "qualia" or consciousness, and the latter that of intentionality, "aboutness," or "content." Thus a dissociation of phenomenality and intentionality can seem to be written into the very terms of their discussion. So, for example, it may be assumed that "qualia," if we have them, are never intentional features, where the term 'qualia' is used in a way indicating it is supposed to capture what I am calling the phenomenal character of experience (see, e.g., Tye 1992). And classic texts in the philosophy of mind seem to have presupposed and promoted such a nonintentionalist view of phenomenal character. For instance, in Gilbert Ryle's discussion of "sensation and observation," he entertains the idea that observation (e.g., seeing) requires, among other things, the having of a "sensation," and that this component of observation might be listed in an "inventory" of one's "stream of consciousness" (1949, 203–5). By classifying the only part of perception he allows might be in one's stream of consciousness as sensation, Ryle assimilates the conscious "part" of perception to itches, tickles, and what he calls "pangs, twinges, and flutterings"—the sort of thing that, as he says, cannot be said to be "correct or incorrect," or "veridical or nonveridical." And so we may assume Ryle would not consider differences in the character of one's sensations to constitute what I have called intentional features—they would not be features in virtue of which one is assessable for *accuracy* and *inaccuracy*. Further, he isolates the only part of perception he would consider treating as an occurrence of consciousness in such a manner that this is never to be thought of as "an exercise of a quality of intellect or character," as he puts it. More broadly, he says, these sensations are such as we should not be "too proud to concede to reptiles"; they are such that an inventory of them could provide "no possibility of deciding whether the creature that had these sensations was an animal or a human being; an idiot, a lunatic or a sane man." This conception of conscious experience as a collection of brute sensations, whose inherent character tells us nothing of the power to perceive accurately or inaccurately possessed by those to whom they belong, or of their varying capacities for intelligent recognition—a way of thinking about consciousness with roots in British Empiricism—has been widely influential in Anglophone philosophy.

Confining differences in the character of conscious experience to a supposed realm of brute, unintelligent sensation can lead one to take a rather dim view of consciousness. For once this is totally dissociated from intentionality (and thus from intelligence, and character—or even from what makes us importantly different from reptiles), it may well begin to seem odd to say we are conscious in this sense, and of questionable significance—so much so that we may begin to doubt that we are, and seek somehow to dispose of this irksome philosophical peculiarity that has nothing to do with the main business of mind. However, to others it has seemed obvious that the connection between consciousness and intentionality is quite robust; they assume it is fairly clear that phenomenal consciousness bears an internal or logical relation to intentionality or intentional content. Colin McGinn, for example, says, "Content, we might say, is internal to phenomenology; the link here is anything but contingent" (1991, 35–36). And Searle, after explaining that all "intrinsic" intentional states differ in "aspectual shape" (the "aspect" under which a belief, intention, or perception is "directed at" an object or state of affairs), writes, "It is reasonably clear how this works for conscious thoughts and experiences, but how does it work for unconscious mental states?" (1992, 157). Searle's answer to the question of what makes one a possessor of intrinsic intentionality—that this requires consciousness—assumes that consciousness logically determines aspectual shape.

I will take this sort of basic disagreement about the relation between sensory consciousness and intentionality as a sign that this matter could bear more looking into. The need to achieve clarity on this issue is made pressing also by the recent prominence of "representationalist" theories, according to which the phenomenal character of sense-experience is not other than the manner in which it represents (Dretske 1995; Tye 1995). Though these may seem to harmonize with Searle's and McGinn's views, on closer inspection they appear to involve an understanding of 'consciousness' that, by my lights, ultimately excludes from consideration what I (and, I suspect, Searle and McGinn) would take phenomenal consciousness to be. And this leaves us with the question of whether one will see the intentionality of sense-experience as inextricably bound up with its phenomenal character, only if one leaves phenomenal consciousness, as I understand this, out of the picture. Once we fully acknowledge phenomenal consciousness, should we distinguish phenomenal features entirely from intentional ones?

In this chapter, I argue that we should not. On the contrary: our lives are full of phenomenal sensory features that are also intentional features. And once we have understood that, we are prepared to appreciate the wealth of differences in the phenomenal character of sense-experience, and to see that such differences may indeed distinguish sensory lives belonging to people, and species, with varying kinds of intelligence. If there are truly brute or raw differences among sense-experiences manifesting no difference in intentional features or intelligence (we should, I think, be skeptical of this), they by no means exhaust such phenomenal differences in sense-experience as we can know.

7.2 FRAMING THE ISSUE

To address the question of how vision's phenomenal character bears on its intentionality, I need to review what I mean by the terms in which the issue is posed. Let's start with 'phenomenal character.' The phenomenal character of vision is how it seems for it to *look* some way to someone—for example, the way it seems to me for it to look as if something has a certain color, or shape. And its seeming to me certain ways for it to look as if something is, for example, red, or yellow, or X-shaped, or O-shaped, is my possession of various phenomenal features.

The phenomenal features here invoked differ from one another, since the way it seems to me for it to look as if there's something red, differs from the way it seems to me for it to look as if there's something yellow, both of which differ in turn from the way it seems to me for it to look as if there's something X-shaped, while each of these also differs from the way it seems to me for it to look as if there's something O-shaped. To have such differing phenomenal features is to have experience with differences in its phenomenal character. That my experience differs in its phenomenal character in various ways, I can know with first-person warrant; I have first-person knowledge that the way it seems to me for it to look as if something is colored or shaped in a certain manner differs from the way it seems to me for it to look as if something is colored or shaped in another. Furthermore, only episodes of phenomenal consciousness can differ from one another in just this way. Whatever would happen in a hypothetical blindsighter's nervous system that would not be an occurrence of consciousness, but that we may suppose could enable her to discriminate visual stimuli spontaneously in respect of their color or shape, would not differ from other states or events in just the ways I have mentioned. Thus a phenomenal feature is not to be identified with the conjunction of some general feature, consciousness (or, having a conscious experience), and some *other* feature, which, while specific to having some kinds of experience but not others, is a feature one may have *without* this constituting an episode of consciousness. In other words, the phenomenal character of experience is not just its being conscious, plus its having some other feature, which may belong to what is not a conscious experience.

As the last chapter shows, we must take special care not to misunderstand this talk of how it seems to us in identifying phenomenal features. When I say it seems to me a certain way for it to look as if there is something green, I do not mean there is, distinct from its looking to me a certain way, a way this looking seems to me. That is, I do not mean that its looking this way to me—this experience—appears to me, so that I might say that the way my experience appears to me is accurate, or inaccurate. And I do not mean that it seems to me *that* it looks to me as if something is green, where this is understood to mean: I think or judge that it looks this way to me. So when I say it seems this way to me, I am not attributing to myself some mentally self-directed intentional feature. Its seeming this way to me *is* its looking this way to me. The locution is not merely redundant, however, because it furnishes us with a linguistic device for identifying the first-person knowable ways in which only conscious experiences may differ, which is of general application, across the range of such experience, and which allows us to recognize that there may be differences describable as ones in the way it *looks* to us, that are not *phenomenal* differences.

So much for what I mean when I speak of the phenomenal character of vision, or of visual phenomenal features. But now again, what do I mean when I talk about the intentionality of vision, or visual intentional features? On my view, it is sufficient for a feature to be intentional, that it be one in virtue of which its possessor is assessable for truth or accuracy (as explained above in 6.2). The way this works in the case of vision is this. I may attribute to myself a certain feature by saying that it *looks* to me as if something is the case. Such statements can be understood as the attribution of intentional features, because, for example, when it looks to me as if there is something X-shaped in a certain place, then there is some condition C such that if it looks this way to me and C obtains, it follows that the way it looks to me is accurate. That condition is: there is something X-shaped in that place. And the assessment for accuracy follows, when C obtains, though C is not rightly regarded as furnishing its looking this way to me with an *interpretation* (as the condition, by uttering "u" x means that p, supplies x's utterance of "u" with an interpretation). C is not an interpreting condition of the feature with respect to which I am assessed for accuracy here; rather, it is a condition of accuracy of this feature. Also, it is sufficient for the claim about how it looks to me to be the attribution of feature in virtue of which I am assessable for accuracy, for there to be such a condition C, that—without supplying an interpretation—together with the attribution yields the consequence: the way it looks to me is *inaccurate*. And there is such a C, namely, that there is nothing X-shaped in that place. Thus to speak of how it looks to someone may be understood as an attribution to that person of a feature in virtue of which he or she is in this way assessable for accuracy, that is to say, an intentional feature. Since such statements are true only of the *sighted*—it does not, in this sense, *look* as if anything is so to the blind—we may speak here of the attribution of *visual intentional* features, or visual intentionality.

Given that this is how I want talk of visual phenomenal features and visual intentional features to be understood, the question may now be posed: How are they related? I propose we look at this as follows. First, consider some instance of its seeming to you as it does for it to look as if something is shaped and situated in a certain way, such as its seeming to you just as it does on a given occasion for it to look as if there is something X-shaped in a certain position. If it seems this way to you, then it appears to follow that it does look to you as if there is something X-shaped in a certain position. If this is right, then its seeming this way to you is a feature in virtue of which you are assessable for accuracy—that is to say, it is an intentional feature. For, from what we have said, if it seems to you as it does for it to look this way, then, if it is also the case that there is something X-shaped in a certain position, it follows that the way it looks to you is accurate. That this follows is enough, according to the conception of intentionality introduced at 6.2, to make the phenomenal feature in question an intentional feature. For if you have this visual phenomenal feature, there is some condition that, when its fulfillment is added to your possession of that feature, entails the truth of a correlative assessment for accuracy (one about the accuracy of how it looks to you). And the fulfillment of this added condition does not secure this consequence by furnishing the attributed phenomenal feature with an interpretation. If it is correct to think assessment for visual accuracy follows in this manner from its seeming to one as it does to us for it to look as if things are shaped and situated in certain ways—then we should say that *enormously many visual phenomenal features are intentional features*. For if you are normally sighted, then for most of the time you have your eyes open, you will have some intentional phenomenal feature, and which such feature you will have will change with the way shape, position, and size visually seem to you.

The question, then, is whether it is better to assert or to deny that assessments for visual accuracy do follow from the possession of visual phenomenal features in the way suggested. Now, it seems to me that there are surely *some* conditions that, when added to one's having visual experience of such a phenomenal character, will entail the truth of correlative assessments for visual accuracy. And what is entailed—that the way it looks to one is accurate, or that it is inaccurate in some respect—will entail that one has a conscious visual experience that is accurate or inaccurate, for its looking some way or other to one is a phenomenally conscious visual experience. The issue is whether, to reach this conclusion that the way it looks to one is accurate or inaccurate, additional conditions need to obtain that are rightly regarded as *interpreting conditions*, and not just the fulfillment of *conditions of accuracy*.

Now, if we broadly survey sane suggestions for reasons to believe we need some condition to perform this job of supplying the phenomenal character of visual experience with an interpretation—with intentionality—and we find such suggestions, upon examination, to be inadequate to support this conviction, then it seems reasonable to conclude that there just is no such job that needs doing. The phenomenal character of visual experience does not need to be supplied with intentionality by adding interpreting conditions, because it already has intentionality.

On the other hand, suppose we find reason to believe there are conditions that could fail to obtain, though one had the sorts of phenomenal features in question, but that need to obtain if one is to be assessable for accuracy with respect to them, and that are reasonably regarded as interpreting conditions. Then visual phenomenal features would be, in a fashion, assimilated to the status of linguistic utterances. For in that case, phenomenal sensory features would need, like linguistic utterances, something like an interpretation, if they are to be features in respect of which one can be assessed for accuracy or truth. You neither *truly* nor *falsely* utter, "It's raining"—regardless of the weather—unless by this utterance you mean (or the sentence uttered means) that it's raining. Just so, it might be held, your conscious visual experience is neither accurate nor inaccurate, regardless of what visible shapes and sizes are to be found in your vicinity, unless some further, separable condition obtains that "invests" your experience (or experience of that type) with meaning. You may imagine a better analogy here would be pictorial (rather than linguistic) representation. Lines and blobs of color on canvas might be arranged just as those on portrait and landscape paintings are, without representing anything accurately or inaccurately. For they do this only if they are also "taken" or interpreted in a certain way by those who make them or view them (as they might not be). Similarly (so the suggestion would go), you might have whatever phenomenal sensory experience you like, but nothing will appear either accurately or inaccurately to you, unless your experience is also taken or interpreted in the appropriate way.

But what is at issue here fundamentally is not whether there are some ways in which visual experience is like or unlike linguistic or pictorial representation, but whether it is like either of them specifically in this respect. The sounds or shapes of utterance, and the colors and shapes of a picture, need something more if what has them is to be assessable for truth or accuracy. The question is whether something also needs to be added to the phenomenal character of visual experience, to make its possessor assessable for accuracy.

7.3 IS THE PHENOMENAL HOLISTIC ENOUGH TO BE INTENTIONAL?

One might object to my way of counting phenomenal visual features intentional because one thinks that the phenomenal character of visual experience is, in a sense, inherently fragmentable—one can isolate "pieces" of it from each other (at least conceptually) while preserving their character—and this, in a way that is incompatible with such features being intentional ones. For intentional features are "holistic"—they cannot be possessed, even in principle, in total isolation from one another, or in just any old combination. So, we might say, a kind of phenomenal visual atomism put together with a holism regarding visual intentionality would give us the conclusion that the sorts of visual phenomenal features I ask us to consider cannot be intentional features. They must, therefore, stand in need of some interpreting condition before their possession gives one experience that can be accurate or inaccurate of anything.

Let me try to make this out in a little more detail. The idea is, it could seem to someone just the way it seems to you on some occasion for it to look to you as if there was something X-shaped in a certain position, even though that someone had no other phenomenally conscious sensory experience whatsoever. This would be someone with a *radically monotonous* history of phenomenal sensory features. Or else it could seem this way to someone whose phenomenal history, though varied, was *severely fragmented*. We might suppose this history to consist entirely in the kind of visual experience we would have in watching a succession of differently shaped and sized items appear on a screen with no experience of continuous change in shape, position, or movement. Another way in which one's experience might be severely fragmented: one has experience in different sensory modalities, but these are not coordinated with one another at all. So where it *looks* as if there's a shape is never where it *feels* as if there's one, and it is never visually or tactually apparent where what sounds, tastes, or smells some way is located. Now, if the visual phenomenal features I ask us to consider are such as could be a part of a radically monotonous experiential history, or if they could belong to a severely fragmented one, then this might seem to show they are not intentional features. For it may seem that the creature whose phenomenal life consists only of the visual experience of an X-shape would not properly be said to have an accurate visual experience, provided there was an X-shape, or an inaccurate one, provided there was nothing X-shaped before it. And similarly, it may seem that this experience, in the context of a certain kind of experiential chaos, would not be properly regarded as accurate or inaccurate of anything. Why? Perhaps (and this is only a suggestion) because appearances can be accurate or inaccurate only if some can, in some sense, be "corrected" by others by failing to "integrate" or "cohere" with them, which they can do only if appearances generally relate to others sufficiently coherently. The atomist worry is that the phenomenal visual features I speak of are isolable in a way that deprives them of the sort of coherence prerequisite to being intentional visual features.

In reply to this kind of worry, I want to say first that I do not think the phenomenal character of visual experience is atomistic or fragmentable in the way this would suggest, and second, that even if we think it is, the claim I am concerned to make can be readily reformulated so that this kind of phenomenal atomism provides no obstacle to its acceptance.

So, first notice, when you consider most actual cases in your experience of its looking to you as if something is shaped and situated a certain way, that part of the way it seems at this time for it to look somehow situated is to be identified with reference to the way what *surrounds* it looks as if it is situated and differentiated in space, at this same time. For it seems to you as it does for it to look as if what is X-shaped is somewhere in relation to what is differently shaped around it. And the way that this seems differs from the way it seems for it to look as if something X-shaped is differently related in location to differently appearing surroundings. Thus it would not seem to someone just as it does to you, in a typical case, for it to look as if something X-shaped is situated in a certain fashion, if it did not at the same time seem to this someone as it does to you, on this occasion, for it to look as if what is surrounding something X-shaped is shaped and situated a certain way. How it visually seems to you as if an X-shape is situated cannot be ripped out of context, and attributed to an imaginary person who lacks visual experience phenomenally like your experience of an X-shape's surrounds. To suppose a subject has a visual experience of an X-shape against a completely homogenous background extending to the limits of her visual field, is not to suppose that it seems to her just as it does to you, in a typical case, for it to look as if something X-shaped is situated in a certain way.

Now, a similar point can be made regarding the relation between how it seems to you at some time for it to look as if something is somehow shaped and situated and the way it *seemed* to you at the immediately preceding time for it to look as if something is somehow shaped and situated. If it seems to you as it does for it to look as if something X-shaped is moving continuously in a trajectory (or increasing in size, or changing shape), then the way it seems to you for it to look as if some shape is somehow situated at any later stage of this episode will need to be identified relative to its earlier having seemed as it did for something shaped to be somehow situated. For otherwise, if the visually apparent situation of the shape during each subinterval is identified only relative to its apparent surrounds during that subinterval, we will be thinking of a series of appearances in different positions. And that would be a way of thinking of a kind of appearance of jerky, discontinuous movement or alteration in size or shape: first this shape is here, then this here, then this here. But the way it seems to us for it to look as if something is moving or altering in jerky, discontinuous fashion differs from the way it seems to us for it to look as if something is moving or changing smoothly or continuously. So we are thinking of experience with the latter sort of phenomenal character only if we think of the visually apparent situation of the shape during a subinterval in relation to its visually apparent situation at a previous interval. (I believe analogous points could be made, not only about the perception of movement or alteration in size or shape, but also about the visual experience of different facets of something stable: the continuous, unjerky change in visual appearance with change in perspective is conceivable only if how it seems to you for something to look from one angle during a given time is not identified completely independently from how it seemed to you before.)

What this shows, if correct, is that we cannot conceive of some subject having visual experience of how something is shaped and situated with the same phenomenal character as ours, by taking a "time slice" of our experience and attributing it to this subject in isolation from experience of the phenomenal character ours had prior to the "slice" in question. For typically, the phenomenal character of our visual experience during a given time, of how something is situated, will be identifiable only relative to the phenomenal character of experience lying outside that time.

Something along the same lines, I think, may be said with regard to the suggestion that the different sensory modalities could be uncoordinated with one another in various radical ways, though the phenomenal character of any one of them would be just the same as it is in the case of our coordinated visual experience. It is far from clear that it could seem to some x just the way it does to us for it to look as if things are shaped and situated in certain ways over time, though it did not seem to x as it does to us for us to *feel where our bodies are*, amidst what visually appears shaped and situated, or though it never seemed to x as it does to us for it to *feel as if something is where it looks to us as if it is*. (We might approach this issue by asking, for example, whether the difference in the phenomenal character of subjects' visual experience before and after putting on lenses that [re-]invert the retinal image—the difference between how it seems for things to look oriented to such subjects—can be properly understood independently of how things seem to them kinesthetically and tactually. Do "seems right-side up" and "seems upside down" have meaning for us independently of coordination between the phenomenal character of different sensory modalities?) I would suggest that the way it visually seems to us as if things are situated cannot ultimately be divorced entirely from the way it kinesthetically and tactually seems to us as if our bodies and other things are situated, so that our visual experience cannot be ripped out of its phenomenal context and reinserted into a radically different one while entirely preserving its phenomenal character.[1]

For reasons of this kind, I do not think that phenomenal features of the sort I want to claim are intentional can be yanked out of our lives conceptually, and attributed to possible subjects in chaotic or monotonous arrangements that we might plausibly think incompatible with their possession of visual intentionality. If we should be holists of some sort about sensory intentionality, then this gives us no reason to doubt the intentionality of visual phenomenal features, *unless* we have warrant for thinking these latter are so unholistic as to preclude their being intentional. But we do not. And, though the issue needs further consideration, it seems we have warrant for thinking that they are sufficiently holistic in relevant ways.

I will sometimes conduct my discussion on the assumption that the kinds of visual phenomenal features we can identify by thinking of how it seems to us, on a given occasion, for it to look as if things of a certain shape are situated in certain ways, are features relevantly holistic enough so as not to be precluded from being intentional features, by reason of some kind of sensory intentional holism. But if you think a real worry along these lines is to be had, you may note that I can alter the sorts of visual phenomenal features I put up as candidates for intentional status so as to avoid it. For if the kinds of visual phenomenal features of which I speak are isolable in ways that disqualify them from being intentional features, we can consider visual phenomenal features of a larger scale, which are inclusive of the allegedly isolable ones, but presumably not subject to the same worry. For example, if it seems to me as it does on a given occasion for it to look as if there is something X-shaped in a certain position, there is another phenomenal feature in which this is included, namely, its seeming to someone as it has seemed to me my entire life thus far for it to look to me as if things were shaped and situated. That feature presumably cannot be isolated or combined with alleged visual experiential fragments in such a way as to preclude visual intentionality. And if we say its intentionality *can* be precluded by isolating it from or combining it with a phenomenal history of *tactual* and *kinesthetic* experience radically unlike the kind that I have, then I would beg us to consider the phenomenal feature: its seeming as it has to me thus far for it to look as if things are shaped and situated, *and* for it to feel to me as if things are shaped and situated, in certain ways. Presumably, the worry that certain phenomenal sensory features are isolable from other such features in such a way as to remove sensory intentionality will not be a worry that applies to *that* phenomenal feature.

So, then, we would have to ask whether there is any new reason to think having such a feature needs any conditions beyond its being the case that there is an X in a certain place, to yield the result that the way it looks to its possessor is accurate. For phenomenal atomism provides us with none. My main concern is just to show that the sorts of phenomenal sensory features we have most of the time we are awake are sufficient for having sensory intentionality. So, to meet the worry raised by combining phenomenal atomism with intentional holism, it would be sufficient to confine my thesis to such ("super-macro") phenomenal sensory features. If there is some reason to think that we need to add interpreting conditions to the possession of phenomenal sensory features to derive assessments for visual accuracy, then it will have to come from some other quarter, and it will have to apply to even these sensory phenomenal features.

7.4 SENSE-DATA INFLATED (AND EXPLODED)

I would now like to clear up a potential misconception that would block our understanding how intentionality is inherent in the phenomenal character of vision, and could serve as an objection to my way of exhibiting the intentionality of phenomenal visual features. This is what I will call a "sense-datum" interpretation of our claims about the phenomenal character of our experience. On this view, one would hold that whenever it's true that it seems to S the way it does for it to look as if there's something X-shaped in a certain position, there *is* something X-shaped there, which looks X-shaped to S (though perhaps we should say: something X-shaped in "inner" space, a "mental object"). And the same holds for every phenomenal feature one might distinguish, by speaking or thinking of how it looks to someone as if something is shaped or positioned. I call this a sense-datum interpretation because, if this view were correct, there would be entities of the sort for which philosophers conjured up the term 'sense-datum': items that sensorily appear to us—for example, look to us—in some way, but that cannot appear as other than they are—objects whose appearances (whose looks) never mislead.

Such a view would provide an obstacle to appreciating the relation between phenomenality and intentionality, because it would prevent us from indicating the conditions under which conscious visual experience is *inaccurate*. I want to say that if it seems to me the way it does for it to look as if there is something X-shaped in a certain position, but there is nothing X-shaped there, then the way it looks to me is inaccurate. But we cannot endorse that view if we take the sense-data line, for then, the report of the phenomenal character of my experience would entail the falsity of the condition I would propose we combine with it to yield the consequence that the way it looks to me is inaccurate. Thus I could not in this manner indicate how the way it looked to me on some occasion might be inaccurate, since the condition by which I would seek to do so would be inconsistent with my report of the phenomenal character of my visual experience. It just would not be possible for my visual experience to be inaccurate in the way I have indicated.

But now we do need *some* understanding of how visual experience can go wrong, if we are to understand the relationship between the phenomenality and the intentionality of vision. Perhaps we cannot simply dismiss as incoherent the notion of a kind of appearance, in some way analogous to sensory appearance, but that is necessarily accurate. Even so, we would, I believe, not understand the notion of the accuracy of appearance at all, if we could conceive of *no* sort of inaccurate appearance. (Similarly, we would not understand what it was to judge truly if we could not conceive of anyone's ever judging anything falsely.) Further, if we cannot admit the possibility of inaccuracy in regard to *sensory* appearances, I do not know where we *could* admit it. And if we have no understanding of what it means to say that something appears accurately, I, at least, have no grip on what it could mean to say that vision has intentionality.

Perhaps someone happy with the sense-datum view would say that it does not prevent us from understanding how visual experience can go wrong, since we can conceive of how the way it looks to us may be inaccurate in a way other than that I propose, compatible (as mine is not) with the belief in sense-data. Maybe (if you have been reading John Locke) you will suggest that when it looks to you as if there's something X-shaped, this is inaccurate, if the X-shaped thing that looks this way to you (the one "immediately perceived" by you) is not caused by a *further* X-shaped thing (that does not look any way at all to you—is not "immediately perceived"). Or maybe (if you have been reading George Berkeley) you will suggest that, though the way it *looks* to you cannot, strictly speaking, be inaccurate, still you may *judge* that things will look to you in other ways, under other conditions, and these judgments may be mistaken (so, based on the way it looks to you now, you might be inclined to judge it will still look to you as if there is an X upon closer inspection, though this turns out to be false). But I believe these traditional approaches to sensory error cannot adequately account for it, and not just because of the standard difficulties that have been brought up for them. For consideration of the phenomenal character of visual experience will show us that any view starting with the premise that something that ("directly" or "immediately") looks some way to us is never other than the way it looks, will fail to give us a satisfactory conception of how visual appearance may be inaccurate.

So, I will argue that attention to vision's phenomenal character will lead us to recognize that a sense-datum view would commit one to a conception of sensory error incompatible with the facts any would-be account of it needs to acknowledge. Thus a sense-datum view of visual experience should not keep us from understanding the intentionality of visual experience as I have proposed.

Sense-datum theories have suffered a massive drop in philosophical popularity in the last half-century. But that by itself is surely not a good enough reason for me to reject them. And much of the reason for the unpopularity of sense-data seems to be that they are not up to performing the roles for which they have been cast in this or that theory of meaning or knowledge. Even if sense-data would play these roles ineptly, this would not show that they do not exist. Some would object to sense-data on general metaphysical grounds—one might argue that they require a type of dualist theory of mind that is to be rejected because of various metaphysical problems to which it gives rise. But if a correct understanding of the phenomenal character of sensory experience leads us to believe that there are sense-data, then we cannot get rid of them merely by showing this gives rise to problems we don't know how to solve—maybe there just are metaphysical problems we don't have any decent idea of how to solve, or that can't be solved at all. I do

accept the claim, often made, that the acceptability of inferring the existence
of sense-data from statements about how it seems or looks to someone is not
at all evident, and should not be granted. But that is not enough; we need to
understand better why such an inference is unacceptable. Further, I am concerned that a legitimate and healthy suspicion of sense-data may be wrongly
taken to warrant a reluctance to acknowledge our possession of phenomenally conscious sense-experience. But the lover of the phenomenal need have
no fondness for sense-data. And again here I want to emphasize that we may
(and should) embrace phenomenal consciousness without endorsing any
sort of "inner-perception" doctrine about it. (Here such a doctrine might
have us say that conscious visual experience involves the appearance [hence
perception] of mental objects, items "in our minds," since they—unlike
things in the ["external"] world—always are the way they look.) So I think
it is worthwhile seeing that the sense-datum view is actually at odds with the
phenomenal character of our visual experience, not only because this will
open the way for an understanding of sensory error we need if we're to
understand the relation of phenomenal character to intentionality, but also
because it will help us further disentangle our recognition of consciousness
from traditional theories of mind and associated talk of "innerness" that can
still warp our conception of it.

We will begin to appreciate what is wrong with the sense-datum view,
and so begin to properly grasp the intentionality of visual experience, if we
think about just what kinds of shapes visual sense-data are supposed to
have. On this view, if it seems to me as it does for it to look as if there is
something X-shaped, then there is something X-shaped that looks that way
to me. But do sense-data have only two-dimensional shapes, or are there,
for example, *cubical* sense-data? Suppose I also say that it seems to me as it
does for it to look as if there is something cubical. Should I say then that
there is a cube, which looks cubical to me? Typically, philosophers have
invited us to attribute to sense-data just the shapes we would trace on a flat
surface, if we were making a perspectival drawing of what we saw. But why
doesn't a report of phenomenal character that embeds three-dimensional
terms like 'cube' imply the existence of three-dimensional sense-data? If one
wishes to keep one's sense-data from bulging out beyond two dimensions, it
appears that one needs to say that phenomenal reports like the one just
mentioned, employing the term 'cube,' only attribute the very same phenomenal features as one could in principle attribute in reports that contained *no* such three-dimensional terms. The idea would be that one could,
in principle, eliminate all such terms from the report of how it seems, without neglecting any phenomenal feature one might otherwise have rightly
attributed to oneself. Thus sense-data may be supposed flat, uniformly two-
dimensional.[2] This stance has deep roots in the empiricist tradition, and is
nicely encapsulated in Hume's comment: "All bodies, which discover themselves to the eye, appear as if painted on a plain surface" (Hume 1739,
1.2.5).

But Hume's remark also suggests just what is wrong with this conception. For if one could, without loss, eliminate three-dimensional terms from reports of the phenomenal character of experience, then Hume would be right, and there would be no difference between the way it seems for it to look to me as if things are three-dimensionally shaped, and the way it seems for it to look to me as if there are items having the two-dimensional shapes that belong to pictures of such three-dimensionally shaped things. But this is not correct. "Bodies which discover themselves to the eye" often just do not appear as do pictures of them painted on a plane surface. For example, the way it seems to me, for it to look to me as if there is a figure of a cube painted on a plane surface, differs from the way it seems to me, for it to look to me as if there *is* a cube before me. And this is so, even if we suppose the cube picture is an expertly executed perspectival representation of what I see on this occasion. If it seems to me as it does for it to look as if there is a cube before me, it looks to me as if something is partly nearer and partly farther from me, and this is not the way it seems, for it to look to me as if a cube is painted on a plane surface.

We might make this clearer by noting that not only do things that are not pictures appear otherwise than pictures of them do, but also, in the right circumstances, even what *is* painted on a plane surface may appear as if it is *not*. Such is the case when we are "fooled" by trompe l'oeil paintings. So it might look to me as if there is some floral relief decorating the top edge of the wall, or as if a wall is made of bricks and mortar—that is, it may seem to me as it does for it to look to me as if a surface protrudes here, and is indented there in a certain way—though I am standing before a wall *without* such protuberances and indentations, but painted so as to make it look to us as if there are such. The way it seems to me, when I am subject to such an illusion, is not the way it does for it to look to me as if there is something two-dimensionally shaped there, but as if there is something three-dimensionally shaped.

Perhaps, once I have seen that a certain surface is, after all, relatively flat rather than bulging out and curving in, and I stand in the same spot from which I was previously fooled, it may then indeed appear or look to me as if there are bricks or floral reliefs painted on a plane surface. Now it "looks fake." But now my experience has a different phenomenal character than it did when I was subject to the illusion. Now indeed it seems to me as it does for it to look to me as if there is a flat painted surface before me. But that was *not* how it seemed to me earlier, when the trompe l'oeil worked.

The more general point is this. "Bodies that discover themselves to the eye," that is, whatever things there are that do look some way to us (whether these are supposed to be sense-data, or something else) often do *not* look as if painted on a plane surface—that is, merely two-dimensional—in the sense of this phrase implied by reports of the phenomenal character of our vision. That is, the way it seems to us to see implies that it looks to us as if things are more than two-dimensional. So if such reports of phenomenal character entail the existence of visual sense-data, if they entail that there are things having certain shapes, which look to us as if they have those shapes, then they will entail that these sense-data are three-dimensional. If we are to say there are visual sense-data, we will have to puff them out to three dimensions.

But I think it is no accident that the usual account of sense-data makes them flat; we will see that they cannot withstand this effort to inflate them. Consider again the situation in which one is fooled by a trompe l'oeil painting, and then one becomes "disillusioned," so that the painting's surface looks as if it is a flat painted surface. Over a certain period, its seeming to you a certain way—your vision's having the phenomenal character it does—implies that, during this time, it first looks to you as if there is a bulgy and indented surface, and then it looks to you as if the same surface is flat, but also: *it looks to you as if the surface has not changed shape*. For when you become disillusioned, it does not seem to you the way it does for it to look as if something that is bulgy goes flat. The way it seems for it to look as if a protruding surface either gradually deflates or suddenly flattens is *not* the way it seems to have the experience one does when what looked to one like a brick wall starts to look like a painting of a brick wall.

So, as a consequence of how it seems to you, it looks to you as if there is something bulgy at t_1, flat at t_2, but unchanging in shape throughout. Now, clearly, it cannot be that there *is* something that first bulges out and then is flat, without changing shape in the duration. So even someone who believes in sense-data will have to admit, there is *some* discrepancy between the way it looks to you during this time, and the way it actually is.

But just where does this discrepancy emerge? If we do not believe in sense-data, we will naturally want to say it looks to you at t_1 as if there is something that protrudes in a certain place, but there actually is not such a thing. However, if you take the sense-datum line, you will not be able to locate the discrepancy here. For you always have to infer bulging sense-data from appearances of bulging. Nor will you be able to say it looked to you later as if there were something flat, but there was not. The only place left for you to locate a divergence between how it looks to you and how it is, lies in its looking to you as if something has not changed shape from t_1 through t_2.

So, on the sense-datum view, you would need to say that though it looks to you as if there is something bulgy at t_1, flat at t_2, but unchanging in shape throughout, actually this is not the case: what looked bulgy to you at t_1, and flat at t_2, actually *did* change shape—it was first bulgy, then flat: it deflated. But now if you say this, then you cannot say that the way it looks to you cannot be inaccurate, properly speaking, but at most judgment or inference from visual appearance may go wrong, on the grounds that what looks to you a certain way—your sense-data—never appear to be other than they are. For here you would admit that they look as if they are unchanging in shape, though really they go from being protuberant to being flat. You may say this is consistent with holding that sense-data always have the shape they appear to have at a given time, but you have at least acknowledged that a certain gap can open up between the way things look and the way they are. But now if you admit the possibility of inaccurate visual appearances, then it does not seem that you can avoid counting the following as a realization of that possibility: in the trompe l'oeil case, it inaccurately looks to you as if something is unchanging in shape.

Notice, however, that this would have us locate the visual error of being taken in by trompe l'oeil painting in a very odd place. If we allow that there is such a phenomenon as inaccurate visual appearance, and it is illustrated by cases like those I've mentioned, then we would naturally say in such a case, where (a) it first looked to us as if a surface protruded out in a certain way, and then (b) it looked to us as if it were flat, though (c) it looked to us throughout as if it were unchanging in shape, the experience reported in (a) was found to be inaccurate, through the accuracy of the experience reported in (b) and (c). But the sense-datum view would have us say, on the contrary, that the experience reported in (c) was found to be inaccurate, through the accuracy of that reported in (a) and (b). In other words, the visual illusion of trompe l'oeil painting consists in making it inaccurately look to us as if something *isn't changing shape*!

That the sense-datum view would force us into this strangely inverted conception of the visual illusion involved in trompe l'oeil may already seem bad enough. But worse is yet to come. If we admit cases of visual illusion of this sort at all, we need to understand them as involving a sensory error of somehow taking something to be bulgy that is not bulgy. And the introduction of sense-data tells us that insofar as there is an inaccurate *visual appearance* in such a case, it is not the appearance of protuberance—that's just fine—but the appearance of shape constancy. But then how, on the basis of such a conception, are we to understand the error regarding the shape of the wall's surface at all? The suggestion will be, I take it, that we falsely judge or infer from the bulgy item that looks bulgy to us, that there is something else that is also bulgy (the wall in the "external world"). Thus the error in question is not to be understood as one of inaccurate visual appearances, but as one of false visual judgment. And how is this error to be revealed or recognized as an error? Again, on the sense-data view, we cannot judge from the *accuracy* of the appearance of shape constancy and flatness that the appearance of protuberance was *inaccurate*: that is denied. The claim is that neither the appearance of protuberance nor that of flatness was inaccurate, but the appearance of constancy was. In order to discover the sensory error, it seems then that we must somehow infer that our judgment that there was something protuberant was a mistake, on the basis of our realizing that what visually appeared to us was protuberant and then flat, and thus that it inaccurately looked to us as if it were unchanging in shape. We must somehow judge correctly that there was something unchanging in shape that did not appear to us, by inferring this from the fact that something that did appear to us, inaccurately appeared unchanging in shape. We somehow correct our judgment about the wall by inferring that things that do not appear to us, really *are* the way things that do appear to us only *inaccurately seem* to be.

This account of the sensory error involved in trompe l'oeil is grotesque. But apart from that, it would clearly fail in any case as a description of what goes on when we are subject to and discover such illusions, for it would attribute to us beliefs or judgments in such situations that we simply do not have. First, few people who have undergone such illusions, or discovered them, have made the judgment that is supposed to be essential to the error: that there is something that does not look bulgy to one, but stands in a certain relation to that which does (perhaps that it causes and resembles it). Maybe a few philosophers over the centuries have thought this upon being struck by this sort of illusion, but this is hardly the standard case. What we normally think in such cases is: something looks like it bulges out in a certain way, and it does. Second, probably nobody (including philosophers) has ever held the beliefs that would be required to correct the alleged error, on the sense-datum view. We simply do not judge or believe or think or assert on such occasions that something that was bulgy flattened out, so although it looked like it did not change shape, it really did, and *therefore* that *something else*, however, was not bulgy, but flat, and did *not* change shape. It seems highly unlikely to me that anyone has ever even tried to infer the flatness of a surface on which such a painting was found from the belief that something else appeared to be unchanging in shape, but *really* went from bulgy to flat. Thus, if we assume the sense-data view, we will have to conclude that no one (except maybe for some philosophers who held that view) has ever experienced the kind of sensory illusion in question here, and probably not even those few philosophers have ever discovered and corrected their sensory error. A conception of sensory error with such consequences is, to put it mildly, unsatisfactory.

I took up the sense-datum view of visual experience in order to remove the obstacle it would provide to my way of conceiving of how inaccurate sensory appearance is possible, thereby blocking also my way of understanding how sensory features can be intentional ones. Part of this obstacle lay in the thought that since what ("directly") looks to us somehow always is the way it looks, there can be, strictly speaking, no inaccuracy in the way something looks, but only in the judgments or inferences based on this. However, even if we thought that whenever it looked to us as if there were something with a certain shape and position, there was such an item that looked that way to us, we should need to admit the possibility of a kind of discrepancy between how something looks and how it is. For such a view would require us to recognize that these items sometimes may appear to us to be unchanging in shape, when really they are not. So this sense-datum story cannot be used to criticize my approach to sensory error on the grounds that, properly speaking, there is no such thing, but *only* errors in sensory judgment. Moreover, the story is untenable in any case, because it permits us no credible way of describing the state of mind of those who discover and correct certain kinds of sensory error. For it would have us do this by attributing to ourselves false judgments or beliefs that few if any have ever had, and would have us discover and correct the error in a bizarre manner that probably no one has ever attempted.

It may have appeared to some unnecessary to argue against sense-data, since so few avow belief in them any more. But we oughtn't to underestimate the lingering effects of the philosophical tradition that gave rise to this notion, and the ways it may shape assumptions about consciousness despite all the criticisms it has suffered. And since I regard it as essential to understanding the relationship between the phenomenal character of sense-experience and its intentionality that we understand how experience can be inaccurate, it is important to identify how I think the conceptions of this suggested by past philosophy (still influential in ways we perhaps do not recognize) keep us from doing so—how they keep us from understanding sensory intentionality.

7.5 Sensory Intentionality Is Not Bestowed by Judgment

We might happily concede that it is a mistake to conjure up X-shaped items "in the mind"—sense-data, ideas, or impressions that always are the shape they look—out of visual experience of X's, and so we may admit such notions should not prevent our thinking of intentionality as inseparable from phenomenal character. But still we may persist in thinking of the phenomenal character of visual experience as being in a way quite contingently related to its intentionality or "representational" features. We might say: the problem is not, as one might suppose from the sense-datum view, that for it to look to you as if there's an X, is merely for you to have an X-shaped item in your mind, so that this (like an X written on paper, or scratched in wax) can be accurate or inaccurate of anything, only if something new is added to it that makes it a representation of something. Rather (one might say), the problem is that the way it feels to have a sensation does not, any more than the shapes or sounds of language do, constrain the "interpretation," the intentional or semantic features that may be given it—that is the truth buried in the sense-datum view. And sensory experience with the phenomenal character ours has needs to be "given" such features. For one may have whatever phenomenal sensory features you please, though the way it looks (sounds, feels, etc.) to one is neither accurate nor inaccurate of anything, and one's sense-experience is so much uninterpreted noise.

So again, the question to pose here is this. Consider sensory phenomenal features of the sort you can identify by thinking of how it seems to you for it to look as if things are shaped and situated in certain ways. What conditions must obtain if it is to be the case that, when you have such features, the way it looks to you is accurate? What must obtain if it is to be the case that the way it looks to you is inaccurate? Is it necessary that certain other conditions obtain, which could fail to do so when one had those phenomenal features, but which refer back to them so as to make of them features with respect to which one is assessable for accuracy? The answer is no if, to reach the conclusion that the way it looked to you was inaccurate, it is enough that some condition such as the following obtain: *there is nothing X-shaped there.* If that is enough to make true the correlative assessment for accuracy, then the phenomenal feature in question is *already* intentional, and does not need to have intentionality *bestowed upon* it. On the other hand, some such condition would be required if we had to add to one's visual experience, say, the condition that one makes a certain sort of *judgment* about it, which one might not make, before the way it looked to one could be inaccurate.

Let's take up this last suggestion. Suppose someone said, "Okay, so the accuracy or inaccuracy of vision does not depend on our judging that little bulgy things in our minds stand for bulgy things out in the world. But still, the phenomenal character of sensory experience needs to have something added it might lack, of a distinctively *intellectual* character, that would supply these sensory materials with a meaning, an interpretation: one needs, in some sense, to *take* the sense-experience to *represent* things in the world, or else it has no intentionality at all."

Now, I do not want to deny that through thought we in some sense "interpret" our sense-experience, and bring to it what it cannot supply of itself. What I want to question is whether some separable intellectual component that could be entirely missing, though the phenomenal character of sensory experience was the same, is something essential to sensory intentionality, that is, necessary for experience to be accurate or inaccurate. The initial suggestion that it is essential, I have left deliberately vague, but let's try to make it clear enough to discuss. What might it mean to "take your visual experience to represent" something? If this is some sort of attitude separable from the way it seems for it to look some way to you, then I suppose it would have to be something we would classify as a thought or belief or judgment or intention about or directed toward its looking to you as it does. One can indeed have conscious sense-experience without taking such attitudes toward it. And I will take it that to believe or judge or intend your experience to *represent* something will be for you to believe (or judge, etc.) that it is accurate under certain conditions, and inaccurate under others. Otherwise I do not know what talk of "representation" here would amount to. I leave to the side (for I do not know how to make sense of) any suggestion that the relevant attitude in the sensory case would be a sort of *intention*. I assume that what we would want here would be something on the order of belief, judgment, or thought.

But why should we think beliefs or judgments about the conditions of accuracy of our sense-experience are essential to its having them? I suspect that whatever attraction we might feel here comes partly from not having left sense-data far enough behind. We think something like judgment is needed for visual intentionality because we haven't yet fully shaken off the influence of views about sensory experience that force us to locate sensory error in the inferences we make about how objects appearing in our minds relate to things in the "external world." But once we've extricated ourselves from this mess, is there some other reason we might have for thinking some separable interpreting judgment must be added to the phenomenal character of our experience before we have sensory intentionality?

We might have a reason for thinking this, if we thought that what conditions of accuracy a given visual experience (for example) had, could be entirely changed by changing what one took (believed, judged) its conditions of accuracy to be. Consider how this works in the case of language. We think that the expression 'cruciform' is true of something only if it has the shape of a cross, and that the expression 'circular' is true of something only if it has the shape of a circle. But we might switch this around for some reason, so that it is true to say of an O that it is cruciform (and false to say it is circular), while of an X it is false to say it is cruciform and true to say it is circular. Ordinarily there would be no point in this, of course, but nothing in the form of the expressions involved prevents us from doing it. Could we do something analogous with the visual experience of crosses and circles? That is, when it seems to me as it does for it to look as if there is something X-shaped in a certain place, could I make the way it looks to me such as would be *inaccurate* if there is an X-shaped item there, but accurate if there is an O-shaped one, by somehow simply believing or judging that this is so?

I do not think anyone would want to say that, as I look at the X on the page, I could make the way it looks to me *inaccurate* just by somehow stipulating that, if there is no O there, the way it looks is inaccurate. It surely would not be enough for me merely to say the words by which this thought would be expressed. What would it take for me to believe that, when it visually seems to me as if there is something X-shaped there, the way it looks to me is *inaccurate*, if there is in fact an X there? It's not clear anything would count as believing *that*. The closest I can come to conceiving of this is to suppose I believed that, under certain circumstances (perhaps involving experimental interference with my normal brain processes), its seeming to me as it does for it to look as if there's an X in a certain location actually correlates with the presence of an O there. So I might take my visual experience of an X as a *sign* or as an *indication* that there was an O there. But it does not seem that this would amount to my believing that the way it looks to me is inaccurate if there is an X, or accurate if there is an O. I would want to say that in such a case my visual experience is regularly inaccurate in such a manner as to allow me to judge accurately how things are, from the assumption that they are systematically other than the way they look. So, similarly, once familiar with certain visual illusions, I might take the fact that two lines look to me as if they are curving out from one another as an indication that they are straight, since they look to me as they do in the presence of *other* lines I believe ordinarily make straight lines look bent. However, in doing this, I do not think that the way it *looks* to me is accurate.

But even if I did not object to this odd idea that, by forming these sorts of inverted beliefs about what conditions correlate with the phenomenal character of your experience, you would actually change their conditions of accuracy, I would still, for the most part, find myself unable to do much to change the conditions of accuracy of experiences in this way. I consider the variety of differences in the way things look shaped, sized, and positioned when I have visual experience of fairly ordinary phenomenal character—as when I see my desk and the jumble of books and papers scattered upon it, or I see through my windshield other cars approaching, or I see a garden hose coiled sloppily in the grass. And I find I simply have available to me no way to identify a set of specific spatial arrangements remotely as complex as those visually apparent to me, which I might try to regard as *correlative* to these, unless this involves thinking of those arrangements visually apparent to me—that is, the shape, size, and position it currently visually seems to me as if things have. Just look about you at any normally variegated scene, and try to think of a set of spatial arrangements you could suppose correlative with those visually apparent to you, so that you could infer that things in your surroundings *in every case* had certain shapes, positions, and sizes other than what it visually seems to you they have. I believe you will find you lack the resources to think of the variety of spatial characteristics you need, to the degree of specificity you need, without thinking of those that are visually apparent to you. But this indicates you have failed to form a suitable alternative belief about what would make your experience accurate. For in order to do this, you were to try to think of spatial characteristics that were in every case wholly other than those visually apparent to you. You will not escape this problem by going for help to other sensory modalities—not just because they will not make *as much* spatially apparent to you *as quickly* as vision does, but also because, by and large, they will not give you spatial arrangements to correlate in thought with visual appearances that are at variance with those visually apparent to you.

The question has been whether you can form an alternative "interpretation" of your visual experience—an alternative "assignment" of conditions of accuracy to it—based on odd assumptions about how the phenomenal character of your visual experience correlates with the spatial character of things around you. Two problems have emerged. First, though you might believe the fact that it looks to you a certain way indicates that things are actually quite otherwise, this seems insufficient to change what makes your experience accurate or inaccurate. Second, if you are, as I observe I am, helpless to form the sorts of thoughts about spatial characteristics and relationships that would be necessary to construct radically nonstandard assumptions about experience-world correlations, then you cannot change the conditions of accuracy of your experience by changing your beliefs about these. So we have found here no reason to think that the conditions of accuracy of our visual experience depend on ("interpretive") judgments or beliefs about what these conditions are.

Is there perhaps some other reason to think this? There might be, if consideration of the beliefs one has about the conditions of accuracy of one's experience played a part in assessing the accuracy of one's vision. But this is another dry hole. The optometrist may want to find out how accurate your vision is, but inquiry into what you *believe* the conditions of accuracy of your visual experience are, or even into whether you have beliefs of this sort, plays no essential role in her job.

Finally, if one would insist that having beliefs about what makes your vision accurate or inaccurate is essential to its being so, then one would arbitrarily rule that those creatures who either are not yet or never will be able to reflect on their own minds, and who hence have no beliefs about how things appear to them (as opposed to beliefs about the things themselves), are creatures unable to see anything either accurately or inaccurately. In that case, then, talk of the accuracy or inaccuracy of young children's or animals' vision would be some kind of philosophical mistake. But it seems to make good sense to speak of the accuracy of animals' and small children's vision. Is there some reason to suppose otherwise? You might think so, if you think that (1) it can look accurately or inaccurately to x, only if x is able to *distinguish* its somehow looking accurately to x, from its inaccurately looking some way to x; (2) this is possible, only if x can form *the belief that* it looks accurately to x (and the belief that it looks inaccurately to x); and (3) there can be creatures with experience who have the phenomenal character of our spatial vision, but who are unable to form such beliefs. However, (1) is plausible only if construed quite broadly, so that any difference in the way a creature responds to accurate versus inaccurate appearances would count as "distinguishing" them, as when, for example, an animal ingests a hallucinogen, and acts differently—acts in ways that reveal the inaccuracy of how things appear to it. Also, an animal might, I suppose, suffer a mirage when thirsty, and then, after approach, turn away. This is different from what it would do if, when on approach, it still seemed to the creature as it would for it to look as if something lay on the surface ahead. But then, when we read (1) this way, the jump to (2) appears unwarranted. To form beliefs about the accuracy of one's visual experience, it is not enough that one is merely able to respond somehow to one's visual experience in ways that differ, depending on whether the experience is accurate or inaccurate. And even if we thought (improbably) that responding in distinguishable ways to accurate and inaccurate appearances were sufficient for having beliefs about their accuracy, then we would have trouble affirming (3)—what's required for having such beliefs would be so little, it would be hard not to have them.

So, I find no reason to think that experience with the phenomenal character of our vision will lack intentionality, if it does not get this from some kind of interpretive judgment directed upon it, which might not be so directed. And there is reason to think such judgment is not necessary. But maybe someone will say that still, *some* connection with judgment, of a sort that might be missing, is essential if sensory experience is to have intentionality. Perhaps the error was just in thinking that the kind of judgment or belief required is *reflective* or *higher-order*.

Presumably, if any other kind of judgment is required, it will be sensory judgment. And we have distinguished, for example, conscious visual experience from visual judgment. Mightn't one then have phenomenal visual features but make no visual judgments? Perhaps, if this is possible, someone might take it to illustrate the possibility of a phenomenal sensory existence without any intentionality. Certain ways of interpreting this proposal clearly make it untenable. For example, it would be no good maintaining that a visual experience with a certain phenomenal character is accurate, only if it causes its possessor to judge that its conditions of accuracy obtain when they do, and inaccurate only when it causes one to judge falsely that they do. This would have us say that it inaccurately *looks* to me as if there is something X-shaped in a certain place, only if my experience causes me to *judge* that there is. This won't work, because if you accept this, you make it impossible for yourself to judge correctly that the way it looked to you on a given occasion was inaccurate. I could never rightly say that, though one line is actually the same length as another, it inaccurately looks to me as if one is longer. For the fact that I judge the lines to be of the same length would indicate that my visual experience did not cause me to judge one to be longer than the other. And, if I hold that visual experience is inaccurate only if it causes the appropriate judgment, I must think that the way it looked to me was *not* inaccurate.

Maybe we will want to try saying that its seeming to me as it does for it to look as if there is something X-shaped on my left is inaccurate, only provided that this experience is *disposed* to cause me to judge that there is something X-shaped there, *unless I have some reason to think there isn't*. One problem with this is that it's not clear that being disposed to make me judge this really is separable from having experience of this phenomenal character. It is not clear that one could have visual experience of this phenomenal character, without being such as would think that there was an X there, barring reason to think there was not. And unless we are confident one could, we have here no reason to think that visual experience might retain its phenomenal character while being stripped of its intentionality. So what we would need is a conception of visual judgment sufficiently demanding that it would be clear to us that something that had visual experience with the phenomenal character of ours might yet lack this sort of visual judgment. We might do this, for example, by saying that creatures without language lack *concepts*, and so cannot, properly speaking, make visual *judgments*—while maintaining they *can* have phenomenally conscious visual experience of the relevant sort. However, if we accept something like this, it would seem at least as reasonable to take it to show that this conceptual visual judgment is not necessary for visual intentionality as to take it to show visual phenomenal features are insufficient for this—really, it would seem more reasonable. For again, there would seem to be nothing wrong with speaking of the accuracy or inaccuracy of such creatures' vision.

In spite of all this, something like the following considerations might still keep alive *some* temptation to make the intentionality of visual experience depend somehow on a potentially missing judgment. Visual experience is not simply accurate or inaccurate without qualification, but accurate in some ways, and inaccurate in others, and accurate or inaccurate to a greater or lesser extent. What I mean here is first, that what we will naturally want to treat as one experience may be accurate in some respects but not in others. So, for example, when I see two lines, it may accurately look to me as if there are two lines not touching one another, but also, it inaccurately looks to me as if one is longer than the other. And it would seem strange to treat these as distinct experiences. For it's not as though it could have seemed to me as it did for it to look as if there were two lines, without its looking as if they had some length; and it could not have looked to me as if they had some length relative to one another, without its looking to me as if they were distinct. Now second, when I say experience is accurate *to a greater or lesser extent*, I mean that even visual experience we want to call accurate may fail to discern differences in things seen, and hence be said to fail in accuracy by some measure or standard. For instance, it may look to me as if there are three figures of the same color, shape, and size, each the same distance from the other—but there are in fact (relatively small) differences in color, shape, size, and location among them. We could perhaps say there is then *some* inaccuracy in the way it looks to me, even though it accurately looks to me as if the three are *about* the same color, shape, size, and distance.

We may feel some inclination to describe this in terms that make it appear as if some judgment is essentially involved in the accuracy of the experience. We might want to say something like—*taken as a sign* (or indication) of the *number of lines* (and so as evidence for a judgment about this), the experience was accurate (for the indicated judgment about this was true), but taken as evidence for a judgment of their *relative length*, it was inaccurate (for the indicated judgment about this was false). Or again, similarly: taken as evidence for a judgment of the proximity of the figures to the nearest centimeter, the experience was accurate; but as evidence for making a more exacting judgment, it was inaccurate.

But this reference to judgments based on the experience is really not essential to specifying the respect in which, and the extent to which, experience is accurate. One can say: it accurately looked to me as if there were two lines, but inaccurately as if the top were longer. And: it accurately looked to me as if the figures were about the same distance apart, but inaccurately as if there were no difference in proximity among them at all. Here there is no reference to the experience as sign, indication, or evidence for the truth of some judgment or belief. To be sure, the experiences are reported by use of a sentence that would be used also to express or report the judgment they might be taken to warrant (e.g., "The figures are about the same distance apart"). But that does not show that any actual judgments so expressible or reportable need be made for the experience to be accurate or inaccurate in the respects and to the extent described. Nor will it show that an experiencer lacking the talent to make such judgments would lack both accurate and inaccurate visual experience. Thus we find no reason in what we might loosely call the "relativity of visual accuracy" for making some potentially missing judgment, or disposition to judgment, essential to the intentionality of sense-experience.

One residual worry: I earlier focused on the suggestion that the one who has the experience needs to make some judgment or hold some belief about its conditions of accuracy, before there can be sensory intentionality. But mightn't someone try saying that what is essential is merely that *someone* make some judgment based on or about the experience for it to be accurate or inaccurate of anything? And maybe this could be someone *other than the experiencer*—an observer. However, if there is no requirement that a separable judgment be somehow directed on or formed from the experience *by the one who has it*, I see no reason why we should think it necessary for *someone else* to do so then. If there are or can be creatures who have conscious visual experience but lack the ability to form the sort of judgment (thought, beliefs) concerned, then their vision will be accurate or inaccurate even when no observer happens to be around to take an interest in their experience, or even if they never have encountered and never will encounter such an observer.

We will not, I conclude, find reason for detaching the phenomenal character of experience from its intentionality by noting some way visual experience may be detached from the likes of visual judgment, or belief, or thought. Similar considerations would show that this will not be done through some separation of sensory experience from attitudes on the order of desire or intention. It is unclear, to say the least, that some creature might have a phenomenal sensory life such as ours without having any desires or intentions. And to the extent we're willing to trust a shadowy inkling that it might, this would appear to count against the view that such attitudes are essential to visual intentionality as much as or more than it would against the view that visual phenomenality is not sufficient for it.

So I see no prospect of our locating a reason for thinking that sensory phenomenal features need to have added to them certain relations to attitudes (or mental representations, if you like) that they could lack, if what has conscious experience of that sort is to have sensory intentionality, sensory features in virtue of which one is assessable for accuracy. For we have found no reason to believe there are either attitudes toward one's sensory experience or attitudes toward one's surroundings such as might be missing while the experience remains, which are necessary for having accurate or inaccurate visual experience of things.

7.6 MIGHT ESSENTIAL ENVIRONMENTAL AND BEHAVIORAL LINKS BE MISSING?

It has been sometimes proposed, suggested, or assumed that having attitudes, intentional mental states, or mental representations somehow requires that they be linked, in the subject or organism that has them, in a certain way ("the right way") to his, her, or its *behavior*, or *environment*, or both. Without the right behavioral or environmental links, there is no intentionality. So perhaps here we can find a type of interpreting condition that might not obtain though one had our sensory phenomenal features, and without which one's sense-experience could be neither accurate nor inaccurate of anything. Perhaps potentially missing behavioral or environmental links are needed to endow sense-experience with intentionality.

Let's take environmental links first. The idea here would be, roughly, that unless sense-experience is rightly causally linked to the sorts of environmental conditions that make it accurate, then it has no conditions of accuracy at all, it has no intentionality, it does not "represent" anything. However such a theory is worked out, it obviously has to allow somehow that one may have a sensory experience of some sort even when it is not linked to the fulfillment of its conditions of accuracy *in that instance*. For if we said, for example, that its looking to me as if there is something X-shaped there is neither accurate nor inaccurate, unless it is caused by there being something X-shaped there, then we have the problem that it can never inaccurately look to me as if there is something X-shaped. And so if we made this tight an environmental link prerequisite for sensory intentionality, we would make inaccurate sensory appearances, misperception, or misrepresentation impossible. But there can be no accurate sensory appearances if inaccurate sensory appearances are impossible. And if there can be no accurate sensory appearances, there can be no sensory intentionality.

A likely response to make here is that some regular connection has to be established between the type of experience had and the sorts of environmental conditions that would make it accurate; but this connection need not obtain on every occasion in which the experience occurs and has those conditions of accuracy. So its looking to me as if there is an X there may be such as would be accurate if there were an X there, even though, on *this* occasion, there is none, because it is a sort of experience that has (or has had) some regular connection with environmental X's on *other* occasions.

Perhaps, then, using some such notion, we will try to conceive of a break between sensory phenomenality and intentionality by supposing that an environmental link of this sort—allegedly essential to the intentionality of experience—is ruptured. So, on this suggestion: the phenomenal character of some sensory experience might remain the same, though it lacks the right causal connection with instances of certain sorts of conditions that would make it accurate, were that connection in place. Thus: it might seem to some subject as it seems to you for it to look as if there is something X-shaped somewhere, but when this other has had experience of such character, this has not been causally connected with X-shaped things in its environment such as would make experience of that sort accurate, were there such a connection. And if that causal connection is missing (on this proposal), the experience is not such as would be made accurate by the presence of local X-shaped figures. But if that were someone's situation, it seems, such a subject's visual experience of shape and position *generally* would have to be similarly estranged from the shape and position of things in the environment. For if one was generally phenomenally estranged in this way from X-shaped items in one's environment, one would be similarly estranged from the shapes of other things in one's environment.

Now, if we want to say that where such environmental links are broken, sense-experience loses what with them would have been its conditions of accuracy, its intentionality, we might want to draw the conclusion either that it would then have no intentionality at all, or else that its conditions of accuracy would now relate to whatever it was regularly causally linked to in the subject's environment. If we are thinking of this in terms of the old "brain-in-a-vat" scenario, we will imagine that somehow a disembodied human brain could be hooked up to a machine that would stimulate it in such a way as to give it phenomenally conscious sense-experience of the same character as ours. And then the idea would be either that the brain's experience is not accurate or inaccurate of anything whatsoever; or that when it seems (to the brain?) the way it seems to us for it to look (for example) as if there's an X there, what makes this accurate is some condition of the brain-stimulating machine, and that condition may not involve the existence of X-shaped items, or (I suppose) have any essential connection with shape at all.

Does this give us a way of prising intentionality apart from sensory phenomenality? Such scenarios, radically disconnecting the character of one's sensory experience from the character of one's environment, have been a staple of philosophical reflection since Descartes. It may be questioned whether we really can conceive of this sort of possibility. In any case, I have not made recognition of the reality of phenomenal consciousness dependent on our being able to do so. But even if we are confident we have a grip on this sort of scenario, it is inadequate to show that the relation between phenomenal sensory features and intentional ones is merely contingent. For if we think we can contemplate the situation of others to whom it seems just the way it does to us for it to look as if there are things around us situated and shaped thus and so with respect to us, but who, nevertheless, are located in environments where things are never then situated and shaped thus and so with respect to them, we will likely find it natural to describe them as suffering from a systematic and total *hallucination*—that is, we will want to say, the way it looks to them is wholly inaccurate. But if we wish to describe it that way, we are saying that the environmental links do not, after all, determine the conditions of accuracy of the experience. The point is, if we suppose we can conceive of the kind of situation in which the break between environmental character and phenomenal character is this radical, we would have as much or more right to take this to indicate that the missing environmental link is *unnecessary* for sensory intentionality, as we would to take it to show that sensory phenomenal features are *insufficient* for it.

Maybe here this concern will be raised: one can be subject to normative assessment—one can be such as to do something rightly or wrongly, well or poorly, and accurately or inaccurately—only if what one does (one's thinking, acting, speaking, or perceiving) is somehow available for *public* appraisal. But visual experience with a character so totally estranged from that of the experiencer's actual environment would not be so available. So it can be neither accurate nor inaccurate of anything. However, it is not altogether clear we have adequate reason to accept a publicity requirement quite this sweeping (or, for that matter, any such requirement at all). But even if we did, we might just as well take it to cast into doubt the possibility that one could live such a deeply environmentally estranged phenomenal life, as find in it support for the view that the experience of such a subject would be neither accurate nor inaccurate of anything.

It does not fundamentally change matters, should we find ourselves attracted to some version of a view that says environmental links are essential to intentionality, since sensory intentionality can be possessed only by beings in whom experience has an evolutionarily ordained function of indicating external conditions. Again, *if* we are firmly convinced that sensory phenomenal features like ours might belong to a being with no evolutionary history behind it (perhaps a created being, or a member of a species that has always existed in its present form), then we may as well take this as reason to doubt that evolutionary heritage is essential to sensory intentionality after all, as count it as evidence that sensory phenomenality of our sort could occur with no intentionality. Alternatively, if we are so sure of a necessary link between visual intentionality and evolutionary adaptation, we may just as well decide to give up the idea that an unevolved being could have a visual experiential life phenomenally like ours, as elect to affirm this possibility, while denying the creature would ever see anything accurately or inaccurately.

Thus, generally, doctrines maintaining the necessity of environmental links for sensory intentionality do not furnish us with adequate reason to think that having visual phenomenal features of the sort we can identify in our own case must be supplemented with separable conditions relating their possession to appropriate environmental causes, before they will be the features of one with visual intentionality. So we have inadequate reason to think that otherwise "uninterpreted" sensory experience needs to have intentionality bestowed upon it by a kind of link to the environment that it could lack while retaining its phenomenal character.

Earlier I said that some see an essential link between intentionality and *behavior*, and this might suggest we could subtract all the intentionality from visual experience while leaving its phenomenal character intact, by supposing it deprived of the relevant behavioral connection. This raises no new issues for us, if we suppose that a failure of the appropriate behavioral links would bring with it a failure of the kinds of environmental links just considered. But is there some way of conceiving of an experiencing being whose experience does have the sort of regular connection to the conditions in its surroundings that would make it accurate (were it ever accurate), but who is, nevertheless, incapable of the sort of *behavior* we might imagine essential to intentionality? Perhaps the hypothetical race Galen Strawson (1994) calls the "Weather Watchers" would provide a model here. Strawson invites us to imagine a group of beings, richly endowed with phenomenal experience much like our own, but who have no dispositions to observable behavior at all—for they are forever rooted rigidly in the ground and constitutionally incapable of doing anything that would enable an observer to attribute such experience to them. Someone might say that such beings are conceivable, but lacking behavior, they would entirely lack intentionality: they would have mere sensations. Strawson himself would not say this—he has his imaginary beings observing and keenly interested in the weather conditions around them. However, we might consider whether Strawson's story could be put to this use.

It is worth noting that the sensory phenomenal features of any such entirely sessile beings would be quite different from our own. For their visual experience would not display the sort of continuous integration of changing visual perspective generated by one's own movement, nor would it manifest the kind of integration with experience of one's own motion, and exploratory tactile experience, that ours does. So if such as the Weather Watchers would be deficient in visual intentionality, this may be due to some deficiency in the phenomenal character of their experience, and not (or not solely) on account of their *behavioral* incapacity. And so, we cannot conclude from their case that the phenomenal character of our vision can be divorced from intentionality. Also, suppose we set aside any doubt that we really have a grip on the notion of Weather Watcher experience (though I confess I'm not sure I do), and we are confident that visual intentionality does not depend on the kind of phenomenal integration they would lack. What would the possibility of such a scenario show us? Again, in that case, it would seem to supply us with as much if not more reason to doubt the necessity of the link between behavior and sensory intentionality, as it would to exclude intentionality entirely from the phenomenal character of experience.

7.7 The Intentionality of Color Experience

I have found no reason to think that our visual phenomenal features, if they are to constitute sensory intentionality, need any help from conditions that might be missing in their presence—whether these are thought to involve links to judgment, or environment, or behavior. But I have concentrated on the spatial aspect of visual experience—of how it seems to us for it to look as if things are somewhere, somehow shaped, and of some size. If we focus on this aspect of visual experience, perhaps it is difficult to think of it as raw or uninterpreted sensation, needing to have intentionality somehow infused into it. But what about the way it seems to see *color*? This seems to require direct discussion, since undoubtedly whatever intuitive appeal lies in thinking the character of visual experience separable from its intentionality comes largely from the notion that our experience of color, or "color qualia," is a matter of sensation alone. Mightn't we fairly maintain that its seeming to us as it does for it to look red, or yellow, or blue to us is a matter of "pure" sensation, a nonintentional phenomenal feature?

It may or may not be possible to have an experience of color devoid of intentionality—a "pure sensation of color"—but I think that, in the light of our reflections about the experience of shape, it will become clear that typically, at any rate, the phenomenal character of color experience is also intentional. For typically, true reports of the phenomenal character of one's visual experience will combine color and shape talk so as to make it clear that the difference between having and lacking certain conscious color experience is a difference in intentionality.

When you can truthfully say, "It looks (e.g.) yellow to me," and also "It looks (e.g.) triangular to me," you can sometimes say as well, "It looks to me as if something in a certain place is triangular and yellow." Thus one does not merely experience color *simultaneously* with shape; the color looks somehow distributed inside (or outside) the shape. It looks to you as if what has this shape is colored a certain way, as if that color is here, or as if this area is so colored. Now, we are agreed that its seeming to you as it does for it to look as if something is shaped and located a certain way is an intentional feature. And surely no one will dispute that there is a difference between the way it seems for it to look to you as if something shaped and situated in a certain fashion, and the way it seems to you for it to look to you as if something is shaped, situated, *and colored* in a certain fashion.

Now, we have to ask: Is this kind of variation in consciousness that comes with color experience also a difference in intentional features? Consider the following two statements.

(a) It seems to me as it does to look as if something in a certain location is triangular.

(b) It seems to me as it does for it to look as if something in a certain location is yellow and triangular.

Both (a) and (b) are attributions of intentional features, and they are attributions of distinct phenomenal features. But are they attributions of distinct intentional phenomenal features? They will be, unless we can somehow analyze the difference between (a) and (b) so as to isolate what (b) adds to (a) from the attribution of any intentional feature. So we would need to analyze (b) as something like:

> (b*) It seems to me as it does for it to look yellow to me, *and* it seems to me as it does for it to look as if something is triangular.

Only if (b) and (b*) are logically equivalent can we say that the difference between what (a) and (b) attribute is a difference in phenomenal features merely, not a difference in intentional features. For only then will we have a way of representing the contribution 'yellow' makes to (b) *without* representing the difference it makes *as* a difference in intentional features attributed. However, (b*) and (b) are *not* logically equivalent; (b*) does not entail (b). For (b*) might describe a situation in which it seemed to me as it does for it to look as if a red triangle is surrounded by yellow. Or it might describe a situation in which I am looking at things through yellow-tinted lenses—when it does not look to me as if any *surface* is yellow. And in either of these cases, (b) will be false, while (b*) is true. Therefore (a) and (b) not only attribute distinct phenomenal features, they attribute distinct *intentional* phenomenal features.

Thus the phenomenal features of ordinary color experience, which would be missing from achromatic conscious vision, are intentional features. Typically, the phenomenal character peculiar to color experience is logically inextricable from what we have agreed is the essentially intentional phenomenal character belonging to experience of shape. For this reason, we may mislead ourselves by speaking of the experience of color as visual sensation. For we sometimes contrast *sensation* with *perception*, so that the latter is "directed outward," while the former either is not "directed" at all, but is entirely without intentionality, or else is the perception of one's own body. But if a sensation is necessarily an experience of this latter type, then in seeing things other than ourselves, we do not have "visual sensations" of color. Maybe we could have a kind of visual color experience utterly devoid of intentionality. But such experience would have a radically different phenomenal character from that belonging to typical color experience, which is, by contrast, ineliminably spatial and intentional.[3]

7.8 VISUAL EXPERIENCE: UNTOLD RICHES

I have been arguing that it is an error to confine consciousness to some category of unintelligent, uninterpreted, inherently "meaningless" sensation, partly because I believe this has sometimes abetted a lamentable tendency, in theories of mind, to underappreciate the richness of conscious experience. However, there are other ways in which this richness of conscious experience is liable to be ignored, which my continual appeal to relatively simple examples—X's and O's, and colored triangles—will have done little to discourage. I would now like to remedy this to some extent. My repeated talk of a few simple shapes should not allow us to forget that the way it seems for it to look to us as it does on a given occasion differs in *many* respects from the ways it seems to us on other occasions. For the differences in shape, location, and color it looks to us as if things have, as a consequence of how it seems to us, are very many (and uncountably so). And the countless ways in which it seems to us for it to look as if there are things variously shaped and colored are differing phenomenal intentional features. This is what I mean by saying that the phenomenal character of visual experience is rich.

Consider again the sunflower, some ordinary encounter with it, and the lush spatial-chromatic intentionality distinguishing the conscious perception of it. It not only looks yellow to me, but this bright, intense yellow looks as if it belongs to what radiates out from a dark, fuzzy, round center, all of which is poised, tilted a certain way, and situated amidst a variegated profusion of other colors and shapes. All this belongs in a report of how it seems to me to have the experience I do. If we see the absurdity in trying to strip intentionality entirely away from how it seems to have visual experience of a simple figure, so as to leave behind some unaltered phenomenal residue as the mere "qualia" of "visual sensation," how much more evidently absurd it will seem for us to do this to the more elaborate forms of conscious perception with which our everyday lives are replete—the phenomenal luxury in which we live most of our waking lives.

But we can be led to understate grievously the wealth of phenomenal consciousness, if we are drawn to the view that we consciously perceive rather little, or only rather intermittently. To help keep us from underappreciating consciousness, it is worth pausing to consider this view, how it may attract us, and how to ward off its false charms. Expressed simply and directly, such a claim might appear to us strange and obviously false, but it is more often implied or suggested than baldly stated. Consider, for example, what Jaynes says, in the course of trying to convince us that "consciousness is a much smaller part of our conscious lives than we are conscious of." He tells his readers, "Right at this moment . . . as you read, you are not conscious of the letters or even of the words or even of the syntax, or the sentences, and punctuation, but *only* of their meaning" (1976, 26; my emphasis).

Jaynes does not expect us to accept this amazing claim as a result of merely stipulating some specially restrictive sense of 'consciousness.' Rather, he thinks this is something we can easily appreciate based on an understanding of 'consciousness' such as we might possess before exposure to his particular theories about it, and clearly he intends the just-quoted remarks to characterize how things ordinarily are, when we read. But hasn't he gone just a little overboard here? Are we really to think that typically when we read we are conscious of *nothing* except the meaning of text?

If we assume, as seems fair, that in saying we are conscious only of the meaning, Jaynes is denying that we consciously see the book, the page, or anything printed on it, then it seems what we are asked to believe is this:

typically when we read, we function with a kind of premium-grade blind-sight. Here the light stimuli from the characters on the page, instead of, for instance, triggering merely the measly thought that there is an X there, rapidly and continually produces, from the time we open the book until the time that we close it, (conscious) thoughts concerning whatever its text is about, though all the while, as we sit with our eyes open before the marks on the page, we *consciously see* no more than we do in a lightless room with our eyes shut tight, that is to say, absolutely nothing.

If this were true, then the phenomenal character of vision would be *considerably* less rich than I want to claim, for it seems conscious vision would be rather infrequent. If we typically do not consciously see anything when we read, then when do we? To take Jaynes's remarks seriously, surely we would have to consider phenomenally conscious vision a rather occasional and spotty affair. However, I find this extreme denial of visual consciousness, once made plain, very strange, and just about as obviously false a remark as one could make about visual experience. But it may be instructive, and help counteract some potential sources of ingratitude for our visual-phenomenal bounty, if we ask ourselves how Jaynes might ever have found it plausible to say such a thing.

There is some sense in which it sounds right to say that we are not typically conscious of, nor do we consciously see, each of the letters printed on the page as we read. At least, I want to say something like this: when I read, I am not conscious of, and do not consciously see, each letter individually. I don't know what could lead Jaynes to say what he does, if not, in part, a thought we might express in this way. But what would we mean by this? In what circumstances *would* it be accurate to say one is conscious of, and sees, each letter individually? Read a line of print in this way—*look at* the first letter on the line, *attend* to it, and say what letter is there, silently or aloud; then do the same for the second letter, then for the third, and so on. The way it seems to one to see when reading in this way is not the way it *typically* seems when reading as a fully competent reader would—though someone just learning to read, or a brain-damaged reader, might typically have something like this kind of experience.[4]

This helps us to understand why, when one has just read a page of text, one might be inclined to say that none of the letters on the page belong in an inventory of "what one was conscious of." For the kinds of claims such an inventory would contain would seem most appropriate in reporting the conscious vision of someone reading in this brain-damaged, letter-by-letter fashion, visually attending to each letter, one at a time. To take a page of text you have just read, and to say you were, as you read, conscious of, or consciously saw, an "a," and an "n," and a "d," and so on, going through all the letters on the page, would seem to imply (or at least suggest) that it seemed to you to see what was before you as it does when you consecutively visually attend to each letter of the text. And normally, of course, it does not seem this way at all.

But if this explains why we might want to say that we are not conscious of the letters on the page as we read, it does not quite account for why Jaynes should be moved to say that one is conscious *only* of the meaning of the text. We might say—sure, as we read, we are paying or devoting more attention to the meaning than to the printed characters on the page, we are attending more to the meaning than to these, but still, we are visually attending somewhat, if not to each letter individually and consecutively, then to larger chunks of print on the page, and we are visually conscious of—we consciously see—groups of characters.

It seems if we want to go along with Jaynes's denial of conscious vision when reading, we need to say that while we devote some attention to what is on the page as we read, we are not paying *enough* attention to this to be visually conscious of anything there. There is, one might suggest, a threshold of attention that must be reached before one can consciously see one's visual stimuli, and this threshold is typically not reached when one is reading. But this does not yet make it clear how anyone could have thought it plausible to think such a thing. One will just want to say that, if there is such a threshold, then yes, it obviously typically *is* reached when one reads.

How can we make Jaynes's attitude here comprehensible, then? Notice that when one is reading, normally one not only (in some sense) pays less attention to what is on the page than to what it means or what it is about, one is also shifting visual attention rapidly. And as the degree of attention to visual stimuli lessens, and shifts in attention become more rapid, one's ability to say with warrant exactly what from among the things before one's eyes one is conscious *of*, and when, diminishes considerably. So, neither while one is reading, nor after one has read some text, can one with much warrant and precision fill in the blanks in an inventory: "First I was visually conscious of . . ., then I was visually conscious of . . ., then I was visually conscious of . . . ." One can say only something like: "I was visually conscious of some of the left side of this line before some of the right part, and of part of this line before the one beneath it." One cannot say: "I was conscious of just this string of characters first, then I was conscious of just this string of characters . . .," and so on. By contrast, if we stare at one letter at a time, visually attending to each—as we normally do not—then we have warrant for giving a less vague inventory of just what we are conscious of, and when.

I strongly suspect this accounts for Jaynes's wanting to say something that implies he does not consciously see anything when he reads. The vague way of saying what he is conscious of is so vague as to be beneath his notice, and thus the relatively low level of rapidly changing visual attention that is involved here accordingly does not seem to him clearly to count as conscious sight.

But if this helps to make it comprehensible how Jaynes could say he consciously sees so little, it does not justify his claims. There is something true to which Jaynes is being sensitive when he makes the remark I have quoted, but it ought not to lead us where it apparently leads him. I consciously see, only if am conscious *of* something that is in my visual field. And I think it would be right to say that typically I am conscious of something in my visual field, only if I visually attend to it, to a degree that would be sufficient to enable me to *say* I was conscious of it, if I tried to say what I was conscious of. I do not take this to imply that only a being capable of saying what it is conscious of can consciously see. The point I want to concede is just that, typically, if one does have the general ability to say what one sees, then one is conscious of something one sees, in a given instance, only if one visually attends to it to a degree that would be enough to enable one to exercise this ability in this case, were one to try to do so.

However, even granting this, it is clear that often one is visually conscious of something, and consciously sees it, during times when one attends to what one sees in such a way and to such a degree that one can say only *vaguely* what one was visually conscious of, and when. It is a mistake to suppose that conscious vision is just absent, unless you are devoting the sort of attention to what you see that would enable you to state relatively precisely what you are conscious of, and when.

Jaynes's error may seem rather idiosyncratic, and his remarks about the experience of reading easily dismissed as careless. But I think the sort of mistake noted here can crop up in forms less stark, where people are more likely to be misled by it, so as drastically to underestimate how much we consciously perceive. For there is a wide range of examples sometimes produced to persuade us how much we do "without consciousness" that can wrongly create the impression that consciousness occurs only rather intermittently or "intervenes" in our activity only in rather special cases, where we need to devote a particular kind of attention to what we perceive.

I have in mind here activities of the sort we engage in virtually every day, involving movement of a kind needed to do more than merely perceive one's surroundings. We move from place to place without smashing into things; we open and walk through doors and go up and down steps; we ride bicycles, drive cars, type letters, hammer nails, dig holes, cut vegetables, play musical instruments, and so on. It is sometimes said that we often or typically accomplish such feats "unconsciously." Now, I suppose this is correct in *some* sense, for to say that one consciously F's, for some values of F and in some contexts, either implies or suggests that one F's as a result of some kind of conscious *deliberative thinking*, or as a result of a conscious *decision to F*. It may not be adequately clear exactly what conscious deliberation or decision is, but it seems right to say that often enough we do the sorts of things I have just mentioned without conscious deliberation about how to do them, or decisions to do what will get them done. Nevertheless, it would be at the very least misleading to say that we engage in such activities "without consciousness," as I think our discussion of Jaynes's remarks about reading will help us to appreciate. Consider something else Jaynes says, in describing the piano playing of a skilled musician:

> Here a complex array of various tasks is accomplished all at once with scarcely any consciousness of them whatever: two different lines of near hieroglyphics to be read at once, the right hand guided to one and the left to the other; ten fingers assigned to various tasks, the fingering solving various motor problems without any awareness. (1976, 25)

And so on. It may seem the same sorts of remarks can be made of virtually any skilled activity. We want to say, for example that often one is not *conscious of* one's hand or one's foot, as one shifts gears in the course of driving a car, nor is one even *conscious of* the knob on the gear shift, or the clutch pedal. But we should be careful not to let these sorts of remarks confuse us into saying that in the course of such activity we consciously perceive little or nothing, and this plays no part in enabling us to engage in it. What we noticed in the case of reading we can often see elsewhere. When we read as skilled readers do, we are usually visually conscious of vaguely identifiable groups of characters, and not of specific letters individually and consecutively, as would be beginning or brain-damaged readers. And generally, often when one *skillfully* performs an activity, one is perceptually conscious of relatively vaguely identifiable things, which have as components the sorts of less vaguely identifiable things of which one is perceptually conscious only when one engages in that type of activity *unskillfully*—as a novice, or as someone struggling to compensate for brain damage, would. We might put this by saying that when handling things skillfully, we do not need to *partition things perceptually* in the way we do when merely learning or struggling. But this is not to say that we do not need to consciously perceive our situation.

So, when I am learning to drive, I am conscious of putting my foot on the clutch pedal, of gripping the gear shift, and so on, when I shift gears (or try to), just as a beginning reader may be conscious of each letter, one after the other. When I know how to drive, though it is no longer true to say I am conscious of these things, it would be a mistake to say I consciously perceive nothing whatsoever, and drive by blindsight. But what *do* I consciously perceive? It is difficult to say exactly. I might rather vaguely say I am conscious of driving a car in certain surroundings, of cars in front of me, without being able to say I was conscious of anything—such as movements of my body, parts of the car I am in, specific cars around me—that in some way goes to *comprise* my driving a car in these surroundings. But we should not let the vagueness of my identification of what I was conscious of make us suppose I had no conscious perceptual experience during this time, and hence that such experience played no part in enabling me to drive down the road without crashing into anything. And the vagueness of what I say about what I was conscious of does not show that my visual experience itself was vague, in the sense of being fuzzy or lacking in acuity.

Nor—and I want to emphasize this—is it right to say I was conscious of "scarcely anything" or "very little." One can, in a way, be conscious of "quite a lot" during a given time, even if a list of items one was conscious of during that time would not contain a large number of entries. Looking at the pattern in a Persian rug, conscious of this pattern, I cannot list a great number of things *in it* I am conscious of—maybe none—but I may consciously see, and be conscious of, quite a lot there, relative to what I see, for example, when looking at a blank wall. I am suggesting that something like this is the case as we engage in skillful activities of various kinds; we are perceptually conscious of quite a lot (as when we see the rug), even if there is not much detail we can give, in saying what we are conscious of. Only in other cases the "pattern of the rug" unfolds noticeably in time, and is something like driving a car in certain surroundings, playing a piano, cutting vegetables, or walking down a street.

Reflection on Jaynes's remarks has led us to recognize that it is not the case that whenever we have perceptual experience with a highly variegated phenomenal-intentional character, we should be able to give some definite and elaborate inventory of what we are conscious of, and when. And it is a mistake to suppose that your visual experience is only as rich as the items you could precisely identify for your "conscious of . . ." list are numerous.

That we are largely inarticulate before the splendor of ordinary visual consciousness is not just a matter of not being able to put many entries in an "I was conscious of . . ." inventory. We generally find it hard to say much of anything about what distinguishes the phenomenal character of a given stretch of space and color vision. And what we have trouble saying, we may find tempting to ignore when theorizing. So perhaps it is worthwhile to remind ourselves of this.

For example: I am sitting in a room writing, and I pause and happen to look up and out a nearby window, and for a few moments I look, in desultory fashion, at a tree outside, and sees its intricate network of bare winter branches splayed out against the sky. Now it looks to me as if some branches are somewhere, and form a kind of pattern, and have some size and shape, as a consequence of its seeming to me the way it does. But if you ask me, "*Where, what* pattern, *what* size, *what* shape?" there is not much I can actually say, except to appeal to your visual experience of the same or similar trees from similar angles in similar circumstances, and say: it seemed to me like *that*. The simplicity of this indexical report, and the massive uninformativeness of its utterance outside a shared context of experience, may conceal the complexity of what is indicated here.

We might think that, if we assume the way the tree looks to me is accurate, we could, in principle, find another way of describing how it looks to me through constructing a detailed description of where it actually is, by plotting the position of every part of it in some system of coordinates. But one problem here is that, obviously, I did not see *that* much detail, partly on account of the fact that I saw the tree from somewhere, and not—impossibly—"from everywhere." And it is not clear how we are to go about appropriately selecting, from an ideally complete description of the tree's shape, size, and position, just the part that would allow us to say how it seemed to me for it to look as if something was in a certain way shaped, and arranged, during a certain time. I surely cannot give a complete description of all I see as I see it, nor can I rely on a memory from which details quickly vanish. I may be tempted to *keep looking* at the tree to give a description of how it *had looked* to me. But as I continue to look at the tree, my eyes jump around so as to give me perhaps greater detail than was previously experienced, and it seems hopeless to try then to say precisely how much of the tree I had consciously seen already, and what more I saw when I looked at it longer. (Though of course, I can know that I am discovering some things I had not noticed.) And, in any case, there is the further worry that any "objective" metrical description of the things we see we would be asked to accept here, no matter how it is truncated or edited, would never, even in principle, yield an accurate description of how what is in space actually *looks* to us, as distinct from how we have come to be able to *think* about spatial relations.

This raises difficult issues. However, what is clear is that there are lots of detailed spatial features belonging to the tree and its branches, such that it would be incorrect to say that it looked to us as if there was something that had *those* features, or that its looking this way to me was a consequence of its seeming to me the way it did. There will always be quite a lot we can say, in principle, about the spatial configuration of a tree, which goes far beyond what we can say that a person was visually conscious of, or consciously saw, when seeing that tree, on a given occasion. However, we can recognize this, without denying that vision has the sort of phenomenal richness I have pointed out, and again, we should not be inhibited here by the fact that we can say so little in identifying the phenomenal character of visual experience in a given case. Visual consciousness of the shape of a tree is not poor, just because it is somehow partial and inarticulate. And though we can see little detail in what is before us, unless our eyes' constant (mostly unnoticed) darting about brings enough light from the stimuli into contact with the most receptor-rich parts of our retinas (the foveas), that does not show (as Dennett [1991] appears to say) that typically we consciously see rather little—or that what we see is extremely "gappy." For often our eyes do move enough, and the changes in what we are not focused on at a given moment are slow enough, that we can consciously see quite a lot. Frankly stated, the error of thinking otherwise seems improbable—but it can sometimes sneak in, by way of suggestion. Consider what Dennett has to say in this passage about his own little episode of tree-viewing, which he had earlier described for us:

> It seemed to [the author] . . . as if his mind—his visual field—were filled with intricate details of gold-green buds and wiggling branches, but although this is how it seemed, this was an illusion. No such "plenum" ever came into his mind; the plenum remained out in the world where it didn't have to be *represented*, but

could just *be*. When we marvel, in those moments of heightened self-consciousness, at the glorious richness of our conscious experience, the richness we marvel at is actually the richness of the world outside, in all *its* ravishing detail. It does not "enter" our conscious minds, but is simply available. (Ibid., 407–8)

Now, I am not at all clear on what it means to say that a plenum comes into one's mind. And it may very well be in some sense incorrect or misleading to say that when one sees such a tree, one "represents" its intricate detail "in one's mind." Moreover, I would certainly grant Dennett that there is much intricate detail in his wiggling budding maple tree that he does not consciously see (if that is what is meant by denying it "enters his conscious mind"). And there is surely nothing wrong with our marveling at all the intricate detail merely available for one to see, which is yet unseen. But if recognition of the "glorious richness" we do not consciously see is supposed somehow to suggest that there is nothing so glorious we do consciously see, it should not. It is *not* an illusion to think that the way it seems to see things is gloriously rich, even if, in certain ways, the things themselves are richer—and there is no reason why we cannot marvel at the richness of both.

I have drawn attention to Dennett's remarks, and earlier, to those of Jaynes, because I think recognizing the impoverishments of conscious vision they try to encourage us to accept, understanding how such claims might arise, and correcting them, can help make us aware of the wealth of vision's phenomenal intentionality. This awareness is a prerequisite to acquiring any sound understanding of visual consciousness, and fairly assessing its importance.

7.9 OTHER FORMS OF PHENOMENAL VISUAL WEALTH

But even if we acknowledge that its looking to us as if things are highly complexly shaped, positioned, and colored follows from differences in the way it seems for it to look to us as it does, and we acknowledge that we commonly have visual experience of such variegated phenomenal-intentional character throughout most of our waking lives, there are still ways it seems to us to see that we may miss. There is more to the kind of variation of which the phenomenal character of vision admits than the ways in which it looks to us as if things are shaped, positioned, and colored. I will just briefly indicate some respects in which I think this is so.

I might say, when I see a sunflower, not only that (a) it looks to me as if there is something shaped, situated, and colored a certain way, but also that (b) it looks to me as though there is a *sunflower* in a certain place. Now suppose this certain way of being shaped and colored in (a) just happens to be a way in which sunflowers are typically shaped, etc. And suppose that both (a) and (b) are used in true reports of the phenomenal character of my experience (by each being plugged into the ellipsis of "It seems to me the way it does for . . .," with appropriate grammatical alterations). The phenomenal features attributed to me are intentional features, we are assuming. But can I understand these reports to attribute *distinct* phenomenal features to me? If so, then the phenomenal-intentional features of visual experience are rich in a way not yet indicated.

It may not initially be clear that there is a phenomenal difference we could mark with (a) and (b). For if it looks to me as though something is shaped, situated, and colored this certain way, then it may well appear plausible to say that there is no *phenomenal* difference between its looking to me as though there is something of this shape, situation, and color, and its looking to me as though there is a sunflower in a certain location. One may want to say that there will be no difference in the *way it seems* to me to have experiences so reported.

But this would be too quick. There is, I want to say, a difference between the way things look to us when they merely look somehow shaped, colored, and situated, and how they look to us when they look recognizable to us as belonging to certain general types or as certain individuals encountered in the past. Then are we to say that flowers look different to the person who knows how to visually recognize the difference among sunflowers, daisies, dandelions, and other flowers, than they look to those totally ignorant of such distinctions? And should I say that Irene looks different to me now that I know her than she looked to me when we were strangers, or than she would look to me were I afflicted with amnesia, so I would say—"She looks totally unrecognizable, totally unfamiliar, to me"? Yes, I think this would be accurate, though this may seem less clear for recognition of types than it is for recognition of individuals.

It may not be just obvious that your visual experience of sunflowers differs phenomenally depending on whether or not you can recognize sunflowers as sunflowers. One will probably be unable to *compare* the way it seems to see them now with the way it seemed to see them before one learned to recognize sunflowers. But generally I think we can say that the way things look to us alters when we come to recognize what types of things they are. And this difference in how things look is a difference that follows from a difference in the way it seems to us for it to look to us as it does. This is not just a matter of its looking to us as if things have colors, shapes, and positions that they did not look to us as if they had before. It has to do also with what aspects of shape, color, and position "stand out for us as significant," and "go together." There is a way it seems to us to see sunflowers not just as some more shaped and colored things, but as what has a distinctively sunflowery look. This point may be more readily appreciated if we think of how it seems to us when we fail to recognize things we see only briefly or with parts hidden or from unfamiliar angles or in (what we would consider) unusual orientations. How it seems to us before we visually recognize them differs from how it seems to us when what we see becomes recognizable to us. And this is not always a matter of seeing more spatial detail, but sometimes just a matter of "seeing the whole thing in a different way." It is natural to suppose that it is this sort of phenomenal character that is missing from the visual experience of people who suffer from visual agnosia. Oliver Sacks's brain-damaged "man who mistook his wife for a hat" stares at a glove and cannot say it is one—he can only think to describe it as "a continuous surface . . . infolded on itself . . . [with] five outpouchings" (1987, 14). One imagines that to him, the glove does not look recognizable as a glove—and this is a matter of its not *seeing* to him as it did before his brain pathology. Another way to explain this point: think of a shape that may belong equally to different letters, distinguishable by their different orientations relative to other letters: an M, and a Greek sigma. The way it seems to one changes when one looks at the figure and recognizes it now as one, now as the other of these letters. The way it seems to me for it to look as if something is recognizable as M-shaped differs from the way it seems to me for it to look as if something is recognizable as sigma-shaped. And this difference need not involve my seeing the figure in different orientations.

It is difficult to be clear about these kinds of phenomenal differences. But I assume we can understand what it means to say that something "looks recognizable to someone as something," so that the following holds. I could employ (a) above in a true report of the phenomenal character of my experience—it could seem to me the way it does for it to look as though there is something of a certain shape, color, and position—even if what looks this way does not look recognizable to me as a sunflower. *And* that could be so, even if we assume this certain shape, etc., just happens to be one typical of sunflowers. However, (b) may be interpreted so that I could not use it in a true report of phenomenal character—it would not seem to me the way it does for it to look to me as though there is a *sunflower* there—*unless* it looks to me as though there is something *recognizable* as a sunflower there.

That the ability to recognize what one sees involves a difference in the phenomenal character of vision may, as I said, be more striking where recognition of individuals is concerned. Think of the change in experience when you suddenly recognize someone who first looked unfamiliar, since you haven't met in a long time. (It is not just that the visual experience is "accompanied by" some "feeling of familiarity"—the way the face *looks* to you changes.) And think of how individual people look different to you after you have gotten to know them than they did when you first met. Notice how different your neighborhood looks to you now that you have lived there for a while, than it did on the day you first arrived. This kind of variation in the phenomenal character of visual experience, where what one sees is recognizable as of a certain type, or as a certain individual, shades into, and is perhaps never wholly separable from, a sort that relates to differences in what "lies beyond" what one sees—that is, both what literally is *located* somewhere else, and what lies beyond the *actual* condition of what one sees, in *possibilities* in which it figures.

For example, that what I see in this neighborhood looks recognizable to me as a certain place has to do partly with its seeming to me the way it does for it to look as if certain *other* places are to be found from within it, depending on where I move. To recognize one's surroundings is to see them as the gateway to somewhere else. And one sees them in this way, as a consequence of the way it seems to one to see. To lack experience of this sort is to experience a lack of orientation. When you are oriented, the way it seems to you to see your surroundings is not merely the way it seems to you for it to look as if things are shaped, positioned, and colored before you in a certain manner. The temporarily disoriented person may see where things are around him accurately, but not recognize his surroundings—and when he does, the character of his experience changes.

When a chess player looks at the board in mid-game, while it looks to her as if there are before her things arranged, shaped, and colored thus and so, and while it looks to her as if there are things recognizable as a pawn, a queen, a knight, and so on, it also seems to her as it does for the game to be in a certain state of play—so that certain areas look like they provide an opening for attack on certain "vulnerable" pieces from other "threatening" ones. So the way it seems to her is shaped partly by its relation somehow to what is no longer the case, and to what might be the case. And when the car mechanic lifts the hood, and looks inside, the way it seems to him for it to look as it does differs from the way it seems to the person who is unable to recognize the parts of a car's engine—but this phenomenal difference has partly to do with its looking to the mechanic as if there are things before him that can come apart and fit together in certain ways. So it does not look to him as if what lies before him is a complicated jumble—but as if there is something that is ordered or organized in a certain way, and this way in which it looks ordered is related to a certain way in which it can be partitioned and assembled. So, again, it seems not just as it does for it to look as if things are actually arranged, shaped, and colored thus and so, but as if things before him are *arrangeable* in *other* ways.

But is this to say that it looks as if there are things that one can arrange differently, or merely as if there are things that can be in different spatial configurations? There is a subtle issue here, about whether it is part of the phenomenal look of things that they look to us *reachable, graspable*, and *manipulable* in certain ways—and not merely shaped and located in a certain manner. And this is tied to a yet subtler question: If we do say it phenomenally looks to us as if things are graspable and manipulable, are we to say that how they look shaped and positioned relative to us is distinguishable from this "pragmatic value" they appear to have, so that this latter may be somehow derived from or founded on the former?[5]

My efforts to point out certain potentially neglected aspects of the phenomenal character of vision have gradually led us into more difficult territory. That is, the sorts of phenomenal differences I have been discussing lately—those involved in it looking to us as if things are recognizable as types and individuals, and in its looking to us as if things have others "lying beyond them," both in literal space and in the "space of possibilities"—are caught up in a lot of hard issues concerning their description and relations, and bring up questions about the relation of perception to thought and action. But if my brief forays into this territory leave us still largely unsure of just how it lies, I hope at least to have drawn attention to some dimensions of vision's phenomenal character (however we should best think of them ultimately) that add considerably to its richness.

7.10 SUMMARY

My aim in this chapter has been to draw attention to certain aspects of the phenomenal character of vision, especially its relation to visual intentionality. My discussion has taken a number of turns, so perhaps it would be helpful to summarize its course.

Some intentional features, on my view, are features in virtue of which their possessor is assessable for truth or accuracy—that, at least, is a sufficient condition of being an intentional feature. And I take it that some sorts of sensory features we possess are assessable for accuracy—we can rightly speak of the accuracy or inaccuracy of someone's vision, for example. The question is whether we are assessable for accuracy in virtue of our *phenomenal* visual features. I want to allow that phenomenal visual features might be intentional ones only in some sort of holistic fashion. But this does not prevent our regarding our phenomenal visual features as intentional ones, since many of the differences in the way it seems to us to see are not rightly regarded as so atomistic as to preclude their being differences in intentional features, and, in any case, we can always shift our consideration to phenomenal features of such a scale that the atomist worry will not arise.

The issue then becomes whether there is anything we need to add to the situation of one with phenomenal visual experience of the kind we can identify in our own cases before it can be said to belong to a being with a form of sensory intentionality. I have assumed that if there are conditions that, when added to the fact that one has such visual phenomenal features, yield some true assessment of accuracy with respect to these features, and those conditions need not include any we should regard as furnishing an interpretation of those features, then they are intentional features. The question is whether what needs to be added is something that shows that phenomenal visual features always stand in need of something whereby they are somehow *assigned* conditions of accuracy, or whether they are *already* intentional.

In order to explore this terrain, we need a conception of how it is possible for sense-experience to go wrong—how, for instance, it may look some way or other to us inaccurately. For if we have no understanding of the possibility of sensory error, we have none regarding sensory success, and in that case we would have, in my view, no grasp of sensory intentionality. I think we can see how inaccurate visual experience is possible, by considering a situation in which it seems to us as it does for it to look as if something has a certain shape in a certain place, when in fact, there is nothing of that shape in that place. Even more, I believe this allows us to see that such visual phenomenal features are intentional ones. For I think that when you add to your having such a phenomenal feature this second ("there is nothing of that shape") condition, it follows that the way it looks to you is inaccurate. And if that follows, phenomenal features are intentional ones, for then it is clear that nothing like interpreting conditions need obtain, if correlative assessments of their possessors for accuracy are to hold true, once one has had visual experience of the right phenomenal character.

But we will be barred from this way of thinking about sensory intentionality if we are drawn to some form of sense-datum view about visual experience—where sense-data are supposed to be denizens of our minds that always appear as they are. So I argued against such a view about visual appearance, by showing how it can give us no acceptable conception of sensory error—in spite of the fact that we have traditionally been urged to seek justification for a belief in sense-data primarily in phenomena of illusion and hallucination.

Getting rid of sense-data helps us properly address the issue regarding sensory phenomenality and intentionality, but it does not yet allow us to conclude our discussion of it. For even if understanding the inaccuracy of visual experience does not require that we explain how an X-shaped thing in our minds comes to represent an X-shaped thing in the world, one might still maintain that it requires something analogous. One might say it is not enough for inaccuracy that one has a conscious visual experience of an X on one's left, when there is no X there; again, the experience has to be related to something else that may be lacking, if it is to be such as can be inaccurate or accurate of anything.

If conscious sensory experience needs some interpreting condition to bestow sensory intentionality upon its possessor, I presume this will have to be sought in some breakable link it may have either with other features that are already intentional—attitudes such as judging, thinking, believing, or intending that something be so—or else with the environment or behavior of the one who has the experience. But if the sorts of attitudes allegedly needed to give intentionality to sense-experience can be genuinely detached from its phenomenal character, we have no reason to think they really are essential to sensory intentionality. We cannot reason that one's experience needs to have conditions of accuracy assigned to it through judging (believing, etc.) that it has them, by saying that since changing such attitudes can change what makes the experience accurate, this must somehow depend on the attitude we take toward experience. For to the extent we can imagine shifting our attitudes toward our experience in the relevant fashion, it would seem inadequate to effect the change, and we cannot, in any case, alter our attitudes in this manner to any great extent. Moreover, we have this reason for thinking such interpretive attitudes are *not* needed: to say they are would be to deprive unreflective creatures of the ability to perceive their surroundings accurately or inaccurately. If we alter our approach, so that the interpreting condition is sought in a disposition to form certain kinds of judgment about (not sense-experience but) sensory stimuli, then we will run into a similar problem. If we render the prerequisites for such judgments weak or unclear, we cannot confidently say that a being with sensory consciousness might be entirely indisposed to make them. On the other hand, if the prerequisites for such dispositions to judgment are clearly more demanding than those for the relevant sort of conscious sense-experience, then we would have as much right to think that breaking their link to such experience indicates they are not really *necessary* for sensory intentionality, as we would to believe the break showed phenomenality *insufficient* for it.

Finally, an analogous problem would keep us from using the possibility of broken environmental or behavioral links to show one may have our sort of phenomenal sensory experience without its being accurate or inaccurate at all. Either the links cannot really be broken in the radical way called for, or they can—but this may just as well be thought to tell us that the links are not required for sensory intentionality after all, as to show that conscious sense-experience needs to draw its intentionality from somewhere else.

Thus we can conclude that our visual phenomenal features are intentional features. In this sense, we might say that visual experience is inherently significant.

Now, since visual phenomenal features—the ways it seems to us for it to look as if things are shaped, colored, and situated somehow—are typically complex, many, and varied, we can say that the phenomenal character of ordinary vision is remarkably rich. We should not allow ourselves to neglect or deny this richness on account of the relative poverty that often character-izes what we can *say* in identifying the distinctive way it seems to us during a given period of time. And there are other subtle and extensive forms of variation in our visual phenomenal features we should acknowledge—such as those involved in our capacity to recognize sameness of type and of indi-viduals—variations that include but go beyond what is indicated by talking of how things look as if they are shaped, colored, and positioned. Again, we may not be able to match the richness of our vision's phenomenal intention-ality with utterances of appropriately corresponding complexity so as to report just how it seems to us to see. And there is, of course, much detail in what is there to see, which one does not consciously see. But this need not make us oblivious to the abundant and nuanced differences in how it looks to us, typically, when we open our eyes for even a short time.

We are now quite far from confining the phenomenal character of vision to "raw feels" or sensations, undifferentiated in ways that would distinguish creatures of different characters and levels and forms of intelligence. The phenomenal visual life of lizards will differ significantly from that of humans, and that of (some kinds of) geniuses (e.g., painters, film directors, architects) will differ from that of (some kinds of) idiots (visual idiots, we might say), in ways revealing important differences in degree or kind of intelligence. For how it seems to us to see is quite indicative of the kinds of intelligent capacities we have that other creatures may lack, such as the capacities to perceive space, and color in space, as well as we do, accurately or inaccurately, and to recognize things visually. The exercise of intelligence in a way that depends on vision is manifest in vision's own phenomenal character, as well as in the motions of our hands and the words we speak.

But if this cures us of trivializing the phenomenal character of perception by making it out to be nonintentional and unintelligent—brute sensation— still, it leaves unresolved many questions about just what differences in intentional features are differences in phenomenal features. One wants to know whether our experiences do or can differ in respect of intentional features, without differing in phenomenal character, and if so, what sorts of intentional features these are. I said earlier that though there is a difference between its looking to you as if the tire has enough air, and its looking to you as if it does not, we may not want to say that how it seems to you for it to look one or the other of these ways differs. I did not commit myself on this, but I think that if we recognize a distinction between the visual experience and visual judgment, we will not want to say that the way it seems to have the visual experiences one might report in these ways differs. So there could be a difference in intentional features here, without any difference in the phenomenal character of *visual experience*. There is some difference between the way it seems for it to look to you as if the tire has enough air, and the way it seems for it to look to you as if it does not, only if there is some difference between the way it seems to judge visually that it does, and the way it seems to judge visually that it does not. Another way to make this point: when it looks to me as if the tire has enough air, but a gauge shows it to be decidedly low, I would not want to say that my *visual experience* was revealed to be inaccurate in some way—only that my judgment was faulty.

If we are to understand the relationship between the phenomenal character of experience and the kinds of intentional features attributed in remarks about how it looks to us of the kind just illustrated, it seems we need to shift our attention away from sensory experience, to what appears more properly to belong to the category "conscious thought."

Conscious Thought

8.1 CONSCIOUS THOUGHT: ICONIC AND NONICONIC

To understand phenomenal consciousness, we must distinguish sensory *ap-pearance* from sensory *judgment*. But this, I've argued, should not make us think that intentionality can be stripped from sense-experience, so as to leave only some "raw feel." Sensory appearance has intentionality of its own, inseparable from its phenomenal character. But if we find in sense-experience a kind of intentionality, distinct from that of judgment, do we exclude judgment from phenomenal consciousness? More generally, we might ask: Does thinking also have phenomenal character? If so, how is this related to its intentionality?

Here I have just slid from talk of judgment to talk of thought. But this blurs a distinction that needs taking into account if we are to understand what, other than sensory experience, is phenomenally conscious, and how it varies in character. For we may speak of *thought* and *thinking* about things, both where this involves imagery of such things, and where it does not. And what we say about the phenomenal character of thought will differ, depend-ing on which of these two kinds of thought—imagistic or nonimagistic—we are considering.

We can get a grip on the distinction between these kinds of thought by noting this. Often the questions, "What were you thinking?" or "What were you thinking of (or about)?" are correctly answered: "I was thinking that p," or "I was thinking of (or about) A," even though you did *not* visualize, auralize, or otherwise "image" that p, or A. So, for example, "I was just thinking about the things I need to get at the store" does not entail "I was just visualizing the things I need to get at the store." (Maybe, for instance, I was repeating to myself a list, without visualizing the items listed. And I was not just *auralizing*, either: I was thinking of [or about] the things I needed to buy.) Also, "I was just thinking that traffic is going to be heavy now" does not entail, "I was visualizing that there will be heavy traffic." (The thought just occurred to me, as it might to someone—say, someone blind from birth—not even capable of visualizing such a scene.)

So, clearly, there can be thinking without imagery. On the other hand, often one will correctly answer inquiries about what one was thinking, by speaking of something one *did* visualize or image. (I may well have pictured a box of laundry soap when I was setting out for the store.) If one *does* visualize or otherwise image something, or that something is the case, one has (I will say) an "iconic thought."[1] While if one does *not* image what one is thinking (or thinking of or about), one has a "noniconic" thought. Only where there is noniconic thinking does it seem right to speak of judgment and judging.

Now, on my account, phenomenal consciousness is not restricted to sensory states (even if these are taken to include imagery), for noniconic thoughts are (often) occurrences of consciousness, in the same sense as iconic thoughts (or imagery) and sense-experience. This may not be adequately clear; it is a point to which I will devote much of this chapter. But to understand what I am saying, one needs to realize that on this view, one and the same occurrence of conscious thought can be *both* iconic and noniconic, under different descriptions. I auralize an utterance ("It's going to rain"), and this is an iconic thought, but I also thereby think what I *mean* by that utterance, namely: *that it's going to rain*—and so I have a *noniconic* thought as well. For though, as I look up at those dark massing clouds, the thought does occur to me that it's going to rain, I do not on this occasion (we may suppose) visualize or otherwise form an image of its raining. Though perhaps I am then able to visualize rain coming down, battering the plants, splashing on wet sidewalks—in the same sense of 'visualize' in which I can visualize a triangle, but not (as Descartes pointed out) a thousand-sided figure—I just do not on this occasion exercise this ability, when the thought occurs to me that it is going to rain. In such an event, my thinking may be identified either relative to the utterance I auralized, and thus as an iconic thought or episode of imagery, or relative to what I mean by this utterance, as a noniconic thought. And under either description, it can be correct to say this is an occurrence of consciousness. When I consciously think (auralize the words), "It's going to rain," I consciously think *that it's going to rain*.

In explaining and defending this conception, I will first discuss the phenomenal character of iconic thought, that is, the way it seems for us to have imagery experience, and its relation to intentionality. Then I will go on to consider how consciousness relates to nonimagistic thought, and to its intentionality. Only after we have added to our understanding of sensory phenomenal features an understanding of the kinds of phenomenal features involved in conscious thought, can we begin to address properly questions about the importance of consciousness.

8.2 INTENTIONALITY AND VISUALIZATION

If I am going to ask how the *phenomenal* features we have, in having imagery, relate to the *intentional* ones we have, in having this kind of experience, I had better first be clear that imagery does involve our having both sorts of features. Here I will follow the usual practice when addressing the topic of imagery, and focus, as earlier with perception, on the visual modality.

We need not belabor the point that visualization experience does have phenomenal character, in the sense explained in Chapter 3. For you should have little trouble recognizing this is so, if you were willing to accept the framework for discussing these matters assembled there, and grant what was said about visual experience in the last chapter. If you acknowledge that the way it seems to you for it to look as if there is something X-shaped differs from the way it seems to you for it to look as if there is something O-shaped, then surely you will need no great prodding to admit that the way it seems to you to *visualize* something X-shaped differs from the way it seems to you to visualize something O-shaped. And I assume you will grant that these first-person knowable differences in the way it seems to you to have such experiences are such as could distinguish only occurrences of phenomenal consciousness.

So visualizing has phenomenal character—but does it have intentionality? If features we attribute to ourselves in saying what we visualize are features in virtue of which we are assessable for accuracy, then they are intentional features. So this is an indication that they are intentional: it seems we can rightly speak of either *accurately* or *inaccurately* visualizing something. If saying this sounds a little odd, I think that is only because often we do not concern ourselves with whether there is anything we visualize or auralize accurately, when we visualize or auralize something. But we *can* make the accuracy of imagery a concern—for instance, when we *try* to visualize something. You might ask me to visualize a figure with a certain type of shape— for example, the type exemplified by an outline of the boundaries of the state of Texas ("Texas-shaped"). And I will either more or less accurately or inaccurately visualize the shape of Texas. I might tend to visualize it more accurately if I visualize it in the "normal" orientation (as in a map with north at the top), and less accurately (to some extent and in some respect inaccurately) when I visualize it on its side, or upside down (or when I try, as they say in psychology, to "rotate the image 90, or 180, degrees"). Perhaps when I try to visualize the shape of Texas in some of these orientations, the end of the line that would form the eastern boundary of the panhandle and the end of its western boundary are too nearly level; perhaps I visualize the western or southern tips ending too bluntly; perhaps when I rotate the image, the eastern part of the state distortingly "balloons" out, tumorlike—in any of these ways I might less accurately visualize this type of shape.

But even though we may in this way speak of accurately or inaccurately visualizing a type of shape, it may not seem this shows us how, in speaking of what one visualizes, one attributes intentional features. For it may appear that only where one *tries* to visualize a shape (or perhaps, only where one *intends* to visualize a shape) does one become in this way assessable for accuracy. And so, one might suggest that while you are assessed for accuracy with respect to your visualizing, properly speaking, it is not the visualizing in virtue of which you are assessed, really. Rather, it is in virtue of trying to visualize, or intending to visualize, that you are assessed: to say you visualize a certain shape relatively accurately is just to say that you were relatively successful in visualizing the type of shape you were trying or intending to visualize. One's trying or intending bestows conditions of accuracy on one's visualization, where otherwise it would have none.

However, I do not think this is right. Clarifying this point will help introduce the claim I want to make about the relationship between the intentionality and phenomenal character of visual imagery. Let's go back to visual (not visualization) experience for a moment. Notice first that the shape it *looks* to you as if something has, may be the shape of Texas, though it does not look to you as if something is Texas-shaped. This may happen, for instance, where you do not *recognize* the shape it looks to you as if something has, as Texas-shaped. So: if the figure is presented to you in some peculiar orientation, even though it looks to you as if it has a certain shape, and, in fact, the shape it looks to you as if it has *is* the shape of Texas, that is, Texas-shaped, still, since it does not look to you as if the figure is *recognizably* Texas-shaped, it does not look to you as if a figure is Texas-shaped. Similarly, we might say, even if the shape it looks to you as if something has is sigma-shaped, or the shape of a duck's profile, it may not look to you as if something is sigma-shaped, or duck's-head-shaped. Suppose, for example, the shape it looks to you as if something has belongs to an inscription of the letter sigma. But this inscription is turned on its side, so that to you it looks as if something is M-shaped (not that it is sigma-shaped)—for in this orientation you do not recognize the figure as sigma-shaped. Or consider the famous duck-rabbit drawing. Suppose you are seeing it "as a rabbit." Then, at that time, while there is a shape it looks to you as if a line forms, and this type of shape could rightly be said to be the shape of a duck's profile, it wouldn't be right to say it looks to you as if some figure is duck's-head-shaped.

I want to say that something analogous holds in the case of visual imagery. The shape you visualize a figure having may indeed be the shape of Texas, but it does not follow that you visualize something *as Texas-shaped*. If you have just seen the shape in some abnormal orientation—one in which it does not look as if something is recognizably Texas-shaped—then, when (closing your eyes) you visualize what you just saw, you are liable not to visualize the figure as (recognizably) Texas-shaped. Similarly, when visualizing the sigma-shaped figure, which you recognized not as sigma-shaped, but as M-shaped, it may be true to say of you that the type of shape you visualized is the shape of a sigma, though you did not visualize it as sigma-shaped. And though the type of figure you visualized was the shape of a duck's profile, you did not visualize a figure as duck's-head-shaped.

However, it is not essential for you to visualize something as having a certain type of shape, that you possess the (or a) *concept* of that type, or of that type of shape, if this entails that you have certain kinds of belief about things of that type, and about shape. For instance, you may visualize something as recognizably Texas-shaped, even if you do not, as we might say, have the concept of being Texas-shaped—because you lack the concept of shape generally. We might say this, for instance, of a young child of whom we could not rightly say that she believes: that shapes are not sizes; that things may differ in size without differing in shape; that they may differ in shape without differing in size; that turning something upside down does not change its shape; and that (for example) square and circular are shapes, not sizes, while big, small, long, and short are sizes, not shapes. She may not *disbelieve* these things, but still we might reasonably think, she simply has not yet acquired such beliefs, and so she lacks (has not yet acquired, understood) the concept of shape. (We might also say, I suppose, that she "has no concept of Texas"—since she does not believe that Texas is a state, or that a state is a part of a country, and so on. But again, we might say that as 'Texas' is a proper name, it does not express a concept, and having beliefs about Texas need not involve possessing the concept of a state, or anything similar.) But in any case, the point is: a child innocent of such beliefs about shape might still visually recognize the shape of Texas, and might visualize something as having that shape. The same goes for sigma-shaped: you may visualize something as sigma-shaped, even if you do not have the concept of shape, or the concept of a sigma (and hence lack the concept of something's being sigma-shaped). You might lack the belief that a sigma is a symbol or a letter, much less a Greek letter—and still be able to visually recognize and visualize something as sigma-shaped.

With this behind us, we're ready to grasp a point about the intentionality of visualization. If, in the sense just illustrated, you visualize something *as* having a certain type of shape, then you visualize that shape accurately or inaccurately in some respect and to some extent. If you visualize something as Texas-shaped, then you will visualize more or less accurately, depending on the ways in which the type of shape you visualize conforms to what is most truly Texas-shaped, that is, depending on how Texas-shaped the shape you visualize is. If you visualize something as sigma-shaped, then you visualize accurately or inaccurately depending on how closely sigma-shaped the shape you visualize is. (Suppose you visualize a figure as sigma-shaped, but "sloppily"—as you might sloppily draw it—the angles formed by the lines at the figure's extremities being too wide, so that although you visualize something as recognizably sigma-shaped, it is just barely so. In another instance, you more accurately, and less inaccurately, visualize a sigma-shaped figure.)

Now, I wish to point out that one may, in this sense, visualize a figure as having a certain type of shape, even though one has not *tried* to do so, or *intended* to do so. Suppose someone tells you that Texas license plates have little Texas-shaped dots in the middle of the license number. You may picture this—visualizing a Texas-shaped figure in the middle of a license number, and visualizing it *as* Texas-shaped, even though you did not try to do so, or form an intention to do so. The visualization just occurred to you, without your trying or intending, much as when you read or hear a story you sometimes just find yourself visualizing what is described, though you made no effort and formed no intention to do this. Similarly, when you rotate a sigma in your imagination, you may then visualize a figure (not as sigma-shaped, but) as M-shaped, when you suddenly recognize it as M-shaped. But this just happened: you did not set out to visualize a figure as M-shaped.

Thus, when we say that someone more or less accurately visualized a kind of shape, we are not just commenting on their success (or failure) in doing something they were either trying or intending to do. And so the feature of visualizing in this way counts as an intentional feature in its own right; we are concerned here with an intentionality of visual imagery that is not derived from the intentionality of having aims or intentions to visualize. Further, these kinds of intentional features are commonly found wherever visual imagery is found. Even where you *are* trying to visualize the shape of Texas, if you succeed to some extent, then you visualize something as Texas-shaped, in the sense you might have done, and done accurately, even without trying. Also, when you remember something, accurately or inaccurately, by visualizing it (as often happens, with or without trying), then you will visualize a figure as recognizably shaped in some way or other—and you more or less accurately visualize some type of shape. So, I remember the house in which I lived when I was five years old, by visualizing it. And I remember it accurately in this or that respect, only if I visualize something as recognizably shaped a certain way, and that type of shape (one that something other than my old house might have) is one I visualize somewhat accurately.

Now—here is what I want to say about the *phenomenal character* of the imagery experiences distinguished in the manner I have indicated. Let the "F" and the "G" in "F-shaped" and "G-shaped" be replaced by whatever terms will form expressions that make the observations I have made above about visualizing something as shaped in a certain way true, and in such manner that someone may visualize something as F-shaped without visualizing it as G-shaped, and vice versa. The way it seems to us to visualize something as F-shaped will differ from the way it seems to us to visualize something as G-shaped. There is a difference in the phenomenal character of such imagery experiences. So I may, after being presented with an upside-down outline of Texas, visualize what I saw—but visualize it not as Texas-shaped, but only as *that* shape (the one I saw a moment ago). And then, when I visualize the figure with a different orientation, I suddenly recognize it as Texas-shaped, I visualize it as Texas-shaped—so the way it seems to me to visualize it changes, somewhat as my visual experience might phenomenally change when, with the map reoriented, I say, "Oh, I see, it's Texas." The change here is not due merely to a difference in the way it seems to visualize a figure in different orientations. Notice: when we go from visualizing something as M-shaped, to visualizing it as recognizably sigma-shaped, the way it seems to us to visualize differs, even though the orientation visualized does not. Again: we may see the duck-rabbit figure as a rabbit, and then visualize that type of figure as rabbit's-head-shaped, and *then* visualize the same type of figure as duck's-head-shaped. And the way it seems to visualize—the phenomenal character of our visual imagery—changes as well.

Now, here is what I want to say about the relationship between the phenomenal character of visual imagery and its intentionality. If it seems to you as it seems to me to visualize a figure as recognizably shaped a certain way, then you do visualize a type of figure as recognizably shaped that way. If it seems to you as it does to me to visualize something as Texas-shaped, then you do visualize something as Texas-shaped. And, if one visualizes something as recognizably shaped a certain way, then one *accurately* visualizes a certain type of shape to a greater or lesser extent. So, from your having a certain phenomenal feature, it follows that some assessment for accuracy is true of you, of a sort that indicates that this phenomenal feature is a feature in virtue of which you are assessable for accuracy. Thus the phenomenal features that we often have, in having visual imagery, and that we can identify by thinking of how it seems to us to visualize, are intentional features.

To assess this claim, we should try to consider whether having visualization experience of the character ours has really is enough to have the kind of imagistic intentionality I have indicated: the more or less accurate visualization of types of shapes. For this, we should try to consider what reasons we might offer for thinking other conditions need to be added to the phenomenal imagistic features, to confer intentionality upon them. Suppose we can find some warrant for holding there are conditions that (a) might fail to obtain, even though one had such phenomenal features, *and* (b) are essential to one's visualizing something as recognizably shaped in a certain way (and thus essential to the intentionality of imagery). Then we will have reason to regard the phenomenal features in question as somehow standing in need of interpreting conditions, before their possessor is to have conscious visualization experience that is intentional. On the other hand, if we can turn up no good reason to think the phenomenal character of visual imagery needs something else to bestow intentionality upon it, then, assuming that phenomenal visualizing is somehow either more or less accurate visualization of types of shapes, the best conclusion will be that we simply do not need to add anything to the phenomenal character of visual imagery to make it intentional. The phenomenal features we can think of, when we think of how it seems to us to visualize, are *already* intentional features.

We might first try to motivate the view that the phenomenal character of imagery is not enough for intentionality, by taking quite closely the analogy between visualizing something (forming a mental image of it) and drawing or painting something (making a nonmental image of it). For we may want to say that when we visualize certain shapes, we bring into being *mental objects* having those very shapes—inspecting with the "mind's eye" what we make (with the "mind's hand"?). And we may then say that these mental items have (as do ordinary pictures, photographic images, and video displays) not only certain shapes, but also representational features. But in no case is the possession of certain shapes by itself logically sufficient to make them *representations of* anything. Having a shape is not by itself an intentional feature. So one might then propose that the phenomenal character of visual imagery determines only what *shape* mental images have; it does not endow these with *intentionality*, any more than the mere production of blobs of paint or ink marks or pixel arrays by itself will suffice to make representations. The way it seems to visualize merely throws shapes and colors on the mind's canvas; it does not make these images *of* anything. Or so runs the suggestion.

But this provides us with insufficient reason to deintentionalize the phenomenal character of imagery. For one thing, we should not accept the claim that it follows from its seeming to you as it does to visualize something as Texas-shaped, that there is a Texas-shaped item of some sort, which you are visualizing, and which would not exist without being visualized, or could not be visualized by another—a Texas-shaped mental object. But even if this did follow, it would not license us to detach visualizing's intentionality from the way it seems for us to visualize. For the phenomenal character of the visualizing may change, even though the putative mental object does not. In the example given earlier, the way it seems to visualize something as M-shaped will differ from the way it seems to visualize something as sigma-shaped, but it need manufacture in my mind items no differently shaped. One and the same drawing would serve to indicate what I visualized in either case, and so presumably, switching from visualizing a figure as an M to visualizing a figure as a ("lazy") sigma need not change the shape of any mental object. But then we cannot say, as was suggested, that differences in the phenomenal character of visualizing can determine only differences in the shapes of the "vehicles of representation" (mental images), not differences in "what they represent"—their "content." A similar reply would be in order if someone argued, not that seeming makes "little pictures" in one's mind, but that differences in visually imagistic phenomenal features in a certain way *correspond* only to differences in the *nonrepresentational* features of pictures whereby they represent (that is, their color, arrangement, shape)—and so also stand in need of interpretation before they can picture anything to us. For, as we have seen, we can appreciate a difference in the phenomenal character of visualization, where there would be no analogous difference in the nonrepresentational features of the relevant (real, nonmental) pictures. So we cannot find a reason to regard the intentionality of visual imagery as quite separate from its phenomenal character, via some analogy between differences in the way it seems for us to visualize and the nonintentional features of pictures, through which they represent things.

Our next move, then, might be to consider, as before with vision, a kind of phenomenal atomism—this time about visual imagery—coupled with an intentional holism. Perhaps someone will suggest that the sorts of phenomenal features to which I refer are essentially isolable in a way that is incompatible with their being intentional. So you might say there could be a subject to whom it seemed the way it does to me to visualize something as recognizably

Texas-shaped, but who had no other phenomenal experience whatsoever: someone condemned to the phenomenal monotony of visualizing the shape of Texas, and nothing else, *ever*. Or you might suggest that there could be someone with more phenomenally varied visual imagery, but without any other sort of phenomenal sensory experience. And, in either case—you might say—one would not be visualizing something as Texas-shaped; one would not have this intentional feature. For one could not recognize the shape of Texas if one had, experientially, nothing with which to contrast it, nor could one recognize shapes one visualized, if one never had more "vivid" sensory experience of shape: for example, the kind reported by saying it *looks* to one as if something is shaped a certain way.

Though the matter is obscure, I am inclined to grant this sort of intentional holism. However, once I grant it, the phenomenal atomism seems to me quite unwarranted. If it is granted that you cannot visualize something as recognizably Texas-shaped without other sorts of experiences, it is not clear to me that it can *seem* to you as it does to visualize something as recognizably Texas-shaped without other sorts of experience. If you think you can conceive of its seeming this way to someone in isolation from other conscious experience, this carries no more weight than someone's thinking she can conceive of a subject's visually recognizing the shape of Texas, though completely deprived of any other capacities for visual recognition.

In any case, we could avoid the question of this sort of atomism and its import for the present thesis, by altering in a certain way the sorts of phenomenal imagistic features with which we are concerned. If certain kinds of phenomenal variety in imagery and sensory experience are essential to having intentional visual imagery, then suppose, instead of considering just (for example) the way it seems to you to visualize something as sigma-shaped, you consider the feature of its seeming this way to you, *and* your having whatever other phenomenal imagery and sensory experience is essential to your visualizing something as sigma-shaped. We can then change our thesis to the claim that *this* phenomenal feature is intentional, as its possession entails one visualizes accurately or inaccurately in some way. To do so would not be to trivialize the thesis, by including in this (macro) phenomenal feature sensory ones we have already acknowledged to be intentional. For the kind of intentionality I would claim the present feature has, is not just that of its looking accurately or inaccurately some way to one, but the intentionality of imagery: one's visualizing accurately or inaccurately. However, for simplicity's sake, I will not reformulate my thesis in this way in the discussion that follows, but will proceed as if we could assume that the phenomenal character of visual imagery was already sufficiently holistic to block any challenges to its intentionality from suggestions of phenomenal atomism.

At this point we might suggest that the phenomenal character of visual imagery needs to have added to it something in the way of *judgment*, something in the way of *noniconic* thought, something distinctively *intellectual* or *conceptual*, as opposed to merely sensorial, to provide an interpretation of it, to make it intentional. But what is the required judgment supposed to be about? Will we require that one make (or be disposed to make) judgments about one's own visualizing? Then we would appear to rule out imagistic intentionality for creatures who lack the power of reflection on their own imagery experience—who lack the concept of visualizing. If, then, we say that the required judgments are not mentally self-reflexive, or higher-order, but rather are judgments about the types of things visualized, we will hit this problem. We have already acknowledged that the intentionality of imagery does not need judgment of this sort. For we have accepted the claim that one can visualize something as recognizably having a certain type of shape, without having the concept of that type of shape. (Again, one can visualize something as recognizably sigma-shaped, without having the concept of shape or the concept of a sigma.) And if one says that we are concerned here with a *nonconceptual* or a *preconceptual* kind of judgment about the types of shapes visualized, then it will become unclear how this is supposed to be something different from what is already possessed by anyone to whom it seems as it does to us to think iconically, and that needs to be added to this.

Will someone say that conscious visual imagery is, in a certain sense, meaningless—nonintentional, uninterpreted—unless one targets the right sorts of *intentions* upon it? But we have already disposed of this suggestion as well. For it is not necessary that one intend to visualize a certain shape for one to visualize something as recognizably having that type of shape. And the latter is sufficient for the intentionality of iconic thought. So the intentionality of the phenomenal features with which we are concerned will not be impugned by noting the potential absence of such intentions.

But mustn't a creature have intentions, or aims, or goal-directed states of *some* sort, in order to have intentionalistic imagery? Maybe so, but then, it is not clear that a creature could have the sorts of phenomenal features we are discussing without having any sort of goal-directed intentionality. So it is not clear that these sorts of states are something possibly missing, that need to be added, for imagistic intentionality. On the other hand, if you are so firmly convinced that intentions and aims could be entirely missing from a phenomenally visualizing being, it is not clear why, then, you should not take this as evidence that having intentionality of a goal-directed sort is not really essential to being able to visualize certain types of shapes accurately, after all.

Finally, someone might urge that imagery experience has to be linked in the right way to behavior or to the subject's environment for it to be genuinely intentional, and the phenomenal character of imagery could remain while these essential links were broken. But here I would respond much as I did earlier in a similar context, regarding visual consciousness. I do not think we have reason to believe this conjunction of claims: there are certain behavioral or environmental links essential to the intentionality of imagery, *and* they could be missing, while the phenomenal character of imagery is held constant. Whatever support these two claims might appear to have, each seems independent of the other. Have we convinced ourselves that there is no accurate visualizing of types of shapes without such and such behavioral or environmental connections? Then why should we not use this conviction to defeat whatever impression we may have that these links might be absent, where it still seems to the subject the way it seems to us to visualize figures as recognizably having certain shapes? On the other hand, if that possibility seems to us undeniable, why not turn it against the claim that the behavioral or environmental connections are necessary ones, instead of against the thought that, if it seems to me as it does to visualize something as recognizably sigma-shaped, then I do visualize something as recognizably sigma-shaped?

However, in the case of imagery's intentionality, there might seem to be a special reason to insist on the importance of environmental connections that could be missing without phenomenal change. For you might say:

> You visualize the house where you were five years old. But there is something you accurately visualize, only if there is the right sort of *historical-causal* connection between a particular building, and your current visualization. But that connection is surely not something that can be guaranteed by the phenomenal character of your experience. And if you merely freely fantasize a house, well, there is no particular of which we can say: you accurately visualized *that*—even if, as it happens, there is somewhere a house of the kind you visualized. All of which goes to show that imagistic phenomenal features are not assessable for accuracy in this way, without assuming that possibly missing historical-causal conditions do obtain, which confer this intentionality on the mental images—make them images *of* these particular things.

But first, I am not so sure of the claim here. Suppose, in reading tales or fables, I visualize something as recognizably unicorn-shaped, and then, exploring a hidden valley, to my astonishment I come upon an actual unicorn. "It's just as I imagined it!" I exclaim. Mightn't this be a case where there was something I accurately visualized, even though I lacked the allegedly necessary historical links to this something? (There was—as it happened—a unicorn I accurately visualized, even before I made my journey into the valley.) However, setting this aside, it is not in any case essential for me to deny that historical links—of a kind that the phenomenal character of imagery cannot guarantee—are necessary for there to be individuals one accurately or inaccurately visualizes. For again, my claim concerns itself with accurately or inaccurately visualizing *types* of shapes.

I conclude that there just is no good reason to think that the phenomenal character of visual imagery requires the addition of conditions that interpret it or confer intentionality upon it, in order for it to have any intentionality at all. There seems to be nothing we might reasonably want, whose absence is compatible with the truth of, "It seems to x as it does to me to visualize something as recognizably having a certain shape," that must be added to the truth of this before we can infer that x visualizes something as recognizably having a certain shape. And, since this is enough to make it the case that x visualizes a certain shape either more or less *accurately*, it is enough to make the phenomenal features we can consider, in thinking of how it seems to us to visualize intentional features.

But if this shows us that intentionality is inextricable from the phenomenal character of iconic thinking, it still leaves us wondering what to say about noniconic thought. Recall that, in Chapter 7, I said that though we might leave open many issues about the kinds of intentional features the phenomenal character of visual experience gives us, we could still recognize that its powers are in a certain way limited relative to those of noniconic thought. For even *visual judgments* may differ where the phenomenal character of *visual experience* does not. For instance, the way it seems to you for it to look as if a tire is low, and the way it seems to me for it to look as if it has enough air, may in certain cases differ, if they do, only if the way it seems to you to visually *judge* that the tire is low differs from the way it seems to me to visually judge that it has enough air. Here we are concerned with the phenomenal character of thought, not that of visual experience. And it will not surprise anyone to say that the phenomenal-intentional character of visualization is similarly limited. I could visualize the tire in question, and whether the tire had looked a little low to me or not, the way it seemed to *visualize* the tire would be no different.

8.3 Conscious Thought: Not Just Imagery

I have said I do not want to give the impression that *only* imagery and sense-experience are conscious—though I focused on these as rather obvious examples. For on my view, *thinking*, where this is distinguished both from sensory appearance and from mere imagery, is phenomenally conscious, in the very same sense identified through these examples and the blindsight thought-experiments. So not only the thinking we keep to ourselves, and express at most in silent speech, but also the thinking we do out loud, and audibly express, is phenomenally conscious—we consciously think when we are talking to other people. This should not be seen to suggest that our audible speech is accompanied by some "stream" of imagery—often there is little or nothing of this sort going on. The point is rather that noniconic thought is conscious too. This is to say that it has phenomenal character. Differences in the way it seems for us to think are not just differences in the way it seems for us to visualize, auralize, or otherwise image things. And these phenomenal features are intentional features.

But this might not be clear. Though one may admit the way it seems to sense and to image is not to be reduced to some "raw feel" of sensation, one may still cling to the segregation of intentionality from consciousness where nonimagistic thought is concerned. Such a view, I take it, is expressed by

Ray Jackendoff, when he says, "The *only* form of linguistic representation available to awareness is, of all things, phonological structure."[2] His point seems to be that the thinking we express when we mean what we say is not conscious, but only the perception or imaging of utterance. Less overtly and more diffusely, such a view seems to be part of a general philosophical attitude toward consciousness influenced by Wittgenstein's (1953) attack on the notion that understanding is an "inner state" or "inner process"—it may seem that to suggest understanding what one says and thinks is somehow experiential, is to regress to some view this and similar critiques have put us past. And although Tye (1995) insists that we not separate the phenomenal character of sensory experience from its representational character, he also holds that phenomenal character belongs properly only to sensory and imagery states.

Certainly not all who consider the relation between thought and phenomenal consciousness would divorce them in this way. (See, for instance, the discussions of Strawson [1994] and Flanagan [1992].) I want here to add my voice to those who would have us recognize the distinctive phenomenal character of noniconic thought. Phenomenal consciousness and intentionality are indissoluably bound not only in sensory experience and imagery, but also in the domain of judgment, conceptual thought, and linguistic understanding. To help clarify and appreciate this point, we need first to consider how we can identify something distinctive about the phenomenal character of noniconic thinking—that is, something about the way it seems to us to think. The first point to grasp is this. The way it seems to auralize or hear a sentence by which one means or understands something as the utterance is made—and thus the way it seems to one to think noniconically—differs from the way it seems to one to auralize or hear an utterance made or heard "senselessly," just as a pattern of (real or auralized) sound. And so, it also differs from the way it seems to one just to have imagery experience. I believe you can appreciate the relevant sort of contrast in phenomenal character if you think of circumstances in which you are reading or speaking a language you are just learning or of which you have only modest knowledge. You can easily find yourself just sounding out a sentence, or speaking it silently to yourself, without just then understanding or meaning anything by it. And it seems different to have the experience of this, than it does to have the experience you have when you read or speak the sentence and "get it"—when it then means something to you.

We may also notice this sort of phenomenal contrast when reading something written in a language we *do* know, especially if the syntax is complex, or the text is difficult to follow, and especially if we are reading aloud for an audience. I may utter the words of my speech while attending so little to what I am saying—that is, to what it *means*—that I lose track of this, cease to follow it, cease to understand what I am saying as I am saying it. We might say, in a sense: I cease to read *comprehendingly*. This does not entail that the sentences I utter are not ones that I understand, or know the meaning of. But it can happen that, though I do understand the sentences in the text I am reciting or reading—I do know what they mean—I do not *follow their meaning as I am reading or reciting them*. As I am reading or reciting in this uncomprehending manner, I may then start to concentrate on what the words I am saying mean, and slip back into understanding, but the way it then seems to me to hear and understand what I am saying as I'm saying it differs from the way it seemed merely to hear my own utterance.

In these cases, this sort of difference in how it seems does not have to do with what words we are reading or hearing—we may be repeating the same text, and hear it just as well, and yet it seems in this way different to us. And we may recognize what words we are reading, both when we read comprehendingly and when we do not; yet there is this difference in the phenomenal character of experience. And clearly this does not have to do with whether or not it seems to us as it does to *image* different things. For there may be no difference of that kind. Nor is it enough to say here that the words sound different to us when we understand than they do when we do not (although this would, I think, generally be true). For they sound different to us, not just in any old way, but in certain ways. And the phenomenal difference here must be identified not just relative to the sounds or sights of utterance, real or imagined, but relative to what is *understood* by them. It seems to me not only the way it does to hear uttered a certain string of words, nor only the way it does to hear and recognize what words or phrases are uttered, but the way it seems to me to hear a certain utterance and understand what is being said in a certain way, as it is said. Thus I should say not just that it seems to me the way it does to think (to say to myself silently), "Bob is driving home from work," but that it seems to me the way it does to say this and, as I say it, understand by it that Bob is driving home from work; that is: it seems to me the way it does to think that Bob is driving home from work. So we can say that there is a phenomenal character distinctive of noniconic thought. For the way it seems to one just to hear an utterance differs from the way it seems to one to hear and understand something by it as one hears it. When the latter occurs, we may say that one's noniconic thinking is phenomenally conscious.[3]

Here is another way to appreciate the phenomenal difference between iconic and noniconic thinking: attend to instances in which a thought occurs to you, when not only do you not *image* what you think or are thinking of, but you also do not *verbalize* your thought, either silently or aloud, nor are you then understanding someone else's words. Striking examples of thoughts occurring, conscious, but in the absence of verbal expression or imagery, are to be found where there is what we might call an abrupt shift in the direction of thought. Suppose you are sitting and reading one morning, and suddenly you remember some incipient appointment—you wonder when exactly it was, feel anxious that you may have missed it, and look at your watch. The thought of the appointment and when it was is an occurrence of consciousness, but it may not be verbalized silently or aloud. You may not have said to yourself—"I have an appointment around now, don't

I? When was it? Did I miss it?" You may not even have said something fragmentary, like: "Appointment! When? Miss it?" And you may not have visualized or imaged any item or event at the time of this thought, such as the person with whom you had the appointment, or the place at which you were to meet. But this little wordless episode of noniconic thinking—your suddenly recalling that you had an appointment—is phenomenally conscious, and the way it seems to you to have this thought differs from the way it would seem to you to have imagery experience of some sort.

A similar example: you are standing at the door to your house, reaching in your pants pocket for the door key, and you find it empty. You feel a sudden panic; you think perhaps you have locked yourself out; you try to remember where you put the keys, then recall switching them to your coat pocket earlier; you reach and find them there—relief. Such little episodes often do not involve any imagery experience—one needn't have *pictured* being locked out (whatever that would mean), or the door key, in having had such an experience, and one needn't have said, "Maybe I've locked myself out!" or something of the sort, on such occasions. Cases of sudden wordless thoughts that, like the examples I have just chosen, involve a sudden surge of anxiety, may be relatively easy to notice and recall, but we can take note of the occurrence of such noniconic thoughts even where they involve no such marked change in one's emotions. Suppose you are riding a bicycle, approaching a green traffic light far ahead, and it suddenly occurs to you that the light will change soon, and you wonder whether to speed up to make the light—but this experience involves no remarkable change in your emotional state. You may have known this thought—that the light's about to change—occurred to you and that it is conscious, though you did not utter to yourself the words, "The light is about to change," or visualize the light changing.

Though the thoughts in these examples are fairly simple, wordless noniconic thoughts can be relatively complex. Walking from my table in a restaurant to pay the bill, I was struck briefly by a thought, gone by the time I reached the cashier, about my preoccupations with this book's topic, the effects of this, and its similarity to other preoccupations and their effects. Asked to state more precisely what this was, I would have to say something like: "My preoccupation with the topic of my book has made the world seem especially alive with examples of it, references to it, so that it can't help but seem to me that the world is more populated with things relevant to it than previously. And it struck me that this is similar to the way in which new parenthood made the world seem to me burgeoning with babies, parents, the paraphernalia of infancy, and talk and pictures of these." Somehow this thought of my philosophical preoccupations and parenthood, and an analogy between their effects, rather complex to articulate, occurred in a couple of moments while I approached the cashier, in the absence of any utterance.[4]

I think you will, if you try, be able to recognize examples from your own daily life, similar to these I have mentioned, of unverbalized noniconic thought. These are sometimes fairly primitive or simple, and sometimes re-markably complicated, so that to *say* what one was thinking would require a lengthy syntactically complex utterance—but in either event thought oc-curs, wordlessly, without imagery, condensed, and evanescent.[5] If you agree that you have such unverbalized noniconic thoughts, and the way it seems to you to have them differs from the way it seems to have imagery and sensory experience, then you will agree that noniconic thinking has a phenomenal character distinct from that proper to iconic thinking and perception.

But to put it this way might suggest for a moment that there is something unvarying or uniform called "the phenomenal character of noniconic thought." We can imagine someone proposing that having experience with this phenomenal character is merely a contingent, unvarying accompani-ment of our thinking about things without imagining them. Perhaps one would want to say that where one speaks or hears comprehendingly, one has some "feeling" or "sensation" of meaning or understanding, and where one thinks without words or imagery, one has a "feeling" or "sensation" of thinking noniconically. I think we can see that would not be an acceptable way to describe matters. It is not the case that there is some single unvarying way it seems to hear or speak with comprehension, or to think noniconi-cally. It will not do to say that the way it seems to have noniconic thoughts is just the same, no matter what these thoughts are about—as if, absurdly, whenever we understand what we say or hear, or whenever we think of something unimaged, this were accompanied by some humming or buzzing sensation, absent when we spoke or heard "emptily," or when our minds lay idle.

One way to make this clear to ourselves: on some occasions someone utters a sentence, and you momentarily understand it one way—you take its meaning one way—and then are struck by the realization that the speaker meant something else altogether. So, we might imagine, someone says to you, "Don't be mad," and you think she is asking you not to be *angry*, but then in a moment you realize she meant: don't be *crazy*. We might suppose such a momentary misunderstanding could arise if you are a speaker of American English and she a speaker of British English. But we needn't sup-pose that you uttered to yourself, silently or aloud, the words "angry" or "crazy"—perhaps what happened was simply that, without uttering a word, you first understood her utterance one way, and then a different way. The thought that occurs to you when you switch interpretations might be such as you could express by saying—"Oh, you mean 'mad' in *that* way." Or simi-larly, on sitting down to dinner, your host might say, "I hope the food's not too hot for you," and first you think he means: hot in temperature—but then, in the next instant, you realize he means: "spicy hot." Again, no words need have "passed through your mind" on such an occasion.

I have chosen simple examples, and so it may seem to you that the hearer in my story is a little dense, but I doubt any of us are totally unfamiliar with the kind of experience of which I speak, where one momentarily takes a speaker's utterance one way, and then switches to a different way of understanding it. When one has an experience of this sort, the phenomenal character of one's experience undergoes a sudden change—it is not uniform throughout. We might illustrate this point also by reference to slightly longer utterances. Consider, for example:

> Before she had a chance to pass the bar, she decided to change directions, but she was not so pleasantly surprised with where she wound up.

This might be taken as a story about an aborted legal career, or as a story about someone getting lost near a drinking establishment. One can read it either way, and I would say, as one reads it comprehendingly, concentrating on the meaning and not just senselessly reciting it, one can note a difference in the way it seems to understand it, depending on which way one takes the story. And this is so even if one does not picture anything differently, or picture anything at all, as one interprets it differently. Again, the way it seems to think as one reads comprehendingly is not some phenomenally monotonous experience, but differs with the way one understands what one is reading.

If you have difficulty granting this point, you might ask yourself this. Given that you can read the story one way, and then read it the other, if we are to say its seeming to you as it does to understand the passage as you read it is just the *same* in either case, what are we to say *constitutes the difference* between your reading it one way or the other? It will not do to propose that what makes it the case that you are reading it in the "lawyer" rather than the "drinking establishment" way is that you are then able to elaborate on the story, or answer questions about it only in the way appropriate to the lawyer interpretation, but not in the way appropriate to the other. You are quite able to do this in ways appropriate to *either* interpretation. Shall we say that, when you are reading it the lawyer way, you are *inclined* to continue the story in certain ways rather than others, or would be *surprised* to have it continued in certain ways (e.g., "So she went back to the bar and ordered a drink")? But when you read it the lawyer way, you may not be *likely* to continue the story in any way at all, unless *asked* to do so. And then, once aware of the ambiguity, you may very well simply be inclined to say— "Which way do you want it to go—law-bar story or drinking-bar story?" Also, you may not be *surprised* when someone offers to finish the story in either way—regardless of which way you just read it. But still there is a difference between your reading the story one way and your reading it the other way. My point here is not that we need to "postulate" some difference in the character of the experience in order to account for a difference in the way the reader understands the passage. Rather, I am suggesting that once you realize that there is nothing you can plausibly substitute for the difference in the phenomenal character of understanding in such a case, so as to characterize *that* as the difference between reading the passage one way and reading it another, you will be better able to recognize this phenomenal or experiential difference involved in understanding, and not ignore it, or confuse it with something else.

It may help clarify matters here to block this misunderstanding. Suppose someone said:

> Yes, I know what you're talking about here, this is the sort of experience I want to describe by saying, "Something clicked." But then, that's not a difference between the way it seemed to have two thoughts—it's rather that two thoughts were separated (punctuated, you might say) by an experience of a special phenomenal character: the experience of a "click."

This would clearly be a misunderstanding of the "click" metaphor. Surely we usually do not actually hear or auralize a clicking sound on such occasions where we have what we might call "the experience of interpretive switch." Rather, it is appropriate to say "Something clicked," because (to elaborate on the figure slightly), something "falls into place"—namely, what someone means—with a remarkable suddenness, such as occurs when two pieces suddenly fit together with a "click." The phenomenal contrast between the two thoughts when there is such an interpretive switch does not consist in the fact that one happens before, and one after, a *third* experience—something like hearing a click. For there is nothing like *that* which happens on such occasions. The contrast, rather, is between the way it seems to have different noniconic thoughts, different ways of understanding what the speaker has said to you. The experience of an interpretive switch in thought is not phenomenally somehow akin to hearing a low hum, then a brief high-pitched beep, then a return to the hum. Rather, it is more like the kind of change that occurs when one goes from seeing the lines on the paper merely as a bisected diamond, to seeing them as forming a picture of a pyramid, or from seeing a curved line plus a dot as a picture of a duck, to seeing it as a picture of a rabbit—a "Gestalt switch."

We might make this a bit clearer still by considering again the sorts of examples I used to illustrate the notion of unverbalized noniconic thought. The way it seemed to me to think suddenly that I had locked myself out differed from the way it seemed to me a moment hence to think that my key was in my coat pocket. It was not as though the way it seemed to me to think what I thought during this time was totally *unvarying*. When I was riding my bike and it occurred to me that the light ahead was going to change, and I wondered whether to speed up, the way it seemed to think this differed from the way it seemed, a moment later, wordlessly to think to look inside the parked car up ahead, in case someone in it was about to fling a door open in my path. And the way it seemed to me to think my compressed thought about my writing, parenthood, and the parallel between them, as I approached the cash register at the restaurant, differed from the way it seemed to me to wonder, a moment later as I stood with my bill in hand, where the cashier was—though this thought was equally unverbalized (I did not say aloud or to myself—"Where is that cashier?"). In cases such as these stories illustrate, there is a change in the phenomenal character of experience, which is neither some change in the way it seems to visualize or image something, nor some phenomenal change in one's perceptual experience.

Thus, whether we consider the kind of "interpretive switch" I spoke of a moment ago, or these examples of changes in what one is wordlessly thinking, we see that there are variations in the phenomenal character of thought, distinct from differences in the phenomenal character of imagery and sense-experience. So, in thinking noniconically, we have phenomenal features over and above those we have just in consciously imaging and perceiving.

Now, it would be phenomenologically obtuse to say such phenomenal variation is *confined* to the kinds of cases I have used as examples—to cases where one switches one's understanding of what one hears or reads someone else say, or where there occurs an episode of changing wordless thought—as if *elsewhere* the phenomenal character of noniconic thinking were entirely uniform. To see that this would be a mistake, it may help to notice these two reasons for rejecting an attempt to confine these differences in character of experience to the kinds of situations I have used to illustrate it.

First, we cannot reasonably say that the experience of interpretive switch occurs only in cases where the subject is the hearer or reader, not the speaker. You can assert a sentence interpretable in a way other than that in which you understood it when you said it, (e.g., "He caught a fly"; "I cleaned my glasses"), and it can occur to you just afterwards that it can be taken in this other way—so that the way it seems to you to understand the phrase then differs. Second, it would be absurd to hold that the experience of understanding any given phrase is uniform, *unless one happens to switch one's understanding of the phrase*. Suppose when you read the "bar" story above for the first time, you took it to be about a near-miss at lawyerdom, but then I give you the punchline—"So she went back to the bar and ordered a drink"—and you have an experience of interpretive switch, and suddenly understand the phrases you have just read in a different way. Now, if the experience of understanding is uniform unless an interpretive switch occurs, it seems we will have to say this. *Until* at t_3 you switched your interpretation of the phrases you had just read at t_2, the way it seemed to you to understand those was just the same as the way it seemed to understand some preceding phrases you read at t_1, such as, "We might illustrate this sort of point also by reference to slightly longer utterances." But then, suppose you had experienced the interpretive switch in reverse order—first taking the story in the "lost near a drinking establishment way," and then (after a different punchline, say—"She had a job as a clerk at a convenience store"), you switch interpretation in the opposite (lawyerly) direction. If we assume the way it seems to understand is uniform until an interpretive switch occurs, we will have to say that when interpretation proceeds according to the first order (law-bar, then drinking-bar), the way it seems to understand the story as lawyerly was just the same as the way it seemed to understand what was read at t_1. But we will have to say the phenomenal character of those experiences would be different, were the order of interpretation reversed (drinking-bar then law-bar). *Then*, we would have to say that the way it seems to understand the story in the drinking-bar manner is just the same as the way it seemed to understand the earlier phrase, "We might illustrate this sort of point also by reference to slightly longer utterances."

However, this is absurd. It is absurd to hold that the phenomenal character of an experience of understanding a passage in a certain way is just like that of almost any other experience of understanding when it *is* first in a sequence of switches, but differs from that of almost all others when it *is not* first in sequence. If the phenomenal character of the experience depended entirely on the order of its occurrence in this way, there would be no difference between the phenomenal character of your experience when you understood the passage first as law story, then as drinking story, and the phenomenal character of the experience you would have if you understood it first as drinking story, then as law story. For either way, whatever experience came first in the switch would be phenomenally like those preceding, and whatever came next would be different from them. But there *is* a difference in how it seems to switch interpretations in one order rather than another. There is a difference between (a) the way it seems to me to understand "He caught a fly" first as about baseball, and second as about an insect; and (b) the way it seems to me to understand this phrase as first about an insect, and then about baseball. The order of an experience of interpretive switch is not indifferent to its phenomenal character.

Having come through these reflections, we are in a position (if we were not already) to acknowledge that generally, as we think—whether we are speaking in complete sentences, or fragments, or speaking barely or not at all, silently or aloud—*the phenomenal character of our noniconic thought is in continual modulation, which cannot be identified simply with changes in the phenomenal character of either vision or visualization, hearing or auralization, etc.* If this is unobvious to us when we turn our attention to verbalized thought, I suggest that is because its phenomenal character is so enmeshed with changes in the phenomenal character of our imagery or perception. For when we speak our thoughts, we either auralize or hear the words with which we express them, and so the changes in the phenomenal character of our noniconic thinking do not occur independent of changes in the phenomenal character of our verbal perception or imagery.

Please notice that my claim here is *not* that verbalized conscious thought is two things stuck together: on the one hand, the experience one has when a thought occurs to one without words or imagery, and on the other, the experience one has when one perceives or auralizes the utterance of a certain sentence, a sentence by which one means something. Noniconic thought is often conscious, silent or audible, verbalized or wordless, but that does *not* mean that when I audibly say what I think, there occurs to me, as I consciously perceive my own speech, "alongside" of this, some conscious "nonverbal thought" expressed by what I say. At least, it would be a mistake to describe the way it seems to think a verbalized thought that p as follows: it seems to me just as it does (a) to think wordlessly that p, while also (b) making some utterance, by which I mean that p. For the (a) and the (b) parts of this seem to contradict one another. If it seems to me as it does to think *wordlessly*, it does *not* seem to me as it does to hear or auralize an utterance. However, one might want to say: "But, as you pointed out, it might seem to one as it does to make some utterance, by which one means that p, even when it does *not* seem to one as it does to *understand what one is saying as one says it*. And what we *add* to the first to get the second is some kind of experience at least similar in its phenomenal character to thinking wordlessly what one understands by this utterance." But this, too, is at least misleading. It is not as though, when I speak comprehendingly, I can distinguish two different aspects of the phenomenal character of my experience: one that is similar to the way it seems to think wordlessly, and one that is like that of hearing or auralizing, uncomprehendingly, utterances of a kind one understands—so that the phenomenal character of the experience is accurately represented as the mere co-occurrence of these two aspects. Without breaking the experience into such components, I would simply say that it seems to me as it does to understand what I am saying as I say it (and *not* as it does to recite a speech or read a text I understand, but whose meaning I do not follow as I speak). Further, the way it seems to me to understand what I am saying as I am saying it changes with what I understand myself to be saying, and these changes are not merely changes in how it seems to me to hear or auralize the words I'm saying, and they are not changes in the phenomenal character of imagery I'm having of what I'm speaking about. Finally, if it seems to me this way, if I have experience with this phenomenal character, then I consciously *think* what I understand by what I am saying. *That* is how I would ask you to interpret my claim that noniconic, verbally expressed thought is phenomenally conscious.

8.4 The Relation of Phenomenal and Intentional Differences in Thought

Where the phenomenal character of thought varies, it often varies with the intentional features peculiar to noniconic thinking. For we have supposed you might think that you've locked yourself out, and then think that your key is in your coat pocket, and we have said that the way it seemed to you to think these thoughts might differ. And to think these noniconic thoughts is to have intentional features. For if you think that you've locked yourself out, and you have locked yourself out, then what you think is true. Thus, in the sense explained in 6.2, you are assessable for truth in respect of this feature: thinking that you have locked yourself out—so it is an intentional feature. And the same could be said of your thinking that your key is in your coat pocket. Similar remarks would show that the other examples we have been discussing also involve a variation in both phenomenal and intentional features distinctive of one's noniconic thinking. If these examples illustrate what is quite common in actual experience, and if we are to say that this kind of variation also characterizes our verbalized noniconic thought, then we will conclude that the phenomenal character special to noniconic thought varies with its intentional features quite ubiquitously.

But you might accept this, and still say that the relation between the phenomenal character of thought and its intentionality is *merely contingent.* You might say one could have experience with the very same phenomenal character as that distinctive of noniconic thought, even though one did not (noniconically) think anything at all. So the suggestion would be that it might seem to one *just* the way it does to me to *say,* "Bob is driving home from work now," and to *think* that Bob is driving home from work now, even when one did not have this thought, *or any thought at all.* The claim would be: it might seem to one precisely as it does to you to speak or hear an utterance and mean or understand something by it as you hear it, even though one understood nothing by it whatsoever.

I believe this would be deeply mistaken. The link between the noniconic phenomenal features involved in thinking and thought's intentionality is not rightly regarded as merely contingent, and such phenomenal features are themselves intentional features. Before I defend my way of looking at the matter, let me first set it out in a little more detail.

My claim is this: the sorts of phenomenal features we can identify by thinking about how it seems for us to think noniconically—what we might label "*noetic* phenomenal features"—are intentional features. More specifically, I want to say the following. If during some period of time t, it seems to x as it seems to me on some occasion to think noniconically that p, then there is some q, such that it is either true, or at least accurate, to say that, during t, x thinks that q. That is to say: there is some q such that x consciously thinks that q. In other words, any such phenomenal counterpart of mine is a noniconic thinker. Furthermore, both for me and for any such phenomenal counterpart of mine, there will be some condition (not necessarily the same condition) such that, when it obtains, and one has the noetic phenomenal feature we share, it follows that what one thinks is true. And this condition is not such as we can reasonably regard as giving an interpretation to the phenomenal feature, or to its possession—it does not make it a feature with respect to which its possessor is assessable for truth, where otherwise it would not be. Therefore, these noetic phenomenal features I can identify in my own case are features in virtue of which one is assessable for truth—intentional features. And, I would maintain, you may say the same of phenomenal features you can identify by thinking about how it seems for you to think noniconically.

That, in outline, is the way I propose we look at the relationship between the way it seems for us to think and what we think. It is less simple than some possible views of the matter, and I suppose the reader is likely to wonder why I do not make the relationship between noetic phenomenality and the intentionality of thought a more straightforward affair. Why do I say that what follows from its seeming to x a certain way is that it is either true, *or at least accurate*, to say of some q, x thinks that q? Why don't I simply say it follows that this is true? And why do I say what follows is that *for some q*, x thinks that q? Why don't I just say: if it seems to x as it does to me to think that p, then x thinks that p?

But before answering these questions, I want first to set the stage by clearing out of the way another kind of worry—again raised by the now-familiar specter of phenomenal atomism. Someone might maintain that the phenomenal character of any episode of thought could (1) occur in complete isolation from all others (there could be an entity with radically monotonous phenomenal thought-experience), and (2) be combined or inserted into any phenomenal history whatever without change. But this, one might say, is incompatible with the essential holism of thought. What thought one thinks—and whether one has a thought at all—essentially depends in some way on what *other* thoughts one does or can think. There could not be an entity who never had, nor was ever able to have, any thought but the thought that it is going to rain. (Surely there are some thoughts that cannot be had in complete isolation. For instance, there could not be a thinker capable of having no thought but this: the thought that intentional holism is true!) Also, you cannot just rearrange thought histories and capacities however you like. It could not be that someone limited to the other sorts of thoughts and thought-propensities of a medieval peasant, one day just had the thought that the moon's gravitational force is responsible for the rising of the tide. Given only what else he thinks and is disposed to think, that thought just couldn't be available to him, we want to say. Perhaps we will also want to say that certain thoughts will be available only to a subject in whom they are in some appropriate way related to sensory perception. So, in sum, the objection is: the phenomenal character of thought is essentially *atomistic*, while thought itself is essentially *holistic*. Therefore it cannot be that someone to whom it seems as it does to me to think noniconically must also be a genuine noniconic thinker.

Perhaps something like this objection will be motivated partly by familiarity with Wittgenstein's famous attack—alluded to earlier—on the notion that understanding is a special sort of "inner process." For I take it that part of what Wittgenstein criticizes is the notion that there is a certain sort of experience you have, essentially isolable from everything else about you, that insures you understand what you say in a certain way, and somehow accounts for your doing so.

Now I do maintain that having experience with the phenomenal character ours has is sufficient for one to have understanding. However, I do not believe this entails that understanding is an "inner process"—but maybe that depends on how one interprets this phrase. In any case, what I have said does not, I think, commit me to the view that processes occurring *literally inside one's body or brain*—for example, patterns of neuron firings—of such type as could occur in a variety of radically different "external" circumstances, are logically sufficient for one to know what one means by one's utterances. Am I then perhaps saying that understanding is an *inner* process in some other, figurative way? I will leave that question for someone who has a better handle than I do on what that kind of "innerness" involves. However, I am not claiming that understanding is a *process*, inner or otherwise, if this implies that understanding always involves something like implementing a procedure that constitutes or results in understanding. But finally, as for the idea that understanding consists in having some essentially isolable experience, I would say: the view I am proposing simply needn't assume this sort of atomism regarding the phenomenal character of thought. What's more, such atomism seems to me quite wrong.

I think the phenomenal character of the "stream" of thought *cannot* be cut up into neat little packets, which, when separated and rearranged randomly, maintain their identity. (Perhaps this is part of what makes the "stream" metaphor seem right.) The phenomenal character of thought is no less holistic than belief or meaning generally. This claim is entirely consistent with my proposed way of seeing the phenomenal features involved in non-iconic thought as intentional features. We have no better reason to hold that the way it seems to lead our thinking lives can be chopped up, isolated, and rearranged in any old fashion, than we have to hold that the thoughts we think can be completely fragmented and isolated. The notion that the way it has seemed to you to think as you have been reading this paragraph could have clipped out of it some temporal slice, its phenomenal character then preserved in isolation as the sole experience of some possible conscious being (as if God could edit streams of consciousness like audiotape), is a notion that deserves to be taken no more seriously than the idea that a single belief could be plucked from you, and made the sole possession of some hypothetical, maximally monotonous mind. The atomist temptation here—the temptation to suppose a period of conscious thinking is like a spliceable tape—can be traced to a double error: one supposes the phenomenal character of imagery consists in *copies* of shapes and sounds perceived, while also ignoring the distinctive phenomenal character of *nonimagistic* thought. And then the stream of verbalized conscious thought becomes like nothing so much as a sequence of recorded sounds that might be broken up and rearranged in whatever manner. But once these errors are recognized, and this confusion undone, the spell of phenomenal atomism is broken.

Should such an atomistic view of thought's phenomenal character still hold some appeal for you, note that there is another way around the problem it presents for my proposal. We can leave undecided the issue of how the phenomenal character of thought can be fragmented, and just focus from the start on the character of thought-experience that is *not* phenomenally fragmented in such a way as might disqualify it from being the experience of a genuine thinker of noniconic thoughts. So suppose x is my *total phenomenal twin*—x has, has had, and is disposed to have, experience with phenomenal character indistinguishable from my own. Then the claim will be that when it seems to such an x the way it seems to me to think that p on some occasion, there is some q, such that x thinks that q. Presumably the phenomenal character of x's experience will not be so fragmented or isolated as to preclude x's being a thinker of noniconic thoughts. Since the atomist worry does not arise for my phenomenal twin, we sidestep the atomist concern.

The move here is similar to that I made at similar junctures in considering atomist objections to the phenomenal intentionality of vision and visualization. The point is that phenomenal atomism plus intentional holism represents no insurmountable objection to my proposal, for not only is it reasonable to believe that phenomenal atomism is false, but also I have available a reformulation of my thesis that can be true, whether or not phenomenal atomism is. If this reformulated thesis is false, and my phenomenal twin may still have no thoughts, it is not because the "pieces" of his experience are so isolated or inappropriately arranged that he cannot be a thinker.

Now, for the sake of convenience, in what follows I will often discuss my thesis as originally formulated, and generally not make explicit the line of defense just suggested, in response to atomist-style objections, wherever it is plausible to think these might be made. But suppose you think the phenomenal character of one's experience could be broken apart without changing the character of the pieces, in ways that would inevitably remove noniconic thought, or otherwise falsify my claim about the relation between thought's phenomenality and intentionality. So you think the reformulation of my thesis I have just suggested is needed. Then by all means, in what follows you may reformulate my thesis into one that explicitly concerns only *total* phenomenal twins, and take that to be the crucial claim at issue.

But now let's go back to an earlier question. Why do I say no more than that the phenomenal character of thought determines that there is *some* noniconic thought it would be accurate to attribute to one? Why not simply say, if it seems to x as it does to me to think that p, then x thinks that p?

Part of an answer to these questions will be found in considering again cases of unverbalized noniconic conscious thought. Suppose that, driving to work, twenty minutes down the road, it suddenly occurs to me (wordlessly) that I left my briefcase at home. I feel annoyed, wonder whether I should turn around to retrieve it, or whether I can get along without it, and so on. At least, an episode of noniconic conscious thought occurred, and this is how I am first inclined to report it. But was that really the precisely correct report of what I thought? Perhaps it would have been more accurate to say the thought that occurred to me was: that my briefcase was at home (not that I *left* it at home). Am I sure that my *leaving* it there, as opposed to its simply *being* there, was part of my thought? And I said that I left the briefcase at *home*. Couldn't this be distinguished from thinking that I left it *at my house*? Perhaps this was the thought I really had then? Also, I said rather vaguely that "it *occurred* to me that . . .," but I might have also said, "I *thought* that

. . .," and this way of reporting it, while also rather vague, suggests the question of just what sort of commitment to what I thought was involved in this thought's just occurring to me. It is not that I just *entertained the possibility* that my briefcase was back at home—but was the commitment as strong as would be implied by *asserting* outright that I left my briefcase at home? Just how strong was the commitment?

I want to suggest that no definite answer to such questions lies somehow in the phenomenal character of the episode of thought to which they refer. Nor, for that matter, does it lie anywhere else, I think. There is an indeterminate (though perhaps not very large) number of possible alternative and equally accurate answers to the question: just what noniconic thoughts, what intentional features of this sort, did I have when I had thought-experience with the phenomenal character mine had? The various answers suggested by the questions I just raised together indicate the kind of thought, the kind of intentionality I had on a certain occasion. Figuratively speaking, they indicate the "space" of intentional features in which to locate what I was thinking at that time. But it would not be right to insist that one of these alternatives provides the uniquely right answer to the question, "What was I thinking then?"—unless the phenomenal character of such thought-experience possessed greater definiteness than we have warrant for saying it does.

I am certainly not suggesting that just anything goes. If I cannot select one of various alternative accounts of what I was thinking then, constrained by the way it seemed to me to think, still, there are many more possible accounts I can with warrant reject. It did not suddenly occur to me that I left my jacket at home, still less was I just then thinking about the danger of global warming. And if I have trouble somehow pinpointing the nature of my commitment to what I say "occurred to me," or what I "thought"— taking refuge in the vagueness of these expressions—still, my commitment was *greater* at that time than it would be to a mere supposition or hypothesis, and *less* than it was a few moments later when I said, "Yes, dammit, I *did* leave it." So, even if, as far as the phenomenal character of my experience can determine, there is an indeterminate number of equally right answers to the question of what I was thinking at that time, still, the differences among these are relatively subtle, they are relatively few, and there is a *vast* number of clearly *wrong* answers.

This then is why I say that if it seems to x as it does to me to think that p, then there is *some* q, such that it is accurate to say of x, x thinks that q. For at least where unverbalized, or only partially verbalized, thought is concerned, the way it seems for me to think does not determine that "I thought that p" provides the uniquely correct answer to the question, "What were you thinking?"—nor does it determine a precise way of characterizing the kind of thinking (e.g., mere supposal, or confident affirmation) going on. And so x's sharing this phenomenal character with me will not determine that this is the uniquely correct answer to the question, "What was x thinking?" either. But I maintain, there will be some accurate answers to give in either case that attribute to us some thought, and it would be false to say of either of us: he thought nothing whatsoever.

The situation is not quite the same when we shift our attention from the case of completely unverbalized occurrences of thought to occasions on which thought is quite verbally articulate—when it is expressed in complete sentences. Suppose I do not just wordlessly think, but come right out and say, "I left my briefcase at home," consciously thinking what I understand myself to say. This would appear to remove some of the indefiniteness that I pointed out in the other, unverbalized, case. Fully verbally articulate thoughts are, it seems, not as inchoate and shadowy in their intentionality as are those verbalized only in grammatical fragments, or not at all. Here, it would appear, it is true (and not merely accurate) to say that I thought I left my briefcase at home. Since this is what I *said*, and what I understood myself to have said, such a report of my thought definitely wins out over alternatives like: "I thought my briefcase was still at home," or "I thought I left my briefcase at my house." So why do I not propose something like: "If it seems to x as it does to me to hear myself utter or auralize 'p' and as I do this, understand by this that p, then x thinks that p"?

We may want to raise a worry for this by wondering, roughly, whether there is any way to verbalize *exactly* what one was thinking during a given time—nothing more, and nothing less. We might feel uneasy about the idea of a fully verbalized, or fully articulate, thought. For consider this. If some annoying person—a philosopher, probably—were to question me about what I meant by saying that I left my briefcase at home, I would assent to various claims. For example: that I moved away from the briefcase, while it remained stationary (and not the other way around); that the thing I left at home is a container in which I carry books and papers; that the place at which I left it is the place where I live, where I habitually sleep and eat, and that I share with my family. Now, it appears we can continue on indefinitely asking questions of the sort that elicit such responses. I said I moved away from the briefcase, which was stationary—but stationary relative to what? And is a briefcase just any container in which one might carry books and papers, or a special kind? What kind? And what sort of paper is a briefcase for carrying? Any kind? I might be able to provide answers to some of these questions, but undoubtedly I will just give up at some point. And I am likely, somewhere along this route, to want to point at examples for answers: "Look, a briefcase is something like *this*, not something like *that*." But in any event, the issue I want to pose is this. Is there some definite point in this process of question-and-answer where I can with warrant say: "Now I am no longer telling you what I *already understood myself to have said* back when I originally said that I left my briefcase at home, now I'm *adding something new*." There doesn't seem to me to be such a point. I do not see how we would warrant the claim that at a certain point I have passed the limit after which I am no longer telling you what I already meant prior to a certain time, but am adding something to what I then meant. And thus I do not see with what right I would claim that there *is* some such limit in any given case—any more than that there is some definite number of hairs you might pluck from my head that would make me bald. There is, I think, *this* kind of indeterminacy to meaning (if not some of the other kinds alleged).

If that is right, we may wonder if there is ever any precise, definite answer to the question, "What were you thinking?"—even in cases where you say what you thought in a complete sentence, meaning what you say. For if there is no way to draw a line between what I already meant, and what I later meant in addition, when questioned about what I meant, we can at least stipulatively draw a line in one place rather than another, and distinguish meaning (and thinking) only what lies on one side of this line from meaning (and thinking) also what lies on the other. But then there is no fact of the matter as to *which* of the thoughts so defined *I* had. And if we say this, then we will say that neither the phenomenal character of my past and present experience, nor that of the experience I am disposed or have been disposed to have, will determine with complete definiteness which of two distinguishable thoughts I had. Maybe this will seem to introduce the need to say that reports of thought are no more than accurate, even where we say what we think by making assertions in complete sentences.

I do not think this would be right. For I do not think the truth of the report that I thought I left my briefcase at home *requires* that what I meant when I said, "I left my briefcase at home," can be determined with the kind of precision I just suggested is lacking here. So I do not think that worries of this sort give us reason to say that the possession of noetic phenomenal features, and dispositions to these, do not determine that something of the form "x thinks that p" is true of someone. In a given case, I can distinguish meanings, and hence thoughts, with a greater degree of fineness than I can truthfully say has been determined by the way it has seemed to me to have the experience I had, and by the way it would seem to me to have the experience I was disposed to have. But it does not follow that it is not true, but at most merely accurate to say, for instance, that I thought I left my briefcase at home. For the intentional feature attributed to me in such a statement is not itself so finely differentiated from others as would give one a right to this complaint: that the facts about my experience fail to resolve the differences between these features sufficiently to make this statement true.

But if this is my view, then it is still not clear why I do not claim: if it seems to x as it does to me to think that p, then it is either true or accurate to say that x thinks *that p*. What I have said so far does nothing to justify my reticence to say this, and to limit myself to saying merely that if it seems this way to x, then there is some thought that q—perhaps distinct from the thought that p—such that it is true or accurate to say x thinks that q.

To see why I think it is worth qualifying my thesis in this way, consider this reason why someone may doubt the phenomenal character of thought determines what one thinks, a reason having to do with the way in which what one thinks—the content of thought—is identified or individuated in ordinary attributions of attitudes. Suppose there is a pad of paper on my desk, and I think that *this* paper is yellow. My phenomenal twin, meanwhile, also has a thought he would report by saying, "I think this paper is yellow." But what "this" refers to, in the two different reports, is in each case different. (Suppose we live on different planets.) So if *what* we think is identified partly by means of indexical expressions like "this," which refer to different items in our respective environments, then one might reason: what we think—the content of our thoughts—is different. And which thought I have cannot be determined by the phenomenal character of my experience, for, *ex hypothesi*, this does not differ between my case and the case of my twin, who nevertheless has a different thought. Thus where p = this paper is yellow, it can seem to my twin just the way it seems to me to think that p, though it is not the case that he thinks that p.

There are other ways—besides the one I have illustrated with my indexically expressed thought about some paper—in which one might argue that differences in what is thought are *extraphenomenally* fixed. So—as I will discuss a bit more in a moment—there are those who would say that the nature of the kinds of things found in a thinker's surroundings (for example, water, gold, lemons), as this nature is determined by scientific theories about that kind, fixes the content of the thinker's thought in a way that may vary independent of the phenomenal character of experience. And there is also the view that facts about one's social environment—in particular, facts about what linguistic community one belongs to—determine differences in what two persons think, quite independent of the phenomenal character of their experience. For, so the story goes, though they be phenomenal twins, if they belong to different language groups, what they think will differ.

Now, we may object that these "externalist" stories about content do not really give us the proper way to individuate thoughts. (One might worry, for instance, that *thoughts* are not items such as may have pieces of paper stuck in them.) But I do not want to get lost in a debate about just what considerations generally should govern some theory about the individuation of thought-contents, and how such an account relates to our recognition, in ordinary discourse, of differences in what people believe, when we talk about whether two people share the same belief or hold different beliefs, and how this relates also to whether what they believe is true or false, as well as to what they mean by their words, and to what their words mean. I confess I find the notion of content, and the matter of just what accounts of content are supposed to tell us, fairly unclear. But I believe that we can find a way of recognizing the intentionality inherent in the phenomenal character of thought without attempting to sort these matters out entirely.

That is not to say I will be able to set aside entirely consideration of the points that have been made in support of externalist views of content. Rather, it is just that I want to state my thesis regarding the connection between the way it seems for us to think and what we think in a manner that can allow us to count thoughts or "contents" in such a way that these may vary independent of the phenomenal character of thinkers' experience. So my point will be that even if my phenomenal counterpart and I will be said to have different thoughts on account of our differing natural or social environments, still, the phenomenal character of our experience is enough to make us both genuine noniconic thinkers, and the conditions whose fulfillment would be enough to make it the case that what we think is true do not include any that are rightly regarded as furnishing our phenomenal features with an interpretation. And that is sufficient to make our shared phenomenal features intentional features.

8.5 THOUGHT'S SEEMING: INSEPARABLE FROM THOUGHT

On my proposal, if one has experience of a certain phenomenal character, and certain other conditions obtain, then it follows that one thinks something truly or falsely. These conditions need not include any that bestow intentionality upon it. No conditions need to be added to the possession of noetic phenomenal features I can identify with reference to my noniconic thinking, to make them features with respect to which their possessors are assessable for truth.

But suppose someone wishes to maintain the contrary. How should I defend *my* view? I will proceed here much as before. If I can find no reason to think that the phenomenal character proper to noniconic thought is not already intentional, but needs somehow to get intentionality from "elsewhere," through its relation to something that might be missing from it, then I will conclude that no such additional interpreting conditions are required. Just as the phenomenal character of sensory experience needs no interpretation for it to be accurate or inaccurate, so the phenomenal character of thought needs no interpretation to belong to an experience of thinking something truly or falsely.

The issue, as I see it, may be posed as follows. (1) Might it happen that, though some x has experience with the same phenomenal character as that belonging some time to your noniconic thinking, x then *has no thought at all*? (2) Is it the case that, even if x is your noetic phenomenal counterpart, a correlative assessment of x for truth will not follow, unless conditions obtain, reasonably regarded as supplying this phenomenal feature you and x share with an *interpretation*? If we find that, as near as we can settle such questions, we should return a negative answer to both (1) and (2), then we should conclude that those like us in noetic phenomenal features would also be noniconic thinkers, and that noetic phenomenal features are features in virtue of which one is assessable for truth—thus, intentional features.

So, let's first have a look at (1). I think we need to start by recognizing that initially, the possibility envisaged in (1) does not, once we are clear about what is involved in it, seem conceivable. What I mean is this. If I am asked simply to consider how it seems to me to think the thoughts I actually think on some occasion, and then suppose that there is someone else to whom it seems the very same way, but who then just *thinks nothing whatsoever*—well, I find I simply do not know how to comply with this request as things stand. Someone might say to me, "Consider the way it seems for you to think, lying awake in bed at night, about what you're going to need to do tomorrow at work (or if you prefer—*what it's like* for you to think about these things). Now suppose it seems the same way to another person, but when it seems to him as it seems to you, really, he just has no thoughts at all." The problem is, if I try to suppose this, nothing happens that I can recognize as success. Nothing happens that I can recognize as successfully conceiving of its seeming to my phenomenal counterpart just as it does to me to think noniconically and understand what I'm saying as I'm saying it, though all the while *he* thinks *nothing*, and understands nothing at all. To put this another way: I do not know how to distinguish its *seeming* to me as it does for me to think noniconically from *really thinking* something, so as to conceive of a situation in which only the former, but not the latter, occurs.

My only hope of doing so, it would appear, is to try to discover some conditions essential to genuine thought, that I recognize could clearly be missing in the case of my phenomenal counterpart. In other words, since the dissociation of phenomenality and intentionality needed for a "yes" answer to (1) does not initially seem conceivable, if I am to give such an answer to (1), I need to identify some condition C of which I believe that (a) it is possible that C not obtain, though x has phenomenal experience with the character of my noniconic thought during some time, and (b) it is necessary that x thinks noniconically at that time, only if C obtains. Without finding some such condition, I do not see how to conceive of my phenomenal counterpart's being literally thoughtless.

You may think it is easier than I do to conceive of such a situation, but only because you misconstrue what you are being asked to conceive. Remember, it is not enough here to think of someone's having imagery experience that is phenomenally like some of your own, but without thinking any noniconic thoughts. For we are concerned here with the kinds of variation in phenomenal character proper not to imagistic, but to noniconic thinking—judgment. So it is beside the point to say that you can conceive of someone's saying to herself the same words you do, but not understanding or thinking anything by them.

Also, we need to take care not to misdescribe certain phenomena as cases of its seeming to one as it does to think, but without thinking—when really they are not. So, for instance, we are required here not just to think of cases in which one speaks with only a "flawed" or "partial" understanding of what one is saying. Bob, having recently read something about this, might say ("as if he knows what he's talking about") that hemophilia is due to a problem with the X chromosome, and that this is why it shows up more in males than females. But when he is questioned about what X chromosomes are, and why something to do with them should be more likely to affect males, he falls into confusion, and flounders around, making a lot of false and muddled claims. Confronted with his ignorance, he is embarrassed, but also taken aback—if he is frank, he will want to say, "I thought I understood this, but now I see that I didn't know what I was talking about." We may perhaps be tempted to think of this as a case in which it seemed to Bob the way it does to us to have a noniconic thought, though he actually had no such thought at all. But to describe such situations in this way would be to overshoot the mark by quite a bit. In this kind of situation, it would not be right to say that Bob didn't really think anything at all, when he was confidently babbling away about X chromosomes, but just had, at most, some "feeling" of a sort that we (supposedly) have when they think certain thoughts. For (in all fairness to Bob) we should want to say that he did have *some* understanding of what he was saying. For instance, we find that he believes that chromosomes are tiny, are found in living things, and are somehow responsible for inherited characteristics.

But what if we found that he did not have even these beliefs, or in fact *any* further beliefs whatsoever that he might express with the terms 'chromosome,' 'hemophilia,' 'male,' and 'female,' beyond what he just putatively expressed by saying the words, "Hemophilia is due . . . etc."? Then, that would, I think, indeed be a case in which Bob did not understand anything by his utterance, and literally made it thoughtlessly. But once we are clear that *this* is the kind of state Bob is in—he is just "mouthing the words"—I believe we will be disinclined to suppose that one has a grasp of the possibility that it might, on such an occasion, seem to Bob just the way it does to us to say comprehendingly that hemophilia is due to a problem with the X chromosome—to think consciously what we understand ourselves to say.[6]

Thus, to judge the issue I'm posing here fairly, it is important to grasp fully what one has to try to conceive of, in order to conceive of someone with experience having the same phenomenal character as one's own thought, but who is literally without any thought, for excessive haste here can readily lead to unwarranted results. For instance, Putnam (1981, 17) says it is easy for him to imagine that he had a "feeling of understanding," but discovered then that he did not really understand anything, upon being awoken by a hypnotist. And the point of this, it seems, is to persuade us to agree that the relation between the phenomenal character of experience and conceptual thought is merely a contingent one. We are now in a position to see why such a conclusion should not be drawn from such considerations.

First, it is misleading at best to speak of a *feeling* of understanding here, because that suggests that the way it seems to speak comprehendingly is phenomenally similar to a feeling of warmth, or an itch, or other experiences that form our paradigms of the category "feeling." But it is not. So we should not let the disconnection between the phenomenal character of such paradigmatic feelings and conceptual thought guide our judgments about the relation between the way it seems for us to think and thinking. And this "feeling of understanding" talk suggests that the phenomenal character of understanding is uniform—but it is not; as we have seen, it changes with what one thinks. So speaking of the phenomenal character of understanding as a kind of "feeling" quite distorts our judgment here, and should be set aside.

Second, we need more detail before we can be clear about the coherence of Putnam's scenario. Just what is supposed to make it clear that one discovered one did not really understand anything by one's words, when previously it seemed to one as it does to understand? Is it the mere fact that one was hypnotized? But I assume one can speak under hypnosis without failing to understand what one is saying. Is it that when one comes out of the hypnotic trance, one cannot answer questions about what one was saying of a sort that shows one was to a surprising degree confused, in a way one was not able to recognize while hypnotized? But—as the Bob case above illustrates—being rather confused about what one is saying is not the same as a complete lack of understanding. Perhaps the scenario is: I come out of the hypnotic state and discover that the whole time I was only muttering what now seem to me to be a string of nonsense syllables, even though earlier it seemed to me throughout just as it now does to understand what I am saying. Now, it is not nearly so clear that this is conceivable. The way it seems to talk while in a hypnotic trance is presumably not just the same as the way it seems to speak and think normally—somewhat as this is also phenomenally different from dreaming, or a hypnogogic state (Cartesian "dreaming skepticism" aside, these clearly are phenomenally different from normal waking experiences). So even if it is conceivable that it could in some sense "seem to me as it does to understand" while in a hypnotic trance, when really I understood and thought nothing, that does not show it could seem to me the way it does to understand in a normal, unhypnotized state, without understanding or thinking at all. Are we to say then: "Yes, but just as the experience had while dreaming could *conceivably* be phenomenally not at all dreamlike, isn't it at least *conceivable* that you could be hypnotized in such a way that there was no change in the phenomenal character of your experience?" This is hardly clear. But anyway, I suppose it is also *conceivable* that under hypnosis I could speak and understand a language I was incapable of speaking or understanding when not hypnotized. And if I am supposed to conceive of a rather odd situation in which, under hypnosis, my noniconic thinking is phenomenally much like it is without hypnosis, but out of hypnosis the words I was uttering seem meaningless, then it appears that what I am conceiving of is the (also odd) case where there is a language I can understand only under hypnosis.

The kind of scenario from which Putnam seems to want us quickly to conclude that the connection between the phenomenal character of experience and conceptual thought is merely contingent, seems to have that force only because of the cursory manner in which it is considered. This should help us to see that, once we recognize clearly that there is variation in the phenomenal character proper to our noniconic thought, we will appreciate the difficulty in conceiving of our phenomenal counterparts' thinking absolutely nothing, and the need, if we are to conceive of this successfully, to identify some condition that we think (a) could be missing from our phenomenal counterparts' situation, and (b) is essential to noniconic thinking.

But what might this be? I will not spend much time on the suggestion that the possibly missing essential condition here involves some kind of *judgment*—some thought or belief about one's thought-experience so as to make *it* about something. It is clear enough that we do not, as a matter fact, target all our conscious thoughts with occurrences of higher-order interpretive thoughts or judgments of the relevant sort. Do we think that, in any case, it is essential to consciously thinking that p, that one always have some dispositional belief about the thought-experience one has, to the effect that experience with this character is an instance of thinking that p? The case for this (b)-type claim would need to be made. And then there is also the question of whether the (a)-type claim can be defended. Have we here found a condition that might be absent when experience with the phenomenal character of our conscious noniconic thought occurs? Only if we also can say that totally unreflective beings could have experience with the phenomenal character of our noniconic thinking. But it seems, on the face of it, no easier to conceive of this than it is to conceive of someone's having experience phenomenally just like our thinking, who never thinks anything at all.

But someone may well propose that there is some *other* sort of possibly absent condition, which needs adding to one's phenomenal thought-experience to give one genuine thoughts, involving an appropriate relation (perhaps causal) of the experience to one's *behavior*, or to one's *surroundings*. The idea would be: our counterparts' phenomenal experience might lack a certain relation to their behavior or environments (because, perhaps, they have always been sessile, or they are brains in vats)—and lacking such behavioral or environmental links, they would think and mean nothing.

The initial problem facing such a suggestion parallels that discovered at a similar point in the discussion of sensory experience. Since at first it appears inconceivable that our phenomenal counterparts would be devoid of thought, to the extent we are confident we have identified a condition that might be missing from their circumstances—a condition meeting requirement (a)—we will seem to have reason to doubt that this condition meets requirement (b)—that it is essential to genuine thought. (So: do we really think that our phenomenal counterparts might be brains in vats? Then maybe the lesson to draw is that the environmental or behavioral connections they would lack are not essential to thought after all.) If, on the other hand, we are confident we have found some condition that must obtain for our phenomenal counterparts genuinely to think, this, together with the difficulty in supposing them thoughtless, appears to give us reason to doubt that the condition fulfills (a)—that it is a condition that might fail to obtain in the case of our phenomenal counterparts. (So: are we sure that no brain in a vat could think or mean anything by its "private" utterances? Maybe, then, we should say it also could not really seem to such brains as it does to us to think and understand.) The difficulty is, it is unclear what is supposed to warrant our maintaining that (a) and (b) are *jointly satisfied* for some condition C, in such a way that we can use them together to convince ourselves that we really can conceive what here appeared to us inconceivable.

Perhaps someone will try to meet this challenge by appealing to certain externalist accounts of meaning and belief. So, one might hold, borrowing from Putnam (1975a), that what we mean by 'water,' for example, is: what has the same underlying nature as demonstratively indicated samples ("For instance, *this* stuff," we say, holding up a glass of what we have poured from the tap, or pointing at a nearby puddle). And then one might argue as follows. If such demonstrative utterances find no referent, subjects express no thought through them. But in that case, *they also express no thought by utterances of the term 'water.'* Now it might seem to certain subjects—who are brains in vats—as if they made utterances aloud though really they did not—it merely sounded to them as if they did, or they merely auralized them. But although one can mean something by apparent or auralized utterances, the apparent utterances of brains in vats would find no referents, and hence would express no thoughts—and so, too, with their apparent utterances of 'water.' But the failure of demonstrative reference surely would not prevent its seeming to such subjects as it does to us when we successfully make such references. And such subjects might be (not just our phenomenal counterparts but) our phenomenal twins—but they do not ever think anything when they apparently utter 'water.' And the same goes for a vast number of general terms it appears to them as if they utter (like 'gold,' 'salt,' 'lemon,' 'tiger,' etc.).

This might be combined with another similar argument drawn from Tyler Burge's (1979) views. One might say that by 'arthritis' (for example), we each mean, roughly, what speakers we would count as experts about arthritis mean by the term. But (one might argue) if subjects are unable to identify any such experts in their environment—or indeed, any other speakers—they lack the kind of membership in a language community necessary for expressing thoughts by utterances of 'arthritis.' And our phenomenal twins might be in such a predicament—for they might be brains in vats—and though it seems to them as if they are uttering, "I've got arthritis," and so on, they express no thoughts thereby. And this is not a special point about the term 'arthritis,' but applies to a vast number of—perhaps all—general terms we use ('brisket' and 'sofa' are a couple of Burge's favorites).

From such arguments one might conclude that our phenomenal twins (if environmentally estranged in the way brains in vats would be) would never express any thought by the use of general terms, and from this one might infer that, on account of their lack of the right connection to the environment, they might have *no noniconic thoughts at all.*

But I do not think such arguments would come anywhere near establishing that conclusion. And this, even if we grant quite a bit. Suppose we grant, for instance, that a pair of phenomenal twins may rightly be said to have different thoughts expressible using general terms, if they belong to environments relevantly different in their physical nature, or if they belong to language groups whose experts' usage of terms differs. And suppose we waive any objection to the idea it could seem to the environmentally alienated brains in vats just as it seems to us to speak comprehendingly of water and arthritis. Still, there are difficulties. For first (in regard to the Putnam-derived argument), I do not think we should assume that we cannot express a thought using a demonstrative term when a referent is missing. (Hallucinating, I might say, "That snake is getting nearer," and voice a thought thereby, though "that snake" meets with no referent.) And even if *this* point is waived, and granting the claim about what we mean by 'water' and other "natural kind" terms, it does not follow that, if an utterer's relevant (apparent) demonstrative utterances find no referents, he or she just means *nothing* by such general terms (like 'water'). Consider: I may be said to have *some* notion or concept of water other than just: what shares the same underlying nature as *this* (and other) stuff. For there are appearances whereby I group together the various samples I indicate, and recognize them as samples of water—what we might characterize as "watery" appearances—and this forms part of my notion or concept of water. So part of my concept of water is that it is watery. Now, if we are willing to accept that our phenomenal twins may be brains in vats, we have no business rejecting the supposition that such twins may enjoy the same sorts of appearance—and the notion of water I have based on appearances by which water is recognizable to me is, we may say, how they understand their apparent utterances of 'water.' Thus, in their case, this notion or concept determines what they mean by 'water.' Even if we say this leaves them expressing a different thought with 'water' than we do, it does not leave them expressing no thought at all. We have found no reason to think that our vatted phenomenal twins would suffer a lack that left them unable to think using our "natural kind" terms.

Similar remarks apply to the argument derived from Burge. Even if we are inclined to defer to the usage of experts in our use of the term 'arthritis' and many others, it does not follow that, if our phenomenal twins can identify no experts to whom they can defer, or any other speakers at all, they just mean nothing by 'arthritis' at all. For I have *some* notion of arthritis other than just: whatever the medical experts say it is. And my phenomenal twin might also have this notion, and understand his apparent utterance of 'arthritis' by means of it. So we may say that, in the absence of other speakers with whom he can align his usage, that notion determines what he means and understands by 'arthritis.' And if he means something, he thinks something.

Thus the considerations at play in Putnam's and Burge's externalisms do not really furnish materials for meeting the challenge of identifying some

condition we can rightfully claim both to be possibly missing from our phenomenal twins' situation, and to be essential to noniconic thought. And so
they do not help us to overcome the difficulty in conceiving of our phenomenal counterparts as literally thoughtless. But without being able to conceive
of this, we have no reason to think there is any condition they might lack,
lacking which, they lack noniconic thought. So we have no reason to think
that, where the phenomenality of thought is present, something more needs
adding before its intentionality is present, too.

We might seek out other sources of motivation for dissociating the phenomenal character of thought from its intentionality. We might look to
some theory holding that since meaning must be *public*, thought must be
communicable, and some claim that since our vatted phenomenal twins
could not communicate, they could not think. But it is unclear, to say the
least, why we should accept some "communicability" requirement of the
strength needed here, something like: for all x, x has thoughts at all, only if
x's thoughts are communicable to others, *in x's actual environment*. (Our
vatted twins would be able to communicate their thoughts, if taken out of
their vats and put into human bodies—why is that not enough?[7]) In any
case, we again run up against the question: if we are so sure thought must be
in this way communicable, why not use that assumption to reject the view
that brains in vats could have experience with the same phenomenal character as our thought, rather than assuming they could, and using that to reject
the view that our phenomenal twins would also be noniconic thinkers? That
second option would leave us with a result at least as counterintuitive. The
first route then seems at least as attractive. And if we take it, we have no
argument from the necessary publicity of meaning and thought to the conceivability of thoughtless phenomenal twins.

At this point, one may go back to take up the other strand of opposition
to the picture I am offering of how the phenomenal character of our thought
relates to what we think—(2) above. One might say: "Our phenomenal
counterparts would not be literally thoughtless. But still, what must be
added to our possession of the phenomenal features we share, to yield a
correlative assessment of us for truth—say, something of the form 'What x
thinks is true'—are conditions that *interpret* these features, and make them
features with respect to which we are so assessable."

What we must ask, then, is whether there is reason to think that what
must be added to our possession of such noetic phenomenal features are
interpreting conditions. Someone might suppose it is enough for this, to hold
that, according to externalist ways of counting or individuating thoughts (or
contents), what I think and what my phenomenal counterpart thinks will be
different. One might say, "Your phenomenal twin would clearly be your
phenomenal counterpart. But when you think *your* keys are in *your* pocket,
your phenomenal twin thinks *his* keys are in *his* pocket. And this is to say
you have distinct thoughts. At least, what would make your twin's thought
true is different from what would make your thought true. Doesn't it follow

that we must add to your possession of the noetic phenomenal life you lead something like an interpretation, to yield the consequence that what you think on a certain occasion is true?"

I don't think that it does follow. For what is it that needs to be added to its seeming to me as it does to think my keys are in my pocket, for it to follow that what I think is true? No more than this, we might say: *that my keys are in my pocket*. And what needs to be added to its seeming to my twin as it does to me to think that my keys are in my pocket, for it to follow that what he thinks is true, is just this, I would suggest: *that his keys are in his pocket*. But now, in neither case does it seem that what has to be added is reasonably regarded as an interpretation of the phenomenal feature we share, or our possession of it. The fact that my keys are in my pocket does not of itself entail anything about this phenomenal feature, its seeming to me as it does to think my keys are in my pocket, or about my possession of it. It is just a fact about my keys. It does not make me assessable for truth with respect to this phenomenal feature as I otherwise would not have been, though I had this experience.

However, you might wonder: how could what follows from *my* having this phenomenal feature be different from what follows from *my twin's* having it? Can we explain why, when we add to the fact that I have this phenomenal feature, the further fact that my keys are in my pocket, it follows that what I believe is true, but this does *not* follow when what is added is the fact that my twin's keys are in his pocket?

The question is whether, in order to explain this, we need to suppose that one's possession of this phenomenal feature needs an interpretation. It doesn't seem that we do. For one might offer an explanation along these lines. If it seems to me as it does to think my keys are in my pocket, then I think something, and *what* I think I could *say* by saying, "My keys are in my pocket." But the truth of what I would say in this way, and thus the truth of what I think, depends on what such an utterance of "my keys" and "my pocket" would refer to: the keys and pocket of the one who could express this thought in this way, namely, me. And so, when I possess this phenomenal feature, what would make what I think true is *my* keys being in *my* pocket, and not my twin's keys being in his. A similar account could be given of why, when my twin has this phenomenal feature, what would make what he thinks true, is his keys being in his pocket, rather than mine being in mine. (And if we are worried that one could have this phenomenal feature in such atomistic isolation that it could not follow from one's having it that one had a thought one could express by saying, "My keys are in my pocket," then we can switch to the claim that it is being my total phenomenal twin from which this follows.) The point is, we can admit that what would make what my phenomenal twin thinks true differs from what would make what I think true. But this does not by itself show that phenomenal noetic features are not features with respect to which their possessors are assessable for truth, until they are furnished with an interpretation. And we can conceive of an account of why the thoughts of different possessors of this feature have different truth-conditions, and thus why (by a certain reckoning) they are distinct thoughts, without assuming they are not themselves intentional features. For the account I have just sketched is compatible with the assumption that they are intentional features.

So the challenge is still to find some condition that could fail to obtain in the presence of the noetic phenomenal feature I would share with my counterpart, but that is essential to deriving some correlative assessment of us for truth, and that is reasonably regarded as an interpreting condition. And again, someone will likely float the suggestion that the relevant condition must relate the experience with that character to some environmental circumstances, perhaps causally, in a way it might fail to be so related. One may (once more) think of the suggestion that brains in vats might have experience phenomenally like our own, and then haul out some theory according to which what such brains would be thinking is determined by their causal connections to the brain-stimulating machines sustaining their activity. How might this work? Again, borrowing from Putnam, I might say that if my phenomenal twin is a brain in a vat, he (it?) would (seem to itself to) say something like, "By water, I mean whatever is the same in kind as *this*," but what the demonstrative 'this' refers to here is determined by what state of the machine causes the brain to have experience with the phenomenal character of my thinking. And then what the brain means by 'water' (and, one may go on to argue, what thoughts it has generally) will be totally different from my own—it will always be thinking about some state or other of the machine to which it is hooked up. So even if my phenomenal twin and I will inevitably be noniconic thinkers, what we respectively think is determined by the interpretation of our experience provided by its causal relations to our environment.

But this is unconvincing—even if we concede that our phenomenal twins might be brains in vats. For if we believe (as we should) that when the man who hallucinates a snake crawling into his bed says, "Get this out of my bed!" his utterance of 'this' fails to meet with a referent, we should say also that the vatted brain's utterance of 'this' fails to find a referent. And so it will not be correct to suppose that the brain in a vat demonstratively identifies (and thus thinks about) some state of the machine that stimulates it. We should either deny that such brains could have experience of the same character ours has, or else deny that the causal relation between the stimulation machine and the vatted brain would supply its experience with an interpretation in the suggested manner.

But maybe there is another way to put Putnam-ish reflections to work here. Suppose I tell the following story. By 'water,' Bob (like other English-speaking earthlings) means whatever is of the same kind as certain samples he indicates demonstratively. Bob, however, is quite ignorant of the chemical nature of water. And he has a phenomenal twin on some other planet (Twin Earth) where stuff that appears watery is not of the same nature as the stuff Bob indicates (namely, H_2O)—for it is XYZ. From this we see that the beliefs and thoughts Bob's phenomenal twin expresses by use of the term 'water' are not the beliefs and thoughts Bob expresses by use of the term 'water.' Thus here—so the story goes—is a difference in what is thought that is left quite indeterminate by the phenomenal character of thought. One might tell a similar story regarding any number of "natural kind" terms. Does that not suffice to show that some causal relation between one's environment and one's experience confers an interpretation on the latter, so as to determine what thoughts one has?

We might add to this a Burgean tale about 'arthritis.' By 'arthritis,' Irene means whatever sources she would count as expert mean by it. She, however, is far from an expert herself—for she mistakenly thinks that one can get arthritis in the thigh. But Irene's phenomenal twin lives in a linguistic community whose medical experts use the term 'arthritis' to refer to rheumatoid ailments generally (and not just those in joints). And this would make Irene and Twin Irene have different thoughts: for what Irene thinks when she says, "Arthritis sometimes occurs in the thigh," is false, but what her twin thinks when she says this is true. Does this show that the relation between one's linguistic community and one's experience confers an interpretation on the phenomenal character of one's thinking?

The answer to both questions, it seems to me, is "No," even if we are willing to grant that thoughts can vary independent of phenomenal character in the way suggested. Consider Bob first. Why should we not say that all that needs to be added to its seeming to Bob as it does to think noniconically that there is water in his glass, so that it will follow that what Bob thinks is true, is simply this: *there is water in his glass*? And all that needs to be added to the fact that it seems to Twin Bob just as it seems to Bob to think this, so that it will follow that what Twin Bob thinks is true, is simply: *there is twater in* his *glass* (where *twater* is what has the property picked out by Twin Bob's use of the term 'water'). Now, these conditions do not appear to have the status of *interpretations* of their experience. The fact that Bob's glass is full of water does not of itself imply anything about the phenomenal feature Bob and Twin Bob share, or its possession, and so it seems it cannot reasonably be said to confer an interpretation on that feature or on the experience of thinking that Bob has.

However, one might suspect that we will not be able to explain why it is that what makes what Bob thinks true differs in this way from what makes what Bob's phenomenal twin thinks true, unless we assume that their possession of the phenomenal feature they share needs an interpretation of some sort, without which having that feature is not having a feature with respect to which one is assessable for truth. But this suspicion seems unwarranted. We might say that if it seems to Bob the way it does to think that there is water in his glass, then what would make what he thinks true, is that something of the same kind as watery stuff he has been able to identify demonstratively (provided there is some) is in his glass. And the watery stuff he has been able to identify demonstratively is stuff in *his* environment. So what would make what Bob thinks true is the presence of something with the nature of watery stuff in his environment—namely, water. Similarly, if it seems to Twin Bob the way it does to Bob to think there is water in his glass, what would make what Twin Bob thinks true is that something of the same kind as watery stuff he has been able to identify demonstratively is in his glass. And the watery stuff Twin Bob has been able to identify is a certain stuff in his environment, namely twater. (If, in order to make this work, we need to assume that the phenomenal feature we are concerned with here includes the subjects' entire phenomenal histories, then we can state the account in a way that makes this assumption explicit.) Thus it seems we can imagine an account of why what makes what such phenomenal twins think true differs (and hence why, on a certain reckoning, what they think is different), which says nothing that requires us to abandon the view that the phenomenal feature they share is an intentional feature.

Similarly, we might say of Irene and her twin: what needs to be added to its seeming to Irene as it seems to her to think one can get arthritis in the thigh, for it to follow that what she thinks is true, is just: *One can get arthritis in one's thigh*; whereas in Twin Irene's case, it would be enough to add: *One can get tharthritis in one's thigh* (where tharthritis is the ailment sources Twin Irene treats as expert call 'arthritis'). In neither case does one need to add anything to their phenomenal conditions that could reasonably be seen as an interpretation of the phenomenal feature they share. And it seems we can conceive of an explanation of why the truth-conditions of these twins' thoughts differ, which involves no assumption that the phenomenal feature they share is not intentional. If it seems to Irene as it does to think one can get arthritis in the thigh, then what would make what she thinks true, is that the thigh can be afflicted with what the sources she has recognized (or has been inclined to recognize) as medically expert—if there are any—would call 'arthritis.' (If it appears we need to change this to the claim that this follows from Irene's complete phenomenal history and dispositions, assume that revision is made.) And we might say something similar about Twin Irene: it follows from her having the phenomenal life she shares with Irene that what would make what she (Twin Irene) thinks true, is that the thigh can be afflicted with what the sources *she* has recognized (or has been inclined to recognize) as medically expert (provided there are any for her to recognize) would call 'arthritis.' Again, it seems there is available to us a way of understanding why there is a difference in truth-conditions, and (if you like) a difference in thoughts, even though there is phenomenal twinhood, without denying that noetic phenomenal features are intentional.

Now, it seems we should say that phenomenal features are not ones with respect to which their possessors are assessable for truth, *independently of who those possessors are*. Only once the possession of phenomenal features is fixed, is it also fixed what would make what their possessor thinks true. But I do not think we have to assume that genuine intentional features must be somehow assessable for truth independently of the context of their possession. I conclude that Putnam-style or Burge-style externalist reflections about content do not give us good reason to suppose that noetic phenomenal features are not intentional features.

We may continue to cast about among other accounts purporting to tell us what external conditions fix or determine the contents of our thoughts, which do not lend themselves to the treatment just suggested, looking for reasons to hold that the phenomenal character of our thought is not intentional without interpretation. But this, I believe, will lead us back to the sorts of problems earlier met with in trying to de-intentionalize the phenomenal. For instance, if we are truly convinced that no one could possibly have thoughts of a certain sort, without the appropriate evolutionary heritage, it is unclear why we shouldn't use this to cast doubt on whatever conviction we may have that differently evolved beings might be our phenomenal twins. And, if we are so sure that differently evolved beings might be our phenomenal twins, why shouldn't we use this to cast doubt on the thesis that these evolutionary differences would entail differences in what we think?

Thus, we have found no convincing reason to think that there are conditions, possibly missing from the lives of those to whom it seems as it does to us to have nonimagistic thought-experience, that are also essential to noniconic thought, or that are needed to confer intentionality on experience. So the better view is that there are no such conditions. Thus it still seems to me that the proposal I made earlier about the relation between thought and thought's phenomenal character is a good one. The phenomenal features we have in consciously thinking nonimagistically do not stand in need of some kind of interpretation before they are the features of genuine noniconic thinkers. *Without interpretation*, they are already features *with respect to which* we are assessable as having thought something true or false, and so they are features *in virtue of which* we are so assessable—intentional features.

Perhaps one will not be entirely happy with this conclusion, because one wants a sharper notion of what I have called "interpreting conditions," or because one wants some more precise and general characterization than I have given of the difference between features merely *with respect to which* their possessors are assessable for truth or accuracy, and features *in virtue of which* we are so assessable. And I suppose this complaint might be made not only regarding my discussion of conscious thought, but also about my discussion of visual consciousness. My response would be this. Though we are assessable for truth and accuracy somehow with respect to our conscious experience, I can find no good way to understand the distinction between features *merely with respect to which*, and those *in virtue of which*, we are so assessable, that would put our phenomenal features entirely in the former category, so as to assimilate them in some measure to the nonrepresentational features of linguistic or pictorial representations. For, as near as I can tell, nothing we need add to the circumstances of someone who has phenomenal features we can identify in our own lives, which yields assessment of such a one for accuracy or truth, has the status of a condition that *confers* assessability for truth or accuracy, where otherwise it would be absent. Thus, at a minimum we may say this. Our phenomenal features are at least ones with respect to which we are assessable for truth and accuracy. In the face of this, the burden of argument then rests on anyone who would yet deny that such phenomenal features are genuinely intentional features, to explain this latter notion in such a way that will justify that denial.

8.6 CONCLUSION

To understand the relationship between phenomenal character and intentionality, it was necessary first to take into account the distinction between iconic and noniconic conscious thought. Taking the former—imagery experience—first, and focusing on visualization, I argued that visualizing has its own phenomenal character, and is intentional, and its intentionality is not separable from its phenomenality. Then, turning to consider noniconic thought-experience, I argued that this has a distinctive and richly variable phenomenal character inseparable from the intentionality we have, when what we consciously think is nothing we visualize, auralize, or image.

Once we accept this, we will not be liable to think of consciousness as something that occurs only when one is engaged in silent soliloquy, or when one has some other kind of imagery, or sense-experience. For it typically belongs even to public, noisy, unimaged thought. So we cannot reasonably say that consciousness does not matter to the thinking we do in speaking, in meaning and understanding something by our utterances. Putting this together with prior results, we can conclude that phenomenal consciousness pertains to what has been generally held to be of core interest to philosophy and psychology, namely, perceptual intentionality, and linguistic understanding.

That this should have been unobvious to some gives us no good reason to doubt it. For recognizing the distinctive phenomenal character of noniconic thought, and its relation to intentionality, is a delicate business. One can easily be oblivious to the subtleties involved, or drastically misled by cursory reflections, especially if one has become comfortable with, or wary of challenging, the habits of generations of professional thinkers trained to set their faces against consciousness. One can come to agree with the account I have given of these matters, I think, only if one is willing to consider them with unhurried and repeated reflection on one's own experience, and what one can know of it, unpressured by philosophical prejudice against finding in it what I describe. The likes of Ryle and Wittgenstein have long warned us off the error of assimilating thought and understanding to mental imagery. But we ought not to correct Humean confusion on this point, only to persist in the empiricist tradition's equally noxious error of supposing thought and understanding to be *experiential*, only if *imagistic*.

However, I do not wish to suggest that nothing but the weight of philosophical tradition keeps us from appreciating how the phenomenal fabric of noniconic thought is—like that of perception—richly various. The patterns of thought's phenomenal character tend somehow to turn hopelessly fragile in our thick-handed theories. There is something about the phenomenal—perhaps an inherent elusiveness to regimentation—that tempts us, when we turn theory upon ourselves, to ignore such experiential differences, or without realizing what we are doing, to replace them with something a little less slippery, like pictures or symbols, which need to be interpreted to have meaning. Though we in some way weave the fabric of thought's seeming nearly throughout our waking lives, to weave it we need not be able to describe it well, and when we stand back and try to lay hold of it, we are liable to tear it clumsily to shreds. I am aware my description of thought's phenomenal character has not done it full justice. But I hope I have helped keep it from intellectual oblivion.

The Importance of Consciousness

9.1 DOES CONSCIOUSNESS MATTER?

I have tried to save consciousness from the neglect it may suffer in various theories. But mightn't someone doubt the rescue worthwhile, even if successful? I can imagine a grudging, equivocal concession:

> All right, so we have omitted phenomenal consciousness, in your sense, from our theories, and we cannot show it is not real. Still, we do theorize about something—for example, a certain collection of discriminatory, regulative, and evaluative talents; higher-order thought; or information access to speech-producing or self-representational or planning subsystems. There's no law against labeling our accounts of these "theories of consciousness"—and what these would explain more deserves our attention than does your *phenomenal* consciousness. That we *do* leave out—*but so what*?

There may not be much to say to someone with such an attitude. Phenomenal consciousness may strike *me* as what's most fascinating about the world, but if it really leaves you completely cold, perhaps I could do nothing to warm you to it. Even so, we must be careful not to confuse a lack of interest in consciousness (or a perplexity about how to design a scientific theory about it) with a reason for thinking it does not occur.

Then again, there may be something more to say here. My discussion may have already removed some obstacles to granting the importance of consciousness. For instance, perhaps you felt inclined to agree with or helpless to resist the Rylean suggestion that being conscious consists in nothing more than having a stream of sensations, such as would not much distinguish a human from a reptile, or a genius from an idiot. You may then very well have held consciousness in rather low regard. However, if you are now convinced that phenomenal features are diversely and richly intentional, you will see that they involve differences in what one thinks and perceives that separate us from other animals, and that distinguish humans manifesting different sorts of intelligence and character from one another. So now consciousness will not, I take it, appear so unworthy of your esteem. Also, perhaps you would have had troubling acknowledging you cared much about phenomenal features, because you had difficulty in distinguishing these from others, or because you were inclined to identify belief in them with belief in "qualia," which term you linked to a bevy of doubtful or murky doctrines to which we are not, in fact, committed in believing we are conscious. If my discussion, or some other, has relieved you of these problems, then it may have enabled you to recognize, as you otherwise might not have, the importance of consciousness.

However, a worry about whether consciousness matters may come from another source: a concern that *it does not make a difference to what happens*. One may want an argument that our possession of phenomenal features can rightly be used to explain why certain things happen, or—if this amounts to the same thing—how such features can be causally efficacious. To address this concern adequately, I would need to discuss just what we count as an explanation of why things happen, and to examine the kind of argument that would lead to an epiphenomenalist denial of the efficacy, not just of phenomenal features, but of the mental quite generally. I would also need to consider the variety of reasons someone might say that, while mind in some guise is genuinely explanatory, consciousness has just some diminished or doubtful part to play in producing our behavior—or perhaps none at all.

This is not a project I want to take on now. I will, however, remark that unless one radically (and misguidedly) restricts the scope of perceptual consciousness, it will at least appear that what we are able to do depends pervasively and enormously on the phenomenal character of our perception. For example, if I take off my glasses, this changes the phenomenal character of my vision considerably, and also—apparently not coincidentally—the quality of my performance at many tasks. So if you need a ride to the airport, you would be unwise to take your chances with me until I put my glasses back on. The reason seemingly is: My driving will be terrible, since things look all blurry to me. And, evidently, not only driving, but countless other abilities are also systematically related to the quality of my conscious vision. What colors and spatial relations of visual stimuli can I spontaneously discriminate in thought and motor behavior? For the most part, those of which I have conscious visual experience.

However, one might argue that loss of our motor abilities systematically *correlates with*, but is not at all *explained by*, loss in our visual consciousness, if one can isolate the visual guidance of our behavior from the generation of our conscious visual experience, so that the latter is seen as a mere by-product—a branch-line—of the route from stimulus to response. But this is doubtful. The studies of blindsight to which I have alluded suggest that the kinds of discriminatory responses to visual stimuli we can make without consciously seeing them are somehow, given the character of the human brain, very limited. As Dennett emphasized in the passage I quoted earlier, blindsighters' responses are only to "simple widely dispersed properties," and allow them to do little spontaneously, without "forced choices." This is some evidence that, in us at least, conscious visual experience cannot, for the most part, be separated from the vision that guides spatial abilities. And this, together with the systematicity of the relation between conscious vision and behavior, supports the belief that our coordinated responses to visual stimuli are explained in part by how the stimuli look to us: we can respond as we do to differences in the stimuli, because we consciously see them.

We may resist this, if we think that the lack of gaps in what physics can ideally explain somehow reduces to nil the explanatory value of all other ways of explaining what occurs in the world: since in principle we could dispense with these other forms of explanation, and leave no occurrence unexplained, they do not really explain after all. But then, this problem would not *specially* afflict the idea that talk of how things seem to us genuinely explains how we act; it would threaten to render all explanation outside of physics spurious. So if the faith that physics can explain everything it can describe does not demand we say that no genuine explanations are found apart from physics, such evidence as I have mentioned supports the view that our phenomenal features do make a difference to what happens.

Against this, it may still be urged that even if *actual* blindsight is relatively feeble in what it can do, we cannot rule out the *possibility* of more sophisticated forms of visual function without visual consciousness. Indeed, I have said we would entirely rule out a blindsight more sophisticated than any apparently actually encountered, only on pain of denying the reality of consciousness. Now, the hypothetical forms of blindsight I have said we oughtn't to rule out may still be relatively weak and limited—but here again the question will be raised: Why stop there? Can we rule out the possibility of *premium-quality* blindsight? And couldn't there be, in principle, self-guided human-shaped creatures indistinguishable from us in their manifest behavior—zombies of a certain sort? If there could be, in either of these ways, elaborate, apparently intelligent responses to visual stimuli, in the *absence* of conscious vision, how could its *presence* be responsible for such behavior?

In reply, one might argue: premium blindsight and zombies are strictly impossible. But, again, I see no acceptable way to establish this thesis, even if recognition of consciousness does not clearly bar us from holding it. There are various reasons it can be somewhat *difficult* to imagine premium blindsight, or self-guided nonconscious humanoids—but these do not, as near as I can tell, show us we just cannot conceive of such, or that they are strictly impossible in some way.[1]

However, I think we should beware of taking such possibilities to show that the phenomenal character of our experience does not affect what we do. Even if there could be, *in some possible world*, blindsighted tennis players and gem cutters, or whole nations of humanoid zombies, in whose behavior conscious visual experience plays no role, one may well doubt it follows that what *we* do in the *actual* world depends in no way on our having it. (From the claim that a's capacity to F depends on and is explained by its possession of feature G, it surely does not follow that in no possible world may any x have the capacity to F without possessing G.) And it seems we can refuse to identify the concept or the property of having conscious visual experience with either the concept or the property of being in just whatever state plays a certain causal or functional role in a system, and yet not commit ourselves to saying consciousness never plays that role in anyone. Though being a conscious experience is not being the occupant of a functional role, experience may yet play a role—or many roles—in us, on account of its phenomenal character.

These matters need more examination. But, as I have indicated, I do not wish here to focus on this aspect of the importance (or unimportance) of conscious experience—the question of whether or not it explains or causally affects what else happens. Rather, I want us here to attend to a way in which the phenomenal character of experience is important to us that we can recognize without assuming it accounts for the occurrence of *something else we regard as important*. I want to focus on a way in which the possession of phenomenal features is valued *for its own sake*, and not just for the sake of having what other features we think come with it. Thus I will argue that even if we suspend judgment on the *efficacy* of consciousness, after we have recognized its *reality*, we will find no excuse for refusing to recognize its *importance*.

9.2 EXPERIENCE FOR ITS OWN SAKE

If you agree that you do have phenomenal features in the sense I have explained, you will probably also affirm that you value having them. That is, I think most of us will agree that we think it better that there are ways it seems to us to have the experience we do on some occasions, than that such experiences are then missing, given what else we think is likely to be the case, on each of these two options. We think it sometimes better to have such experience than not to have it. So, we value its looking, sounding, smelling, tasting, and feeling to us as it does on many occasions. And we value the exercise of our ability to think consciously—whether iconically or noniconically, whether in wandering reveries or in disciplined inquiry.

That is not to say, of course, that absolutely everyone who has phenomenal features prefers to have them, or that we would rather have than lack any of them anytime we can get them. People who want to commit suicide, believing and hoping that there is no afterlife, may be said not to value having conscious experience any more. And, obviously, we may not value having experience of a certain phenomenal character at a certain time or place (e.g., I'd rather not listen to music right now), and there are phenomenal features (e.g., the way it seems to be in excruciating pain) that many of us would prefer *never* to have. However, if you are not burdened by suicidal despair, and you would not deny that you have phenomenal features, I believe that, if you consider examples, you will readily acknowledge that you do value *sometimes* having *some* phenomenal features. Furthermore, unless you are astonishingly indifferent to the condition of others, you will likely agree that you think it better that other people sometimes possess rather than lack some forms of phenomenal consciousness. You also value *their* perceiving and thinking consciously in certain ways. So, I think it is clear that in this way, we value our own and others' possession of phenomenal features.

But it may not initially be clear whether this is due entirely to our believing they are needed for the possession of *other* features we value ourselves or others having. I say that, given what else I think is likely to be the case on each of these options, I would rather consciously see than not. But perhaps it is precisely and entirely because of what *else* I implicitly assume will differ between the situation where I have certain phenomenal features, and the one in which I do not, that I prefer the former to the latter. That is, likely I was assuming that, in suffering some change or loss of phenomenal visual features, I would also be losing certain nonphenomenal features I value as well—such as the ability to pilot a car so as to reliably reach a given destination without loss of life or property. And perhaps it is only for the sake of having such nonphenomenal features, which I value and assume would be lost along with the phenomenal ones, that I value having the latter. Similarly, while of course I do want others to be able to see consciously as well— maybe that is only because, for instance, I want them not to crash into me. But I said I wanted to come up with a way in which we value the possession of phenomenal consciousness that did not rest on assuming it makes a certain difference to what else we possess, or what else comes with it and is missing in its absence. Thus there seems to be a problem here about confirming that we do indeed value consciousness not just for what else (we think) its possession confers, but in this other way: "for its own sake."

However, even if we assume the phenomenal won't be lost, without loss of nonphenomenal features for whose sake we value it, isn't it just *obvious* that we value having the experiences themselves for its own sake, and so not simply for what they bring with them? For example, it is surely not simply on account of what it enables us to do that we like things to look colored to us. There is, for instance, a delight we take in the sunflower's dense flaring yellow, and in the untrammeled, impenetrable blue of a clear bright sky, that we would lose did it not seem as it does for it to look to us as if there is something yellow or blue. Surely this loss does not derive just from the fact that, missing such experience, we would no longer be able to say, "It's blue," when turning our eyes to the sky, and "It's yellow," when gazing upon the flower, or to say whether this blue and this yellow are similar to or different from other samples of blue to which we are exposed, point to the brighter yellow, and so on. We would, most of us, miss the way yellow and blue looked to us, and not just what else their looking that way enabled us to do.

But it is not sufficiently clear yet what is meant by saying that we value having experience of a certain phenomenal character for its own sake, and in what such an attitude is manifest. Does this imply, for instance, that we would still rather have certain phenomenal features than not, even if deprived of the ability to have any *other-than-phenomenal* features we value having, whose possession we think ordinarily accompanies our having such conscious experience? If I would still prefer having a certain group of features over not having them, even when deprived of all others for whose sake I value them, then I cannot value the features in the first group merely for the sake of having some in the second; I must then value their possession for its own sake. Is *this*, then, what we have in mind if we say we value having experience for its own sake—that we would still rather have it, even if we lost all other things for whose sake we value its possession?

While preferring to keep conscious experience even then presumably *would* show we value it for its own sake, it is doubtful whether such a preference is widely or strongly held. For it seems we should test for this preference by asking ourselves how our evaluation of phenomenal features would be affected by our believing we would lose the nonphenomenal benefits we normally think coincide with their possession. So we would need to consider what we would think of retaining the phenomenal experience while its nonphenomenal benefits are wiped out. Let's try this. Suppose you thought you faced these options: either (a) you will no longer have any phenomenal experience at all, and will be dead (or, if you prefer, you will remain alive in a vegetative state), or else (b) you will continue to have phenomenal features of the sort you would ordinarily be expected to have in the future, but now only under this rather un-ordinary condition: *your sense-experience will never be accurate of what is in your actual environment.* Thus your experience will not bring with it the sort of capacity to make contact with your surroundings you assume it ordinarily does. So: you keep the phenomenal, without nonphenomenal benefits. To suppose you confronted this option (b), you might imagine some such device as what Peter Unger (1990) calls an "experience inducer," or else some scenario such as philosophers have conjured up in "brain-in-a-vat" arguments for skepticism. In either case, you may suppose there is some mechanism by which you can be given sensory experience of the phenomenal character yours actually has had or will have, but without its being brought about by the sorts of conditions that would make the way it seemed to you accurate.

Now, would I still value having phenomenal features even if I thought the way my body and the character of my surroundings were to appear to me would forever be radically at variance with the way they actually were? Perhaps I would just as soon be dead. Whether or not I would still want to go on at all if I really believed I faced this prospect, I would at the very least find it acutely disheartening. For I do not merely want to have experience; *I want my experience to be engaged with the world in which I am.* Maybe having phenomenal features is not by itself enough to make a life worth living. If the claim that we value conscious experience for its own sake is made to hang on the notion that we would still rather have it than not, even if deprived of all else for whose sake we value it, then the truth of this claim will be, for many of us, in doubt. And though we may so degrade our environment and our own characters that we would gladly embrace the chance to spend the rest of our lives in "virtual reality," entertained by hallucinations, I wouldn't want to depend on such proclivities to show we value experience for its own sake.[2]

I want, then, to try a different way of revealing this kind of evaluative attitude, working from the following two premises. First, I take it, the fact that we do value having phenomenal features for the sake of having other, nonphenomenal ones does not preclude our valuing their possession for its own sake as well. For example, the professional coffee or wine taster values its seeming to her as it does to taste coffee or wine, because she thinks without such experience, she would lose her livelihood. So she values the possession of phenomenal features, for the sake of having nonphenomenal ones. But I assume it does not follow from this, that she does not value its seeming to her the way it does to taste things, along with having other conscious experience that comes with this, *for its own sake as well*. Second, I think we can say that we value possession of phenomenal features for its own sake, or "intrinsically," if we value at least *someone's* having *some* phenomenal features, *and* if it is *not* the case that we do so only (or merely, or solely) for the sake of someone's (or something's) having nonphenomenal features. If we do value the possession of phenomenal features, but not solely for the sake of the nonphenomenal, then we value the possession of conscious experience (at least partly) for its own sake.

Let me clarify this second premise. I assume that one does not value each possession of a phenomenal feature F that one values, only for the sake of some further, distinct possession of a phenomenal feature G. Thus I assume there is not an infinite regress of valuing with regard to experiences—so that one values some experiences only for the sake of other experiences, which in turn one values only for the sake of yet others, and so on. It may be that we value one group of experiences for the sake of another, and that second also for the sake of the first (so that our valuing of the phenomenal ultimately doubles back on itself). But in that case, we do not value the first experience *only* for the sake of the second. (If I value x's being F for the sake of y's being G, and y's being G for the sake of x's being F, then it is wrong to say I value x's being F *only* or *merely* for the sake of y's being G.)

Further, I will assume that we value the possession of some phenomenal features, not merely for the reason that their loss would (we think) lead to our having certain *other* phenomenal features that we would prefer *not* to have. For example, I think that if I lost conscious vision, I would feel depressed, but it is not only in order to avoid feeling depressed that I would rather keep having visual experience. For I would feel a way I would rather not feel—a way I *disvalue*—upon the loss of phenomenal vision, partly because, if I felt that way, I would think I had lost something I value. Generally (I assume), if I value x's being F because I think that without this, x will be G (which I disvalue), and *also* I think that it would be worse for x to be G than not, partly because I value x's being F, then it is not true that I value x's being F *solely* because I think it is worse for x to be G. For then I think x will be in a condition I disvalue—being G—at least partly because I value x's being F. Roughly: if the *value* I attribute to one thing is due (at least in part) to the *disvalue* I attribute to a second, but also, the disvalue I attribute to the second is due (at least in part) to the value I attribute to the first, then it is not the case that I value the first *solely* because I disvalue the second. And, I believe, often where we prefer the possession of some phenomenal features partly because we prefer *not* to have certain others—"bad feelings"—that we think the loss of the first would bring, the situation is like this: we prefer not to have these others also, at least partly because we value the possession of the first group of features. For example: I think feeling depressed at the loss of visual consciousness would be a bad thing for me, partly because if that is the way I felt, I would think I had lost something it is *good* for me to have: visual consciousness.

The upshot of the last three paragraphs is this. I take it that if: (1) there are some phenomenal features you think it is better to have than to lack (given the assumptions you make about what either option is likely to involve); (2) there is no infinite regress of experience valuation; (3) you do not value the possession of some phenomenal features, only because you *disvalue* the possession of others; *and* (4) you do not value conscious experience only for the sake of some possession of *nonphenomenal* features; then (5) *you value conscious experience, but not only for the sake of something else.* And so, you value it, at least partly, *for its own sake.* Now, since I will assume that (1)–(3) do hold true for those of us who recognize the reality of phenomenal consciousness, in order to make it clear to ourselves that we value experience for its own sake, we need only to establish (4). So: we can see that we value the possession of phenomenal features for its own sake, if only we can see that we do not value this merely for the sake of someone's or something's having *nonphenomenal* features.

But still, how can we make *this* evident to ourselves? We might again be tempted to say: it is clear that we do not value the phenomenal solely for its nonphenomenal rewards, if we observe that we would still rather have certain phenomenal features than have none at all, when either way we would lack any of the nonphenomenal features for whose sake we value them. But again, I would not want to count on a willingness to say life spent in an "experience-inducer" would be better than no life at all to show us that we intrinsically value conscious experience. However, we may yet make this clear to ourselves if first we ask: what would support (4)'s *denial*—the claim that we valued ourselves or others' having phenomenal features, *only for the sake of something else nonphenomenal*? It seems this would be evidence of such an attitude: whenever we considered the possession of some phenomenal features we took ourselves to value, we found ourselves disposed to say, not just that we value these for the reason that, if we had them, we would (given the circumstances) also have certain nonphenomenal features whose possession we value, while if we lost the phenomenal ones, we would lose the others as well. We further found ourselves inclined to assert that it is *only for this reason* (or only because of this) that we value them at all. But I think if we consider cases, we will find not this—but just the opposite.

So consider again, for example, the case of color vision. You would say, I assume, that at least given what you would take to be involved in these two options, you would rather have conscious visual experience of color, than find yourself subject to achromatopsia. That is, you would rather continue on with normal color vision, than lose it (such that, though you would still have acute visual experience of spatial relations, and recognitional capacities, things would no longer look red, green, blue, yellow, and so on, to you—but only black and white and varying shades of gray). And I assume that you would agree that a reason you have this preference, a reason you would say you had for thinking it better to see in color than to be an achromatope, is that with visual experience of color comes many nonphenomenal features that you would lose with this sort of color blindness: certain abilities to have nonphenomenal features, which you value having—abilities to respond to colors, in verbal and other behavior. A simple example: you think that with conscious color vision you will be able to brake and accelerate your car appropriately in response to the color of traffic lights, but without conscious vision of color, you would lose this ability.

But now: would you also agree that the *only* reason you would rather see in color, is that doing so leaves you with this and other nonphenomenal features, while color blindness would deprive you of these? I take it this would be unusual. It would be unusual to say:

> I'd rather consciously see red, green, blue, etc., but only because I'd rather be able to go and stop at the right times at intersections with traffic lights, and only because I'd rather be able to match a blue shirt to blue pants, say "It's blue" when asked what color it is, and so on. And if I consciously see color I will have these abilities, and I will lose them, if I lose conscious visual experience of color. That is, I prefer phenomenal experience of color to its absence, only because I think, without it, I will lose certain *nonphenomenal* benefits I would otherwise have.

I would *not* be disposed to any such assertion, though I assume the loss of many nonphenomenal benefits would probably come with this sort of color blindness. And I think you are likely to find the same. What's more, I think it is likely you will find that you, like me, not only would not assert this, but would affirm the very contrary:

> It's *not* that case that I prefer phenomenal experience of color to achromatopsia only for the reason that, on the first option, I'd have certain nonphenomenal benefits (such as the capacity to make verbal and other motor responses to colors), which, on the second option, I'd lose.

Someone might ask: but if not only for this reason, then what other reason might we have for this preference? Well, just this: we think it is simply *better* for us to *have* color experiences (and perhaps other phenomenally conscious thoughts and feelings these afford us) than to *lack* them. But now, if we think this, and we believe we do not think it is better to have, rather than lack, color experience, only for the reason that this loss would involve the loss of valuable nonphenomenal features we would otherwise have, then we should agree: we value the possession of some phenomenal features, *but not only for the sake of possessing some nonphenomenal ones.* So (given the assumptions spelled out earlier) we believe that *we value having some phenomenal features for its own sake.* And if we believe this, then, barring good reason to think we are mistaken about our values, or our reasons for holding them, we are justified in concluding that we do indeed intrinsically value the possession of some phenomenal features.

I will come back in a little while to what might count as a good reason for saying we are wrong to think we do not value phenomenal consciousness merely for the sake of something else. First, I want to point out that this same pattern of thought, which I have applied to the example of color experience, can be applied more widely, to support the claim that we intrinsically value many different phenomenal features. Consider now not just the *chromatic* aspect of conscious visual experience, but its *spatial* aspect as well. Presumably we would say that there is a vast range of abilities to discriminate spatial relationships verbally and in other behavior that we would lose, and sorely miss, if we were deprived of conscious spatial vision (by becoming either legally or "stone" blind). But we would not say that it is *only* for the reason that our loss of phenomenal spatial vision would behaviorally handicap us, or strip us of other nonphenomenal blessings we would otherwise have, that we think it better to retain sharp and subtle visual experience of space. On the contrary, I think we would *deny* it was *merely* for this sort of reason, and, if pressed about what further reason we could have, we would say: having rich conscious visual experience of space is just better than not having it.

Consider also taste. I suppose most of us tasters (professional and non-professional alike) will say that we think it better for it to seem to us as it does for things to taste to us as they do, rather than for us to be entirely bereft of such conscious experience. And I suppose we would agree that there are nonphenomenal features we would rather have than not, which we think we would normally lose in losing the phenomenal character of taste-experience, and this gives us reason to prefer to keep phenomenal taste. So maybe I think that if food and drink did not taste any way to me. I would become so unmotivated to consume them that I would run the risk of mal-nourishment. And, also for reasons of health, I would like to be able to say whether food or drink tasted normal or spoiled. Thus I think that if I lost gustatory consciousness, I would be less likely to eat regularly and healthily, and for this reason I would prefer having taste-experience to losing it, other things being equal. But I certainly would *not* say that it is *solely* for the reason that I think I would lose these or other nonphenomenal benefits that I would rather keep taste-experience. Again, I would deny that it is only for such reasons. And I think it is unlikely you will find mine an eccentric attitude, or fail to share it.

We will perhaps be even more struck by such thoughts, if we consider the sorts of phenomenally conscious feelings that are part of human sexuality. I would rather it felt to me as it does to caress and be caressed, to kiss and be kissed, and experience sexual union and orgasm, than to be phenomenally dead in these respects. Am I inclined to say that I think it is better for me to have experiences of such phenomenal character than lack them, *only* for the reason that, were I to lack experience, I would be unable (or less likely?) to make certain kinds of behavioral responses to stimulation? No. Though I definitely value the ability to respond in the appropriate ways, and (I suppose) I value the experience partly for the sake of its contribution to such response—I would deny that I value the former entirely or merely for the sake of the latter. And again, I would be fairly surprised if the contrary attitude were widespread.

Of course, there may be people who would rather that it did not feel this way to them, because of the difficulty in reconciling sexual desire with other aims; or there may be people who would honestly say that they valued the way it feels to them to engage in sexual activity, only for the sake of (for example) the procreation it makes more likely. Similarly, some people might actually say that they would prefer to be rid of the phenomenal character of taste-experience, for then they would have less trouble confining their diet to nutritious foods, and wouldn't have to fight off cravings for ice cream, steak, and rich sauces. But it is enough for me to make my point if, first, there are at least some phenomenal features you have, or are able to have, such that you believe sometimes it is better to have them than not, given what you believe likely to come with having or lacking them; and if second, when reflecting on these cases, you are inclined not to *assert*, but to *deny* that it is only for the sake of some possession of nonphenomenal features that you value and think you would lose along with the phenomenal experience, that you consider it better to have the experience.

I therefore encourage you to consider in this way whatever kinds of experience you value having. I do not assume that, in doing so, we will all discover we think we intrinsically value precisely the same kinds of phenomenal experience, but I would be surprised if there were many who could not find a considerable variety of phenomenal features to value having in this way. It may help us to understand this variety, and what sort of variety it is, if we take note of this. The kinds of conscious experience we are likely to find that we take ourselves to value in the way I have suggested by no means confine themselves to those appreciated by some sort of crude sensualist, wallowing in the enjoyment of sensations someone might say we share with brutes and idiots. Rather, as the diversity of experience is unfathomably extensive, so, too, is the range of phenomenal features we value, *and* these features will vary in many ways embodying differences in understanding, intelligence, and talents.

So, to value in this way the phenomenal character of your *visual* experience will likely be to value the distinctive way of perceiving space and color that only one endowed with our species' abilities may enjoy, and also to value ways of seeing one has developed, which other people (not to mention other animals) can be without. You may think here of whatever pleasures, in whatever degree and direction refined, you take in the sight of color, shape, or movement in nature, in the human form, or in artefacts. These may be the sort found in a brief interlude, gazing at clouds out the window, or those had over many days hiking through some stony wooded wilderness. One may find them in attending to the visual detail in a leaf, a hand, or a piece of jewelry, or in surveying some vast spectacle from a rooftop or cliff. The experience may or may not be distinctively *aesthetic*—however that is made out. One may well think here of the visual experience of painting, sculpture, film, or dancing, but also of sports, or of the sight of anything done well or gracefully—seeing the surgeon, the craftsman, or the cook in action. We may also include not just the spectator's visual experience, but that of the agent as well. And without attending to art in even the broadest sense (or perhaps attending only *with* what art teaches us), we can appreciate the expressive nuances revealed every day in how someone's face, gesture, walk, or posture *looks* to us.

Similar remarks may be made regarding each sensory modality. (Think of the kinesthetic enjoyment afforded by a vast range of culturally conditioned activities, from dance to sport to yoga, and think also of hearing music, poetry, or the sound of a friend's voice.) In valuing conscious sense-experience for its own sake, what we value is certainly not limited to crudely differentiated brute sensation; it includes but is not confined to what the aesthete and the gourmet know and seek, so as to encompass all sorts of subtly various experience in which human sensory intelligence is manifest.

It should be said as well: even should you be so rare as to disdain all such attachment to sense-experience as the province of mere lovers of sights and sounds, or bestial slaves to food and sex, you may value the phenomenal character of experience for more than what else it provides. For in the same way that we find ourselves valuing sense-experience for its own sake, we can and no doubt will find ourselves intrinsically valuing conscious *thought*. So, since we have seen that thought has its own intentional-phenomenal character, and consciousness is not a purely sensory phenomenon, even someone unwilling to indulge any but an austere enjoyment of experience found in thinking about logic or mathematics, or in scientific, philosophical, or religious reflection, can discover in the way I have suggested that the possession of phenomenal features is valued not merely for the sake of something else. For again here, as elsewhere, when we ask ourselves whether the phenomenal features we value having, we value only for the sake of the nonphenomenal benefits we think we would lose without them, I believe we will find ourselves inclined to the negative answer that reveals the nature of our attitude.

This last point is addressed not just to those of an ascetic bent. Maybe you quite willingly admit you find sensory experience valuable, or maybe you would be suspicious of an attempt to separate its appreciation entirely from that of thought and understanding (perhaps because there is something ineliminably *aesthetic* involved in the latter). Or maybe "abstract thinking" holds little or no appeal for you. Even so, you can, of course, value for its own sake the possession of phenomenal features involved in thinking. So, if intrinsically valuing the kind of *thought* involved in the appreciation of literary, musical, dramatic, or visual arts is bound up with our also valuing in this way forms of *sense-experience*, or even if we can never extricate our evaluative attitude toward thought entirely from that toward sense-experience, we can find we value for its own sake experience with the phenomenal character of thought. Also, clearly, the thinking we value having in this way need not be anything recondite or learned—the conscious thinking we do in many kinds of everyday speaking, to others and ourselves, can be included. And I take it that practically everyone would rather speak sometimes to someone about something than never to anyone (even oneself!) about anything. Since this will hold true in circumstances where, if we acknowledge the phenomenal character of spoken thought, we will want to say we value this not merely for whatever nonphenomenal benefits we take it to have, virtually all of us can in this way find that we value having the phenomenal features involved in thinking.

These reflections on our sensory and thought experience will, it seems to me, lead us to recognize that, regarding a wide variety of phenomenal features that we have and can have, and that we value having, we believe we do *not* value having them *only* for the sake of the nonphenomenal rewards we take them to occasion. And it seems we should hold that the things we *believe* we value, and what we believe is the character of our reasons for valuing them, coincide with what we *do* indeed value and *how* we do so, *unless we have good evidence to the contrary.* So, since, if we value the phenomenal not solely for the sake of the nonphenomenal, we value the former for its own sake as well, in the absence of that contrary evidence, we should conclude that we do indeed intrinsically value the possession of phenomenal features.

So the next question is: What would be contrary evidence here? What should convince us that, even if we think otherwise, really we value the phenomenal character of our experience only for the nonphenomenal benefits we believe come with having it? It seems what we need to find is some indication that our interest in our phenomenal features would wane if we thought we would receive—even in their absence—these nonphenomenal rewards we ordinarily assume are attached to them. The most powerful indication of this would be that when we actually offered people the choice of *having the relevant nonphenomenal features*—notably, certain verbal, behavioral, and discriminative capacities—while *removing the phenomenal features* they claimed to value having for its own sake, we discovered this:

they always chose this option over the retention of phenomenal features—or else, they at least always were indifferent between it, and the option of retaining the phenomenal features in question. This would show that really they do not care about consciousness, as long as its absence does not require them to forfeit something else for the sake of which they would otherwise value it. But clearly, this is evidence we are not in a position to collect. We cannot actually offer people the option of this sort of *pheno-ectomy*; we cannot offer to turn them into partial or total "zombies," retaining the same manifest nonphenomenal powers they had with conscious experience, while being deprived of this. Even apart from the ethically objectionable nature of performing such an operation on human beings (obviously there would be great risks—and to what end?), there is also the problem that no one now knows how to do it, and it seems highly improbable that there *is* any feasible way of doing it.

Thus it seems that any experiment by which we can gather evidence of this sort against our belief that we value experience for its own sake, will have to be conducted *in thought alone*. Let's try it then. Suppose you thought you faced the choice between (a) continuing on leading the sort of phenomenally conscious life you expect to live, or (b) undergoing a radical pheno-ectomy, which will make you permanently unable to have conscious experience, but will leave you (or your body) in possession of those features, for which sake you ordinarily value possession of phenomenal features: thus the nonphenomenal benefits will be the same on either option. And suppose you set aside any concerns having to do with the risks that the procedure may not work as planned. Then, if you still prefer the retention of at least *some* of them (you think [a]—the consciousness plan—is better than [b]—zombification), you do value having phenomenal features for its own sake. On the other hand, if you find that you would be *indifferent* to (or even *prefer*) the total loss of consciousness, when convinced that this would lose you none of the nonphenomenal benefits you assume would come with consciousness, then you find that you do not value consciousness for its own sake after all. For in that case, it turns out you would just as soon *lose* it, if you thought this would *cost you nothing with respect to the other things* for the sake of which you value it.

Now again, even though we cannot find out what we will do when faced with this choice in reality, we can run the experiment in thought. We can ask ourselves whether, if we *thought* we faced this choice, it would affect our interest in remaining conscious, so as to reveal that we were all along interested in it only for what else we thought we would have only with it, and not for its own sake. However far-fetched the prospect of effectively "zombifying" a human being may be, it seems we can at least conceive of ourselves *believing* we faced this prospect. And if we can do that, then we can look for the proposed sort of evidence that we do not really value being conscious for its own sake, but only *think* we do.

But what do we find? *I* certainly find myself without hesitation opting for the consciousness plan over zombification. And if you are like me in this regard, then you, too, will have failed to find evidence that you do not really intrinsically value conscious experience after all. Now you might refuse to play this game altogether. You might say:

> The suggestion that conscious human beings might be forever deprived of all capacity for phenomenal experience, so that never again did anything look, smell, feel, sound, or taste any way at all to them, so that never again did any conscious thought or feeling occur to them, though still: they continued on, moving and making utterances much as they otherwise would have—that I find so thoroughly incoherent that I literally cannot conceive of so much as *thinking* I faced that prospect. So I cannot say whether or not it would affect the value I accord remaining conscious, if I thought I had such a choice.

But before you dismiss the thought-experiment I am suggesting, take care to notice: it does not require you to believe that such zombification is possible, "metaphysically" or otherwise. All it requires is that you can conceive of someone thinking that zombification is an option. Now do you really believe you cannot do even *that*?

If you believe you cannot, notice also that you will still then say that, like me, you have not turned up a reason to conclude that you only thought you intrinsically valued conscious experience, but really do not. So, if you responded to the earlier questions so as to reveal that you think you value being conscious not merely for the sake of its nonphenomenal concommitants, but for its own sake as well, then you still have more reason to hold that this is indeed how your values stand than you have for holding the contrary.

But further, if you do admit you are able to conceive of thinking you face a choice between (a) and (b) above, and if this leads you to the same verdict as it does me, then not only do you leave quite unscathed such reason as before was found for thinking you intrinsically value consciousness, you add to this a new one. For then, were you to think you would receive the same nonphenomenal rewards as accrue to you with consciousness, but in its absence, you would still think life as a conscious being better. And this by itself gives you reason to say that you do not value phenomenal features only for the sake of nonphenomenal ones. So, when we put this together with the fact that you do value having phenomenal features, we come again to the conclusion that you value having them for its own sake.

Suppose someone resists this argument as follows.

> The reason we fail to find ourselves indifferent as between (a) the consciousness, and (b) the zombification options, is not that we intrinsically value *being conscious*, but rather this: we intrinsically value *our own continued existence*, and we think that, without consciousness, *we* won't exist. Though we suppose that our

zombified bodies will carry on much as we ourselves would have when conscious, we also think that those nonconscious beings with our bodies, whatever they are, are *not us*. Even if what results from my pheno-ectomy is still a person, that person is not me. Thus this thought-experiment shows that I do value being phenomenally conscious for the sake of something else: my own existence.

I myself find plausible the view that phenomenal consciousness is in this way (and perhaps others) essential to personal identity: if I am phenomenally conscious, no future being that completely lacks the capacity for conscious experience is me. However, we can grant that, without spoiling the point that we value experience for its own sake. First, even if I do value having phenomenal features for the reason that I think that, without the capacity to have such features, I will cease to exist (and I prefer continued existence to the alternative), still, it does not follow that I value phenomenal experience *only* for that reason. Second, let me be firmly convinced that my permanent loss of consciousness is a permanent loss of me, regardless of how my zombified body is supposed to carry on. Still, if I can conceive of thinking zombification is an option, I can surely conceive of thinking zombification with personal survival is an option. If I have trouble, all I have to do is to read Unger's (1990) book on consciousness and identity. Then I will see that someone might indeed think that, even though his brain be altered so as to render him permanently without consciousness, he would still exist, if his brain were also still capable of directing behavior so as to keep him moving and uttering in a way manifestly indistinguishable from that in which he otherwise would have. For Peter Unger apparently thinks this. So surely I can ask myself how my evaluative attitudes toward phenomenal consciousness would be affected if I not only thought I faced the choice between consciousness and zombification, but also shared Unger's view of personal identity. And I find again: consciousness wins. It won't do to say that my response to the thought-experiment reveals only a concern with my own continued existence, since, even if I thought *that* held constant between (a) and (b), I would still plump for consciousness. So the reason I go for (a) is not that I think it is the only way I will get to stay around. Thus, once more: not only do I not find here a source of evidence for thinking I do not really intrinsically value having conscious experience, I find just the opposite: a reason to think that I do.

Finally, even without supposing myself persuaded of Ungerian views of personal identity, I can adjust the thought-experiment so as to retain much the same result. For I might suppose that the option (b) offered me, not a *completely*, but only a *partially* zombified future. Suppose, that is, on plan (b) I would lose the capacity for some (but not all) types of phenomenal experience (let's say, for instance, I would lose conscious experience of color), but without loss of the sorts of nonphenomenal features I value having, and for which sake I value having just those types of phenomenal features. Since I would survive such a *selective* pheno-ectomy with the capacity for other kinds of conscious experience intact, there is no worry that option (b) deprives me of a future altogether. Now we might say this. Suppose I thought I faced a choice between (a) conscious life, and (b) one or another such selective pheno-ectomy that left intact the nonphenomenal benefits I would otherwise think I'd receive along with the targeted phenomenal features. If, whenever I suppose I think I faced some such choice, I find no preference for (a) over (b), then it turns out that I do not value having phenomenal features intrinsically. For it turns out I would never care for them, if I thought I would get *without* them the nonphenomenal goods I take to come *with* them. On the other hand, if I find that for at least some such selective pheno-ectomy, I still prefer the consciousness option to the consciousness-deprived option, then this shows that I do value having the relevant phenomenal features for its own sake. For it shows I do not value them merely for the sake of some nonphenomenal payoff.

Now again (assuming you are willing to suppose you think you face the prospect of zombification) I think you will find that such thought-experiments reveal that you value having phenomenal features for its own sake: and this, not just for a few, but for a wide variety of such features. Of course, there may indeed be some such choice before which you would be indifferent—or in which you would even prefer to take the loss of consciousness. For example, suppose you were someone, like our old friend Connie, with an amblyopic crescent of conscious visual experience of what is in your left visual field. You may very well *not* prefer being in *that* state over being someone like Belinda, who had all the nonphenomenal benefits of this experience one would care for, but without the experience. You might even find Connie's sort of experience irritating, and prefer its extinction. But I would be surprised if you did not find many sorts of conscious experience, whose retention you would prefer over their loss in some partial-zombification scenario.

To revert back to our earlier examples: most of us would, I imagine, much prefer that things looked colored to us, rather than always black and white and varying shades of gray, even if we believed we had the option of lacking such phenomenal features, without lacking whatever discriminatory capacities we think go with them. Even if we thought the loss of conscious color vision would leave us with superb blindsight capacities to discriminate colors, we still rather consciously see in color.

Consider also that most of us would not be indifferent to a choice between the option of (a) keeping the capacity for it to seem to us as it does for what we eat to *taste* various ways, and (b) losing such experience—even if we thought we would still have whatever powers of discriminatory response to food and drink we think having experience with this phenomenal character affords us. So, suppose you thought you had the option of being able spontaneously to classify verbally different types of food or drink that met your tongue, without its seeming to you as it does to taste these at all—a kind of gustatory analogue of spontaneous premium-quality blindsight. Though robbed of the phenomenal character of taste-experience (somewhat as when you have a bad head cold, but worse), it would nonetheless just occur to you to say things, as a result of stimulation to your taste receptors, that would constitute rather fine discriminatory judgments. Perhaps, oddly, you think you would, for example, even be capable of telling us the vintage of a wide range of wines splashed on your palate, though there was no difference in the way it seemed to you to taste these, because appropriate stimulus-triggered discriminatory judgments nevertheless would pop into your head. However, even if you thought you would retain such prodigious discriminatory powers while the phenomenal character of taste-experience was lost, you would probably still much rather keep the *seeming* of taste as well.

Similar remarks could be made regarding each of the sensory modalities, or regarding sense-experience in general. You would, I think, be rather unusual, if there were just *no* type of conscious sensory experience, and *no* context in which it is had, where you would rather have the experience than not, even if you thought the nonphenomenal bounty for the sake of which you value the experience available without it. Probably few of us would generally rather be without phenomenally conscious sense-experience during sexual encounters, even if we thought without it we would still "perform" just as well.

And as before, you can arrive at similar results even if (improbably) you are either evaluatively neutral or hostile to the charms of the senses. For in that case, you may consider the value you accord conscious thought. Suppose you like thinking about mathematics. Would it suit you just as well (or even better) if you always got the same valuable results as you get from conscious mathematical thinking, but *without* the conscious thinking? Is it all the same to you if you always acquire the ability to produce a proof or the solution to a problem so as to write this out, and actually express these conclusions, *only while totally devoid of conscious thought*? I imagine no one who likes mathematics would be just as satisfied doing it only while in some zombie-ish state, any more than one who likes sex would just as soon have a zombified sex life. As for other kinds of reflection someone might value while professing to find no intrinsic value in *sensory* experience—I will only remark that as frustrating as philosophy (for instance) can be, and however mixed a pleasure it may be for some of us (even if it was otherwise for Plato), surely no one it has captured would just as soon speak or write about it only while lacking phenomenally conscious thought altogether.

But also (as before), this sort of point about the intrinsic value accorded conscious thought needn't be addressed only to those with a disregard for the value of sensory experience, nor need it be made just with reference to modes of thought seemingly far removed from sensory experience. *Whatever* you enjoy talking and thinking about, ask yourself: would you still rather have the experience of thinking of such matters, with the phenomenal character that this has, rather than lack it, if you thought that would cost you nothing in the way of nonphenomenal goods? Most of us enjoy talking or writing, with others or in solitude—even if we vary widely in what we like to talk about and how. And we would, I am confident, often much prefer to have the conscious experience involved here, sensory and otherwise, than not, even if we thought we had the option of receiving its nonphenomenal rewards without it. We might actually prefer to have a job interview, or give court testimony, while temporarily bereft of consciousness, if we thought this could be successfully done. But we *typically* would prefer not to be totally devoid of conscious thought and perception while speaking, even if we thought we would be capable, while totally nonconscious, of somehow responding so as to appear to hold up our end of the conversation as well as we ever do. If your life makes you want to say otherwise, all I can say is: that is very sad.

Let's review the argument. What it is to be phenomenally conscious, and whether or not we are, is no longer in question here—the issue is, given that we are conscious, in what way do we see this as good? I think you will say, upon considering cases, that you value having phenomenal features, but not solely for the sake of some occurrence of nonphenomenal features. If you do, then, I have argued, you should agree: you value having phenomenal features for its own sake. And if you think this is so, then in the absence of compelling evidence to the contrary, you are warranted in thinking it is so. What would give you evidence? This: you find you would never prefer to have rather than to lack phenomenal features, if you thought either way you will receive the nonphenomenal rewards for the sake of which you value experience. But either you will find you are simply unable to conceive of yourself so much as thinking such a choice lay before you—in which case you do *not* find evidence against your belief that you intrinsically value experience—or else, you can suppose you thought you faced such a choice—in which case not only do you fail to find evidence *against* your belief, you find more evidence in its *favor*. For then you find you would prefer to have phenomenal features, even if it made no difference with regards to some nonphenomenal payoff.

Now, I do not see any other way we might look for a reason to think we do not really intrinsically value experience, but only think we do. For where are we to look for evidence of our values, if not in our sincere avowals about them, and in our response to real or hypothetical choices? Thus I conclude that we do indeed value having experience for its own sake. And we have found a way of making this evident to ourselves that does not depend on our regarding as settled the question of the *efficacy* of consciousness—the question of whether or not our possession of phenomenal features accounts for what else happens in the world.

Notice I started off (at the beginning of this section) talking about our valuing the possession of phenomenal features generally—both our own *and others'*. But I then framed the argument just in terms of questions concerning the value one accords *one's own* experience. This was partly because I assumed we would all be egoistic enough that, if we would recognize intrinsically valuing experience in *any* case, we would most readily recognize it in our own. But now it is time to acknowledge as well that none of us is likely to be *so* egoistic that we do not value other people's experience in much the same way. The process of reflection we carried out by considering what we take to be our evaluative attitudes toward our own experience, can be reapplied, with consideration of our attitudes toward *other people's* possession of phenomenal features. The details of this I leave to you, but I would be surprised if there is no one of whom you could truthfully say: "I think it's better that he or she have some phenomenal features than not—and not only for the reason that this would affect the occurrence of nonphenomenal features I value." And I would be surprised if, no matter who other than yourself you considered, you never found you preferred their remaining with some phenomenal features over their undergoing pheno-ectomy, if you thought this would not disturb nonphenomenal features whose occurrence you would rather see than not. We intrinsically value *others'* possession of phenomenally rich sensory and cognitive lives as well—not only our own.

9.3 The Importance of Being Conscious

Imagine that to all this someone said:

> Yes, phenomenal features are fun and very nice for all of us to have, no doubt. And maybe as a matter of biological fact, we can't do very much in their absence. But it's still not clear *how much* we value them, beyond our valuing what else we think goes with them. Perhaps, in addition to whatever derivative value they have, they have for us only something like the value of an ornament, decoration, or frill—a nice extra.

Probably no one would seriously propose that the intrinsic value of consciousness is no more important to us than this suggests. Again imagine you thought you faced a choice between consciousness, and its total loss. I am assuming you would prefer consciousness. But how much—only a little? Surely if you want a future at all, you are not anywhere close to being indifferent between a conscious one, and one devoid of experience. To say you think the first "much better" undoubtedly will seem an understatement.

But is it necessary to your having a strong preference, that you value the possession of consciousness for its own sake? Or is it only because of nonphenomenal features you would lose that you have a preference this strong? Perhaps this isn't clear. We may say here, somewhat as before, we find at least that we *believe* that we value having conscious experience *to an enormous extent*, and that it is partly for the reason that we intrinsically value having it that we value it so much. And, in lieu of a reason to think otherwise, it is right for us to believe this. Also, somewhat as before, we can look for a reason to think otherwise in a consideration of hypothetical options. Again, I think not only will we find no reason to doubt our initial belief—we will find reason to support it.

So, suppose you thought you would survive a radical pheno-ectomy without loss of the nonphenomenal features, for whose sake you value being conscious. If the enormity of your preference for retaining consciousness were due solely to the value you accorded the nonphenomenal features for the sake of which you value consciousness, then, if faced with this option of having the nonphenomenal without consciousness, your preference for consciousness would no longer be enormous. But would thinking you had this option remove your enormous preference for a *conscious* future? I would say it would not remove mine. So then not only do I fail to find that I think the enormity of my preference for consciousness is due solely to my thinking its loss would involve a loss of valuable nonphenomenal goods, I find instead that I think it is *not* due solely to this. Then I think it is *also* due partly to the loss of phenomenal goods involved. And if I think this is an additional reason, then I am committed to thinking: I enormously prefer consciousness to its lack, partly for the reason that I value having it for its own sake.

Now, I believe you will also fail to find evidence here that the enormity of your preference is due solely to your valuing experience for the sake of something else. For either you will not think you can play this game at all, or else you will think you can, and find, like me, that your preference for the consciousness option is still an enormous one, even if you think the nonphenomenal benefits of consciousness otherwise available. And in that case, you will also find the enormity of your preference for consciousness is due partly to your valuing its possession intrinsically.

But it is a little unsatisfying to say only that the extent to which we value being conscious, on account of our valuing it intrinsically, is enormous. Perhaps we can get some measure of just how considerable this sort of preference for consciousness is, if we reflect on this. Most of us would, I imagine, think that, in a certain sense, an unconscious life is hardly worth living. That is, at least this is true: I think that the only life available to me that is much worth living—that is more than a little preferable to not living at all—is a conscious one, and I expect you are also likely to think that the only life available to you that is worth living is a conscious one. But we may ask: is that only because we think that the only nonconscious lives available to us would be remarkably deprived of nonphenomenal features whose possession we value? I do not regard a nonconscious future as much better (really I regard it as worse) than no future, because I think if I were permanently nonconscious I would be forever in a comatose or vegetative state—and I would just as soon be dead as that. But will I say that this assumption is my *sole* reason for thinking the nonconscious life is not worth living? I would say (and I suppose you will want to say if you have come this far with me): "That I'd rather not be reduced to a state of vegetative torpor is not the only reason. Another is this: I value being conscious for its own sake, and the unconscious life would be completely lacking what I value in this way."

Are we mistaken to say this? What would show we were? Presumably we do think the nonconscious lives available to us are horribly deprived of non-phenomenal features we value having, and for the sake of which we value being conscious. And presumably it is partly for this reason that we think a nonconscious existence is hardly better than death. Suppose then we broaden the range of nonconscious lives we think available to us to include zombified ones. Suppose, that is, we thought that among the lives available to us are nonconscious lives in which we are able to keep the nonphenome-nal features for the sake of which we value consciousness. Would every such enlargement of the range of lives available to us destroy our conviction that the only available life we would much care to have is a conscious one? If so, then this would appear to show we have this conviction solely for the reason that we think the only nonconscious lives available to us are ones deprived of valuable nonphenomenal features. Roughly: give us a zombie life as non-phenomenally good as the conscious one we expect, and, other things being equal, we would always strongly prefer it to no life at all.

But is this true? Suppose you thought you had the following choice:

(a) You will live as a conscious being, more or less as you ordinarily expect or hope to do; or

(b) You will undergo a radical pheno-ectomy, and become zombified, but not lose the valued nonphenomenal features of (a); or

(c) Your body will be destroyed, and replaced by a duplicate of that which would have resulted from a choice of (b)—an exact twin or doppelganger of the zombified you in (b), which is never to be activated, unless your body is destroyed.

So the options now are much the same as in the previous thought-experi-ment, except that we have added (c). If you think consciousness is not essen-tial to your survival, then you will think you survive (b), but I will ask you to assume (very plausibly) that whether or not you think this, (c) will mean your demise. For I am asking you to suppose you think that this zombie double (kept dormant unless your body is completely destroyed), which comes into being through some fanciful biotechnology at the time of your existence, is not you. And I am asking you thus to suppose you think that *its* remaining in existence in (c), is not *your* remaining in existence.

Now, if I thought I had these choices, viewed in this way, I would enormously prefer (a) (consciousness) to either (b) (zombification) or (c) (zombified replacement), whereas I really would not see much to choose between those latter two options. I would have no strong preference for either (b) or (c) over the other. If, in mulling over these choices, you come to a similar result, notice now that, while here you think a nonconscious life is available to you with all the nonphenomenal benefits you are interested in, still you think the *only* available life much worth living is a conscious one. Thus, it is not true then that if you think you have the option of a zombie life nonphenomenally as good as the conscious one you anticipate, you would always strongly prefer it to no life at all.[3] So: first, you do not find evidence for believing that, contrary to initial conviction, the only reason you think life without consciousness hardly worth living is that you think that the only lives available to you without phenomenal features are also poor in other ones. But second, you now have additional warrant for your initial conviction. Your evaluative response to the imagined situation seems to show that you regard life without consciousness as hardly worth living, but not solely because you think that the only available nonconscious lives are poor in valuable nonphenomenal features. For your belief that the only available life much worth living is conscious persists, even in a situation where you think a nonconscious life is available that is rich in the relevant nonphenomenal features. So you think life without consciousness is hardly worth having, but not solely because it is poor in *nonphenomenal* rewards. But then, it is also at least partly because you think the available nonconscious lives are poor in *phenomenal* goods that you view them as little or no better than death. So, you think available nonconscious lives are hardly worth having, partly because you value being conscious, but not just for the nonphenomenal benefits this provides. Thus it is partly for the reason that you value having phenomenal features for its own sake that you think the only available life you would much care to have is a conscious one.

Once we take stock of this, we can see that our possession of phenomenal features is clearly of no small importance to us. For we have found that:

- We value having phenomenal features for its own sake.
- It is partly for this reason that we value having them to an *enormous* extent.
- And, it is partly for this same reason that we consider life without consciousness to be little or no better than death.

Thus we have found that phenomenal consciousness is very important to us indeed, and at least partly on account of our intrinsically valuing its possession. But again I have slipped into urging us to address these reflections only to the first-person case. What happens if we try to cover the same territory, asking how much we intrinsically value the experience of other people?

First, I think it is clear that virtually all of us will find we would say of at least some other people that we would view the prospect of their losing consciousness forever, not just a *little* worse than that of their having a normal conscious life, but *enormously* so. And we would say this is not just because of a loss of nonphenomenal goods for the sake of which we want them to be conscious, but because we value their being conscious for its own sake. This is not cast into doubt, but only confirmed by imagining we think they have available to them a zombified future. For I presume that you would think it was not just a *little*, but a *lot* worse for your friends to undergo a radical pheno-ectomy than to continue on having conscious experience, even if you thought that this operation would leave them with all the nonphenomenal goods for whose sake you wanted them to be conscious. The prospect of your friend's becoming a zombie, with no conscious thoughts, feelings, perceptions, is a horrifying one.

But what do we say when we come to the next step and ask whether we think it is little or no better for them to live as nonconscious beings, than for them not to live at all? We will probably want to say this: that we think that a conscious life is the only life *available* to them that is much worth living. But then again, we face this issue. We assume that the only nonconscious life available to them would be some kind of completely inactive vegetative existence. Is it then only for this reason that we would view the nonconscious life available to them as little or no better than their death? When we try to perform here for others a reflection analogous to that we engaged in a little while ago about ourselves, we come to a complication. For what we ask is this. Do we still think the conscious life is the only one available appreciably better than none, when we consider the choice among:

(a) Others' having the conscious life we expect and hope them to have;

(b) Their having a zombified existence with all the nonphenomenal benefits of (a); and

(c) Their being destroyed and replaced by zombie twins?

Well, if, as above, we describe the situation so as to imply that what emerges from the zombification procedure in (b) is a *person*—as indeed the *same person* as that being who was conscious prior to undergoing the pheno-ectomy—then it seems we should say this. Since that entity would be a person, and since persons are in a sense *strongly irreplaceable*, it is not right to say that (b) is little or no better than (c). For on (c), a certain person is destroyed, and replaced by a duplicate. But on (b), that is not the case. However, it is a extremely bad thing for this to befall persons (I think so anyway). That is the sense in which persons are not to be viewed as replaceable objects. There seems to be a certain asymmetry here then. For when I contemplate *my own* future, the assumption that my zombified body would still be me, and would therefore still be the body of a person, did not keep me from saying that it would be no worse for it (for me) to be destroyed and replaced by a double, than for it (me) to continue on its (my) way.

Thus, as long as we put in place the assumption that a person, post-zombification, does not cease to exist, it seems we cannot come to the conclusion about others that we came to about ourselves: that it is partly for the reason that we instrinsically value others' possession of phenomenal features that we think their living without consciousness little or no better than their not living at all. We will say that their loss of consciousness is a great loss, and say this partly because we intrinsically value their having it, but we may *also* say that it is only because we value this for the sake of something nonphenomenal, that we view their living without consciousness as no better than their death.

But then we may wonder what happens if we do *not* presuppose that zombies are persons. Suppose we describe option (b) in a way that leaves open the issue of whether or not they are: we say simply that on this option, a person's body undergoes a pheno-ectomy, and emerges as the body of a zombie. Then we compare how we rate this situation relative to (c), one in which *that* being is destroyed and replaced by another such zombie, twin of the first. Is there much evaluative difference? I have to say that I do not see that there is. That is, when I suppose that the person's body has really been permanently zombified, it does not seem much worse to me that this is destroyed and replaced by another such zombie body, than that no such switch takes place. On the other hand, if I think the contrast is between, on the one hand, some conscious human being living into the next day, and, on the other, her being annihilated and replaced by a duplicate (either zombified or conscious), there is no question as to which is the worse state of affairs. The first is fine, the second ghastly.

If, when looked at this way, you find your own evaluative responses to these contrasting scenarios similar, and, like me, you view persons as irreplaceable in the way I mentioned, then we have some evidence that we do not think of zombies as persons—that we regard phenomenal consciousness as essential to personhood. This belief is controversial, even among those who would accept the reality of phenomenal consciousness. The relation between consciousness and personhood clearly requires a searching examination; now is not the time. So I will confine myself to this. On reflection, we are likely to discover that we value others' possession of phenomenal features enormously, and for its own sake. This case parallels the immense importance we accord our own possession of consciousness, except in this. Whereas we consider that it is little or no better for us to live without consciousness than to die, partly because we intrinsically value being conscious, and while we also think it little or no better for others to live without consciousness than to die, it is not so clear that we hold this last belief partly for the reason that we intrinsically value others' experience. Whether we do or not, is likely to hinge on whether or not we assume that consciousness is essential to personhood. The most I would claim here, is that our response to these scenarios can reveal—it does in my case—the belief that to think of a being as completely lacking the capacity for phenomenal consciousness is to think of that being as no person at all: without consciousness, no one—no *person*—is there.

9.4 SHOULD WE CARE SO MUCH ABOUT CONSCIOUSNESS?

We have found, in any case, that the possession of phenomenal consciousness—both our own and other people's—is of enormous importance to us, and this, partly because we intrinsically value it. But someone might here point out that all this shows is that this is how our values stand, not that this is how they *should* stand. What could we say to someone who said we were mistaken to value being conscious in this way, someone who said that having experience is just not intrinsically valuable, or at least not to that extent?

I honestly do not know how to try to persuade by argument people who really did not already value being conscious for its own sake that they should start doing so. Nor do I know how to attempt to argue them into valuing others' experience, if they really do not care about this, except insofar as it impinges on other aspects of reality they value. Perhaps that is because we cannot teach others to value something intrinsically, by giving them reasons to do so—we can only help them to have the sort of experience that will enable them to find it instrinsically valuable. But if we do already find being conscious intrinsically valuable, we can say this in our defense. We do value this enormously, and have no good reason *not* to do so.

I say I have no good reason *not* to care about consciousness as much as I do, because the reasons I can think of for supposing I have overrated consciousness just do not seem to me good ones. For example, someone might think that phenomenal consciousness is not very important because it is not strictly essential to doing the jobs we believe it to do. That is, they might think that the coordination of behavior and information-processing that we may be inclined to think depend on conscious perception and thought, can be adequately accounted for without these, and for this reason, consciousness is not valuable or important. But first, it is unclear that human brains *can* do much worthwhile without conscious experience—indeed, it seems unlikely that they can—and hence it is unclear that we should not think phenomenal experience belongs in an adequate account of how we are able to speak, solve problems, and act on perception. And second, the claim that it does not belong in such an account simply does not entail that experience is not enormously valuable for its own sake.

If someone then says that the phenomenal character of experience cannot be so valuable, since it has to do with mere sensation, raw feels, etc., and is not related to the really valuable, more *human* cognitive features, we will say that the premise is false. Differences in the phenomenal character of our experience are not merely differences in raw feels (whatever those are), but are differences in intentional features that reflect many different sorts of cognitive ability, including those we may tend to think of as distinctively human. And so we should be critical of any suggestion that we have overinflated the value of consciousness since it is something too rudimentary to matter so much. For example, it will be at best misleading to say (as does White [1987]) that it is not *consciousness* that is so important to the special value we place on persons' lives, but rather *self-consciousness*. For we have seen that we value the possession of conscious experience for its own sake so much that existence without it is little or no better than death—and this will be so even if an existence without it could, in some sense we decide upon, possess "self-consciousness." So, then, instead of saying it is not consciousness, but self-consciousness, that matters, we should say: even if an unself-conscious life has little intrinsic value, our possession of self-consciousness is of much intrinsic value to us, only if it involves phenomenal consciousness.

Someone might think it pertinent to urge here that there could be persons, and thus beings deserving high moral consideration, that had no phenomenal features: "Zombies are people, too." But first, I should say, I do not believe that zombies would be persons, and I do not think I have any good reason to do so.[4] But in any case, believing in the personhood of zombies is not incompatible with believing that the difference between being conscious and not being conscious is an enormously intrinsically important one. You might think that zombification would not destroy personhood, or the moral status that goes with it, but still believe that, for you or your friends, it would be tremendously worse to become a zombie than to stay conscious.

Further, we needn't worry that by placing a high intrinsic value on experience, we manifest some excessively egocentric focus. There is nothing essentially selfish about valuing the possession of experience for its own sake. We can and do value not only our own experience in this way, but also that of others. To my mind, the real difficulty is not with making sense of how valuing experience can be reconciled with a concern and respect for other persons, but rather with how we are to make sense of that, if we do not think of people as having phenomenal lives at all. (If what demands our respect and concern is not partly the character of other persons' experience, then what is it? If we could clarify some notion of "autonomy" that applied equally well to conscious beings and zombies, it is a further question whether it would be a kind of autonomy that would entitle its possessor to the sort of regard conscious beings deserve.)

Now, once we recognize that we value our experience in this way, and to this extent, we may want to raise questions about just what kinds of experience we value *more* than others, and why. Clearly we consider some kinds of phenomenal lives better than others, most obviously because we would rather have enjoyable than painful ones. But it is not *just* because of that, for we will likely recognize some kinds of phenomenal histories as better and some as worse than others, even if we cannot say that the better ones are in every case more *enjoyable* and the worse more *painful*. A life whose phenomenal aspect is filled with violent, sentimental, or degrading fantasies, and vindictive, unsympathetic, incurious, and self-indulgent thoughts, and in which sensory experience is relatively unformed by the discovery of beauty, or by any but acquisitive desires, will be, other things held equal, a poorer sort of life than one with the opposite traits, and in which the phenomenal character of thought, imagination, and perception manifests affection, passion, and respect for what they reveal. And this is so, I believe, regardless of whether we can say those who live the former sort of life enjoy the relevant experiences less, or have less pleasant and more painful experiences than those who lead lives of the latter sort. However, I have been interested now not in trying to explain or justify such an evaluation of lives and experience, but in the prior task of showing that some sort of phenomenal experience is extremely important to us, and not only in some derivative way.

You may want to complain that this is obvious. Who would deny that they care about whether they have experiences, and what sort they have? I admit that those who acknowledge the phenomenal will often need little encouragement to say that it is important to them. As for those who would not acknowledge it, they would, I imagine, say something like this:

> We enjoy our experiences every bit as much as you do. It's just that we have a rather different idea of what an experience is. You think it involves this "phenomenal character" business, and we don't; we think experience is just a matter of being able to make spontaneous discriminatory judgments (or of encoding maplike representations poised to affect our beliefs, or whatever). But of course we'd also rather see colors, feel caresses, and so on, than not. That is, we'd rather be able to make certain kinds of discriminatory judgments spontaneously (or possess detailed maplike representations, etc.) than not.

However, I am not trying to show that people who would deny they are phenomenally conscious do not enjoy experience. (Though I do have a little trouble imagining that all they enjoy about having [say, sexual] experience is the fact that it represents matrically in great detail, or affords them spontaneous judgments about stimuli.) Of course, they do *have* and *enjoy* conscious experience; I cannot for a moment seriously think otherwise. But the intellect can hide as well as reveal what is valuable about experience. My aim here is to try to make it clear what is valuable about it (its phenomenal character), and in what way we value it (intrinsically). I do this because I think that understanding better what we value and how we value it helps us to *appreciate* its value, as we would not if we did not reflect upon it, or if such reflection only tended to disguise it from us. And such appreciation is itself also valuable.

Finally, discussing the value of phenomenal consciousness openly and in detail helps us to make explicit something we may lose sight of, or only dimly recognize: why disputes over the nature of consciousness are not trivial, however arcane they may appear as we pursue their details. To those of us who accept the reality of phenomenal consciousness as I have described it, what we accept and others deny or neglect will be something we intrinsically value to an enormous extent, something essential to the value we find in our own lives. We should make it clear that consciousness is not something we "posit," out of a desperate need to shore up a sense of our own "specialness," but something we find, whose immense importance to us we then recognize. We resist "theories of consciousness" without consciousness not out of some kind of sentimentality, nor because we shrink at the cold fingers of science on our souls, nor because we imagine our lives will be meaningless unless we hallow some piece of them with the label, "An Unsolvable Mystery." To explain precisely and systematically what gives us phenomenally conscious experience in all its variety would be an excellent thing; should this be interminably elusive, we will have no cause to celebrate. But efforts to show phenomenal consciousness to be some kind of fiction or disposable cultural artefact, or to paint official portraits of ourselves or our minds from which it has been thoroughly excluded, would intellectually rob us of what makes our lives worthwhile, and its appreciation.

Maybe that last remark will only strengthen an impulse to disregard phenomenal consciousness, if one presumes that any grand picture "threatening cherished values" must portend some exciting revelation. "Didn't many great theoretical triumphs threaten belief in what people took to be essential to the importance of their lives? Think of Copernicus, Galileo, and Darwin, and other intellectual pathbreakers. If our denial of phenomenal consciousness seems to some morally offensive, we must be on the right team!"

Perhaps such thoughts are seldom put so baldly, but I suspect they exert some influence nonetheless. If they do, it is curious how, in intellectual matters, as in fashion and music, the fear of nonconformity (we mustn't be on the wrong team!) and the thrill of heresy (sacred idols have been shattered!) can be so effectively bound in a single appeal. Such ways of thinking hint at the view that if our sense of the importance of our lives seems somehow anchored in consciousness, then it is probably illusory and deserves to disappear from our self-conception. That is the sort of suggestion we will probably be able to take seriously only so long as it remains an inexplicit, unexamined insinuation. And, from my point of view anyway, what makes the content of modern cosmology, physics, and biology appear morally threatening is not, as is sometimes thought, how it humbles human pride. (Do you really imagine, for instance, that your sense of the importance of your life depends on the position of our planet in relation to other heavenly bodies, or on how impressive your remote ancestors were? Would it really make any difference to the importance you attach to your own or others' lives if our planet were literally at the center of the universe? Would you feel better about yourself if you thought we were actually much *weaker* and *dumber* than our distant forebears?) What I think has been most truly—though generally indirectly—threatened, morally speaking, by the progress of the sciences in the modern age is not our pride (which is generally pretty resilient) so much as our confidence that we can determine what matters in our lives on the authority of some other person, or some institution. But what I want to protect and promote is not *that*, but only (on the contrary)—*the recognition for ourselves of what we value.* In any case, I hope we can face the issues I have raised without simply being blown around by winds of doctrine, or selling ourselves to the zeitgeist, whatever we take that to be.

9.5 But Must We Talk about It?

Now, some might admit that consciousness is valuable not only for what it provides, but also for much more than that, yet still want to keep intellectually aloof from it. They may admit that consciousness does matter to them a great deal, but perhaps, made nervous by the difficulty of talking about consciousness, and the obscurely ornate and perennially unresolved controversies in which it is caught, they would still prefer not to have to say much about it, at least not when cooking up philosophical or psychological theories about thought, language, and perception. Perhaps even if we do care about consciousness as *persons*, we needn't care about it as *theoreticians of the mind*. For, it will be said, we are—whatever else we are—"cognitive systems" of a certain sort; "our brains encode mental representations." But, it will be added, phenomenal consciousness is not essential to being a cognitive system, or to storing and processing mental representations. Consciousness is, then, on a certain understanding, not essential to mind, and so, when making theories about mental representations—what they are, and how they are produced—we can simply ignore all this funny business about phenomenal character.

I am not going to try to address the issue of whether consciousness *is* essential to mind, or to anything that engages in "cognition" or "mental representation." To do that, I would need to assess ways of trying to explain mental representation that make consciousness inessential to it, in the light of some reasoned view about just what would count as success in saying what the difference is between what has mind, and what merely in some ways behaves *as if* it does. I am not presently able to address this issue to my satisfaction.

However, this may matter less than it seems. For I think that even without embracing some thesis that consciousness is essential to mind, we can see that theorizing about the mind cannot so safely ignore phenomenal intentionality. Though it is not obvious just what we should demand of philosophical and psychological accounts of mind, I assume there is some sense in which we want them to be accounts of perception, imagery, and linguistically expressed thought. Now, even if there is nonconscious mental representation of these sorts, this is not the only kind *we* have. And presumably we would like our theories to account for the kinds we have, and at the very least, they should not be incompatible with affirming that we have the kinds we do. But if we explain in our theories only a form of "mental representation" that is not the phenomenal intentionality we have, then we do not fully account for forms of perception, imagery, and thought that we do actually possess. And if the forms of perception, imagery, and thought attributed to the objects of our theories are not such as we can reasonably maintain belong to those to whom it seems to perceive, image, and think as it does to us, then these theories—however intellectually impressive—fail in a crucial respect: they are not about us.

This is not somehow because its seeming to us the way it does constitutes some infallible inner appearing of mental activity—thought, imagery, and perception; for this is not to be construed as an inner appearance at all, fallible or otherwise. Rather, it is because how it seems to us is at least a considerable part of such activity. Whether we should also speak of nonconscious mental activity, what this means, and whether we should hold that there is somehow much *more* nonconscious mentation or cognition than conscious, I will not now try to say. But I do say that how it seems to us is at least an important, various, and extensive part of our mental activity. Thus, if our philosophical and psychological theories make no place for our phenomenal features, that is a serious failing in these theories.

I will not try to address now the question of just what would make for successful theoretical explanations of our having experience with the phenomenal character ours has. And I won't try to determine whether this or that current philosophical and psychological theory describes perception and thought in ways compatible with our recognition of this character— whether they are, as we might put it, *phenomenologically adequate*. For now, I just want to say that we have no excuse for evading a responsibility to make our theories faithful to the phenomenal character of our experience, should we, for some reason, find this evasion tempting.

9.6 CONCLUSION

I have not come close to exploring fully the question of the importance of consciousness. A more extensive discussion of this issue would require us to take up many large topics not quickly or simply treated, some of which I have already mentioned, such as the explanatory relevance of consciousness, what makes some sorts of experience more valuable to us than others, how consciousness relates to a distinction between genuine and merely as-if mentalness, and how it is involved in what makes one a person. Looking into these issues not only would land us in the middle of a lot of hard questions about cause, value, and identity, but also would require us to go over more thoroughly the territory covered in talking about thought and perception, and to try to say how this or other conscious experience relates to action, intention, emotion, desire, and decision. And finally, entwined with all this are still-lingering questions about the nature of self-knowledge. For though we have by example and contrast identified a distinctive first-person knowledge of our attitudes and experience and gone on to make use of it, I still have not tried to elaborate or defend a positive account of the conditions under which we have such knowledge, even if I have at times revealed certain views about this issue.

Someone might react to this by complaining that I have left the important questions untreated. But I do not think this would be fair. For however sincere our efforts with regard to these questions, and however striking and bold the answers offered, they will be sorely lacking, or even undermined entirely, if we do not come to terms with the issues I have discussed in the preceding pages. If phenomenal consciousness is denied or neglected in favor of something else one labels 'consciousness,' if it is not distinguished as it should be from capacities for discriminatory response, or self-representation, or if it is wrongly consigned to some category of raw feels or sensations and stripped of significance, then we will not be able to make progress with the questions about consciousness and explanation, identity, value, and knowledge that I have left for the future. For we will then start so mired in confusion about consciousness, and so prone to neglect it, that we will misconstrue the questions, or accept poor reasons for answering them in ways disdainful of the phenomena.

On the view presented here, we will address such questions fruitfully, only if we approach them with roughly the following conception in hand. Consciousness is a feature that we know with a distinctively first-person warrant to be shared by episodes of sense-experience (in its various modalities) and thought (silent or noisy, iconic or otherwise). Conscious visual experience of a certain kind is not just a certain discriminatory capacity regarding visual stimuli, nor more generally can it be rightly identified with some disposition to have other manifest features—those of a sort we can with warrant be judged to have without observation beneath our surfaces. This reveals that certain functionalist conceptions of mind embody a neglect of consciousness, to be found also in views (whether professedly "functionalist" or not) that fail to distinguish consciousness from self-representation, or from the access of information to one's capacities to verbalize it or use it to control or plan behavior. These distinctions become clear through considering hypothetical forms of responsiveness in thought and behavior to visual stimuli without conscious visual experience—forms of blindsight.

What would be missing in such blindsight cases is its seeming a certain way to one—for example, the way it seems for it to look to you as if there is something blue or X-shaped. More generally, for a person to be conscious—phenomenally conscious—is for there to be, in this sense, some way it seems to him or her. For it to seem various ways to you, is for you to have conscious experience—episodes of consciousness—of varying phenomenal character; it is for you to have various phenomenal features; and for experiences to vary in phenomenal character is for them to vary in ways only conscious experiences can.

The phenomenal features we have when we perceive, image, and think are not "mere sensations," but are themselves intentional features, abundant and subtly differentiated. And while it seems likely we would be able to engage in rather little intelligent behavior without consciousness, we value phenomenal features for more than what we think they enable us to do; and our valuing them in this way is enormously important for our attitude toward our own lives, and toward other people. Finally, an adequate philosophical or psychological theory of human thought and perception needs to account for, and not conflict with, how it seems to us to think and perceive—our having the phenomenal intentional features we have.

Some may have been inclined from the beginning to grant this picture more or less, and press on to other questions. But I hope by now it is clear that trying to articulate and defend a stance on the points of contention that have arisen is no simple matter, and that formidable minds of great ingenuity and influence have offered views deeply at odds with the picture just sketched. The challenge this presents should not go ignored if we wish to understand consciousness.

I started this inquiry by proposing and defending a first-person approach to it. I have not tried to argue that such an approach is indispensable to understanding consciousness—though maybe that is true—but only that it is available, and that the results it provides deserve to be reckoned with. One may find the attempt to philosophize through reliance on first-person reflection uncongenial; I admit it has its frustrations. But I think we stand to lose more if we shun it out of some sense that firmer ground for dealing with these matters lies elsewhere. If the ground elsewhere does seem firmer, I think it will be only because one loses touch with the issue when standing there, not because one has found a better place from which to deal with it. That is, I think that the difficulties in talking and reasoning about consciousness we find when we engage in the kind of thinking I have tried to promote do not stem merely from adopting this approach; they are inherent in the topic, and if we flee them, we flee it. But we need not turn away from them; I believe we can face these with some success, if while we bring to bear as much dialectical skill and knowledge of relevant research as we can, we cultivate a patient, reflective appreciation of our own experience, reliant on a distinctive self-knowledge.

CHAPTER 1

1. Some Wittgensteinians (see Hacker 1987) will want to quarrel with my taking all of these as examples of occurrences, and calling them "experiences." But just what is at issue here, and where one wants to come down on this issue, will, I hope, become clearer as discussion proceeds. If you agree with me that such episodes of consciousness as I describe from Chapter 3 on do occur, then you will grant me all that I wish in regard to the occurrence of experience.

I might add that when I talk about experience, I do not take this to commit me to any particular metaphysical doctrine about the identity and boundaries of an occurrence of experience. For example, in employing this term I leave it open whether experience is in every case, in some sense, an internal event, and whether we are to say it occurs "in the mind" (or "subject," or "soul," or "self"), as opposed to taking place "outside," "in the world."

2. This depends on how you think the "essentially indexical" character of the first-person belief affects the identity of the belief (see Perry 1977, 1979).

3. Although Descartes does not, I believe, ever explicitly define 'consciousness' as a perception of one's thoughts, he speaks of one's being "conscious of" one's thoughts (or, in other translations, being "aware of" one's thoughts) and of one's "perceiving" them, apparently interchangeably, and seems not to have distinguished between simply having conscious visual experience, on the one hand, and being aware that, or thinking that, one sees, on the other. For a discussion of this point, see Williams 1978, 225ff., 286–87.

4. Descartes (1641) in the Second Meditation: "If I look out of the window and see men crossing the square, as I just happen to have done, I normally say that I see the men themselves. . . . Yet do I see any more than hats and coats which could conceal automatons? I *judge* that they are men." Descartes thinks ultimately that this judgment that these are men (that is, beings with human souls) and not automatons is warranted, but what does he think makes it so? His remarks at the end of Part 5 of the *Discourse* (1637) appear to indicate he thinks that what makes it right for one to regard another human (but not a beast) as ensouled, is that his or her verbal utterances cannot be adequately explained by any physical means, but only as soul-caused. By contrast, we have reason to conclude that beasts probably do not have souls, because their movements can be explained otherwise than by attributing souls to them. A basic assumption here, it seems to me, is that third-person psychological belief is warranted only if it can be justified entirely on the grounds that it provides the best theory of dementalized bodily movements. One should note that this Cartesian view can be distinguished from the more modest assumption that possession of third-person warrant requires that third-person belief somehow depend—via perception—on nonintentional features of persons perceived. We should not be too quick to assume we know the best way to conceptualize this sort of dependence. It is not obvious that we have to suppose that when one perceives other people in everyday life, and forms beliefs about their intentionality, one first perceives the actions of others as mere movements, and then at some later stage in a psychological "process" hypothesizes, or makes some inference to, an explanation of these in intentional

terms. Nor is it clear we must be able to offer a rational reconstruction of some such process, if our belief about others are to count as warranted.

5. For some different (and more elaborate) ways of mapping this territory, with somewhat different use of terminology, see Williams 1978, app. 1; and Alston 1971.

6. See Don Locke 1968, 9–10, 34–36). Although Locke thinks one actually knows only one's own "bodily sensations" (but not one's own thoughts) by perceiving (i.e., feeling) them, he speculates that one could, by being hooked up to another's nervous system, feel, and know by feeling, another's sensations (though this, he says, would not imply that one had or "owned" the other person's sensations). I have to say it is not clear to me how one could feel a sensation without having it.

7. See Wittgenstein 1953, secs. 408, 278, and related remarks starting on 220e. Hacker (1987, chap. 6, sec. 3) extends Wittgenstein's remarks in the manner to which I refer.

8. Hacker 1987, 225: "Indeed, 'I *know* that it looks to me as if . . .' is either nonsense or just an emphatic way of saying that it really does strike me thus, just as 'I know I am in pain,' if it means anything, is just an emphatic way of saying that I am in pain."

9. Malcolm 1954, 84–85: "A man cannot be in *error* as to whether he is in pain; he cannot say, 'My leg hurts,' by mistake, any more than he can groan by mistake. It is senseless to suppose he has wrongly identified a tickle as a pain or that he falsely believes that it is in his leg when in fact it is in his shoulder. . . . The point about the incorrigibility of the utterance 'I'm in pain' lies behind Wittgenstein's reiterated remark that 'I *know* I'm in pain' and 'I don't know whether I'm in pain' are both senseless (e.g., 246, 408). Wherever it is *meaningless* to speak of 'false belief,' it is also meaningless to speak of 'knowledge'; and wherever you cannot say 'I don't know . . .,' you also cannot say 'I know. . . .'"

10. One might want to allow for "nonstandard" cases in which one is mistaken—such as "hysterical pain."

11. Wittgenstein 1953, sec. 244.

12. Malcolm says Wittgenstein does not deny this (Malcolm 1958, 159).

CHAPTER 2

1. From Nisbett and Wilson's abstract (1977): "Evidence is reviewed which suggests that there may be little or no direct introspective access to higher order cognitive processes. . . . It is proposed that when people attempt to report on their cognitive processes, that is, on the processes mediating the effects of a stimulus on a response, they do not do so on the basis of any true introspection."

Notice, however, that this is not to be understood as a general denial of "introspective access" to mind—late in the article, the authors make a distinction between introspection of mental "process," which they say we *do not* have, and introspection of mental "content," which they say we *do*. "We do indeed have direct access to a great storehouse of private knowledge. . . . The individual knows . . . the focus of his attention at any given point in time; he knows what his current sensations are and has what almost all psychologists and philosophers would assert to be 'knowledge' at least quantitatively superior to that of observers concerning his emotions, evaluations, and plans" (ibid., 255). When Nisbett and Wilson deny that we have introspective access to "process," they usually want to deny that we have the same sort of knowledge regarding the correct explanation or predictions of our responses as we have of the aforementioned types of "mental content."

2. Nisbett and Wilson write, "In two of our . . . studies, subjects were asked to predict how they would have responded to stimuli that were actually presented to subjects in another condition. In both cases, predictions about behavior were very similar to the inaccurate reports of subjects who had actually been exposed to the conditions. Thus, whatever capacity for introspection exists, it does not produce accurate reports about stimulus effects, nor does it even produce reports that differ from predictions of observers operating with only a verbal description of the situation. As Bem . . . put it in a similar context, if the reports of subjects do not differ from the reports of observers, then it is unnecessary to assume that the former are drawing on 'a fount of privileged knowledge.' It seems equally clear that subjects and observers are drawing on a similar source for their verbal reports about stimulus effects" (ibid., 248).

Later, in a passage where they indicate that they take 'awareness' to mean more or less the same as 'introspective access,' Nisbett and Wilson make even clearer the general connection they assume between 'introspection' and accuracy of first-person judgment: "The criterion for 'awareness' should be . . . 'verbal report which exceeds in accuracy that obtained from observers provided with a general description of the stimulus and response in question.' Even highly accurate reports, therefore, provide no evidence of introspective awareness of the effect of the stimuli on responses if observers can equal that level of accuracy" (ibid., 251).

3. This shows that it is just not tenable to maintain, as Nisbett and Wilson do, that we have a distinctively first-person knowledge of what attitudes and experience we have—of the "contents" of our minds—but no such knowledge of the explanation of our "responses" (i.e., "mental process"). If one can "introspectively" know the content of one's mind, and one is able to use this knowledge to make accurate explanations and predictions about oneself (Nisbett and Wilson do not deny this), then "introspection" *does* play a role in one's knowledge of "process" as well. Perhaps Nisbett and Wilson fail to appreciate that a difference between the subject's and the observer's knowledge of "content" yields a difference in their knowledge of "process" because of their assumption that any first-person/third-person difference in knowledge must involve a difference in the level of accuracy of first- and third-person reports; perhaps they think that while (at least certain types of) first-person "content" reports are more accurate than third-person ones, this first-person advantage just does not ever happen to make first-person explanations or predictions any more accurate than third-person ones.

This is, in any case, false, but more important, once we extricate ourselves from the confusion of insisting that any difference between first-person and third-person knowledge must involve a difference in accuracy of report, we no longer have any excuse for the erroneous assumption that we have a distinctively first-person knowledge of "content," but none of "process." We should note, then, that it would be misguided to say that Nisbett and Wilson's criticism of "introspection" doesn't have any relevance to the claim to first-person knowledge with which I am concerned, because this claim is about knowledge of content, not process. If Nisbett and Wilson *did* have evidence to show we have no first-person knowledge of what accounts for our responses (which they do not), this would also have to show we have no first-person knowledge of the contents of our minds, since our knowledge of our contents forms part of our knowledge of our processes.

4. However, it is hard to say how effective Nisbett and Wilson's criticisms of their intended target are, since the authors are less than clear about what the target is. What kind of difference in accuracy of reports do they think would be required to indicate that one had the privileged or introspective knowledge of "process" they want to deny we have? Is the idea they are attacking that first-person explanatory/ predictive remarks adverting to certain types of mental states are *invariably* more accurate than those of well-informed observers? Or would it be enough for one to have "introspective" knowledge that one *averaged* greater accuracy for first-person explanations/predictions involving certain types of mental states? Or, would one have the kind of superior accuracy sufficient in their view for "introspection," simply if one had at certain times accurate beliefs regarding certain mentalistic explanations or predictions of one's own responses, when, at those times, well-positioned observers did not, *regardless* of whether this contributed to a higher overall average rate of accuracy of certain sorts of explanations or predictions? Nisbett and Wilson do not make sufficiently clear what they are considering when comparing "levels of accuracy" of reports.

5. Gopnik 1993, 1–2: "According to this [commonsense] interpretation of first-person privilege, our beliefs about our own psychological states do not come from the same source as our beliefs about the psychological states of others. In the case of our own minds, there is a direct link leading from our underlying psychological states to our psychological experiences. It is easy enough to imagine how we might be so wired that whenever we were in a particular psychological state we would have a particular corresponding psychological experience. Because we have no experience of other minds, this link cannot exist in that case, and so our beliefs about the psychological states of others must be indirect."

6. "Suppose the commonsense and philosophical accounts of privileged first-person beliefs about the mind were correct. Then we should predict that, however erroneous children's views of the psychological states of others might be, they would not make similar errors in their understanding of their own psychological states. If they knew anything at all about their own minds, then what they know ought to be substantially correct. This knowledge certainly should not be systematically and consistently wrong" (ibid., 6). "We find that children make errors about their own immediately past states that are similar to the errors they make about the states of others. This is true even though children ought to have direct first-person psychological evidence of these past states" (ibid., 7).

7. Incidentally, the only way in which the examples that manifest first-person knowledge require us to think of first-person belief and knowledge as "immediate" is this: first-person beliefs about attitudes, and these attitudes themselves, are not mediated by observation of the person to whom these belong in the way that third-person beliefs and the attitudes they are about are observationally mediated. That is all. As far as this goes, there may be some other kind of "mediation," or at least some kind of complex relationship, between first-person beliefs and what they are about, or between the person who has such beliefs, and his attitudes. And first-person knowledge may, in some sense, "involve inference." (At least it is plausible to suppose that the first-person knower has to be *able* to make certain sorts of inference, if he is to have beliefs about and knowledge of his own [or anyone's] attitudes.) All that would be ruled out so far regarding the "inferential" status of self-knowledge is the following. Whether or not it is true, as some people say, that third-person knowledge always involves "inferences" from the kinds of observation of others that enable one

to possess warrant for claims about their minds, first-person knowledge is not in this way "inferential." For again, in many instances of first-person knowledge, either *one does not make the relevant observations of oneself*, or *there is nothing of the relevant sort for one to observe*—so one cannot be making the putative inferences from observation.

8. Though one study they discuss does show that subjects' reports that they had certain attitudes in the past are sometimes false: subjects whose opinions on political questions were altered by their exposure to arguments tended afterwards to report that their past beliefs on these matters were much more similar to their later ones than was actually the case (Nisbett and Wilson 1977, 236). But the only defects in subjects' reports of their *current* attitudes and experience, for which Nisbett and Wilson's cited studies provide evidence, involve either an absence of certain true reports (rather than the presence of false ones) or alleged errors, not in reporting that one had certain experiences at all, but in making certain kinds of comparative judgments about them. For example, one study Nisbett and Wilson discuss purports to show that subjects (nonverbally) "evaluated" electrical shocks they were given as "less painful" in circumstances in which they were given only rather weak justifications for undergoing the shocks, than they did in those circumstances in which they were given "adequate" justification for their suffering. This difference in "evaluation" is supposed to be clear from differences in the subjects' galvanic skin response, and from differences in the ease with which they accomplished various learning tasks during their ordeal. What Nisbett and Wilson are keen to point out is that the subjects were not inclined to report the shocks to be less painful on the one condition than on the other (ibid., 234). It is rather unclear, however, that the evidence offered shows that the subjects' reports about their pain are in any sense *mistaken*. That is, it is hardly clear that the evidence show the shocks *felt* more painful to the subjects on the one condition than on the other, which is presumably what they were reporting on.

9. The kind of eliminativism I allude to here (and throughout my discussion) is that represented by Paul Churchland (1981). I find it convenient to use this version of the view as a point of reference, but I believe my remarks here will defend my claims against other varieties of eliminativism as well, which envision replacements for "folk psychology" different from Churchland's and fault our ordinary psychological notions on different grounds than he does—see, for example, Quine 1960, and Stich 1983.

10. I should point out that typically, eliminativists do not put their view to quite the use I imagine here. To the extent they address the issue of first-person knowledge, they tend to be concerned with saying or suggesting that, in their view, first-person claims about mind do not enjoy a kind of privileged status that would block the possibility of an "empirical discovery" that all such claims are false. But I would say the eliminativist needs to do more than deny some form of introspective "privileged access" as usually construed, in order to make his case. For I think he needs also to say first that whatever kind of warrant one has for first-person claims about mind, it is entirely dependent on the kind of warrant others could have for third-person claims, and further, that possession of this third-person warrant depends entirely on the possibility of justifying mentalistic claims as a theory to explain the movements and sounds of one's body, as such. I argue that we have no good reason to accept this epistemological view. This undercuts the case for eliminativism, and so protects the thesis of first-person knowledge from eliminativist attack.

I should perhaps also note why I do not leave the eliminativist issue open, and defend my view in another, more neutral, way. Typically, what eliminativism charts for extinction are "propositional attitudes," so why do I not simply say we at least have first-person knowledge of *experience* (which may not involve having any such *attitudes*), and proceed on this basis to investigate consciousness with reference to such knowledge? For after all, what I want to use first-person knowledge for is a discussion of conscious experience, and (at least some) eliminativists do not say they want to eliminate *that*. I have two reasons: first, I am not willing to leave experience and consciousness vulnerable to potential eliminativist arguments by leaving unchallenged the premises on which such arguments would be mounted; second, I believe it seriously distorts our conception of experience to see this as something distinct from intentionality and attitudes. Thus I would not want to base my approach on any concession to this way of looking at things. I suppose I would say that experiences are (at least sometimes) "propositional attitudes," if all that means is that experiences can be accurately reported using psychological verbs that embed sentences in their grammatical objects. So, "It looks to me as if the X on this side is bigger than the X on that side" can be both a report of *conscious experience*, and a report of a *propositional attitude*. But in any case, on my view, intentionality cannot be entirely prised away from the phenomenal character of experience, as I discuss in Chapters 7 and 8.

11. Paul Churchland appears to propose harsh eliminativism when he characterizes it as "the thesis that our common-sense conception of psychological phenomena constitutes a radically false theory, a theory so fundamentally defective that both the principles and ontology of that theory will eventually be displaced, rather than smoothly reduced, by completed neuroscience" (1981, 601). For it appears that to "displace the ontology" of this commonsense conception is to say that we just do not have any attitudes of the sort that we attribute to ourselves in everyday speech. But Paul and Patricia Churchland have, it is true, expressed their shared views in less straightforwardly "eliminativist" terms, suggesting in fact that talk of *elimination* is misleading, and that *revisionary* materialism might be a better term, saying they "have no ideological stake in the revision being massive or minor, though our expectations lean toward the former. . . . What we do believe is that our current framework is not sacred, that it is neither manifestly nor divinely given, and that 'obviousness' is a familiarity phenomenon rather than a measure of metaphysical truth" (Churchland and Churchland 1996, 298–99).

But just to say that one believes that our ordinary ways of classifying psychological phenomena (e.g., as belief and expectation) are not beyond revision, or even to say one expects them to change a lot, somehow as a result of neuroscience, is quite different from saying that there is reason to say neuroscience will show us that we do not have any of the attitudes we ordinarily attribute to ourselves. The "nicer" view (the Churchlands jokingly refer to it as "good-guy materialism") is harder to criticize, but that is largely because it says so little. When no specific revisions have been identified and proposed, nor rationales for them offered, there is not much to talk about.

I should note that the Churchlands also offer to sum up eliminativist claims in this way: "As science advances, certain 'natural' categories that figured in an earlier theory turn out to have no role and no place in the replacing theory that is taken to provide a correct account of a certain range of phenomena. If those categories are deeply entrenched in common sense, and if they are also routinely used in observation, then the new theory of what is observable will be different from what the ancestor theory assumed to be observable" (ibid., 297). But just to take up the view that theory change in science can lead us to conclude that what once were regarded as observables or data to be explained are to be treated as posits of some false theory, whose existence is denied as that theory is rejected, is not yet to say anything "eliminativist" about the mind. One needs to take some further step, along the lines of proposing that *our ordinary attributions of attitudes and experience to ourselves should be regarded in this way*, as mere posits of a false theory that has become so entrenched we tend to regard such attributions as reporting phenomena to be explained by our theories, when really—now that we have some other theory (sort of)—they are better regarded just as chimerical would-be explainers, like phlogiston, caloric fluid, crystalline spheres, vital spirit, and so on. But once this step is taken, we have a right to ask what reason we have to follow. One can draw whatever lines of analogy one likes between attitudes and experience on the one hand, and nonexistent creatures of past theories on the other; while that may pack some kind of rhetorical punch, we still need to be told just why we should think that the analogy holds in relevant respects. We might point out that many of the Churchlands' stock examples of theoretical detritus (e.g., vital spirit) would not ever have been regarded as belonging to some domain of phenomena to be explained, but always only as something more in the line of explanatory posits. And if we are then told that asking for an explanation of what is described in attitude talk is like asking for an explanation of the earth's immobility (which surely *did* once seem like a datum to be explained), then we will want to know why we should go with *that* analogy. Drawing these analogies does not give us a reason to accept them. Why not draw analogies in a way friendlier to our everyday mind talk? We might also say that asking for explanations of people's remembering, believing, and hoping that things are so, doubting and wondering whether they are, or its looking to them as if things are certain ways, is *not* like asking why the earth is still, but rather like asking why the earth exists at all, or how clouds are formed, or why children resemble their parents, and so on.

12. "What we must say is that FP [folk psychology] suffers explanatory failures on an epic scale, that it has been stagnant for at least twenty-five centuries, and that its categories appear (so far) to be incommensurable with or orthogonal to the categories of the background physical science whose long-term claim to explain human behavior seems undeniable. Any theory that meets this description must be allowed a serious candidate for outright elimination" (P. M. Churchland 1981, 605).

13. Somewhat similar points have been made in more detail in Horgan and Woodward's (1985) defense of "folk psychology."

14. We might also note that where we identify behavior by reference to things in our environment, it seems we still have not purified our conception of behavior adequately to make an eliminativist-style assessment of psychological explanation, as long as we classify these things in ways we understand by drawing on talk of attitudes, as is the case with artifacts. Can we say what makes something count as a shoe, a bed, a house, a road, a knife, a car, etc., without reference to human interests and aims?

15. However, I should say something about one more way in which one might suggest that a third-person perspective can give rise to doubt about our possession of first-person warrant. It has been suggested that externalist views concerning belief (or the content of mental states generally) are in some way incompatible with the notion that we have a kind of "first-person authority" regarding what we believe,

and so their acceptance threatens our claim to such authority, and perhaps also to a distinctive first-person knowledge of mind. But what is the worry here? Perhaps the thought is that we are or can be ignorant that the conditions in our environment obtain that, according to externalism, determine what we believe, and this entails that we are ignorant of what we believe. But one may respond here that one can know that one believes that p, without knowing that a certain condition obtains, even when one believes that p, only if that condition obtains. Perhaps the worry is that a person might be transferred back and forth between two different external situations determining different beliefs, in such a manner as would leave her unable to tell that she was transferred—would she not be ignorant of what she believed then? One may say that if the external circumstances determine the content of her beliefs, they will accordingly determine the content of her beliefs about her beliefs as well—so in either situation, she correctly believes that she believes that p, when she does. But if the concern is that the person undergoing such a switch would not believe that the contents of her beliefs were different, when according to externalism they are, one might question whether, if Irene is to know that she believes that p in situation A, and know that she believes that q in situation B, she must know that her belief that p is different from her belief that q. Also, one might say that while someone who is tranferred back and forth in this manner would be put into ignorance concerning what she believes, it does not follow that someone who is *not* being shunted back and forth would be so ignorant, and we do not have to know we are not being shunted to escape this sort of ignorance.

More generally, I would remark that, if externalist views are somehow inconsistent with the notion that we can form true and warranted beliefs about our own states of mind in circumstances that make it clear we do not have the same sort of warrant for such first-person belief as would ordinarily be had for corresponding third-person beliefs, this is more of a threat to externalism than it is to the thesis of first-person warrant. For first, the presumption in favor of the view that we do often know what we are thinking in such circumstances is at least as strong as any allegiance we owe to the (rather equivocal) intuitive reaction to hypothetical situations supposed to support externalist views of belief. If we have to eliminate one or the other, it seems more reasonable to reconsider our reactions to Twin Earth scenarios, swampmen, and the like, than to throw out the claim that we often know what we are thinking. Second, it seems that if externalism threatens first-person knowledge, it threatens third-person knowledge, too. If I cannot tell the difference between two different content-determining situations I am in, I cannot tell the difference between situations others are in either, and so if an ignorance of my own beliefs ensues, so does an ignorance of others' beliefs. One might say: "But you can come to tell the difference, by empirical investigation." Even if that is right, it is plain we generally do not rely on empirical investigation to determine which sort of world we are in, in order to tell what people believe. So if a failure to do so brings ignorance of their beliefs, we are ignorant. Finally, even if (absurdly) we said we did have to rely on such investigation to determine what we think, that would not show that the way one knows one's own mind does not differ from the way one knows others' minds. Cases of solitary self-knowledge would still show this difference.

My brief discussion here is indebted to more thorough treatments by Burge (1988), Davidson (1984b, 1987), Gallois (1996), and Heil (1992). I should say also that Gallois conducts an interesting and detailed discussion of self-knowledge that, unfortunately, became available to me too late for me to incorporate its study into the present work.

16. There is an echo of this kind of concern in Dennett 1991, where the author justifies his determinedly third-person approach to the study of consciousness (what he calls "heterophenomenology") by saying that the only alternative is to embrace a doctrine of "papal infallibility" with respect to first-person statements about experience (ibid., 96).

17. See ibid., 66–67.

CHAPTER 3

1. For two among the many discussions of this "inverted spectrum" possibility, see Block and Fodor 1972 and Shoemaker 1975.

2. See Chalmers 1996; Searle 1992, chap. 3; and a symposium in *Journal of Consciousness Studies* (vol. 2, no. 4 [1995]), for some discussions of the possibility of what philosophers call "zombies."

3. Dennett 1991, 210ff. For other accounts linking serial processing and consciousness, see Johnson-Laird 1988a; 1988b, chap. 19; and Flanagan 1992, 172–75, 189–91.

4. Sometimes it seems we are supposed to believe that the attractiveness of the "stream of consciousness" metaphor, and the psychological realism of the literary technique so labeled, lend support to the notion that consciousness essentially involves "serial processing." Flanagan (1992, 41) associates this kind of "seriality" with William James's remarks about the "stream of consciousness," equating consciousness's "streamlike character" with its being "von Neumann-esque." And Dennett dubs the von Neumann-style virtual processor in his theory of consciousness the "Joycean machine" (1991, 212).

But what James was after in using this metaphor does not, I think, do much to liken conscious occurrences generally to the steps in a von Neumann-style process. James, I believe, wanted to draw attention to something else entirely: the continuousness of consciousness—the way in which occurrences of consciousness merge into one another, lacking definite natural boundaries separating them from one another, the way in which conscious states resist analysis into precise distinct segments. The appeal of the metaphor also stems from its suggestion that there can be many "things going on in consciousness" simultaneously, with mutual influence on one another, like the currents in a stream. None of this sits at all well with the aim of forcing consciousness into the framework provided by the von Neumann as opposed to parallel architecture.

As for Joyce, it seems to me that one finds little support in *Ulysses* for this serial-processor talk about consciousness, unless one is determined to read the stream-of-consciousness passages as imagined *transcripts* of the character's silent speech, and one assumes such silent speech is supposed to exhaust the episodes of consciousness in their lives. But this is certainly not the only way of reading these passages. We might suppose that, rather than writing an imaginary transcript of silent speech, Joyce generally put *more* words into the stream-of-consciousness passages than actual people would silently utter—though *fewer* than would be adequate to verbalize all that they consciously think, feel, and perceive—in an effort to strike a balance between the need to convey the minimal, fragmentary articulateness of much instantaneously rich conscious thought, perception, and feeling on the one hand, and the need to provide the reader with words enough to suggest this richness, to make the text (sort of) comprehensible, and to give it literary value on the other. In any case, it is difficult to see what is supposed to be so von Neumann-like about these dense associative connections, of which we cannot make any definite and exhaustive list, holding one part of these passages together with another. Why should we find it plausible to think the wandering path of a Molly Bloom's thoughts are determined by her (or her brain) following a set of von Neumannesque instructions?

We should note that Dennett draws some support for his serial-processor approach by reminding us that the von Neumann architecture was conceived of as a way of realizing the principles of the Turing machine, whose conception was inspired by Turing's thinking about the steps he would go through in conscious thought when trying to solve a problem in mathematics (Dennett 1991, 212, 215). But the most this shows us is that conscious thinking can constitute the kind of rule-following captured in the notion of the Turing machine. It does not show that this is true of all episodes of consciousness, or even that it is typical.

Dennett might try to defend his von Neumann-machine idea against my reference to conscious perception partly by insisting that it is an illusion to suppose that perceptual consciousness is as "rich" as I seem to presume—really, there is very little "going on in it" at once—so there is nothing so odd about thinking of the stream of consciousness as passing through a "von Neumann bottleneck," and if this is not always actually "verbalized," it is such as can fruitfully be regarded as though it were. But in response to this, I would insist: consciousness *is* richer than this (see Chapter 7).

5. I have made variants of this point before (Siewert 1993, 1994). Block (1995) independently makes similar observations, with reference also to the case of D.B. and his "amblyopic crescent," and uses them similarly in criticism of Dennett (see my Chapter 5).

6. Chalmers (1996) makes a convincing case that they are not.

7. An example I owe to Bealer (1994).

CHAPTER 4

1. Among other questions Tye's theory is supposed to answer is what would differentiate what he calls a "super-blindsight" subject's spontaneously formed *beliefs* about what he consciously sees, from the *experiences* of a normal subject with conscious vision. Part of his answer is that whereas our visual experiences "represent local surface features throughout the [visual] field," the hypothetical blindsighter's beliefs would not (1995, 142). And this claim is meant to have the force of metaphysical necessity. But how would Tye's theory distinguish Belinda's left-field visual capacity from Connie's? Notice: the question here is not about what distinguishes Belinda's *belief* about what is in her left field from Connie's *experience*, but rather about what distinguishes the kind of visual condition that enables Belinda to form such a belief from Connie's blurry left-field experience. Should we say that, since Belinda lacks a phenomenal state that Connie has, she must represent something in her left field less determinately than Connie does, or that Connie must represent local surface features in the relevant portion of her left field that Belinda does not—as a matter of metaphysical necessity?

Tye does not address this issue directly, but if he were to say this, it would not be satisfactory. For given Belinda and Connie's parity in respect of the capacity to discriminate left-field stimuli spontaneously, there would be no reason to assume that Belinda's visual representations that are (in Tye's terms) "poised for use" by her "belief and desire system" would have to be any less "determinate" than Connie's. So were he to insist that if someone lacked a conscious visual experience Connie has, they couldn't possibly have equally determinate visual representations of their left fields, he would have to deny that there could possibly be a form of spontaneous blindsight like Belinda's.

2. Someone might object that neither this sort of blindsighter nor his observers could have warrant for saying he had visual discriminatory talents of any sort, without internal examination, if we assume that genuinely to have such talents, they must, roughly speaking, "come from within." That is, if the movements and utterances of the subject are caused by some kind of remote-control device, or by continual miracles or divine intervention, rather than (as we take ours to be) by what goes on in us without such external guidance, then the subject does not genuinely have the discriminatory talents, but acts somewhat as an amazing sort of puppet. And one might claim that we have no warrant for thinking that thoughts and behavior are not puppetlike without some internal examination. Then one might say that it wouldn't be right to regard Dennett's proposal as suggesting we identify visual consciousness with possession of some *manifest* talent—for what is "manifest" does not give us warrant for attributing the sorts of talents in question.

However, I think it would be a mistake to say that, until we conduct some internal examination, we have no more warrant for believing that thought and behavior are as endogenous in origin as we take our own to be than we have for thinking they are puppetlike. *Before* looking under the skin, and theorizing about how what goes on there accounts for bodily movement and utterance, our failure to discover any external control of the sort we believe would make someone or something puppetlike gives us more warrant for thinking someone a self-guided or self-moving sort of creature, than for thinking him, her, or it a sort of puppet. That is, at least while we have not yet done any internal examination of a relevant sort, if we find no evident external direction of an appropriate sort (i.e., nothing analogous to the puppeteer's strings), we have more warrant for the "self-mover" claim than for the "puppet" view. So even if we need more warrant for the first claim than for the second before we can attribute, say, discriminatory talents to a subject, that does not make those talents other than manifest features, on my conception. For still it is true that we can have *some* warrant for thinking someone has such talents, prior to internal examination of that someone, or suitably related creatures. And that is enough to make such talents of a manifest sort. Granting this, we might reasonably take Dennett to be proposing that an absence of a certain kind of conscious visual experience is nothing over and above some missing manifest discriminatory, regulative, or evaluative talent.

3. We might want to make quick work of this suggestion by saying that we can, after all, imagine and conceive of the sort of high-powered blindsight Dennett wants to rule out, and that anyone who rules out its possibility is guilty of consciousness neglect. Or we might say that we can conceive of a being shaped as we are, whose movements and utterances are indistinguishable from our own, but who lacks not just conscious visual experience, but *any* conscious experience whatsoever. This

would be one variant of the so-called zombie possibility. And while Dennett would, it seems, want to deny the possibility of such an entity, we might say that this is tantamount to a denial of consciousness. But, as I have already suggested, the step from the forms of blindsight I have invoked to introduce the notion of phenomenal consciousness, to the much more powerful, premium variety, or to the idea of zombies, will perhaps not seem obvious, and opens up potential sources of confusion and uncertainty that I would prefer not to deal with now. For I think that, even without moving in this direction, we will find that this suggestion that the absence of conscious vision is "nothing over and above" some missing manifest talent, if construed nontrivially, cannot reasonably be made compatible with the recognition that we have phenomenally conscious experience.

4. I am grateful to Dan Reisberg and Zeke Koch for making me aware of the need to discuss the suggestions that arise in this section.

5. Similar points apply, if we consider the kind of nonphenomenal pain state Rosenthal would have us take as an illustration of sensory quality. If I ever do think I am, in Rosenthal's sense, in pain, when I do not feel pain, I have a thought that is seemingly *inferential*. From evidence I have that I am in a condition typically conducive to feeling pain, and that some typical effects of this feeling are present, and that I have taken some kind of drug that usually stops one from feeling pain, I infer that I am "in pain." And if, when I do *feel* pain (and thus consciously feel pain), I also think that I am *in* pain—where this just means I am in a condition that gives rise to this feeling but that can persist without it—then that thought is again inferential. But this time I would infer that I am in pain, in this sense, partly from the fact that I feel pain. Thus even if I do recognize a use of the term 'pain' that permits me to speak of a nonphenomenal quality of being in pain, I do not actually on certain occasions seemingly without inference think I have a state with this quality, this pain one can have when one feels no pain.

6. A parallel point again applies in the pain case. If I understand 'pain' so that one may be in pain without feeling pain, then I see no reason why the thought might not spontaneously occur to me that I am in pain in this sense when indeed I am. While receiving pain stimuli, I am debilitated by this, but under the influence of an anesthetic, and without being able to cite all this as a reason for saying so, it occurs to me that I am "in pain," though, all the while, it does not seem to me the way it does to feel pain—I have no conscious pain experience.

7. I should note that I think Tye's (1995) account of phenomenal consciousness generally lacks the resources to distinguish a blindsighter like Belinda from a conscious sighter like Connie, and so fails to recognize the existence of the feature I am calling phenomenal consciousness. Phenomenal experiences are, on Tye's view, matrical or maplike (*not* sentencelike) mental representations, output by "sensory modules," which do not (or do not "need to") "draw on memory representations," and are "poised for use by the cognitive system"—i.e., their content "stand(s) ready and in position to make a direct impact" on belief and desire (ibid., 137–39). That something of this sort could be other than a phenomenally conscious sense-experience is, Tye holds, metaphysically impossible. Now, both Connie and Belinda would have beliefs about what is on their left, arising from the "output" of their "sensory (visual) modules" (I suppose), but one has conscious visual experience of a blurry patch of grayish light on the left and the other does not. Does Tye's theory of phenomenal experience allow for their possibility? The answer is yes, only if Belinda would necessarily differ from Connie in respect of what visually output, matrically represented,

memory-independent information about her left field she had, ready to make a direct impact on her beliefs. However, assuming we grant the legitimacy of Tye's theoretical apparatus, and do not deny the possibility of Connie and Belinda as originally described, there is no reason to suppose Belinda *would* have to differ from Connie in this way. So if we do not rule out the possibility of Connie and Belinda as originally described, it seems we have no reason to rule out the possibility that such a Connie and Belinda would be indistinguishable in respect of what visually output, matrically represented, memory-independent information about their left fields they had, ready to make a direct impact on their beliefs. But Tye would have to deny this possibility, since on his view there is nothing more to having the sort of experience I have attributed to Connie than there is to having visual information of this sort. And in denying this possibility, he gives us no recourse but to deny the possibility of Connie and Belinda altogether, which is tantamount to denying the reality of phenomenal consciousness.

I have already said something about why our two hypothetical subjects would be alike in respect of what they matrically visually represent on the left. About these representations being similarly "poised," I would say this: in either case, the output of their visual systems would be ready to give rise to thoughts, which need not be elicited by "acts of will," about what is on the subject's left, and which the subject is disposed to believe are true.

CHAPTER 5

1. It may help if I illustrate how my comments here would apply, in response to relevant remarks of Tye's (1995, 190–92). He suggests that if you can imagine, and conceive of, some subject having the kind of visual representation he (Tye) identifies with the phenomenal character of visual experience, but without having that experience, you are mistaken. What you are *really* imagining is not what you say you imagine (that is metaphysically impossible), but rather someone who is oblivious to her visual experience in the way a distracted driver may be. And that, he says, is someone who *does not bring "phenomenal concepts" to bear in thinking about her state.* Now, I think Belinda would count (if anyone would) as one who had the kind of visual representation of her left field that Tye identifies with visual experience— but nothing on her left would look any way to her at all. I suppose Tye would say that I have misdescribed what I have imagined: what I have really done is imagine that Belinda is oblivious to how things look on her left—she lacks a certain kind of thought about her left-field visual state that she has about her right. There are two questions I want to address: Is Tye right in his suggestions about what I am imagining? And does Tye avoid the difficulties I have noted in trying to explain the appearance of possibility by alleging that we mistake an absence of a thought about visual experience for an absent visual experience?

Let's start with the second question. If Tye would suggest I am mistakenly supposing the thought that one has experience with a certain phenomenal character to be essential to having experience with that character, I would point out that—on the contrary—this is something that I explicitly deny. If this thought (with its constituent phenomenal concept) is identified relative to the notion of phenomenal consciousness I employ, I would say that people and animals can have phenomenally conscious experience without applying this notion to their experience. That is, if in thinking of one's experience as having a certain phenomenal character, one thinks of oneself as having some feature, the occurrence of which would be denied by someone who denied the possibility of Belinda-like blindsight, then my deeply held conviction is this: it is not essential to having visual experience that one think such a thought about it, or apply such a phenomenal concept to it. So how can I fairly be said to mistake Belinda's lack of this thought for a lack of left-field visual experience? If, on the other hand, in thinking of one's experience as having a certain phenomenal character, one does *not* think of it as having a feature whose occurrence would be denied in denying the possibility of Belinda (that is not part of the concept one employs), then again, I do not believe the thought in question is essential to experience. For it *is* part of the notion I use in thinking about my experience (when, e.g., I think something looks red to me) that it is the notion of a feature that would be denied by one who rejected the possibility of certain kinds of visual discrimination without conscious visual experience. That is something that has, on reflection, emerged about my concept of something's looking some way to me. So when I think about how things look to me, I do not think these other thoughts, employing some other concept, about the conscious visual experience I have. But I believe I have conscious visual experience galore. So how could it be fair to accuse me of confusing the absence of *those thoughts* with an absence of *experience*?

Now, as for the first question, again, I am indeed conceiving of Belinda as someone who does not think she has (in my sense) phenomenally conscious visual experience of what is on her left—in *that* way, and to that extent, I suppose she does not "bring phenomenal concepts to bear" on her state. But that is not *all* I am supposing about her. I am *also* supposing that she does not have the phenomenal experience she does not think she has: not only does she not think it looks any way at all to her on her left—it does not. And I am certainly not imagining her to be in a distracted-driverlike state; for I am not in the least tempted to confuse what it is like to be in that state with what it is like to be someone to whom things do not look any way at all. I will testify under oath that I have always thought it a source of great confusion to take these "distracted driver" stories to illustrate a lack of conscious vision. I suppose Belinda to be a person who, in an unoblivious, undistracted state, will say—correctly—that things look somehow or other to her on her right, but not on her left, though she can spontaneously visually judge about how things are on her left (and judge that she visually judges) as well as Connie can, with her restricted blurry visual experience of her left field. Maybe Tye would firmly insist that I am really imagining some situation other than the one I describe. But unless he can give me a reason to think there is some hidden confusion in my thinking that should make me change my mind, I will have no more call to do so than I would if he just firmly insisted I had *really* imagined a *bearded* man, after I sincerely said I had imagined one clean-shaven.

2. Tye seems to think, on the contrary, that pointing to a difference in concepts in this context not only will explain why we believe a certain situation is possible (when according to him it is *not*), but also will give us reason to think the situation in question is indeed metaphysically impossible. Recall I have argued that if we do not reject the possibility that Belinda and Connie could differ in respect of what conscious visual experience they have of what is to their left, while being similar with regard to their visual discriminatory abilities in the ways I have described, then we have no reason to reject the possibility that two such subjects may not differ with respect to what they visually represent in a "nonconceptual, matrical" fashion to be so on their left, so that this information is "directly" available to belief and desire. And as I understand Tye's "PANIC" theory, this would be metaphysically im-

possible. Thus it seems to me his theory would deny possibility in a way that excludes (what I call) phenomenal consciousness. Now, Tye defends his view both against the worry that we can imagine someone *lacking* the kind of PANIC (Poised, Abstract, Nonconceptual, Intentional Content) with which his theory would identify the phenomenal character of a certain kind of experience, while *having* experience with that character, as well as against the worry that one can imagine the PANIC without the experience. His defense is that appeals to imaginability in support of claims about metaphysical possibility provide only defeasible warrant for them, and the claim to imagine (e.g.) a "felt quality" Q without the theory's specified PANIC, P, *is* defeated. But by what? He says,

> Consider . . . the claim that Q can be imagined without the specified PANIC. Why do we naturally suppose that this claim is true? The answer surely is that in thinking of a state as having phenomenal character Q, we think of it via the exercise of phenomenal concepts. The conception we form of it is the one we have when we introspect it. By contrast, in thinking of a state as having PANIC P, we bring to bear a very different set of concepts. So, we naturally infer that we are thinking of two different things: Q *and* P. But this inference is unjustified. The difference in thoughts can be accounted for solely by a difference in concepts. (Tye 1995, 189)

And then a little later:

> Not only can the PANIC theorist account for the fact that we can apparently imagine Q without PANIC P in an entirely straightforward way (and one that does not presuppose the truth of the theory), but the initial presumption that Q is imaginable without the appropriate PANIC is seriously threatened by the above considerations. . . . Some things that are conceptually possible are metaphysically impossible and hence unimaginable. (ibid., 190)

The idea appears to be that we have reason to believe it only seems, but is not really, possible that Tye's P's and Q's could vary independently, because:

(1) Our concept of the quality Q and our concept of the PANIC P will be different;

(2) It does not follow from (1) that Q and P are distinct; and

(3) It can be explained why we suppose it is true to say that it is possible that Q and P could vary independently: we assume the opposite of (2), and so from a distinctness in concepts we wrongly infer a distinctness in what they are concepts of.

Now if I am right, Tye's PANIC theory of consciousness will be fairly accused of leaving phenomenal consciousness out, unless he can give us a reason why we should believe it is metaphysically impossible that Belinda and Connie differ experientially while remaining the same in their manifest talents, in the ways I have indicated. He needs to argue that it is not possible, for they would necessarily have the same PANICs, and they couldn't be in *that* way the same while differing experientially. But I do not think he has given us a good reason to think this. If I can conceive of Belinda and Connie sharing a certain P while only one of them has a certain Q, you have not given me a reason for thinking the belief that it is metaphysically possible that this happen is false, when all you have done is tell me (1) and (2). I will of course grant that my concept of my experience and my concept of a PANIC are different, and I can recognize a way of talking about concepts and properties that allows it is possible for two concepts to be concepts of one and the same property, so I can grant that a distinction between P and Q does not simply follow from the fact that my concept of P and my concept of Q are distinct. Still, I may well conceive of P occurring without Q, and if I can find no reason to think it is not metaphysically possible for this to happen (this certainly does not follow from [1] and [2]), I will conclude that I have more warrant for believing than for denying it is metaphysically possible for P to occur without Q. For conceivability (plus apparent imaginability, if you like) of something is defeasible evidence that it is possible—and I have not yet found a defeater. But if this is my story, the proposed explanation (in [3]) of my "mistake" fails because it claims my modal belief depends on my accepting an inference I do not accept. And again: even if I think it would be too bold to believe it is possible that P occur without Q, on the strength of thought-experiments, imagination, and lack of evident "defeaters," I would still have the question: Why *should* I believe that it is *impossible* that P occur without Q? Why should I think that here we have one of those cases where two distinct concepts pick out a single property? The truth of that does not follow from (1)–(3). Thus it seems to me this doctrine about concepts *neither* shows that Belinda is impossible (and hence that there is no phenomenal consciousness left out of the PANIC theory, after all), *nor* adequately explains away the belief that Belinda is possible; it certainly does not somehow accomplish both feats at once.

3. Chalmers (1996) has something related and broadly similar to say in response to objections that his zombie thought-experiment violates metaphysical a posteriori necessities, though his remarks are set in the context of a general account of meaning that appeals to the notions of intension, extension, and possible worlds, and to the distinction between a priori and a posteriori ways of knowing. Chalmers's framework seems to me to have many virtues, and of course, I welcome any support that it would provide my comments; though I would also claim that the defense I offer here of phenomenal consciousness against accusations of metaphysical transgression stands independent of such a theory and the notions it employs.

4. Dennett 1991, 141–42. In Dennett's lingo, the first alternative is "Orwellian" and the second "Stalinesque." I leave aside these labels, though, since I find that this way of describing things confuses the issues, and the polemical weight of the epithets is distracting. Similar dilemmas are supposed to arise in regard to rival accounts of the phi-phenomenon (ibid., 141, 465). And these sorts of predicaments are alleged to vitiate the controversy between Benjamin Libet and Patricia Churchland over the former's claim to have determined that it takes at least 500 msecs for a stimulus to give rise to consciousness of it (ibid., 154–67).

5. Dennett 1993, 152: "What I have a *very* hard time imagining is what could induce me to think I could choose ('from the inside') between the hypothesis that I really *had* lost all visual *quality* (but none of the content), and the hypothesis that I had succumbed to the delusion that other people, no more gifted at visual discernment than I, enjoyed an extra sort of visual *quality* that I lacked." I think it is clear that Dennett is not saying that he couldn't imagine something just causing him to choose the denial over the contrary hypothesis—rather, he cannot imagine anything that *should* make him choose it. For he says: "If I found myself in the imagined predicament, I might well panic. In a weak moment I might even convert, and give up my own theory. . . . I can also imagine myself having the presence of mind in these bizarre straits to take seriously the hypothesis that my own theory favors: I'm deluding myself about the absence of visual quality' (ibid., 153). Presumably, one who is not "weak," one whose judgment reflects the virtue of "presence of mind" in this

situation, is one who believes what he has most reason, or justification, or warrant for believing.

6. It at least seems possible (not strictly impossible) to me that there could be self-moving (nonpuppet) humanoid zombies. The possibility that such a being could be physically ("molecule for molecule") type-identical to myself seems somewhat more problematic, mainly because of special worries about epiphenomenalism this raises. (It may seem that if what we actually have, excluding consciousness, could be [as in the zombie case] causally sufficient for securing whatever effects we are inclined to attribute to consciousness, then it is causally sufficient for these effects in our case as well—and so consciousness is causally superfluous to them.) However, the acceptability of that argument, and its bearing on assessing the possibility of this type of zombie, is far from evident to me. I would say, though, that it does not seem possible to me that a zombie could be in every way "functionally equivalent" to me, if this is taken to entail that it would have all the same beliefs about itself that I have about myself. For I doubt that a zombie would be able to understand what 'phenomenal consciousness' means, and so I doubt it would ever believe that it had experience with this or that phenomenal character.

CHAPTER 6

1. I suggested in Chapter 1 that the "perceptual model" of consciousness, the notion that consciousness is in some way "perceiving" one's own mind, or what's "in" it, is part of the legacy of Descartes' philosophy—a by-product of the notion that once one has doubted all one believes about one's surroundings, one still knows one perceives *something*—something, therefore "in one's mind"; an "idea." As I mentioned, John Locke explicitly affirms the perceptual model, though I should say that it is not clear that Locke has a coherent view here: he seems to define both consciousness and "reflexion" as the perception of mental operations, but then implies that young children have the former, while denying they have the latter. Armstrong (1965) thinks a consciousness-as-perception story can be attributed to Kant, on the strength of the latter's claims about "inner sense" (though I am not so sure about this). In any case, Armstrong cites Kant and Locke (though not Descartes) as historical precedents for his own modern functionalist version of the consciousness-as-internal-perception story. Lycan (1987, 1996) also defends an "inner-sense" account of consciousness from a functionalist point of view. And there are other recent views I have previously noted (Johnson-Laird 1988a; Rosenthal 1986) that take consciousness essentially to involve, if not self-reflexive "perceptions," at least some kind of self-representation.

The perceptual model has also been prominent in the twentieth-century "continental" tradition. Brentano ([1874] 1973, book 2, chap. 2) influentially held that all conscious experience involves an "inner perception" of it—each experience is a "presentation" of itself. His student Husserl seems to have adopted this view, with some rather difficult-to-pin-down modifications—that may ultimately, it seems to me, remove mental self-directedness from the story ([1900] 1970, investigation 5, chap. 1, and the appendix: "External and Internal Perception: Physical and Psychical Phenomena"; also 1928, app. 12). Jean-Paul Sartre, under Husserl's influence, developed a (similarly elusive) version of this view (Sartre [1937] 1957; [1943] 1953, Introduction, sec. 3). More recently, David Woodruff Smith (1986) has articulated a position drawn from this lineage.

2. See Bernard Williams 1978, with John Searle 1992, 141–43.

3. Brentano [1874] 1973, 102: "We have seen that no mental phenomenon exists that is not, in the sense indicated above, consciousness of an object. However, another question arises, namely, whether there are any mental phenomena which are not objects of consciousness. All mental phenomena are states of consciousness; but are all mental phenomena conscious, or might there also be unconscious mental acts?

"Some people would just shake their heads at this question. To postulate an unconscious consciousness seems to them absurd."

It seems that Brentano assumes that for a "mental act" to be conscious, it is necessary that it be "an object of consciousness" (i.e., an intentional object) of some kind. For he takes it to follow from its *not* being an "object of consciousness" that it is an "unconscious mental act." By opening his discussion in this way, it seems to me that Brentano prevents himself from ever focusing on the possibility that one may have "mental acts" that are, in my sense, conscious, though they are not "objects of consciousness," that is, their occurrence does not satisfy the conditions of truth or falsity (or of accuracy or inaccuracy) of any intentional features belonging to one's current episodes of consciousness.

Now consider Sartre ([1943] 1953, 11): "The necessary and sufficient condition for a knowing consciousness to be knowledge *of* its object, is that it be consciousness of itself as being that knowledge. This is a necessary condition, for if my consciousness were not consciousness of being consciousness of the table, it would then be consciousness of that table without consciousness of being so. In other words, it would be a consciousness ignorant of itself, an unconscious, which is absurd. This is a sufficient condition, for my being conscious of being conscious of that table suffices in fact for me to be conscious of it."

Thus Sartre tries to persuade us that "all consciousness is consciousness of itself" (ibid., 13–14). His argument depends on our identifying (a) being something that is not conscious (or as he might put it, being "an unconscious"); (b) being a state that is "*ignorant* of itself"; and (c) being a state of which there is no consciousness. But we have seen that the sense in which consciousness of a state is *knowledge* of it may be distinguished from a state's being conscious in my sense. And while knowing that I am phenomenally conscious of a table may be a sufficient condition for my being phenomenally conscious of it, this is not due to some peculiarity of consciousness, but is just because knowing that p implies that p is the case. Further, it is not obviously absurd that there could be phenomenally conscious experience that is "not conscious of itself," if this just means "ignorant of itself." It would be an equivocation to insist this would require us to assume that there could be an "unconscious conscious experience" or "a consciousness" that is "an unconscious." With apparent inconsistency, Sartre himself insists on distinguishing consciousness and knowing, and says that the consciousness of consciousness that (he says) necessarily belongs to all consciousness, is not a "knowing."

4. Dennett, who is sympathetic to Rosenthal's account, seems to recognize this, but instead of taking it as evidence that the "everyday concept of consciousness" has been badly represented by Rosenthal, oddly assumes that Rosenthal's account of this is correct, but that this "folk psychological concept" is defective (Dennett 1991, 314–15).

5. See Block 1994 and Dretske 1995 for arguments against higher-order-thought theories of consciousness that appeal to similar considerations. However, I should note that some appear to be unconcerned about this kind of objection. Carruthers

(1989) advocates a view that, like higher-order-thought theories of consciousness, requires that beings with conscious experience possess intellectual capacities of a sort that nonhuman animals and young humans would seem to lack. But he seems quite willing to embrace the consequence that, according to him, such beings simply lack conscious experience, and operate with a kind of blindsight. (He even wants to say that dogs and babies do not feel pain.) How can this seem acceptable to him? I think we can see how he is led into this by certain erroneous notions. First, his understanding of consciousness is distorted by his vastly overestimating how plausible it is to say that active adult human beings are often temporarily without any conscious sense-experience—he seems to think that when one's attention is deeply absorbed by something other than what one sees (as in the case of routine driving, or dishwashing), one fails to see consciously at all. Now, I can admit that it may be hard to draw a sharp line here, so as to say just what kind of visual experience I lose when my attention is intensely focused on something other than what I see, but I cannot say that my attention has ever been so absorbed elsewhere that I was driving or washing dishes *by blindsight*. Here it appears Carruthers tacitly assumes that when you cannot identify in a definite manner just what items you consciously saw a short time ago, you consciously saw nothing whatsoever, nothing looked any way to you at all then. But one can consciously see, even though able retrospectively to identify but vaguely just what one saw. (See my discussion at 7.8.) The fact that one was paying so little attention to what one saw that one is unable to *say* whether or not one saw this or that item that passed before one's eyes, does not show that one was utterly bereft of conscious vision. However, if one ignores such niceties, one may then be inclined to think of consciousness as something of an occasional affair even in one's own life (though this, too, is a fair leap), and then maybe it will not seem so outlandish to suppose that cognitively unsophisticated creatures lack conscious experience altogether. Moreover, Carruthers seems to think his denial of consciousness to brutes receives considerable support from the conceivability that creatures with pain behavior—avoidance, wincing, etc.—might be without feelings of pain. But this antibehaviorist point simply does not show that pain is somehow the exclusive province of those with relatively advanced intellectual powers. Finally, I think Carruthers denies consciousness to "brutes" more confidently than he should, because he does not appreciate the difficulty that the sort of blindsight thought-experiments I discussed make for his view, which identifies the difference between conscious visual experience and its lack with the difference between an experience whose content is, and one whose content is not, available to the subject to think spontaneously about, in thoughts that are, in turn, available to be spontaneously thought about. For my hypothetical spontaneous blindsighter can have such thoughts about the information she gets through blindsight—without conscious visual experience. It appears Carruthers must say this is inconceivable, or in some way strictly impossible. This suggests that he can find it plausible to deny that young children and nonhuman animals have conscious experience, because his view neglects phenomenal consciousness.

6. I should note that Rosenthal accepts that an animal would need to have concepts of some of the sorts of sense-experience it possesses, in order to have higher-order thoughts about these. He does not think this is a problem for his view, because he thinks all the animal needs are concepts for distinguishing some of its own "sensations," and these should be easy for it to come by (1986, 472–73). Perhaps Rosenthal is suggesting some version of the strategy I consider here: there are no truly unreflective conscious perceivers, because what is required for low-grade reflectiveness about

one's experience is really so undemanding. But his remarks not only leave unaddressed the problem that most conscious experience occurs without our having any warrant for believing it contemporaneously thought about (consciously or otherwise, with crudity or sophistication), they do not really address the concern that more is needed for having concepts of experience than for just having experience. Does Rosenthal think the kinds of beliefs about vision I suggest are needed for having concepts of seeing and visual experience are not really necessary for this? What *would* be enough to have concepts for distinguishing one's own visual "sensations"? Would it be enough just to "distinguish" these somehow? If this is no more than a matter of responding somehow to differences in how things look to one, I do not see why we should regard it as involving having true or false thoughts about, or possessing concepts of, "sensations."

7. Might Sartre offer us some version of the suggestion just raised, that there is a lower-grade kind of "consciousness of consciousness" that is essential to all consciousness? He would be eager to agree that there is, as he would say, "a consciousness" that is not reflected on, and he would not maintain, like Rosenthal, that there is, nonetheless, nonconscious *reflection* in such instances. But he would also say that we need to distinguish between *reflective* self-consciousness that is occasional, and a kind of *nonreflective*, "nonthetic," "nonpositional" self-consciousness that is ubiquitous. Unfortunately, he does not do much to help us understand these latter two adjectives, "nonthetic" and "nonpositional." He does tell us that a nonpositing consciousness is not a "knowing" consciousness, but far from helping, this seems only to create more confusion, since his argument that all consciousness is consciousness of itself seems to depend on just the opposite assumption. In *Transcendence of the Ego*, Sartre explains "nonpositionality" of this sort, by saying that though consciousness is consciousness of itself, it is "not for itself its own object" ([1937] 1957, 40–41). But then, it looks as though Sartre is not maintaining that consciousness necessarily requires some kind of *intentionality* wherein "consciousness" is directed at itself. If so, then he does not offer an account of consciousness of the sort I am criticizing, wherein consciousness essentially involves a kind of self-directedness of mind. But then, it is also totally unclear what it is he thinks he is telling us, when he says that all consciousness is consciousness of itself. And it is extremely misleading for him to say that all consciousness is a kind of "self-consciousness." For it is hard to see what self-consciousness is supposed to be, if not some kind of intentionality directed at a "self" (or, as Sartre would have it: "a consciousness").

CHAPTER 7

1. Merleau-Ponty ([1945] 1962) argues for a view of this sort.
2. See, e.g., G. E. Moore's (1953) discussion of the variously shaped sense-data he maintains those variously situated in the lecture hall see when he holds up an envelope before them.
3. Mightn't we imagine having a thoroughly despatialized, and thus deintentionalized, experience of color? This is not easy to do. We might think of, for example, the visual experience we have when closing our eyes after gazing at a bright light ("after-images"), or the vague experience of light we have when, with eyes closed, we bring them near a strong light source. But in either case it still looks to me as if the color is somewhere, even if this location is vague, and even if it does not look to me as though some *thing* has that color. The color still appears before me, not behind

me; near (or at?) my eyes, not far away, and not at my feet. To arrive at a totally despatialized visual experience, it seems we have to imagine a peculiar, seemingly disembodied kind of "color sensation."

But we may not need to despatialize visual experience completely to conceive of it lacking visual intentionality. In the after-image case just mentioned, there is some plausibility to the claim that the notions of accuracy and inaccuracy are not applicable to this in the way they are to visual experience. But we should not, in any case, assimilate the phenomenal character of visual experience generally to that of this marginal case, of vanishingly meager spatial experience, where vision and vivid imagery are scarcely phenomenally distinguishable. And, even if this sort of experience lacks visual intentionality, and is more like imagery, this does not show that it lacks intentionality altogether. For, as I argue in the next chapter, the phenomenal character of visual imagery is also intentional.

4. Like the patient Zasetsky in Luria 1972.

5. I take it that it is fundamental to Merleau-Ponty's (1945) phenomenology of perception that this question be answered in the negative, for the way we perceive space is inherently practical.

CHAPTER 8

1. I am indebted to Wollheim's (1984) discussion of iconic thought.

2. Jackendoff (1987, 289–90) takes this to exclude what he calls "conceptual structure" from awareness, when we engage in silent speech. I think this would commit him to rejecting my view that noniconic thought, and not just utterance experience, is conscious. He supports his claim primarily with two considerations, both of which seem to me inadequate. First, he says that if "conceptual structure" were conscious, we would not be able to distinguish "linguistic awareness" from "visual awareness." We must distinguish them by saying that visual awareness has conceptual structure, but linguistic awareness does not.

It is difficult to *say* exactly how, or in respect of what, we distinguish perception and thought with first-person warrant (or, if you like, "phenomenologically"). But it is far from clear that Jackendoff's proposal is the only or even the most plausible one. One might take this distinction not as a reason to doubt that thought is conscious, but rather as a reason to doubt that the "content" of conscious perception is just like the "content" of conscious thought. In any case, it seems clear that we can phenomenologically distinguish different sorts of experience with, in some sense, the same content. The ball both looks and feels spherical to me, but that does not make for any difficulty about phenomenologically distinguishing visual from tactile experience.

Jackendoff's second argument is that the "tip-of-the-tongue" phenomenon shows us that "conceptual structure" is generally missing from linguistic awareness, for here, what is missing from awareness is not "conceptual structure," but "phonological structure" (290–91). The idea seems to be that we would not have the peculiar sort of experience of "trying to fill a void" that we have in these cases, if conceptual structure were ever conscious, for then we could just have the conceptual-structure awareness without phonological-structure awareness, and we would not sense any lack, for we would not *need* the phonological structure in awareness, in order to (indirectly) get at the conceptual structure.

But if this is the argument, it is inadequate. First, it does not follow from the claim that one can have conceptual structure in awareness, that one can have it without the appropriate phonological structure. Second, even if one can have a conscious thought without verbal articulation of it (as indeed I think is the case), one may still be aware of a lack of this verbal articulation, when one has difficulty in giving it. Third, even if one can have a thought without verbally expressing it, it may not be the case that one can have it without being *able* to verbally express it (and for this reason, in the tip-of-the-tongue case, one does not have the thought one is searching for, and so one feels a lack). And finally, it may be important to have thought in verbally articulate form if one is trying to communicate it, or preparing to communicate it, or if one is trying to assess its relationship to other thoughts. So there are many reasons we may sense a distressing lack in the tip-of-the-tongue cases, which are compatible with saying something like "conceptual structure" is "in" awareness.

3. This talk of consciousness and understanding needs to be handled with care. From Wittgensteinian considerations Dennett draws the moral that "no conscious experience will guarantee that I have understood you, or misunderstood you" (1991, 57). Interpreted a certain way, this claim is consistent with what I wish to say, but not because of the Wittgensteinian point that imagery is inadequate to account for language comprehension. You say, "The train is late," and I, hearing you, consciously think of the train's being late. This does not guarantee that I understand you, not because my picturing the train stopped somewhere up the track is not enough for me to understand you (though clearly it is not), for my conscious thought of the train need not consist in some such imagery. My conscious experience does not guarantee that I understand you, because I understand you in this case, only if *you mean* that the train is late by your utterance, and no conscious experience *I* am having can entail that *you mean* this. However, this does not show that no conscious experience of mine can guarantee that I understand what you are saying in a certain way, i.e., that I *take* you to mean this or that—even though perhaps you do not mean what I understand you to be saying, what I take you to be saying.

4. Even if I am not completely confident that a perfect silent-speech transcript for these moments (assuming there could be such a thing) would be completely blank, it is clear that it could not have contained more than a couple of relevant words, at most—I just cannot talk fast enough, not even silently, to have said all *that* in a couple of moments. And we must not think this complex thought was not conscious, just a nonconscious thought that explains my supposed auralized utterance of, say, "book" and "baby"—how could this explanatory hypothesis possibly be justified, against an indefinite number of alternatives, by such meager evidence? And yet I do know that I had this thought. So my conscious thought was not an auralized verbalization of my thought, and it was not an episode of visualizing something, either: for how could I *picture* all that I was thinking about here?

5. See also Searle's discussion of example of this sort (1992, 137).

6. Also, we need to be careful not to confuse a case in which it seems to one just as it does to think some thought, with a case in which it seems to one as it does to be *about to* think some thought. We can conceive of the latter without genuine thought occurring—but that does nothing to show we can do this in the former case. Consider the kind of experience one sometimes has—particularly at the end of a long, exhausting conversation—where one is just about to say something, perhaps one even opens one's mouth as if to speak, but then somehow, in some sense, one "loses the thought," and falls into confusion, the thought somehow fails to "coalesce." You might be slightly tempted to describe this as a case in which it seems to you the way

it does to think a thought wordlessly, but in which, as it turns out, you had no thought at all. But this would be a mistake. For the sort of experience to which I allude is phenomenally quite different from the sort we earlier discussed. There is a difference between, on the one hand, the way it seems to me to be just about to think something, or the way it seems to me almost to form a thought (which perhaps might not yet come, or might not get formed), and, on the other, the way it seems to me to have an unverbalized thought. On a certain occasion, it seemed to me the way it did to think that I had locked myself out, not simply the way it would be just about to think this.

7. I owe this point to Kirk Ludwig (see Ludwig 1992).

CHAPTER 9

1. Here are some of the things that make it difficult. You might note, for example, that you cannot conceive of the possibility of zombies by conceiving of *being* one. For to conceive of being x is to conceive of how it seems to x to have the experience x has. And there *is* no way it seems to the zombie, ex hypothesi. However, it is not necessary to conceive of being a zombie, in order to conceive of there being a zombie. One might note also that it is difficult to conceive of becoming a zombie in a piecemeal fashion. For if one is to conceive of becoming, for instance, a partial zombie with "super-duper" blindsight, then one has to suppose one will be able to make "content-rich" visual judgments about the location, shape, and size of visual stimuli—and these will be such as one is unable to express other than indexically ("this shape," "this far," "this big," and so on). But to suppose I say spontaneously, "There is something there with *this* shape, *this* far from something of *that* shape," while consciously seeing nothing there, is to suppose I say this while it seems to me as it would to make these utterances without *meaning* anything by "this shape," "this far," etc. And in that case, I would think I did *not* mean anything by them. And it is hard to imagine really wanting to say such things when I think I mean nothing by them. Also, to suppose you are a premium-quality blindsighter, you will need to suppose you are able to move around spontaneously and confidently, successfully avoiding, approaching, and grasping things as well as you do with conscious sight, although it visually seems to you no different than it would in a totally dark room. And it just is hard to imagine how it would seem to have an experience of such confident and finely coordinated action in such surroundings, where your movements would not, as they normally do, appear to you as appropriate to, or as called for by, what you consciously see around you. These difficulties are not much alleviated by supposing that you no longer experience these utterances and movements as *your own*, your actions. For it also is rather hard to imagine how it would seem to have such an alienated experience of one's own body. But none of this shows that the super-duper blindsighter, or the total zombie, is flat-out inconceivable. Finally, we may find it hard to conceive of nonconscious zombies because to do so, we imagine encountering them, and we find ourselves hard put to imagine, and somewhat repelled by the idea, that we could actually make ourselves believe they were totally bereft of conscious experience. But though it may be true that, if I encountered a zombie, I could not help believing that it was *not* a zombie, but a conscious being, this is not enough to show that I cannot conceive of there being a zombie.

2. Unger (1990) conducts an intricate and valuable discussion of these issues, to which I am much indebted.

3. I imagine someone might say: "But on the whole I'd rather *my body* remain in existence than be replaced, even if consciousness is gone forever, because I *like* my body!" The question is, however, just how strong this preference is, on reflection. Maybe it is rather like wanting some keepsake or heirloom (and not just an exact duplicate) to continue in existence, even after one's death. I think it is unlikely such a preference will seem to be of comparable strength to your preference for conscious, over zombified, existence. One way to see this is to consider: would it be difficult for you to agree to donate an organ from your future zombified body for (potentially somewhat useful) medical research that could not be otherwise carried out, even if this ruled out option (b), and left you only with the zombified replacement option (c)? It would not be hard for me. But I presume the situation would be rather different, if donating the organ meant foregoing an otherwise available conscious future, in favor of zombified replacement.

4. When thinking about these issues regarding value, personhood, and consciousness, it is important to keep in mind that the point is often just to consider the relative worth of the relevant situations, not the rightness of the actions needed to bring them about. Suppose you resist the claim (which I endorse) that if the body of a conscious person becomes zombified, the world in which the resultant zombie continues existence would be little or no better than one in which it is replaced by a zombie twin. Perhaps you would do this because you think: "On that assumption, if I thought *you* were actually a zombie, then it follows that I should then be indifferent to your destruction and replacement. And that seems wrong." But notice that this does *not* follow, partly because of the relevance of epistemic considerations here. Just how good could your reasons ever be for thinking another was actually a zombie? Arguably, if x were radically internally dissimilar to you and other members of your species, then you would have less reason to think x conscious than you otherwise would. But that is not to say you would have *much* warrant for denying x was conscious. So, arguably, your reasons for thinking another being was a zombie would never be good enough to justify your *treating* that being *as a zombie*, even if, as it happens, it were a zombie. Furthermore, there is this consideration: our moral response to other people is not directed by tenuous theoretical reflections about the available strength of warrant for holding that someone we encounter is or is not a zombie. Our concern, respect, and sympathy for others is solicited by the appearance they present to us. And to override our normal sensorily elicited emotional responses to others, on the basis of some abstruse theoretical reasoning, would arguably undermine or degrade our ability to feel the right moral emotions toward others generally. Thus, even if we encountered (or constructed) actual zombies, and even if it would not be worse that they are replaced by twins than it would be for them to continue in existence, it would be wrong for us to *treat* them in this way, destroying and replacing them like toasters, television sets, or computers, because of the way that would ultimately suppress, weaken, or confuse moral sentiments it is good that we feel toward conscious beings.

REFERENCES

Alston, W. P. 1971. Varieties of Privileged Access. Reprinted in Alston 1989.
———. 1989. *Epistemic Justification: Essays in the Theory of Knowledge*. Ithaca, N.Y.: Cornell University Press.
Armstrong, D. M. 1965. The Nature of Mind. Reprinted in *The Mind/Brain Identity Theory*, ed. C. V. Borst. New York: St. Martin's Press, 1970.
Baars, B. J. 1988. *A Cognitive Theory of Consciousness*. Cambridge: Cambridge University Press.
Bealer, G. 1994. *The Rejection of the Identity Thesis*. In *The Mind Body Problem*, ed. R. Warner and T. Szubka. Oxford: Basil Blackwell.
Block, N. 1978. Troubles with Functionalism. In *Minnesota Studies in the Philosophy of Science* 9:261–325. Minneapolis: University of Minnesota Press.
———. 1993. Review of D. C. Dennett 1991. *Journal of Philosophy* 90:181–83.
———. 1994. Consciousness. In *A Companion to the Philosophy of Mind*, ed. S. Guttenplan. Oxford: Basil Blackwell.
———. 1995. On a Confusion about a Function of Consciousness. *Behavioral and Brain Sciences* 19:227–47.
Block, N., and J. Fodor. 1972. What Psychological States Are Not. *Philosophical Review* 81:159–81.
Brentano, F. [1874] 1973. *Psychology from an Empirical Standpoint*. Translated by T. Rancurello, D. Terrell, and L. McAlister. New York: Humanities Press.
Burge, T. 1979. Individualism and the Mental. *Midwest Studies in Philosophy*, vol. 4. Minneapolis: University of Minnesota Press.
———. 1982. Other Bodies. In *Thought and Object: Essays on Intentionality*, ed. A. Woodfield. Oxford: Clarendon.
———. 1988. Individualism and Self-Knowledge. *Journal of Philosophy* 85:649–63.
Calvin, W. 1990. *The Cerebral Symphony: Seashore Reflections on the Structure of Consciousness*. New York: Bantam.
Carruthers, P. 1989. Brute Experience. *Journal of Philosophy* 86:258–69.
Chalmers, D. 1996. *The Conscious Mind: In Search of a Fundamental Theory*. New York: Oxford University Press.
Churchland, P. M. 1981. Eliminative Materialism and the Propositional Attitudes. *Journal of Philosophy* 78:67–90.
Churchland, P. S. 1988. Reduction and the Neurobiological Basis of Consciousness. In Marcel and Bisiach 1988.
Churchland, P. M., and P. S. Churchland. 1996. *The Churchlands and Their Critics*. Edited by R. N. McCauley. Oxford: Basil Blackwell.
Davidson, D. 1973. Radical Interpretation. Reprinted in Davidson 1984a.
———. 1984a. *Inquiries into Truth and Interpretation*. Oxford: Clarendon.
———. 1984b. First Person Authority. *Dialectica* 38:101–11.
———. 1987. Knowing One's Own Mind. *Proceedings and Addresses of the American Philosophical Association* 60 (3):441–58.
Dennett, D. C. 1978. Toward a Cognitive Theory of Consciousness. In *Brainstorms*. Cambridge, Mass.: MIT Press.
———. 1988. Quining Qualia. In Marcel and Bisiach 1988.

Dennett, D. C. 1991. *Consciousness Explained*. Boston: Little, Brown.

———. 1993. Living on the Edge. *Inquiry* 36:135–59.

Descartes, R. [1637] 1985. *Discourse on the Method*. In *The Philosophical Writings of Descartes*, vol. 1, trans. J. Cottingham, R. Stoothoff, and D. Murdoch. Cambridge: Cambridge University Press.

———. [1641] 1985. *Meditations on First Philosophy, with Objections and Replies*. In *The Philosophical Writings of Descartes*, vol. 2, trans. J. Cottingham, R. Stoothoff, and D. Murdoch. Cambridge: Cambridge University Press.

Dretske, F. 1995. *Naturalizing the Mind*. Cambridge, Mass.: MIT Press.

Flanagan, O. 1992. *Consciousness Reconsidered*. Cambridge, Mass.:MIT Press.

Gallois, Andre. 1996. *The World Without, the World Within*. Cambridge: Cambridge University Press.

Gopnik, A. 1993. How We Know Our Own Minds: The Illusion of First-Person Knowledge of Intentionality. *Brain and Behavioral Sciences* 16:1–14.

Hacker, P.M.S. 1987. *Appearance and Reality: An Investigation into Perception and Perceptual Qualities*. Oxford: Basil Blackwell.

Heil, J. 1992. *The Nature of True Minds*. Cambridge: Cambridge University Press.

Horgan, T., and J. Woodward. 1985. Folk Psychology Is Here to Stay. *Philosophical Review* 94 (2):197–220.

Hume, D. 1739. *Treatise on Human Nature*. Oxford: Clarendon.

Husserl, E. [1900] 1970. *Logical Investigations*. Translated by J. Findlay. London: Routledge and Kegan Paul.

———. [1928] 1966. *The Phenomenology of Internal Time-Consciousness*. Translated by J. Churchill. Bloomington: Indiana University Press.

Jackendoff, R. 1987. *Consciousness and the Computational Mind*. Cambridge, Mass.: MIT Press.

Jaynes, J. 1976. *The Origin of Consciousness in the Breakdown of the Bicameral Mind*. Boston: Houghton Mifflin.

Johnson-Laird, P. N. 1988a. A Computational Analysis of Consciousness. In Marcel and Bisiach 1988.

———. 1988b. *The Computer and the Mind*. Cambridge, Mass.: Harvard University Press.

Kripke, S. 1972. *Naming and Necessity*. Cambridge, Mass.: Harvard University Press.

Lewis, D. 1972. Psychophysical and Theoretical Identifications. *Australasian Journal of Philosophy* 50:249–58.

Loar, B. 1990. Phenomenal States. In *Philosophical Perspectives*, vol. 4, Ed. J. Tomberlin. Atascadero, Calif.: Ridgeview.

Locke, D. 1968. *Myself and Others: A Study in Our Knowledge of Minds*. Oxford: Clarendon.

Locke, J. 1690. *An Essay Concerning Human Understanding*. Reprint. New York: Dover, 1959.

Ludwig, K. 1992. Skepticism and Interpretation. *Philosophy and Phenomenological Research* 52:31–339.

Luria, A. R. 1972. *The Man with a Shattered World*. Translated by L. Solotoroff. Cambridge, Mass.: Harvard University Press.

Lycan, W. 1987. *Consciousness*. Cambridge, Mass.: MIT Press.

———. 1990. The Continuity of Levels of Nature. In *Mind and Cognition: A Reader*, ed. W. Lycan. Oxford: Basil Blackwell.

———. 1996. *Consciousness and Experience*. Cambridge, Mass.: MIT Press.

McGinn, C. 1991. *The Problem of Consciousness: Essays Towards a Resolution*. Oxford: Basil Blackwell.

Malcolm, N. 1954. Wittgenstein's *Philosophical Investigations*. *Philosophical Review* 63:530–59.

———. 1958. Knowledge of Other Minds. *Journal of Philosophy* 55:969–78.

Marcel, A., and E. Bisiach, eds. 1988. *Consciousness in Contemporary Science*. Oxford: Oxford University Press.

Merleau-Ponty, M. [1945] 1962. *Phenomenology of Perception*. Translated by C. Smith. London: Routledge and Kegan Paul.

Moore, G. E. 1953. The Introduction of Sense-Data. Reprinted in *Perception and the External World*, ed. R. J. Hirst. New York: Macmillan, 1965.

Nagel, T. 1974. What Is It Like to Be a Bat? *Philosophical Review* 4:435–50.

———. 1986. *The View from Nowhere*. Oxford: Oxford University Press.

Nisbett, R. E. and T. D. Wilson. 1977. Telling More Than We Know: Verbal Reports on Mental Processes. *Psychological Review* 84 (3):231–59.

Perry, J. 1977. Frege on Demonstratives. *Philosophical Review* 86:474–97.

———. 1979. The Problem of the Essential Indexical. *Nous* 13:3–21.

Putnam, H. 1960. Minds and Machines. Reprinted in Putnam 1975b.

———. 1965. The Nature of Mental States. Reprinted in Putnam 1975b.

———. 1975a. The Meaning of 'Meaning'. Reprinted in Putnam 1975b.

———. 1975b. *Mind, Language and Reality: Philosophical Papers*. Vol. 2. Cambridge: Cambridge University Press.

———. 1981. *Reason, Truth, and History*. Cambridge: Cambridge University Press.

Quine, W.V.O. 1960. *Word and Object*. Cambridge, Mass.: MIT Press.

Rorty, R. 1970. Incorrigibility as a Mark of the Mental. *Journal of Philosophy* 67:399–424.

Rosenthal, D. 1986. Two Concepts of Consciousness. Reprinted in *The Nature of Mind*, ed. D. Rosenthal. Oxford: Oxford University Press, 1991.

———. 1991. The Independence of Consciousness and Sensory Quality. In *Philosophical Issues*, vol. 1, *Consciousness*, ed. E. Villanueva. Atascadero, Calif.: Ridgeview.

———. 1993. Thinking That One Thinks. In *Consciousness: Psychological and Philosophical Essays*, ed. M. Davies and G. W. Humphreys. Oxford: Basil Blackwell.

Ryle, G. 1949. *The Concept of Mind*. Chicago: University of Chicago Press.

Sacks, O. 1987. *The Man Who Mistook His Wife for a Hat*. New York: Harper and Row.

Sartre, J-P. [1937] 1957. *Transcendence of the Ego*. Translated by F. Williams and R. Kirkpatrick. New York: Farrar, Straus and Giroux.

———. [1943] 1953. *Being and Nothingness*. Translated by H. Barnes. New York: Washington Square Press, 1956.

Searle, J. R. 1983. *Intentionality: An Essay in the Philosophy of Mind*. Cambridge: Cambridge University Press.

———. 1992. *The Rediscovery of the Mind*. Cambridge, Mass.: MIT Press.

Shallice, T. 1988. Information-Processing Models of Consciousness: Possibilities and Problems. In Marcel and Bisiach 1988.

Shoemaker, S. 1975. Functionalism and Qualia. *Philosophical Studies* 27:291–315.

Shoemaker, S. 1994. The First-Person Perspective. *Proceedings and Addresses of the American Philosophical Association* 68 (2):7–22.

Siewert, C. 1993. What Dennett Can't Imagine and Why. *Inquiry* 36:96–112.

———. 1994. Understanding Consciousness. Ph.D. diss., University of California, Berkeley.

Smith, D. W. 1986. The Structure of (Self-)Consciousness. *Topoi* 5 (2):149–56.

Stich, S. 1983. *From Folk Psychology to Cognitive Science: The Case Against Belief.* Cambridge, Mass.: MIT Press.

———. 1996. *Deconstructing the Mind.* Oxford: Oxford University Press.

Strawson, G. 1994. *Mental Reality.* Cambridge, Mass.: MIT Press.

Strawson, P. F. 1958. Persons. In *Minnesota Studies in the Philosophy of Science* 2:330–53. Minneapolis: University of Minnesota Press.

Tye, M. 1992. Visual Qualia and Visual Content. In *The Contents of Experience*, ed. T. Crane. Cambridge: Cambridge University Press.

———. 1995. *Ten Problems of Consciousness.* Cambridge, Mass.: MIT Press.

Unger, P. 1990. *Identity, Consciousness and Value.* New York: Oxford University Press.

Weiskrantz, L. 1986. *Blindsight: A Case Study and Implications.* Oxford: Oxford University Press.

White, S. 1987. What Is It Like to Be a Homunculus? *Pacific Philosophical Quarterly* 68:148–74.

Williams, B. 1978. *Descartes: The Project of Pure Inquiry.* Harmondsworth: Penguin.

Wittgenstein, L. 1953. *Philosophical Investigations.* Translated by G.E.M. Anscombe. New York: Macmillan.

Wollheim, R. 1984. *The Thread of Life.* Cambridge, Mass.: Harvard University Press.